# OF ME AND OTHERS

Born in 1934, Alasdair Gray graduated in design and mural painting from Glasgow School of Art. Since 1981, when *Lanark* was published by Canongate, he has written, designed and illustrated seven novels, several books of short stories, a collection of his stage, radio and TV plays and a book of his visual art, *A Life in Pictures*.

In his own words, "Alasdair Gray is a fat, spectacled, balding and increasingly old Glaswegian pedestrian who has mainly lived by writing and designing books, most of them fiction."

T0333551

# OF ME
# AND OTHERS

by Alasdair Gray

*for Morag, Mora, Andrew,*
*Bert, Katriona, Tracy, Maff,*
*Jim, Libby and Alexandra*
*in Scotland*
*England and the U.S.A.*

CANONGATE BOOKS

EDINBURGH 2019

# biblio notice

This revised edition published in
Great Britain, the USA and
Canada in 2019 by Canongate
Books Ltd, 14 High Street,
Edinburgh EH1 1TE

Distributed in the USA by Publishers Group West
and in Canada by Publishers Group Canada

canongate.co.uk

1

The author gratefully acknowledges the support of
Creative Scotland towards the publication of this book

*British Library Cataloguing-in-Publication Data*
A catalogue record for this book is available on
request from the British Library

ISBN 978 1 78689 520 2

Printed and bound in Great Britain by
Clays Ltd, Elcograf S.p.A.

# an epigraph

Everyone over middle age
regrets some loss that ageing brings.
My principal regret is this:
I've never tackled handy things.
Before King Louis lost his head
his hobby was repairing locks.
Byron, despite a crippled foot,
wrote epics yet could swim and box.
Sir Thomas Browne, Bill Carlos Bill,
were medical practitioners.
The Reverend Sydney Smith had skill
to doctor his parishioners.
One soldier wrote great words for tunes.[1]
One housewife writes tremendous books.[2]
One postman publishes cartoons.[3]
One mural painter welds and cooks.[4]
One sweeper of streets can etch and paint.[5]
One banker played the bagpipes well.[6]
One fisherman became a saint who
holds the keys of Heaven and Hell.[7]
Ruskin swept stairs and weeded plots.
D. H. Lawrence scrubbed the floors.
Count Tolstoy emptied chamber pots.
Why do I flinch from household chores?
Frosts's farming was not infamous.
Melville and Conrad sailed the sea.
James Kelman drove an omnibus.
No honest toil excuses me.

1. Hamish Henderson 2. Agnes Owens 3. Stuart Murray 4. Nichol Wheatley 5. Alan
Richardson 6. Former manager of the Glasgow Byres Road Clydesdale Bank 7. Peter

# TABLE OF

# CONTENTS

# F o r e w o r d

MY LAST BOOK WAS CALLED *A Life in Pictures*. This one might have been called *A Life in Prose*. It contains reminiscences and essays written between 1952 and 2014 about my own works and those of friends. Marginal and footnotes give dates of writing or publication. The earliest piece is a speculative essay, apart from which the rest describe what I think facts, though readers will dismiss some as opinions. Three, though mainly factual, diverge into fiction for reasons the notes also explain. My life as a professional author connects most of them. I have improved a few sentences so that my younger self sometimes seems to write better than he did, but no other changes suggest I was wiser in those days than I am now.

I thought this book would turn out to be a ragbag of interesting scraps. I now think it has the unity of a struggle for a confident culture, a struggle shared with a few who became good friends and thousands I have never met. Every nation has periods of lesser and greater assurance. When I was twenty-one the Scotland I knew was confident in the many goods it made and exported, but many educated people had very little confidence in Scottish visual and literary art, not because we lacked them, but because our education had stopped us seeing them. I believed all good books by Scots must be published in London and would fail if not praised by English book reviewers;

also that artists wishing to live by their art had better follow the example of Labour politicians and go to London. This explains the querulous tone of many early essays. I felt my nation was treated as a province, even by many who lived here. I wanted that to stop.

Being twelve years old when the 2nd World War ended, I belonged to the first generation to benefit by the welfare state in both healthcare and education. Unlike post-Thatcher children we had grants to attend art schools and universities without getting into debt, and even shift from one to another. From these pre-Thatcher graduates came poets, writers and playwrights who are now part of a very loose literary and artistic establishment at home in their own land, which may again become a nation in 2015.

A Socialist like my father, I loved Riddrie Public Library because it let anyone, but especially me, become a citizen in the world's Republic of Letters. I referred so much to it in these essays that I have deleted most and other repetitions, filling the hole

✳✳✳✳✳✳✳✳✳✳✳✳✳✳✳✳✳✳✳✳✳✳✳✳✳✳✳✳✳✳
✳✳✳✳✳✳✳✳✳✳✳✳✳✳✳✳✳✳✳✳✳✳✳✳✳✳✳✳✳✳
✳✳    with a frame of asterisks like this and the numbers of the earlier    ✳✳
✳✳    pages on which the deleted information has already appeared.    ✳✳
✳✳✳✳✳✳✳✳✳✳✳✳✳✳✳✳✳✳✳✳✳✳✳✳✳✳✳✳✳✳
✳✳✳✳✳✳✳✳✳✳✳✳✳✳✳✳✳✳✳✳✳✳✳✳✳✳✳✳✳✳

Alison Lumsden, my sharpest critic, says my habit of forestalling antagonistic remarks in forewords[1] and postscripts[2] is a cowardly ploy intended to baffle honest criticism. She is right. This ploy will get my work forgotten sooner rather than later.

1. *Such as this.*                    2. *See page 468.*

# Middle Age Self Portrait

O N MONDAY, 18TH MAY, 1987, 10.30 PM. My birth certificate says I am 52 years, 167 days, 40 minutes old. My passport says I am 1.74 metres or 5 feet 9¼ inches tall. According to the scales in the lavatory I weigh 13 stones and 7 pounds in my socks, semmit, underpants, bath robe, national health spectacles and false upper teeth: from all of which a doctor will deduce I am not in the best of health. I have the lean, muscular legs and small bum of the brisk pedestrian but the bulging paunch of the heavy drinker, the fleshy shoulders hunched too near the ears of the asthmatic with bronchial tendencies. The neck is thick; hands and feet and genitals small; the chin strong and double with the underside not yet grossly pendulous; the moustache pale sand colour; the straight nose survives from the years when I was thin all over; the eyes are small and sunken with blue-grey irises; the brow straight and not deeply lined; the hair of the scalp is fading from nondescript brown to non-descript grey and thinning behind a slightly eroded scalp-line. In repose the expression of the face is as glum as that of most adults.

Saltire Society was founded in 1936 by people who wished to see, "not just a revivals of the arts of the past, but a renewal of the life that made them, such as achieved by Scots in the 18th century." It publicized new buildings, good restorations of old ones, while issuing pamphlets on Scots history, law, philosophy, famous writers, usually dead. In the 1980s it started printing autobiographical booklets about modern authors. MacDiarmid & Goodsir Smith were dead, so theirs were edited out of their personal accounts still in print. Naomi Mitchison and I wrote our own. Mine, published in 1988, was last of a series which should have continued while any Scots knew they had a literature.

In conversation it is animated and friendly, perhaps too friendly. I usually have the over-eager manner of one who fears to be disliked. When talking freely I laugh often and loudly without being aware of it. My voice (I judge from tape-recordings) is naturally quick and light, but grows firm and penetrating when describing a clear idea or recollection: otherwise it stammers and hesitates a lot because I am usually reflecting on the words I use and seeking to improve and correct them. When I notice I am saying something glib, naive, pompous, too erudite, too optimistic, or too insanely grim I try to disarm criticism by switching my midland Scottish accent to a phony form of Cockney, Irish, Oxbridge, German, American or even Scottish.

At present I sit on a low comfortable chair in the room where most of my work and sleeping is done. I wear the aforementioned socks, semmit etcetera, and am being painted by Michael Knowles B.A. (Hons.), a quiet-spoken English artist living in Edinburgh who hopes to sell the portrait to the Royal Scottish Museum. I like and fear the idea of becoming a thing with an unliving public shape, but I obviously like it more than fear it for I am embalming myself in words for the *Saltire Self-Portrait* Series while Mr Knowles paints me doing it. I had planned to start less blatantly with a platitude everyone would accept, a platitude told in rhyme to make it seem original. I would then cunningly shift to an account of the people who made me, using old certificates and memories but mostly some pages my father once wrote about his early life in Bridgeton. I was reading these pages an hour ago when Mr Knowles arrived. I laid them down, we

arranged the furniture to let the window-light fall
equally on me and on his canvas, then the pages could not be found though we rummaged for them in all the places I could think of and a few where they could not possibly be. From childhood this habit of slyly, casually hiding valued objects from myself has deprived me, sometimes permanently, of money, travel tickets, useful tools, keys, paintings, notebooks, manuscripts and appliances to assist breathing when the asthma is bad. A psychiatrist once suggested these losses were caused by a hidden wish to attract attention and get proofs of love from those close to me. I doubt it. I have often inflicted such accidents on myself when nobody is close and nobody notices. The cause may be a sneaking appetite for disaster which Edgar Allan Poe calls The Imp of the Perverse and associates with alcoholism, irrational vertigo and procrastination. The older Freud calls it The Death Wish, perhaps too sweepingly. It has done me no lasting harm. Perhaps a defective grasp of solid externals is sometimes not caused by unconscious will, but by too much reflecting on mental innards. I'll find the lost pages eventually. They are certainly within arm's reach, and I may use them to add dignity to an otherwise selfish narrative.

Meanwhile, what am I for? What does this ordinary-looking, eccentric-sounding, obviously past-his-best person exist to do apart from eat, drink, publicize himself, get fatter, older and die? Stars, herbs and cattle exist without reasons, they fit the universe wherever they occur without need of language to maintain their forms, but a born human has no foreseeable shape. It is turned into a Chinese housewife, a neolithic hunter, an unemployed car mechanic or Ludwig van Beethoven by an always changing when and where pressing on a unique yet always ripening or rotting bundle of traits: traits joined by a painfully conscious need to both stay the same and grow different. This need generates ideas, arts, sciences, laws and a host of excuses, because one of our traits is garrulity. Even in sleep we talk wordlessly to ourselves. So what are you for, Gray?

At present I do not know. Until a few years ago I wanted to make stories and pictures. While writing or painting I forgot myself so completely that I did not want to be any different. I felt I was death's equal.
*We live and have lived, die and will die in this place*
*and millions have been and will be forgotten*
*with hearts and faces we struggle to keep*
*until folded in sleep or gone rotten,*
*and most, before dying, give blood to son or daughter*
*and when the bones of these children crumble, remain*
*not even memories – names cut on stones, perhaps:*
*otherwise we are a procession as featureless as water*
unless we get into a lasting image or repeatable pattern of words. But the most necessary and typical people are seldom commemorated in art and history which whore after the rich, the disastrous, the eccentric and love, above all, monstrous folk with one ability, one appetite so magnified that they seem mere embodiments of it – that is how our heroes and gods get made. I tried to tell convincing stories by copying into them pieces of myself and people I knew, cutting, warping and joining the pieces in ways suggested by imagination and the example of other story-makers,

for I wanted to amuse, so my stories contain
monsters. I do not decry them for that, but I have no new ideas for more. Can I entertain with some of the undistorted facts which generated them?

Early last century a Scottish shepherd whose first name is now unknown fathered William Gray, a shoemaker who fathered Alexander Gray, a blacksmith in Bridgeton, east Glasgow, a district then brisk with foundries, potteries and weaving sheds. And Alexander married Jeanie Stevenson, powerloom weaver and daughter of a coalminer. She became his housewife and bore another Alexander, who became a clerk on a weighbridge on a Glasgow dock, then a private in the Black Watch regiment in France, then a quartermaster sergeant there, then worked a machine which cut cardboard boxes in a Bridgeton factory until another world war began.

While some of this was happening Hannah, wife of a Northampton hairdresser called William Fleming bore Henry Fleming who became a foreman in a boot-making factory, and married Emma Minnie Needham. Henry, nicknamed Harry, also became a trade-unionist, and his bosses put his name on a list of men not to be employed in English factories. He and Minnie came to Glasgow where she bore Amy Fleming who first became a shop assistant in a clothing warehouse, then married Alex Gray the folding box maker, thus becoming a housewife.

She and Alex lived in Riddrie, a Glasgow corporation housing scheme where she bore Alasdair James Gray who became a maker of imagined objects, and Mora Jean Gray who became a physical exercise and dance teacher in Aberdeen, and married Bert Rolley from Portsmouth, a chemist who analysed polluted water. Alasdair Gray married Inge Sorenson, a nurse in an Edinburgh hospital, thus making her a housewife in Glasgow, though only for 9 years; and she bore Andrew Gray who became a supplies private in a Royal Air Force base near Inverness. But long before Mora and Alasdair got married all their working ancestors in this crowded little tale were dead, except for their father Alexander Gray. After cutting cardboard for 21 years he became manager of a hostel for munition workers, builder's labourer, wages clerk, persuader of hoteliers to subscribe to the Scottish Tourist Board, a remover of damaged chocolate biscuits from a conveyor belt, wages clerk again, warden for the Scottish Youth Hostel Association, hill guide in mountainous parts of Britain for the Holiday Fellowship, and lastly house-husband in the polite little town in Cheshire on which Mrs. Gaskill based her novel, *Cranford*. He died a month before his 76th year on the fourth of March 1973.

Here follows some of his early memories typed at my request in 1970 or 71. I have rearranged sentences in the first two paragraphs, cut out five conjunctions, replaced two pronouns by nouns, and added three commas and a period.

## NOTES ON EARLY LIFE IN GLASGOW
## BY ALEXANDER GRAY

MY FATHER'S GRANDFATHER HAD been a shepherd on the Earl of Hume's estate at Douglas

Water. His father was a high class boot maker whose shop was in (now) London Road near Glasgow Cross.
My father was the product of an age when children left school at 10 years and were sent to sea to learn the ways of the world. He served on two voyages, one when the crew were men released from Barlinnie prison to man the sailing vessel, while the second ship had to leave Cuba because of the war with the U.S.A. On reaching home he was made drunk by the crew (he being a popular cabin boy) and taken home where his Mother found him at the door, sitting on his box the crew members having knocked on the door and run off. That ended his seafaring education.

By the age of 25 years Father must have become a blacksmith. He made two journeys from London to Glasgow, working his way from job to job, for walking was his passion and his recreation. He had married, had two sons, William and James, after which his wife died. He married again. By his second wife I was his third son and had a sister, Agnes. He died in 1921 aged 70. My mother came from a mining family at Wishaw. I had several uncles and aunts from both sides of the family and it was Sunday afternoon and evening visitations to them or from them that provided the changes in domestic routines, for all were within walking distance or short tram journey distances from home in Bridgeton.

My early recollections are of our room and kitchen in a street off Main Street, Bridgeton, in a dirty grey tenement of three stories. Like most flats up east end Glasgow closes, ours was a two-room and kitchen. My step-brothers slept in the room while Father and

Mother shared the bed recess in the kitchen, the biggest room. Agnes and I slept in the hurley bed, kept below the kitchen bed during the day and rolled out at night. The lighting was on a long piped bracket fixed to the mantlepiece, which could be angled to suit a reader. The light was poor, not white as was later the case when gas mantles were introduced, first with vertical mantles and later by the smaller mantles now used on Calor Gas lamps. The fireplace was black leaded with the door handles and fire-irons in polished steel, the polishing of them being my weekly job, together with the oval dish covers which hung on the kitchen wall below the shelves of crockery and other dishes. In front of the window in the kitchen was the jaw-box or sink with the brass water pipe which provided only cold water, and was another of my weekly polishing jobs.

Father worked in a smiddy between the Clyde and French Street some ten minutes walk from home. These were the days when work started at 6am and breakfast was taken during a break about 8am. Mid-day dinner was around 1pm and work ended around 6pm. Father would have a cup of tea and some buttered bread before work and return for a breakfast of porridge, an egg or other "kitchen" – cooked food like bacon or sausage. Dinner consisted of soup or broth, meat, potatoes, veg, followed by a milk pudding or fruit. The evening meal we called tea would be plain bread, currant bread, scones, cheese and tea, while supper would be porridge or peas brose. During my school holidays Father would have his dinner at the smiddy to which I carried his soup in a can, his main course between plates tied in a towel. There I would pump the bellows so fast that the fire would blaze. Sometimes I would look over the wooden fence to Auld Shawfield, the football ground of Clyde before they moved to the present stadium between Glasgow and Rutherglen. I remember seeing players in red shirts running around, though don't remember if they were training or playing a match.

When the season for girds came round Father would make iron girds¹ and cleeks for my friends and me and we would make the iron ring as we ran round the streets in Bridgeton or made expeditions to the Sauny Waste, the open ground in the loop of the Clyde upstream from Dalmarnock Bridge. From the short street which gave access to works and a piggery on the Rutherglen bank, an earth path followed the riverbank. It was uneven, with hills and dales which required skill with the gird to maintain an uninterrupted run. Hills and hollows of sand filled the rivers loop in the middle of which was a flat hollow in which we could play football.

Often at the two ends of the loop a man would be on the lookout for the police, for in some hollow there would be a pitch-and-toss school of some two dozen men. In the centre a man would swing a leather belt to keep a ring clear while another would be laying bets with the surrounding crowd, yet another balancing two pennies on a sliver of wood or his fingers, preliminary

1. A gird was a thin metal hoop, at least waist-high to the child racing it but the bigger the better. The cleek was a short iron rod ending in a hook or ring, used by the racer as a handle to drive the hoop. The pleasure of this was the pleasure of running as fast as a wheel running beside you, a wheel which depended on your skill in turning corners, dodging obstacles and leaping over holes without you and gird losing speed or falling.

to tossing them high in the air to descend as head or tail, or two heads or two tails. Heads and tails were a neutral toss and had to be repeated till they both came down the same side up. With tails the crowd was happy because it won, with heads it put up with the loss, hoping the tosser could not continue winning forever. Small boys were not welcomed in this game, but we crawled through the grass to the rim of the hollow and peeped down over the heads of the gamblers, running away when we were spotted, to return by the river bank or an adjoining street to our own street.

Football of course was our favourite past-time. This was before the days of tarmac. The streets were cobbled, the ball did not run true but stotted in unexpected angles, except when the wall of the houses was used in passing an opponent and lamp-posts were goals. When each team was of two or three, the near posts on each side of the street would be used, but if more boys were available two near posts on the same side would be used thus providing a longer pitch. Such fun was not looked upon with pleasure by folk living on ground level flats and sometimes above, for windows were often broken. Sometimes a policeman would appear so the ball was snatched up and we all disappeared up various closes to cross the intervening walls of the back courts to adjoining streets and freedom. Leave-O or Kick-the-Can were alternatives to football, while the girls either had wooden hoops or peever and beds otherwise called Hop-Scotch. Sometimes selected girls would play with the boys at Hide and Seek, and the closes and dunnies[2] provided scope for initiative in avoiding discovery.

Father and Mother were deeply religious. Father was involved in the creation of the Congregational Union, i.e. the Union of Congregational Churches[3]. He sometimes took the pulpit when the Minister was ill, was superintendent of the Sunday School, an elder, and when a new church was created, Dalmarnock Road Congregational Church, gave some seven years service as church officer or cleaner as his donation to the new building. The Minister's wife was an invalid so Mother was President of the Mothers Meetings. Both were to my mind examples of Christian living for they not only observed the conventional daily or weekly forms of worship, but in their treatment of people of all religions or none, were helpful and kind and tolerant. We had grace at all meals, and each night before retiring to bed, Father would read the daily lesson from the Bible and Mother would say a prayer, or the roles would be reversed and sometimes I or Agnes would be asked to take the little service.

Father and Mother were both mild of temper. I never heard them raise their voices in discussion or argument between themselves or with others. The first years of this century had no social security or health insurance[4], and doctor's bills were to be avoided. I remember Father coming home with his face and hands

2. A dunny is the ground floor exit from a close into a tenement back yard or green, which was usually some steps down lower than the close mouth or entrance from the paved street.

3. Milton and Cromwell were of this sect, and during the Protectorate it nearly became the legally Established Church of England and Scotland. It resembled the Scottish Presbyterian Church in rejecting Episcopalian bishops, liturgy and ornament, but differed from it after 1688 by insisting that the congregation of each church should elect its ministers, so has never been supported by the revenues of the state.

4. Remember Alexander Gray is writing in 1971.

bandaged after he had been splattered with molten lead at work. He came from hospital where he had the pieces of lead picked from his skin, had his mid-day dinner and went back to work. On another occasion when our home had been burgled and drawers and cupboards ransacked and clothing etc. taken, he returned home to learn of the theft. His first thought was for his working clothes and all he said was, "Well, they left me the best suit, the one I need for my work." After 40 years with the same firm he reached the age of 65 and was told he was getting too old for his work as a blacksmith. Without warning he was handed his weekly wage, which I don't think ever exceeded 30 shillings, was thanked for his long and useful service and given the advice to look for a lighter job. His hand was shaken by the owner and he left, knowing that at his age he would not be able to get a tradesmen's job. In his last five years of labour he was a hammer-man to blacksmiths at Stewart & Lloyds at Rutherglen, much heavier work than that done by the men he was assisting. I never heard him complain. He was a teetotaller and did not smoke. His weekly spending was for butterscotch, the odd tram fare when on his Saturday afternoon walk. Often he would rise on Sunday morning and walk up to ten miles before going to church at 11am. On Saturday afternoons he would take me on walks along the paths round and over the hills which surround Glasgow, the paths which Alexander McDonald wrote about in *Rambles Round Glasgow*. When Mother, after an illness, spent a week at Strathaven, Father and I walked there and back[5] each Saturday having taken the tram to Cambuslang.

One of my treats was to be taken to Celtic Park by Uncle John, who was Mother's brother and manager of the newside at Beardmore's[6] furnaces. The oldside was hand-fed furnaces where Uncle Tom was the leading hand. Both lived at Parkhead. I can still hear the hush of the thousands on the terraces as Jimmy Quinn barged his way toward the goal with his opponents floored by his strong shoulders, to be followed by the roar which exploded when he cannoned the ball into the net.

Mother was good with her hands. She knitted, crocheted, made jam and baked and had time for church work. Her contribution to the family purse always ensured that at Glasgow Fair the Grays had a week's holiday. Never once did we stay at home in that time. Occasionally we also had a day Doon the Watter[7] on other holidays.

In politics my father was a radical liberal, though he never was active as a political worker. He knew Keir Hardie and was instrumental in getting K.H. to speak at Dalmarnock Congregational Church where at that time the minister was the Rev. Forson. Incidentally Father had a Bible class at the Sunday School and from his class came the two Graingers who later were medical doctors in Bridgeton and three Forsons, all of whom became Congregational Ministers, one of whom succeeded his father in my father's own church

5. A walk of at least seventeen miles or 27.3 kilometers.
6. In 20th Century's first half Beardmore & Co. was the largest engineering firm in Britain, building parts of Merchant and Royal Navy warships, locomotive engines, motor cars and aircraft, including the first airship to make a double-crossing of the Atlantic. (See Keay's **Collin's Encyclopeadia of Scotland**.)
7. This was a trip by paddle steamer from Broomielaw, at the centre of Glasgow, to one of the many resorts on the Firth of Clyde and its islands, the trippers usually returning the same day.

church. I went to John Street School as an infant and later into the Higher Grade School, where I was a mediocre scholar, being better with my feet and hands than with my head. I remember the celebration when George the VII[8] became King. We each received a small box with the heads of the King and Queen on the lid. We were marched from school to Glasgow Green for fun, games and sport, but what I did is now beyond me. Glasgow Green was not only where football was played. Part was the bleaching field and the nearby folk after the weekly washing would spread out or hand their clothes and water them for the sun to make them white. It was nearby what was to become the Greenhead Baths. It was also here where we school children were taken for swimming lessons. We would line up outside, having raced from school for first place in the queue where we prepared by partially undressing so that no time would be lost in the boxes beside the pool.

Every New Year all of the Stevenson family (my mother was a Stevenson) visited Granny who lived above a wide pend[9] just beyond the present Tramway garage at Parkhead. All the Uncles and Aunts and their children were present, four families in all. The youngsters sat down first and had steak pie followed by plum pudding in large helpings, then were sent out to play while the parents had their dinner. Through the pend there was a large gable end where we played hand ball. We picked sides and each side in turn had

8. *This is an error. Edward VII was crowned in 1902 when Alec Gray was five. He is remembering the coronation of George V in 1911 when my Dad was thirteen.*
9. *A pend is an passageway into a lane through the ground floor of a tenement, usually with upstairs flats above it entered from the communal close.*

to hit the ball against the gable end, the ball being hit after it stotted once on the ground. The side which failed to return the ball to the wall after one stot lost a point, and the first side reaching perhaps 10 points lost the game. When the elders finished washing up after the meal we all returned to the house and games and song passed the afternoon, each person reciting or singing his or her party piece.

It was on Sunday that the black morning coats were worn for church. Father, Bill who was church organist and choirmaster, and Jim who sang in the choir (he also sang in the Orpheus Choir) also wore their tall hats. When Father died in 1921 I was an outpatient at Bellahoustoun hospital, a military hospital, being given treatment following a war wound. In order to maintain the dignity of the family at the funeral I also had to get a morning coat and tall hat.

END OF ALEXANDER GRAY'S NARRATIVE

---

YOU STARTED READING THIS because you are more interested in me than my father. This essay has become a preface to an autobiography instead of the sketch for one I intended, yet Dad's self-negating account of his first family – even the style of his language – tells a lot about the characters of working people who shaped mine, though the gentle radical blacksmith who taught the Bible to three Bridgeton doctors and a clergyman died 13 years before I was born, and I don't know when his wife died. My Dad only spoke of his life before marriage when I asked about it, which was hardly ever. This reticence included his experiences of fighting in France between 1914 and 18. There was an exception to this in my late teens when I had bouts of asthma. These sometimes made me feel all life and history was a bad disease, a disease which could only be cured by a God of Love in whom I had no faith despite all Christian churches praying to Him. A Socialist and Agnostic, my dad believed with Marx that humanity would one day solve every problem it had the sense to recognise. As he could not persuade me of this he tried to help by introducing me to his parents' God in ways which respected their faith and his own. I made a note of these words, which told some things his written account does not, and eventually I paraphrased them in the 26th chapter of my first novel.

*"My father was elder in a Congregational church in Bridegton: a poor place now but a worse one then. One time the well-off members subscribed to give the building a new communion table, an organ and coloured windows. But he was an industrial blacksmith with a big family. He couldnae afford to give money, so he gave ten years of unpaid work as church officer, sweeping and dusting, polishing the brasses and ringing the bell for services. At the foundry he was paid less the more he aged, but my mother helped the family by embroidering tablecloths and napkins. Her ambition was to save a hundred pounds. She was a good needlewoman, but she never saved her hundred pounds. A neighbour would fall sick and need a holiday or a friend's son would need a new suit to apply for a job, and she handed over the money.*

*But there was something wrong with me. Then the 1914 war started and I joined the army and heard a different kind of prayer. The clergy on all sides were praying for victory. They told us God wanted our government to win and was right there behind us, with the generals, shoving us forward. A lot of us in the trenches let God go at that time with no fuss or remark, as if it were an ordinary thing to do. She got a lot of comfort from praying. Every night we all kneeled to pray in the living room before going to bed. There was nothing dramatic in these prayers. My father and mother clearly felt they were talking to a friend in the room with them. I never felt that, so I believed Duncan, all these airy-fairy pie-in-the-sky notions are nothing but aids to doing what we want anyway. My parents used Christianity to help them behave decently in a difficult life. Other folk used it to justify war and property. But Duncan, what men believe isn't important – it's our actions which make us right or wrong. So if a God can comfort you, adopt one. He won't hurt you."*

This speech – or, to be accurate, the words it paraphrases – did not help me at the time, for words cannot cure a physical pain unless they are a sort of hypnotism. But when my health mended it helped me believe what I still mainly believe: that original decency is as old as original sin and essentially stronger: that those who pray are consciously strengthening wishes which (whether selfish or not) are already very strong in them, and which decide the nature of the god they invoke.

I swear that extract contains no invention, just two bits of condensing and an exaggeration – 10 years of voluntary service are made out of what was less. It also contains an image I used in another piece of writing: the image of a small boy at family prayers who suspects he is at fault because he feels God is not with him. This became part of a play I wrote in 1964 called *The Fall of Kelvin Walker*. It was televised by the BBC in 1968 and published as a novel in 1985, and is a fable about a monstrously pushy young Scot getting rich quickly in London. He is buoyant with energies released by his escape from a nastily religious father who has used the god of Calvin like a rubber truncheon to batter his children into submission. Neither father nor son in that fable much resemble my father, or his father, or me, and none of the incidents in it befell any of us. When copying a thing from experiences of myself or acquaintances I sometimes gave it a context like that where it happened, sometimes did not. My most densely and deliberately autobiographical writing is in books 1 and 2 of *Lanark*. Apart from the encounter with the Highland minister, the encounter with the prostitute, the fit of insanity and suicide, nearly every thought and incident is copied from something real in context where it happened, but so much of my life was not copied that *Lanark* tells the story of a youngster estranged by a creative imagination from family, friends, teachers and city.

I hope this is a convincing tragedy. It was not mine. My family and half my teachers did not stunt my imagination. They encouraged it Scottishly, by allowing me materials and time to paint and write, not praising me to my face but talking about the results of my work when they thought I could not hear. My family and schooling made art seem the only way to join mental adventure, physical safety and social approval. They pressed upon my bundle of traits in a way which made anything but art and writing seem dull or threatening.

The foregoing paragraph is written to indicate both connections and divergences between life and art. The following questions were asked by Christopher Swan and Frank Delaney in August 1982 when preparing a BBC broadcast interview, and may illuminate the same subject.

**Question.** *What is your background?*

**Answer.** If background means surroundings: the first 25 years were lived in Riddrie, east Glasgow, a well maintained district of stone-fronted corporation tenements and semi-detached villas. Our neighbours were a nurse, postman, printer and tobacconist, so I was a bit of a snob. I took it for granted that Britain was mainly owned and ruled by Riddrie people – people like my father.

If background means family: it was hardworking, well-educated and very sober. My English grandad was a Northampton foreman shoemaker who came north because the southern employers blacklisted him for trade-union activities. My Scottish grandad was an industrial blacksmith and congregational kirk-elder. In the 30s, when my father married, he worked a box-making machine in a factory, hiked and climbed mountains for a hobby, and did voluntary secretarial work for the Camping Club of Great Britain and the Scottish Youth Hostel Association. My mother was a good housewife who never grumbled, but I now know wanted more from life than it gave – my father had several ways of enjoying himself. She had very few. They were, from that point of view, a typical married couple. I had a younger sister I bullied and fought with, until we started living in separate houses. Then she became one of my best friends.

**Q.** *What was childhood like?*

**A.** Apart from the attacks of asthma and eczema, mostly painless but frequently boring. My parents' main wish for me was that I got to university. They wanted me to get a professional job, you see, because professional people are not so likely to lose their income during a depression. To enter university I had to pass exams in Latin and mathematics which I hated. And of course there was homework. My father wanted to relieve the drudgery of learning by taking me cycling and climbing, but I hated enjoying myself in his shadow, and preferred the escapist worlds of comics and films and books: books most of all. Riddrie had a good library. I had a natural preference for all sorts of escapist crap, but when I had read all there was of that there was nothing left but the good stuff: and myth and legend, and travel, biography and history. I regarded a well-stocked public library as the pinnacle of democratic socialism. That a good dull place like Riddrie had one was proof that the world was essentially well organized.

*Q. When did you realize you were an artist?*

*A.* I did not realize it. Like all infants who were allowed materials to draw with, I did, and nobody suggested I stop. At school I was even encouraged to do it. And my parents (like many parents in those days) expected their children to have a party piece – a song or poem they would perform at domestic gatherings. The poems I recited were very poor A. A. Milne stuff. I found it possible to write verses which struck me as equally good, if not BETTER, because they were mine. My father typed them for me, and the puerile little stories which I sent to children's radio competitions. When I was eleven I read a four-minute programme of my own compositions on Scottish BBC Children's Hour. But I was eight or nine years old when it occured to me that I would write a story which would get printed in a book. This gave me a feeling of deliriously joyful power.

**Q.** *What sort of things did you draw when you were a child?*

**A.** Space ships, monsters, maps of imaginary planets and kingdoms, the settings for stories of romantic and violent adventure, which I told my sister when we walked to school together. She was the first audience I could really depend on in the crucial years between seven and eleven.

**Q.** *How did your parents react to your wish to become a professional artist.*

**A.** They were alarmed. They wanted art to enrich my life in the spare time left over from earning a wage, but they thought, quite correctly, that living to make it would bring me to dole-queues, and wearing second-hand clothes, and borrowing money, and having my electricity cut off – bring me to the state many respectable working folk are forced into during depressions, for reasons they cannot help. That I should choose to become a seedy parasite in order to make obscure luxury items hardly anybody wanted worried them, as it would worry me if my son took that course. So till a few years ago I was embarrassed when I had to tell people my profession. But that feeling of shame stopped last year when I earned enough to pay taxes, so it was not important.

*Q. Is it possible that your concentration on Scottish subject matter will make* **Lanark** *inaccessible to the non-Scottish?*

*A.* You would not be interviewing me if my book was only accessible to Scots. And all imaginative workers make art out of the people and places they know best. No good writer is afraid to use local place names – the bible is full of them. No good writer is afraid to use local politics – Dante peoples Hell, Purgatory and Heaven with local politicians. I don't think Scotland a better country, Glasgow a better city than any other, but all I know of Hell and Heaven was learned here, so this is the ground I use, though sometimes I disguise the fact – just as Dean Swift pretended to describe an island people by pygmies, when describing England.

*Q. What made you write* **1982 Janine***?*

*A.* A wish to show a sort of man everyone recognizes and most can respect: not an artist, not an egoist, not even a radical: a highly skilled workman and technician, dependable, honest and conservative, who should be one of the kings of his age but does not know it, because he has been trained to do what he is told. So he is a plague and pest to himself, and is going mad, quietly, inside.

*Q. What are the main themes of your painting?*

*A.* The Garden of Eden and the triumph of death. All

my pictures use one or other or both. This is nothing abnormal. Any good portrait shows someone at a point in the journey from the happy garden to the triumph of death. I don't regard these states as far-fetched fantasies. Any calm place where folk are enjoying each other's company is heavenly. Any place where crowds struggle with each other in a state of dread is a hell, or on the doorstep of hell.

*Q. How important to you is religion as a theme?*

*A.* Religion is not a theme, religion – any religion – is a way of seeing the world, a way of linking the near, the ordinary, the temporary with the remote, the fantastic, the eternal. Religion is a perspective device so I use it, of course. I differ from the church people in seeing heaven and hell as the material of life itself, not of an afterlife. Intellectually I prefer the Olympian Greek faith. Emotionally I am dominated by the Old Testament. Morally speaking I prefer Jesus, but he sets a standard I'm too selfish to aim for. I'm more comfortable with his daddy, Jehovah, who is nastier but more human. The world is full of wee Jehovahs.

# Another Not Scotland

NOBODY IS MORE LIKE GOD than a baby. Babies live in eternity, a present tense without past, future and thought. When hungry or in pain their whole universe starves and is wholly evil until it supplies what they need, failing which they abolish it by dying. When fed, comfortable, awake they are fascinated by sensations, smells, tastes, noises, lights, colours – everything perceivable. Slowly they start noticing bodies besides theirs.

As a baby I was taken out in a pram by my mother's sister, Aunt Annie, through Riddrie Knowes near my home. *Knowes* is a Scots word for hills, which for years I thought meant trees, because though she pushed me uphill to reach it, we then went along an unpaved road between high elm and beech trees. Years later she told me that one day a dead crow fell into the pram from an overhead branch, perhaps struck dead by heart failure. This unexpected corpse did not hurt me, but she said that when we passed under that tree on later perambulations I looked up as if expecting another bird to fall from it. This showed I was starting to *associate ideas*, as Hobbes,

The Edinburgh Book Festival Ltd (International, of course) hired me to write this for publication by Cargo Publishing 2012 in a boxed set of four slim hardcover books with the titles **Here** and **There**, **Somewhere** and **Everywhere**. The set was named **Elsewhere**. The writers, asked "to explore what it meant to them to be elsewhere," came up with prose grouped (said said the blurb) so that "**Here** were stories of home, **There** was travel and exploration, **Somewhere** a land of magic and imagination and **Everywhere** was what young adults find elsewhere." My piece was 6th in **Here**. This essay spans more of my life that any other, showing how the more I have aged, the more interesting remote past has become to me. It does. Yes indeed.

Locke and Hume called the process. Pavlov later proved it anatomically by opening dogs' cheeks to show they salivate on hearing dinner bells. More experience of that tree must have taught me that it was not a dependable source of dead birds, but proved I had begun connecting past events, however mistakenly, with future expectations.

Before my son could walk or talk I saw that happening in his face when he was fed his first spoonful of ice cream. First a brief frown – *What is this?* – then a look of shock – *It freezes! Hurts!* His face tensed, mouth opened as he drew a deep breath to bellow out his rage, but before that cry emerged he suddenly stopped – his mouth was thawing the freezing cream, the pain of his cold palate roof was giving way to lovely new sweetness on his tongue. He swallowed, licked his lips, opened his mouth for more. The second spoonful made the first range of expressions happen again, but faster. When the last of the ice cream was eaten he was welcoming the coldness as an introduction to something better. Thus we learn to think, while discovering we are not God, but a body in times and places others share.

Wordsworth is surely right to say that the younger we are the more wonderful appear realities like rainbows, sunlight, storms, flowers, mountains etcetera. So what also arouses our early appetite for tales of magic gifts, impossible monsters, fantastic kingdoms? I seem to remember that no sooner was home a familiar place to me than I wanted stories to take me elsewhere, to extravagantly different places. Two or three centuries ago some authors decided that fairy tales were invented by superstitious nursemaids who used them to fill the minds of respectable people's children with nonsense. They wrote stories for children about children, tales about children who told lies and were disobedient so came to really bad ends, good children who sometimes suffered unfairly but were at last rewarded or else died and went to Heaven.

Two very different poets hated such tales – Sam Johnson, a very sensible Christian, and Sam Coleridge, an intensely intellectual scatterbrained Romantic. They agreed that young children needed tales of giants and magical wonders – "to stretch their little minds" said Johnson. The reason was obvious long before Alfred Adler advertized his inferiority complex. Infants live in a world of giants because even children a year or two older tower over them. They can hardly ever redress unfair treatment so like imagining help from fairy godmothers, an Aladdin's lamp, a Wizard of Oz. As a child in the 1930s and 40s I gloried in such stories and the Disney movies based on them, which were also wise enough to contain believable nightmares – the wicked witch's gloating mockery of the skeletal prisoner dead from thirst, Dumbo Jumbo's mother chained as a mad elephant when she revolts against her child being made a clown, Pinocchio growing donkey ears and tail after joining an orgy of vandalism. My appetite for fantasy was healthily abated between the years of eight and ten when I lived beside a Yorkshire market town.

Our home was a bungalow at the side of a rural lane. On the other side was, a neglected field with trees and clumps of bushes, also an overgrown garden

with an old draw-well smothered in ivy. I don't recall
even a ruined house nearby. Here with one or two school friends I made dens – secret places inside bushes or up trees which we wanted nobody else to see or know about. Much healthy open-air business was enjoyed searching for and making these as we explored the banks of the river Wharf, or cycled on country roads to places like the Jackdaw Crags beyond the town, looking for new ones. I recall nothing wild or remarkable done in these dens, not even stories we told each other there. Then in 1944 our family returned to Riddrie, the housing scheme in North-East Glasgow where I was born, and been as happy as most well-treated children, but which now felt like confinement. Secret dens could not be built in our back green or the adjacent public park. The banks of the nearby Monkland Canal would have done, being sufficiently wild, but were forbidden to me as dangerous. Other boys played outdoors by kicking balls about. I didn't enjoy that. Fantastic fiction became my obsession. I visited Riddrie Public Library four or five times a week, never taking much more than a day to read a whole book.

The genre I preferred began with someone who seemed like me in a commonplace world, who found an exit into a wonderland, a place of exciting adventure. The earliest classics of this genre were Lewis Carroll's *Alice* books, and I had heard others dramatised on the BBC's *Children's Hour* – *The Magic Bedknob*, *The Wind in the Willows*, *The Box of Delights*. A sub-division of this had children who found lost or hidden lands. Prodigiously productive Enid

Blyton wrote a shelf of books about these – *The Valley of Adventure*, *Sea of Adventure*, *Island of Adventure*, and others. In adolescence, I enjoyed similar books written for immature adults – Conan Doyle's *The Lost World*, Rider Haggard's *She*, *The Return of She* and *Allan Quartermain*. There were films about them – *King Kong* and *Lost Horizon*. In a BBC radio dramatisation I heard H.G. Wells's *The War of the Worlds* and at once ordered through Glasgow Public Libraries all his early romances, which I still think are science fiction's unsurpassable best. His *The First Men on the Moon* shows an impossible adjacent planet, yet imagined in gloriously convincing detail that also makes it excellent social criticism. That novel, his *The Time Machine* and *The War of the Worlds* describe exotic worlds elsewhere, but are no more escapist fiction than *Gulliver's Travels* and Orwell's *1984*.

Before leaving secondary school I decided to write a book about a fantastic world of my own invention that would also grotesquely satirise the world I knew. In planning this I was inspired by Kafka's *The Trial*, translated by Edwin and Willa Muir, and also by their foreword saying that Kafka's protagonist, like John Bunyan's Pilgrim, was seeking salvation in a world where neither Heaven nor Hell are clearly signposted. This novel in which a bureaucracy uses a rented bedroom, the attic of a slum tenement, a pub's bar room and a cathedral outside service time to entangle a man could be happening in Glasgow, and the bureaucrats were more humane and believable than Orwell's Thought Police. Kafka's junior bank manager was so ruthlessly selfish that I never doubted his guilt. And now I was also reading books about the growing pains of young men in worlds nearer my own in time and space – *David Copperfield, A Portrait of the Artist as a Young Man, Sons and Lovers*. I realised that books which, as Milton says, *the world would not willingly let die* must present real local experiences such as those Dickens, Joyce and D.H. Lawrence suffered, even if they were combined with strange Heavens, Hells and magic wonderlands elsewhere. Many books in the Bible did that, and most folk tales, the stories of Hans Christian Andersen and poems I loved and knew by heart, especially the *Scottish Border Ballads*. In a public library (Denistoun, not Riddrie) I found Tillyard's *The English Epic and its Background* which, after briefly surveying the great epic poems and histories of Greece, Rome, Italy and Portugal, concluded that since Milton's time, great epics were likely to be in prose, and mentioned Walter Scott's most Scottish novels as almost (though not quite) amounting to a national epic. So I set out to write an epic, and a Scottish one.

Like many Scots children's primary and secondary schooling, mine had said nothing about Scottish culture. Until the 1970s our state schools had generally a broader and higher standard than their English equivalents, but aimed to qualify the smartest pupils for high positions in London, Oxford, Cambridge, Canada, Australia and elsewhere, so in Scotland English literature was taught as if no Scot had contributed to it, though some Irish and American authors were named. We had heard of Robert Burns because most of our parents knew some of his poems and many were sung on the BBC Scottish Home Service, but R.L. Stevenson was dismissed as a writer for very young children and the only Walter Scott novel given to us was *Ivanhoe*. This tells how the Normans in England became acceptable to Saxons they had conquered – a fine lesson for Scottish children! For most of the 20th century the poet Hugh MacDiarmid was treated as a pest by Scottish politicians and ignored as a poet by British academics, though his work and critical writing had won the attention of French and American professors of literature. In 1958, Hogg's *The Private Memoirs & Confessions of a Justified Sinner*, with a preface by Andre Gide, came to Glasgow Public Libraries and me, proving that a Scottish tradition of combining local and supernatural events existed in prose as well as poetry. But to work well in a book, the Scottishness of Scottish characters must be taken for granted. Dostoyevsky slightly spoils some great novels with sentences about Russian-ness. *Gillespie* by MacDougall Hay is a nearly great novel about a dull but cunning, mean, greedy grocer becoming wealthy in a Highland fishing village, blighting lives around him as he does so. This account of late 19th century capitalism at work through interesting people in a small town would be almost as good as Hardy's *The Mayor of Casterbridge* and Brown's *The House with the Green Shutters*, were it not nearly ruined by a first chapter suggesting that Gillespie's parents were doomed to produce a monster by their weird, uncanny Scottish home. I saw that the local setting of my epic, like the supernatural part, must be shown without comment in convincing details.

I was 44 in 1979 when this novel was completed and accepted by an Edinburgh publishing house. Two years passed before it was printed. I did not foresee that it would be a successful book but I knew that a print factory would soon be stamping paper with properly spaced type and binding it into books of 560 pages each. I imagined shelves of them in warehouses and shops, each as solid as a brick yet each containing my soul – my inner being – along with everyone and everything that had helped to make me, including (of course) every story I had enjoyed.

This sense that my main reality would become books that would outlast my body brought peace and relaxation that were helped by a new job that, in return for a little easy, agreeable work, gave me a steady wage and an office with a view across Kelvingrove Park. I was writer in residence at Glasgow University, which meant discussing the writings of a few students who wanted my advice, but did not require me to write anything. Nor did I wish to write. I had no ideas for another story, had no intention of seeking them. I was at last free to enjoy reading for its own sake as I had done as a child. Escapist fantasy no longer interested me. I bought Ezra Pound's complete *Cantos*, having gathered they were great poetry about the good and bad monetary roots of our civilisation, something we should all understand, especially since economists believe only they can do it. I also bought *The Road to Xanadu* by Livingston Lowes, a study of how Coleridge had come to write his great long poem and a fragment of one.

I was not a very productive versifier, but

interested in the working of creative minds.

I found Pound's *Cantos* hard going apart from the denunciation of extortionate money lending (which Marx called Capitalism) as a blight upon well-made art and building. He quoted Chinese and Renaissance scholars, founders of the USA republic and examples of Mussolini's public work schemes in many pages, amounting, in my mind, to a formless, confusing fog. But suddenly a line from one of his Chinese *Cantos* spoke clear sense to me:

*Moping around the Emperor's court, waiting for the order-to-write.*

The last three words were obviously hyphenated because they were translations of one Chinese word. This suggested a highly cultured, hierarchic empire which might train a man from infancy to be its greatest poet, and flatter him with high rank and privileges, yet prevent him from writing a word before it wants a poem to justify the government's most appalling crime. I lifted a pen, wrote these sentences –

*Dear mother, dear father, I like the new palace. It is all squares like a chessboard. The red squares are buildings, the white squares are gardens…*

– and started inventing another new world elsewhere. Livingstone Lowes' book had also stimulated this by showing that more exotic domains than Kubla Khan's had gone into making Coleridge's great poetic fragment. There was the artificial paradise in the Atlas Mountains where assassins were trained, the happy valley where Abyssinian princes were confined, a sacred Himalayan grotto and a source of the Nile. This was reviving in a middle-aged man the pleasures of childhood den-making and every lost, secret, romantic world that had once entertained him in books, comics and films. I enjoyed giving my dumb poet a luxurious apartment, garden and servants, and inventing the cruel education that qualified him for these privileges, and revealing the huge confidence trick through which the vast, exploitive empire was ruled, since the Emperor turns out to be a puppet managed by ventriloquists. I believe that, for its length, *Five Letters from an Eastern Empire* is my best story.

After its publication in 1983 a producer in Scottish BBC Radio decided to broadcast it, and asked if I would like the reader to be a particular actor. I suggested Bill Paterson. "But surely he has a *Scottish* voice?" said the producer, who was English. I said, yes, Bill Paterson *had* a Scottish voice, but there were many Scottish accents, both local and general – my narrator was a high-class mandarin, and Scotland had many mandarins in its universities, and Bill Paterson could easily sound like one of them. "But your narrator is supposed to be the Poet Laureate of a *great empire*!" said the producer, who obviously thought it irrelevant that Britain now had none, so had the story recorded in London by an English actor. That broadcast won the approval of Rodger Scruton, a Conservative critic who thought the story a satire on Communism. A friend who later attended an international literary conference told me he had heard a Chinese and Japanese scholar discuss which of their nations my empire resembled. I told him I thought it was very much like Britain.

# Childhood Reading

THE FOLLOWING REPORT on my reading was made near the end of my 16th year in September 1951, and retained by my English teacher, Mr Meikle, whose widow gave it to me after his death in the spring of 1993.

It was written with a steel-nibbed pen dipped in a squat glass bottle (if I wrote at home) or (if I wrote at school) into an inkwell – a truncated cone of glazed white earthenware less than two inches high, whose wide end was closed by a glazed white earthenware disc, slightly more than an inch in diameter, a disc with a hole in the centre to admit the pencil and a projecting tip all round which let it hang smugly in the circular hole cut for it in our desk tops. In 1951 ball point pens had been commercially marketed for several years, but most British schools forbade their use because it would reduce the quality of our handwriting. In those days most employers still preferred clerks whose penwork was clear and elegant, so schools encouraged it. In 1951 my writing, like nowadays, was very clear but not at all elegant, having changed little since I learned

These are answers to a questionnaire sent to secondary schools, either by the Department of Education for Scotland, or else the Glasgow part of it, to find how much the pupils had read of well respected authors. The questionnaire, headed **Whitehill Senior Secondary School Report on Reading** may even have been devised by the teachers of English (Mr Meikle among them) who gave them out. I made this the start of an essay Robert Crawford asked me to write for a new journal, **Scotlands**, he was editing. The University of Edinburgh was the publisher. It later became **Scottish Studies Review**. First printed in 1994. The article here is a wee bit enlarged. Robert had also been Mr Meikle's pupil when both were at Hutcheson's, the Grammar School, as good 2ndary schools were once called.

to draw words when four or five. The letters are distinctly shaped and connected, but the loops of a, d, g and q are almost circular, with oval ascending loops, as are the ascending and descending loops of f, g, h, j, k and l. All ascenders and descenders are short. I could never slope the vertical strokes slightly to the right as we were urged, so my vertical strokes are exactly so, or incline as much to the left as the right.

I am almost certain the manuscript I gave to Mr Meikle was copied out at home from an earlier, messier attempt. I was as prone then to afterthoughts as I am still, and though the spaces left for book titles after the authors names were all the same size, the titles written in are all written without a blot or correction.

SCOTT – *None.*
JANE AUSTEN – None.
DICKENS – *The Christmas Books. Barnaby Rudge. Little Dorritt. Oliver Twist. David Copperfield. The Pickwick Papers.*
THACKERAY – *The Rose and The Ring.*
CHARLOTTE BRONTE – *Jane Eyre.*
EMILY BRONTE – *Wuthering Heights.*
GEORGE BORROW – *Lavengro. Romany Rye.*
MEREDITH – *The Ordeal of Richard Feverel.*
R. L. STEVENSON – *Treasure Island. Kidnapped. Doctor Jekyll and Mr Hyde. The Master of Ballantrae. A Child's Garden of Verses. Virginibus Pueresque.*
TROLLOPE – *None.*
HARDY – *None.*
BARRIE – *None.*

KIPLING – *Just So Stories. The Jungle Books. Puck of Pooks Hill. Stalky and Co. Seven Seas.*

CONAN DOYLE – *The Casebook of Sherlock Holmes. A Study in Scarlett. The Sign of Four. The Lost World. The Poison Belt.*

CONRAD – *Youth. Casper Ruiz. The Shadow Line. Under Western Eyes. Chance. Last Essays.*

SHAW – *The Black Girl in Search of God.* (Here follows the titles of the 43 plays Shaw had published in 1934, and I had read in a book my father owned, to which I added:) *Scraps and Shavings. An Intelligent Woman's Guide to Capitalism, Socialism and Fascism.*

H. G. WELLS – *The Time Machine. Collected Short Stories. The Invisible Man. The War of the Worlds. The First Men on the Moon. The Island of Dr. Moreau. The Food of the Gods. The History of Mr. Polly. Tono Bungay. The King Who Was a King. A Study of History. An Experiment in Autobiography. The Shape of Things to Come.*

JACK LONDON – *None.*

SIEGFRIED SASSOON – *None.*

H. V. MORTON – *None.*

WODEHOUSE – *None.*

BENNETT – *The Card.*

BUCHAN – *The Thirty Nine Steps. Prester John. The Powerhouse. Greenmantle.*

HUGH WALPOLE – *Mr Perrin and Mr Trail. Jeremy.*

NEIL MUNRO – *The Daft Days.*

OTHER AUTHORS AND TITLES – Voltaire's *Candide.* Sterne's *Tristram Shandy, Sentimental Journey.* Defoe's *Robinson Crusoe.* Fielding's *History of Jonathon Wilde The Great.* Swift's *Gulliver's Travels.* Hugo's *Les Miserables, The*

*Hunchback of Notre Dame.* Mrs. Gaskell's *Cranford.* Poe's *Tales of Mystery and Imagination.* Verne's *Twenty Thousand Leagues Under the Sea.* Carroll's *Alice in Wonderland, Through the Looking Glass.* Kingsley's *Waterbabies,* unabridged. Huxley's *Brave New World, Ape and Essence.* Orwell's *Animal Farm, Nineteen Eighty-Four.* Apuleius' *The Golden Ass.* Boswell's *Life of Johnson.* Ibsen's *The Wild Duck, Peer Gynt, An Enemy of the People.* Edward Lear's *The Complete Nonsense.* Hendrick Van Loon's *Home of Mankind, Story of Mankind, Arts of Mankind, Liberation of Mankind.* Goethe's *Faust Part I.*

The above list was not wholly truthful as I wanted my teachers to think me a greater scholar than I was – a greater scholar than they were. I had read only a little beyond the start of *Barnaby Rudge* and Conrad's *Under Western Eyes.* I stopped reading the first because I am impatient of man-made mysteries and Dickens' 18th century convinced me less than Conrad's. I recoiled from the second because I hated to read of lives ruined early by treachery. Nor had I read Arnold Bennett's *The Card.* I had heard a radio talk on it with dramatized excerpts, and knew I could answer questions on it that would satisfy any adult.

Nor had I read more than a few pages of *The Intelligent Woman's Guide to Capitalism* etcetera. To this day I cannot thoroughly read a work of politics, sociology or philosophy which does not describe particular instances. Shaw's treatise may have had many, but his title made me doubt that. But I had read enough to grasp and believe that the more just society is, the more essential to it is everyone's work, and the more equal are their incomes, which I still believe. And I had only dipped into a few chapters of Well's *Study of History* in the Pelican paperback version.

Explaining how, and where, and when I came to read the other books would take at least a year, so I will comment on very few. The complete plays of Bernard Shaw and Henrik Ibsen stood on the middle shelf of a bookcase in my parents, beside Carlyle's *French Revolution*, Macauleys *Essays*, *The History of the Working Classes in Scotland* and *Our Noble Families* by Tom Johnson, a Thinkers library volume called *Humanities Gain from Unbelief*, an anthropology of extracts from atheists called *Lift Up Your Heads*, a large blue-grey bound volume with *The Miracle of Life* stamped in gold on the spine. This contained essays on *The Dawn of Life*, *What Evolution Means*, *Life That Has Vanished*, *Evolution as The Clock Ticks*, *The Animal Kingdom*, *The Plant Kingdom*, *Man's Family Tree*, *Races of Mankind*, *The Human Machine at Work*, *Psychology Through the Ages*, *Discoverers of Life's Secrets*. The 476 pages (excluding the index) were half given to black and white photographs and diagrams. The middle shelf also held Shaw's *Quintessence of Ibsenism* and *The Adventures of the Black Girl in Search of God*.

The last was perhaps the first adult narrative brought to my attention at the age of three or four. I cannot remember that though was told of it later. I recall discovering it in my middle teens among my dad's books and enjoying it greatly. He then told me he had read it to me when I was wee. The story is an evolutionary fable about human faith, told through the quest of a black girl through the African bush. Converted to Christianity by an English missionary she sets out to find God, but doubting he can be found on earth, and encounters in various dealings the gods of Moses, Job and Isaiah, then meeting Ecclesiastes the Preacher, Jesus, Mahomet, the founders of the Christian sects, an expedition of scientific rationalists, Voltaire the sceptic and George Bernard Shaw the socialist, who teach her that God should not be searched for but worked for, by cultivating the small piece of world in our power as intelligently and unselfishly as possible.

The moral of this story is as high as human wisdom has reached, but I cannot have grasped it then. My father told me that I kept asking, "Will the next god be the real one daddy?" No doubt I would have liked the black girl to have at last met a universal maker like my father: vaster, of course, but with an equal vital sense of my importance. I'm glad he did not teach me to believe in that, for I would have had to unlearn it. But my first encounter with this book was in a pre-history I have forgotten or suppressed, though I returned to it later. It was a beautifully made book with crisp clear black-woodcuts decorating covers, titlepage and text. These were by a young artist called Farrel, obviously influenced by Eric Gill, and like the text it blended the mundane and exotic. A few days ago I learned how closely Shaw worked with Farrel, suggesting some illustrations with preliminary sketches of his own, as Lewis Caroll had worked with Tenniel on the *Alice* books.

This was all on the middle shelf of the bedroom

bookcase. The shelf above was blocked by orange-red spines of *Left Wing Book Club*, four fifths of it being the collected works of Lenin in English: dense text with no pictures or conversations in at all. The bottom shelf was exactly filled by the *Harmsworth Encyclopedia*, because the bookcase had been sold along with the Encyclopedia by the publisher, who owned the *Daily Record* in which they were first advertised. This contained many pictures, mostly grey monochrome photographs, but each alphabetical section had a complex line drawing in front, a crowded landscape in which an enthroned figure representing Ancient History (for example) was surrounded by orders of Architecture, an Astronomical telescope, glimpses of Australia and the Arctic with Amundsen, and an Armadillo and Aardvarks rooting around a discarded anchor. I gathered that these volumes contained explanations of everything there is and had been, with lives of everyone important. The six syllables of the name EN-CY-CLO-PAED-I-A seemed to sum up these thick brown books which summed up the universe. Saying them gave me a sense of power confirmed by pleasure this gave my parents. But the four colour plates showing flags of all nations and heraldic coats-of-arms gave an undiluted pleasure which was purely sensuous. I was fascinated by the crisp oblongs holding blues, reds, yellows, greens, blacks and whites combining in patterns more vivid and easily seen than any where else, apart from our Christmas decorations.

I found a similar but more complex pleasure in Wills cigarette picture cards, gathered for me by my father into slim little squareish pale grey albums

costing a penny, when empty. There was an album for
Garden Flowers, Garden Hints, British Wild Animals, Railway Equipment, Cycling and Aircraft of the Royal Airforce. These cards, five to each page, were windows into places where weather was always a bright afternoon and everything was in best condition. Cigarette card albums, encyclopedias and *The Miracle of Life* are still a source of information and imagery for me, though I have since added others. Together with *The Black Girl in Search of God* they occupied the place an illustrated family bible may have held in the lives of my father's parents, who died before I was born.

From my four and a half years before the Second World War began – or from the five years before it hotted up – I also remember a big book of Hans Andersen fairy tales, well illustrated, which must have been read to me because I cannot remember not knowing *The Marsh Kings Daughter* and *The Brave Tin Soldier* and *The Tinderbox* and *The Little Match Girl* and *The Snow Queen* and *The Little Mermaid* and their mingling of magic with the ordinary urban and domestic, and their terrible sad sense of how quickly things change and are lost to faithful people whose affections do not. There were flower-fairy books, Rupert Bear annuals (also in sunny colours) Milnes' *House at Pooh Corner* and two Christoper Robin verse books. All these books were left behind when we flitted from our home until the war ended, spending the last three or four years of it in Wetherby, a Yorkshire market town.

And there I read with delight Lofting's *Dr Doolittle* books, Kipling's *Just So Stories*, Thackeray's *The Rose and The Ring* (all illustrated by their authors), the *Alice* books, and Kingsley's *Waterbabies* in (as I was careful to mention in the 1951 school reading report) the unabridged version. Also *The Wind in the Willows*, though a chapter called *The Piper at the Gates of Dawn* embarrassed and annoyed me. I dislike mysteriously superior presences. With the exception of *Wind in the Willows* and Thackeray's book all these had (like Shaw's *Black Girl* fable) encyclopedic scope, mingling people, animals and magic, going under the earth and soaring over it, making as free with time and space as any Indian or African creation myth, or *Paradise Lost*, or Goethe's *Faust*, or Ibsen's *Peer Gynt*. And all these books were strengthened by artfully blending the impossible and normal. That the fairy-tale tyrant of Crim Tartary should be a very commonplace Victorian pater familias at home – that, even so, when unexpectedly enchanted by a lovely chambermaid he instinctively proposed in Shakespearian rhyming couplets to marry her after drowning his first wife – seemed to me wonderfully comic. It was incredible but appropriate.

Which brings my reading to the age of ten without even mentioning Kingsley's *Heroes*, Hawthorne's *Tanglewood Tales*, a version of the *Odyssey* for children and *Gods, Graves and Scholars*, a book about the archeological discovery of Troy, Mycenae, Minoa, Babylon, Nineveh, Egypt and Yucatan.

# Childhood Writing and Mr Meikle

AT THE AGE OF FIVE I SAT in a room made and furnished by folk I never met and had never heard of me. Here, in a crowd of nearly forty strangers, I remained six hours a day and five days a week for many years, being ordered about by a much bigger, older stranger who found me no more interesting than the rest. Luckily the prison was well stocked with pencils and our warder (a woman) wanted us to use them. One day she asked us what we thought were good things to write poems about. The four or five with opinions on the matter (I was one of them) called out suggestions which she wrote down on the blackboard:-

> A FAIRY
> A MUSHROOM
> SOME GRASS
> PINE NEEDLES
> A TINY STONE

We thought these things poetic because the verses in our school-books mostly dealt with small, innocuous items. The teacher now asked everyone in the class to write their own verses about one or more of these items. With ease, speed, hardly any intelligent thought I wrote this:-

This story is not fiction, for the dream occurred to me, though I admit adding to the end more poets than I recalled upon waking. I also imagined the last reparteé with Archie Hind. It came last in my book **Ten Tales Tall and True** in 1993, published by Bloomsbury, one of 13 tales. The title page said, "This book contains more tales than 10, so the title is a tall tale too. I would spoil the book if I shortened that, spoil the title if I made it true." Mr Meikle did not live to see the book but I read him the story before he died and drew his portrait, to place as a vignette on the last page. He was pleased about that. I am glad it has the same place here. This was my first book to be type-set by a friend living in Glasgow, Donald Saunders.

*A fairy on a mushroom,*
*sewing with some grass,*
*and a pine-tree needle,*
*for the time to pass.*
*Soon the grass it withered,*
*The needle broke away,*
*She sat down on a tiny stone,*
*And wept for half the day.*

The teacher read this aloud to the class, pointing out that I had not only used every item on the list, I had used them in the order of listing. While writing the verses I had been excited by my mastery of the materials. I now felt extraordinarily interesting. Most people become writers by degrees. From me, in an instant, all effort to become anything else dropped like a discarded overcoat. I never abandoned verse but came to spend more time writing prose – small harmless items interested me less than prehistoric monsters, Roman arenas, volcanoes, cruel queens and life on other planets. I aimed to write a novel in which all these would be met and dominated by me, a boy from Glasgow. I wanted to get it written and published when I was twelve, but failed. Each time I wrote some opening sentences I saw they were the work of a child. The only works I managed to finish were short compositions on subjects set by the teacher. She was not the international audience I wanted, but better than nobody.

At the age of twelve I entered Whitehill Senior Secondary School, a plain late 19th-century building of the same height and red sandstone as adjacent tenements, but more menacing. The playgrounds were walled and fenced like prison exercise yards: the windows, though huge, were disproportionately narrow, with sills deliberately designed to be far above our heads when we sat down. Half of what we studied there impressed me as gloomily as the building. Instead of one teacher I had eight a week, often six a day, and half of them treated me as an obstinate idiot. They had to treat me as an idiot. Compound interests, sines, cosines, Latin declensions, tables of elements tasted to my mind like sawdust in my mouth: those who dished it out expected me to swallow while an almost bodily instinct urged me to vomit. I did neither. My body put on an obedient, hypocritical act while my mind dodged out through imaginary doors. In this I was like many other schoolboys, perhaps most others. Nearly all of us kept magazines of popular adventure serials under our school books and when possible stuck our faces into *The Rover, Hotspur, Wizard* and highly coloured American comics, then new to Britain, in which the proportion of print to pictorial matter was astonishingly small. Only the extent of my addiction to fictional worlds was worse than normal, being magnified into mania by inability to enjoy much else. I was too clumsily fearful to enjoy football and mix with girls, though women and brave actions were what I most wanted. Since poems, plays and novels often deal with these I easily swallowed the fictions urged on us by the teachers of English, though the authors (Chaucer, Shakespeare, Jane Austen, Walter Scott) were far less easily digested than *The Rover* etc.

Mr Meikle was my English teacher and managed the school magazine. I met him when I was

47
IMAGINARY
DOORS

thirteen. He became my first editor and publisher, and a year or two later, by putting me in charge of the magazine's literary and artistic pages, enabled me to edit and publish myself. There must have been times when he gave me advice and directions, but these were offered so tactfully that I cannot remember them: I was only aware of freedom and opportunity. Quiet courtesy, sympathy and knowledge are chiefly what I recall of him, and a theatricality so mild that few of us saw it as such, though it probably eased his dealings with those inclined to mistake his politeness for weakness. I will try to describe him more exactly.

His lined triangular face above a tall thin body, his black academic gown, thin dark moustache, dark eyebrows and smooth reddish hair gave him a pleasantly saturnine look, especially as the cheerfully brushed-back hair emphasized two horn-shaped bald patches, one on each side of his brow. While the class worked quietly at a writing exercise he would sit marking homework at his tall narrow desk, and sometimes one of his eyebrows would shoot up into a ferociously steep question mark, and then sink to a level line again while the other eyebrow shot up. This suggested he had read something terrible in the page before him, but was now trying to understand the writer's frame of mind. Such small performances always caused a faint stir of amusement among the few who saw them, a stir he gave no sign of noticing. Sometimes, wishing to make my own eyebrows act independently, I held one down with a hand and violently worked the other, but I never managed it. Outside the classroom Mr Meikle smoked a meerschaum pipe. He conducted one of the school choirs which competed in the Glasgow music festivals. His slight theatrical touches had nothing to do with egotism. As he paced up and down the corridors between our desks and talked about literature he was far more interested in the language of Shakespeare, and what Milton learned from it, and what Dryden learned from Milton, and what Pope learned from Dryden, than in himself.

Not everyone liked Mr Meikle's teaching. He did not stimulate debates about what Shakespeare or Pope said, he simply replied to any question we raised about these, explained alternative readings, said why he preferred one of them and went on talking. Nor did he dictate to us glib little phrases which, repeated in an essay, would show an examiner that the student had been driven over the usual hurdles. He let us scribble down what we liked in our English note-books. This style of teaching seemed to some as dull as I found the table of elements, but it just suited me. While he told us, with erudition and humour, the official story of English literature, I filled note-book after note-book with doodles recalling the fictions I had discovered at the local cinema, on my parents bookshelves, in the local library. I was not ignoring Mr Meikle. While sketching doors and corridors into the worlds of Walt Disney, Tarzan, Hans Andersen, Edgar Allan Poe, Lewis Carroll and H. G. Wells I was pleased to hear how the writers of *Hamlet*, *Paradise Lost*, *The Rape of the Lock* and *Little Dorrit* had invented worlds which were just as spooky. I was still planning a book containing all I valued in other works, but one of these works was beginning to be Glasgow. I had begun to think my family, neighbours, friends, the girls I could not get hold of were as interesting as any people in fiction – almost as interesting as me, but how could I show it? Joyce's *Portrait of the Artist as a Young Man* suggested a way, but I doubted if I could write such a book before I was seventeen. Meanwhile Mr Meikle's voice absorbed my whole attention. I remember especially his demonstrations of the rhetorical shifts by which Mark Anthony in *Julius Caesar* changes the mind of the mob.

My private talks with Mr Meikle took place before the class but out of its earshot. We could talk quietly because my head, as I stood beside his desk, was level with his as he sat leaning on it. I remember telling him something about my writing ambitions and adding that, while I found helpful suggestions in his teaching and in the music, history and art classes, the rest of my schooling was a painful hindrance, a humiliating waste of time for both me and my teachers. Mr Meikle answered that Scottish education was not designed to produce specialists under the age of eighteen. Students of science and engineering needed a grounding in English before a Scottish university accepted them, arts students needed a basis of maths, both had to know Latin and he thought this wise. Latin was the language of people who had made European culture by combining the religious books of the Jews with the sciences and arts of the skeptical Greeks. Great writers in every European language had been inspired by Roman literature; Shakespeare only knew a little Latin, but his plays showed he put the little he knew to very good use. Again, mathematics were also a language, an

exact way of describing mental and physical events
which created our science and industry. No writer who
wished to understand the modern world should ignore
it. I answered that Latin and maths were not taught like
languages through which we could discover and say
great things, they were taught as ways to pass
examinations – that was how parents and pupils and
most of the teachers viewed them; whenever I
complained about the boring nature of a Latin or
mathematical exercise nobody explained there could
be pleasure in it, they said, "You can forget all that
when you've been through university and got a steady
job." Mr Meikle looked thoughtfully across the bent
heads of the class before him, and after a pause said
he hoped I would be happy in what I wished to do
with my life, but most people, when their educations
stopped, earned their bread by work which gave them
very little personal satisfaction, but must be done
properly simply because their employers required it
and our society depended upon it. School had to
prepare the majority for their future, as well as the
lucky few. He spoke with a resignation and regret I only
fully understood eight or nine years later when I
earned my own bread, for a while, by school-teaching.

This discussion impressed and disturbed me.
Education – schooling – was admired by my parents
and praised by the vocal part of Scottish culture as a
way to get liberty, independence and a more useful and
satisfying life. Since this was my own view also, I had
thought the parts of my schooling which felt like
slavery were accidents which better organization would
abolish. That the parts which felt like slavery were a

deliberate preparation for more serfdom – that our schooling was simultaneously freeing some while preparing the rest to be their tools – had not occurred to me. The book I at last wrote described the adventures of someone a bit like me in a world like that, and though not an autobiography (my hero goes mad and commits suicide at the age of twenty-two) it contained portraits of people I had known, Mr Meikle among them. While writing the pages where he appeared I considered several pseudonyms for him. (Strang? Craig? McGurk? Maclehose? Dinwiddie?) but the only name which seemed to suit him was Meikle, so at last I called him that. I was forty-five when the book got published and did not know if he was still alive, but thought he would be amused and perhaps pleased if he read it.

And he was alive, and read it, and was pleased. He came to my book-signing session at Smith's in St Vincent Street, and said so. It was wonderful to see him again, as real as ever despite being a character in my book. Of course his hair was grey, his scalp much balder, but my head was greying and balding too. I realized he had been a fairly young man when I first saw him in Whitehill, much younger than I was now.

Three years ago I got a note from Mr Meikle saying he could not come to the signing session for my latest novel, as arthritis had confined him to his home. He had ordered a copy from the bookshop, and hoped I would sign it for him, and either leave it to be collected by Mrs Meikle (who was still in good health) or bring it to him myself. I phoned and told him I could not bring it, as I was going away for a month immediately after the signing session, but I would inscribe a copy for Mrs Meikle to collect, and would phone to arrange a visit as soon as I returned. He said he looked forward to that.

I went away and tried to finish writing a book I had promised to a publisher years before. I failed, came home a month later and did not phone Mr Meikle. He was now one of many I had broken promises to, felt guilty about, wanted to forget. When forgetting was impossible I lay in bed remembering work to be finished, debts to be paid, letters to write, phone-calls and visits I should make. I ought also to get my false teeth mended, tidy my flat and clean the window facing my door on the communal landing. All these matters seemed urgent and I often fell asleep during efforts to list them in order of priority. Action only seemed possible when I jumped up to fend off an immediate disaster, which Mr Meikle was not.

Suddenly I decided to visit him without phoning. It seemed the only way. The sun had set, the street-lights shone, I was sure he was not yet abed, so the season must have been late in the year or very early. The close where he lived was unusually busy. A smart woman holding a clipboard came down and I was pressed to the wall by a bearded man rushing up. He carried on his shoulder what seemed a telescope in a felt sock. I noticed electrical cables on the stairs, and on a landing a stack of the metal tripods used with lighting equipment. None of this surprised me. Film making is as common in Glasgow as in other cities, though I did not think it concerned Mr Meikle. It did. His front door stood open and the cables snaked through it. The lobby was full of recording people and camera people who seemed waiting for something, and I saw from behind a lady who might have been Mrs Meikle carrying round a tray loaded with mugs of coffee. Clearly, a visit at this time would be an interruption. I went back downstairs regretting I had not phoned first, but glad the world was not neglecting Mr Meikle. I even felt slightly jealous of him.

A while after this abortive visit I entered a public house, bought a drink and sat beside a friend who was talking to a stranger. The friend said, "I don't think you two know each other," and introduced the stranger as a sound technician with the British Broadcasting Corporation. The stranger stared hard at me and said, "You may not know me, but I know you. You arranged for a BBC camera crew to record you talking to your old school-teacher in his home, and didn't even turn up." "I never arranged that!" I cried, appalled, "I never even discussed the matter – never thought of it!"
"Then you arranged it when you were drunk."

I left that pub and rushed away to visit Mr Meikle at once. I was sure the BBC had made a mistake then blamed me for it, and I was desperate to tell Mr Meikle that he had suffered intrusion and inconvenience through no fault of mine.

Again I entered his close and hurried up to his flat, but there was something wrong with the stairs. They grew unexpectedly steep and narrow. There were no landings or doors off them, and in my urgency I never thought of turning back. At last I emerged onto a narrow railed balcony close beneath a skylight. From here I looked down into a deep hall with several

balconies round it at lower levels, a hall which looked
like the interior of Whitehill Senior Secondary School, though the Whitehill I remembered had been demolished in 1980. But this was definitely the place where Mr Meikle lived, for looking downward I saw him emerge from a door at the side of the hall and cross the floor toward a main entrance. He did not walk fast, but a careful firmness of step suggested his arthritis had abated a little. He was accompanied by a party of people who, even from this height, I recognized as Scottish writers rather older than me: Norman MacCaig, Ian Crichton Smith, Robert Garioch and Sorley Maclean. As they accompanied Mr Meikle out through the main door I wanted to shout on them to wait for me, but felt too shy. Instead I turned and ran downstairs, found an exit and hurried along the pavement after them, and all the time I was wondering how they had come to know Mr Meikle as well or better than I did. Then I remembered they too had been teachers of English. That explained it – they were Mr Meikle's colleagues. That was why they knew him.

But when I caught up with the group it had grown bigger. I saw many Glasgow writers I knew: Morgan and Lochhead and Leonard and Kelman and Spence etcetera, and from the Western Isles Black Angus and the Montgomery sisters, Derick Thomson, Mackay Brown and others I knew slightly or not at all from the Highlands, Orkneys and Shetlands, from the North Coast and the Eastern Seaboard, Aberdeenshire, Dundee and Fife, from Edinburgh, the Lothians and all the Borders and Galloway up to Ayrshire.

"Are all these folk writers?" I cried aloud. I was afraid

that my own work would be swamped by the work of all these other Scottish writers.

"Of course not!" said Archie Hind, who was walking beside me, "Most of them are readers. Readers are just as important as writers and often a lot lonelier. Arthur Meikle taught a lot of readers that they are not alone. So did others in this mob."

"Do you mean that writers are teachers too?" I asked, more worried than ever.

"What a daft idea!" said Archie, laughing, "Writers and teachers are in different kinds of show business. Of course some of them show more than others."

I awoke, and saw it was a dream,
though not entirely.

# An Essay in the Future Tense*

THE NEW EDUCATION BILL will be passed only after much opposition and delay. Strikes, protest meetings, demonstrations will shudder the country, and the Government will be forced into a general election. Nonetheless, the Bill (being conceived by a Scots Minister of Education) will eventually pass into law. Under it, pupils will attend whatever classes they wish and each teacher will be paid according to the number of his pupils.

At the start of the new system, schools throughout the country will pass into a time of wonderful confusion. Pupils will devote the first days of their new freedom to those subjects they enjoy. The gymnasiums and football pitches will be unusually crowded. But by the second week even the most vigorous will have had enough, and will drift into other classes.

This drift will be sustained by the second part of the Bill – the part which has the teacher paid according to the size of his class. While the P.T. teachers are earning £50 per week, the other teachers will have to leave the profession or make their instruction interesting.

They will do this in many ways. Probably a progressive art teacher will lead the way, replacing the drearier cylinders and stuffed ducks of his classroom

*From the 1952 Whitehill Senior Secondary School magazine. The non-coercive secondary school agenda proposed here still strikes me as both practical and humane, on a financial basis that should appeal to lovers of the free market. The 2nd item shows my wish to be in any group discussing big ideas.

with specially hired artists' models. Similarly, the classroom with rows of hard desks, bare walls, and black-boards, will give place to rooms bright with colour, hung with good pictures and interesting apparatus, and well designed furniture. For instance, the maths room of the future will be fitted with working models which explain geometry and algebra in terms of aeroplane designing and boat-building. The walls will be decorated with murals depicting incidents in the lives of famous mathematicians (such as Archimedes leaping from his bath shouting "Eureka"). Cinema and television screens will be in every classroom.

Pupils who naturally dislike a subject, and who have not just been discouraged from it by dull teaching, will not attend that class. Why should they? Should a boy who loves engineering and will eventually make his living by it, be forced to attend classes on painting, unless he wishes to? Force him to study painting against his will and he will hate it. In the same way the artistically inclined pupil will not be taught mathematical problems used in building machinery, unless he enjoys them. Of course, the dull teachers who are not interested in making their subjects enjoyable will have no pupils and no pay, and will leave the profession. They will become what nature intended them to be – bank clerks, commercial travellers, and museum attendants. Similarly, pupils lacking interest in all subjects in the curriculum will leave school and become gravediggers or politicians.

There are many drawbacks to this scheme, but these will be gradually overcome by wisdom, imagination, and experience. By that time Whitehill will have its own canteen, swimming-pool, kitchen-garden, theatre, newspaper, dance-hall, psychiatrist...

## THE STUDENTS CHRISTIAN UNION

The S.C.M wants to make more students consider thoughtfully the teaching of Jesus. It does this through debate. The members discuss different ideas of Christianity, each giving his own view of the matter, whether it is orthodox or heretical. The meeting has a place for many shades of religious (or irreligious) feeling. The only condition of membership is a willingness to listen to the ideas of other people, and to explain your own. The founders of the S.C.M. believe free discussion is a step nearer the truth – which is also a step nearer God.

The Whitehill branch of the S.C.M., at present designated S.C.S. (Student Christian Society), was founded at the start of the year. We began with quite eighteen names on the roll. Through time, the meetings have become more and more select, until now we have an average attendance of six (seven, if you count the chairman). Although this has not impaired the quality of the speeches, it does not make for *variety*, for by this time most of us know what the others think on the most important topics.

This is not satisfactory. We would enjoy the Society more if it had new members with more ideas. If you are an intelligent, talkative person in the Fifth or Sixth Year you may wish to try us. The S.C.S. meets fortnightly in Room 81; usually on Wednesdays at 4.15. Mr. J. M. Hutchison is our chairman. WARNING: Don't come if you dislike discussion of your deepest beliefs, or object to being contradicted.

# Art School Thesis on Epic Painting

EVERY WRITER ON VISUAL ART is condemned to use jargon – a set of words without generally accepted meanings and usually borrowed from other arts and sciences; words like Classic, Romantic, Heroic, Architectural, Literary. This is the penalty of dealing with one art through the medium of another. Such words rarely have the same meaning for two, even intelligent, even educated men. For instance the word "Classical" will suggest to some the culture of ancient Greece; but for one man this culture is represented by the clarity of Euclid and the splendid balance of the Parthenon, while for another it is represented by the doomed interplay of Gods, men and women in the great tragedies. To a third man "Classical" may not be associated with Greece at all, but with the symphonies of Beethoven. Every other word in the jargon of art-writing may be as differently understood.

There is a kind of painting I value above all others. The jargon adjective that fits it best is *epic*, I think – a word that was most commonly used in literature, before Hollywood producers began calling big

*The graduates of art schools were required, beside a show of their work, to have written a thesis before the Scots Department of Education gave them a diploma. This was mine. Epics are dear to me because I had entered art school wanting to make myself both writer and painter of big works. In 1953 (my 2nd year) I decided my book should be, like Dante's big* **Comedy** *and the* **Ulysses** *of Joyce, a national epic, for I had just read Tillyard's* **The English Epic & Background**, *which said that the epic form combined every genre, and that future epics were likely to be novels. The self-conceit of this essay, written in ink upon folded sheets of lined foolscap, amazes the much more conventional old man I have since become. Hey ho.*

films with casts of thousands screen epics. Ezra Pound said the literary epic was poetry with history in it. It was certainly the longest, most ambitious kind of poem, and as written by Homer, Virgil, Dante and Milton, combined the politics of this world with the theology they thought universal. This thesis will describe paintings I think are also of that kind. To avoid as much vague jargon as possible I must clarify the meanings of my words, which can only be done by relating them to a philosophy. The thesis will therefore start by giving mine, thus. First, my view of mankind in the universe. Second, the use of creative artists to mankind. Third, the main artistic categories. Lastly, the epic category and some pictures belonging to it.

## THE CONDITION OF MAN IN THE UNIVERSE
To understand the condition of man in the universe we must first put aside memories of any religious or philosophical system accepted from family or society. Systems are popular less for their truth than their comfort. This does not mean that popular systems are untrue. The men who originally preached them wanted to justify the world's black horrible things, not to minimise them. But unless we begin by divorcing what the eye sees from systems, which try to explain what the eye sees, we will never fully be able to understand these systems, and our acceptance or rejection of them will be glib and shallow.

What we see in the universe is this: Everywhere life is fighting to dominate matter. Matter continually and unmaliciously engulfs life, which in many forms infests, tortures, kills and eats itself. Men exploit and murder each other, often unknowingly or unwillingly. Each one of us encloses thoughts, feelings, intuitions and sensations that frequently co-operate to help us survive but also often contradict each other.

Every philosophical and religious system accepts the truth of this vision, and has various ways of accounting for it. My own system is cobbled together out of bits from the work of various writers. I give it here, not to assert a doctrine, but to give my basis for the statements on painting in the last section of the thesis.

When introspective men examine the bit of the universe they know best – themselves – their proudest discovery is that their basic self is basic to all selves and looks out of all eyes – even eyes that glare belligerently into each other. Many of them also discover that their basic self is basic even to unliving things, as Wordsworth and Blake discovered.

*Each grain of sand,*
*Every stone on the land,*
*Each rock & each hill,*
*Each fountain & rill,*
*Each herb & each tree,*
*Mountain, hill, earth & sea,*
*Cloud, Meteor & Star,*
*Are Men Seen Afar.*

Such discoveries are only made after long terrible periods of self-doubt and self-questioning, and they are accompanied by a feeling of delight which does not last long; but to anyone who feels it the memory of that delight is a guarantee that the discovery was valid. The success of an artist or a mystic depends on his ability to share that delight with those who know his work; or at least to persuade them that he felt it. Those who participate most deeply in the delight are aware of something eternal, fundamental, unvarying and limitlessly generative underlying, supporting and infusing the apparent chaos of the universe, and they are identified with it for a rare moment. The delight is at once a sense of unity and a sense of expansion.

Note that this conviction of the universe's underlying unity can be arrived at by scientific logic. Modern biology teaches that matter was once the womb of life, that our blood is moved by the impetus of its tides, that our feet stand on it's platforms, that life is engulfed by the soil only to be resurrected from it. But when men have not felt this unity as a sensation of delight they cannot be moved by such logic. The fact that their bodies are under the same law as stones and water gives them no feeling of kinship with stones and water: it alienates them from their bodies. Therefore this delight is the one foundation and proof of my whole philosophy. From it I arrive at the three following definitions:

God is the name we give to something eternal, fundamental, unvarying and limitlessly generative, which cannot be proved, only felt. Life is God operating through matter to the extent of it becoming self-conscious. Mind is that bit of God which operates through self-conscious matter.

The difference between life and matter is that God is conscious in one and unconscious in the other; the resemblance is that he is fundamental to both. But in saying that God "is fundamental to" life and matter

I imply that he is not completely identified with them, and there is an element of the universe which is not God. I do not believe this. The unity experienced throughout the delight must be absolute if it is to be true. All the universe is God, and men are parts of God. But if this is so why do we need to discover that God is fundamental to us and what surrounds? Why can we not always feel and see it? It is no answer to say that our sense of impropriety when children and old people are flayed by jellied petrol is founded on a delusion about the nature of things. Why, after accepting this brotherhood in eternity with the avalanche, the microbes of disease, howling wolves and murderers with bombs, must the thinker return to the universe of time and space and flight to eradicate them? Why is there evil?

To me the only answer is, that conflicts within the body of eternity are the conditions of its existence. God could not be, in his entirety, eternal, fundamental, unvarying and limitlessly generative, if his parts were not unbalanced and in unending conflict. Such evil as the deliberate scorching to death of innocent people will always be part of life in the universe of time and space, and so will the struggle with such evil. Without evil there would be no struggle, without struggle there would be no life. Though life can often relax a little while from the struggle it can only finally abandon it by dying. Our inducement to continue this struggle is, that those who are most active and use all their faculties to the fullest stretch are occasionally rewarded by the heightened sensation of eternity stretching itself through them. The delight of this usually justifies life for those who feel it.

65 COMFORT AND DELIGHT

A mind is a piece of eternity enclosing (as a balloon encloses air) an expanse of unknown and evil eternity, which is part of itself, and enclosed (as air encloses a balloon) by an expanse of unknown and threatening eternity of which it is part. Life is the mind's struggle to explore the unknown and lessen the threat. When a mind has done a little of either it recognises its own eternity in what was previously ordinary, remote and horrible, and enjoys the short delight of extended consciousness.

Note: throughout this thesis the words "God" and "eternity" are interchangeable.

THE CONDITION OF THE ARTIST AMONG MEN
Only a few men in any age are capable of the most rewarding sort of struggle to compel eternity from its dens inside the ordinary, the remote and the horrible. The majority prefer the comfort of acceptance to the delight of prolonged struggle. Delight is always a dubious, flickering thing. Comfort is stable, and can be protracted. It is got by accepting the result of a struggle (often somebody else's struggle) and then struggling only enough to stay alive. It is essential that the majority should prefer comfort to delight, because the few who prefer delight are seldom given to that toil which supports a society – they are too busy forwarding it; besides, they often make poor parents. But adherence to comfort sometimes prompts men to muffle the discoveries of those who prefer delight, because acceptance of a new discovery often modifies an old one, and robs us of some of its comfort. When

men need to defend their ignorance with censors, jails and executions it is a virtue to undermine their comfort, for the good has gone out of it.

A short time ago "human progress" was an over-rated concept, now it is an under-rated one. Unluckily so, because it contains an important truth. Both failures to understand the nature of human progress come from measuring it in terms of comfort. Shelley and Wells – who mark the beginning and end of the 19th century optimism – thought they were pioneers of a society where comfort would be universal, struggle unnecessary and delight cheap. They believed they were preparing for a concerted human effort that would plant a garden where the ordinary, the remote, the horrible prevailed. We of the 20th century have learned that life always borders upon these enormities, and that even the bit of eternity which is our birth right can sometimes only be kept with a hard fight, and that without such a fight the unknown and evil can encroach on us and make us bestial. This lesson has been made so hideously true to us by two World Wars that we are inclined to disparage the idea of progress, especially social progress. But if progress is measured in opportunities for delight – or more precisely, in opportunities to struggle for delight – then we have reason to believe that a modern society such as our own is superior to most of the societies preceding it – even the slave-supported but magnificent society of classical Greece. Those who gave our society everything that most furthers it preferred delight to comfort. The great painters belong among such men.

Anyone who classes painting with alcohol,

nicotine and other expensive luxuries will see little
reason to lump great artists with the scientists,
politicians and religious enthusiasts usually regarded
as the pioneers of civilization; for though no society
has lacked great artists it is not easy to see how these
influenced the events of their time. Perhaps artists do
not influence the events of their time to any important
degree. They do something altogether as solemn and
important. They penetrate the external essence of
contemporary events, make a lasting beautiful shape
out of it and let that shape broadcast the significance
of the event. Without artists there could be no history.
Delight can be communicated and preserved through
music, words, pictures and shaped minerals, but in not
many other ways. Without being embodied by art in
something we have made, no social delight would
survive those who first enjoyed it:

> London's pride is tumbled down,
> Down-a-down the deeps of thought,
> Greece is fallen and Troy town,
> Golden Rome has lost her crown,
> Venice pride is nought.
> But the dreams their children dreamed
> Fleeting, wild, romantic, vain…
> These remain.

This poem (I have misquoted it slightly, not
remembering the whole) contains everyone's
justification for making what they do as well as they
can. The artist expresses, and by expressing,
perpetuates, the actions and discoveries by which his
people glimpsed eternity. A society which does not
make such things will add nothing inspiring to history,

and be commemorated only in footnotes to books about other societies, as the Spartans are commemorated.

## THE VISUAL ARTIST CATEGORY

Good pictures are maps of districts where an artist discovered eternity. "This is where I found eternity" says Turner "in rain and steam and speed." Michelangelo found it in the bodies of athletes, the artists of Altamira in the bodies of bulls they hunted. Poussin found it in the organisation of a civilised landscape, Bosch in the tumult of a phantasmagoric subconscious one. Bad pictures are faulty maps of districts where the painter has never been but where he believes eternity is to be found, because some good painter of the past has struggled for it and won it there. Bad paintings shine with reflected delight. Bad artists often find it easier to sell their work than good ones, because they are peddling the comfort of the accepted. They rarely try to crib from contemporary good artists because in doing so they run the risk of joining the struggle and becoming good.

When we look at the world's good paintings with the intention of putting them into categories we are depressed by their variety. Each painting seems a window into a different world, a world with its individual colours, proportions, inhabitants and emotional climate. The only common element is that each painting has an irrefragable unity. No line, tone or colour can be altered in any one without impairing the delight we feel in it. Apart from this it is clear that there are as many different sorts of artist as there are different sorts of men. Any likeness between the artists

of a particular age is imposed by social pressure. The
Byronic anarchic bandit painters of the past 100 years have been produced by a society which has not come to terms with its image makers, just as the priest painters of ancient Egypt were produced by a society which came too thoroughly to terms with them. To discover a way through the diversity of subject matter and attitude we will begin by resorting to the old over-simplifications. Here comes some jargon.

*Visual artists are Classic, Romantic, Realist.*

*Classical artists subdue their passions through cool reasoning, test their subconscious intuitions against social analysis. Such artists ride on their emotions like rowing boats on calm water, their social consciousness adjusting and steering. Their politics are conservative. When they fail it is by turning their best ideas into repetitive academic forms. They often die rich and respected.*

*Romantic artists make their powers of reasoning and social analysis serve their passions and instinctive feelings. They are moved like yachts by the wind of their passions, the conscious intellect working to stop them overturning, which sometimes happens. Their politics are radical, sometimes revolutionary. They sometimes die through poverty and neglect, while delighting posterity.*

*Classical artists convey delight through the equilibrium of broad, general views. Romantic artists convey delight through the impetus of deep, intense views. Realists differ from both by their subject being modern life, using fewer examples from the past.*

Problems arise when we try to enlist painters

under one of these headings. No artist wholly belongs
under any one. The pictures of Giotto, Poussin, David,
Ingres and Cézanne have a carefully constructed
calmness we may call Classical with a capital C.
Giotto lived before that word was used of the visual
arts, but the last four consciously strove to be Classical.
But David – "he of the blood-stained brush," as Walter
Scott called him – was a political revolutionary. There
is a turbulence in the compositions of Michelangelo,
El Greco, Goya and Van Gogh, and this fits with the
often tormented private lives of the first and last two,
yet El Greco was an Orthodox Catholic whose work
was as much commissioned by the Spanish priesthood
as Giotto's by the Italian. How can such words be
attached to the works of Leonardo, Breughel,
Rembrandt, Caravaggio, Velasquez? All the big labels
art historians, journalists and polemicists find so
useful – Realist, Impressionist, Post-Impressionist,
Cubist and Surrealist – are too vague to suggest the
quality of one fine work of art.

Art criticism is most helpful when it is most
empirical, thus we know what is meant when a picture
is called a crucifixion, nativity, portrait, nude,
landscape and still life. When governments still bought
huge paintings for their palaces and museums in the
18th and 19th centuries what were called History
Paintings were thought greatest because they often
used elements of all the foregoing kinds of picture. In
the introduction I said I would describe the main
artistic categories: there are only two: good and bad.
All other categories are built upon individual
preferences and biases among work that is generally

agreed to be good. Therefore when I describe (with examples) the epic category of painting, and even construct a theory of the pictorial epic, understand that I am consciously working inside the limits of an individual psychology. Certain paintings have given me more acute delight than others, therefore I believe their painters had a more intense apprehension of eternity than others, therefore I think their scope sufficiently wide to be called "epic."

## THE EPIC CATEGORY

Grunewald's polyptych at Colmar, Rembrandt's *The Night Watch*, Mantegna's *Crucifixion*, Tintoretto's *Last Supper* and Gauguin's *What are we? Where do we come from? Whither do we go?* are epic paintings. In each of them I feel that the artist looked intensely in and intensely out. He looked into the universe he contained and at the universe containing him, and he realised and explained in his picture a very important thing about the nature of them both. The discovery contained in these paintings is too vast to be merely tragic. They all deal with men in an open space – and that space is the universe. In Rembrandt's painting the psychological depth of the portrait faces is as great and implies as much as the depth of space on the city wall on which they stand. The organization of the crowd is superb. This is not a rabble or a mob. It is not a disciplined troupe. It is moving, but not concertedly. There are drums, weapons, banners being carried and held, but casually. The gestures of the men are also casual, but important. But most significant of all is the unrelatedness of the individuals, the psychological gulfs between each of them. Obviously they are one group, but none of them seem to recognise that the others exist – or they recognise it only casually, almost somnambulistically. They are held together by the gulfs of light and shadow between them.

In Grunewald's crucifixion there is greater awareness between the members of the group around the cross, but the awareness is an agony. Grunewald was terribly conscious of what the flesh was capable of sustaining. The terrible unremitting abyss of the universe. It is really against this that Christ is crucified. On the left side his mother sways back, supported by St John, with Mary Magdalene on her knees at their feet. Both women are working their hands together, in a way which is partly prayer, partly a way to distract their attention from the agony of Christ by making a physical sensual pressure against themselves. On the other side of the cross stands St Peter, feet slightly straddled, pointing to the agony on the cross with his forefinger in a gesture which is so undramatic and pedagogical that the horror of the situation is weighted more heavily.

Each of these paintings, in their own way, describes the condition of mind in the universe in pictorial images. Each is intensely aware of the unknown, the ordinary, the remote, the horrible: the ordinary in The Night Watch, the remote in Gauguin's painting, the horrible in Grunewald's; the inhuman precision of Mantegra's conception exaggerates the everyday nature of the crime of the crucifixion, planted as the cross is in the geological stratas supporting a city; while Tintoretto behind a room whose marble floor is littered with kitchen utensils, shows dim divine presences lurking behind a busy crowd of eating men who seem unaware of their radiant halos.

Each of these paintings (with the possible exception of the Gauguin) is too vast and too stark for comfortable acceptance. Each is too full of the facts of our condition to be accepted with anything less than delight. These pictures are not tragic. Tragedy depends on the feeling that death has perhaps the last word. It is a literary conception. In these paintings life and vacuity, pain and struggle and man's phenomenal persistence are shown as fundamental, eternal, and limitlessly generative. That is why I think them epic paintings.

# A Report to the Trustees

I APOLOGIZE TO THE TRUSTEES OF THE BELLAHOUSTON TRAVELLING SCHOLARSHIP AND TO MR BLISS, the director of Glasgow Art School, for the long time I have taken to write this report. Had the tour gone as planned they would have received, when I returned, an illustrated diary describing things done and places visited. But I visited very few places and the things I did were muddled and absurd. To show that, even so, the tour was worth while, I must report what I learned from it. I have had to examine my memory of the events deductively, like an archaeologist investigating a prehistoric midden. It has taken a year to understand what happened to me and the money between October 1957 and March 1958.

On learning I was awarded the scholarship my first wish had been to travel on foot or bicycle, sketching landscapes and cityscapes around Scotland, for I knew very little of it apart from Glasgow, two islands in the Firth of Clyde, and places seen on day trips to Edinburgh. However, a condition of the scholarship was that I go abroad. I decided to visit London for a

*The original of this is also a sheaf of lined fullscap pages folded together, covered with my manuscript in ink. It was written in 1959 over a year after my return from an unhappy trip to Spain. I took many months to turn the events into a careful account of facts without over-emphasis. The result was a piece of prose so professional that the trustees thought it was fiction. 25 years later, having run out of ideas for short stories, I used it to fill my space in a book of stories I was sharing with my friends, Agnes Owens and Jim Kelman. This anthology was first suggested to me by a Quartet Books editor, but published by Bloomsbury in 1985 with the overall title **Lean Tales**, which is now long out of print.*

fortnight, travel from there to Gibraltar by ship, find a cheap place to live in southern Spain, paint there as long as the money would allow, then travel home through Granada, Malaga, Madrid, Toledo, Barcelona and Paris, viewing on the way Moorish mosques, baroque cathedrals, plateresque palaces, the works of El Greco, Velazquez and Goya, with Bosch's *Garden of Earthly Delights*, Brueghel's *Triumph of Death*, and several other grand gaudy things which are supposed to compensate for the crimes of our civilization. The excellence of this plan, approved by Mr Bliss, is not lessened by the fact that I eventually spent two days in Spain and saw nothing of interest.

On the 31st of October I boarded the London train in Glasgow Central Station. It was near midnight, dark and drizzling, and to save money I had not taken a sleeping car. The prospect of vivid sunshine, new lands and people should have been very exciting, but as the train sped south a sullen gloom settled upon me. I looked at my reflection in the rain-streaked carriage window and doubted the value of a tourist's shallow experience of anywhere. I was homesick already. I do not love Glasgow much, I sometimes actively hate it, but I am at home here. In London this sickness increased until it underlay quite cheerful feelings and weighed so heavy on the chest that it began to make breathing difficult. I had been in hospital with asthma during the three previous summers, but a doctor treating me had said another very bad attack was unlikely and a trip abroad might do me good. I had a pocket inhaler which eased difficult breathing with puffs of atropine methondrate, papaverine hydrochloride, chlorbutol and adrenaline; and for strong spasms I had a bottle of adrenaline solution and a hypodermic needle to inject myself subcutaneously. In London I slept in a students' hostel in a street behind the university tower. The dormitory was not large and held about fifty bunks, all occupied. I was afraid to use the inhaler at night in case the noise of it wakened someone, so used the needle, which should have been kept for emergencies. This made sleep difficult. At night I felt trapped in that dormitory and by day I felt trapped in London.

The main shops and offices in London are as large as ours, sometimes larger, but the dwelling houses are mostly of brick and seldom more than half the height of a Scottish sandstone tenement. Such buildings, in a country town surrounded by meadows, look very pleasant, but a big county of them, horizon beyond horizon beyond horizon, is a desert to me, and not less a desert for containing some great public buildings and museums. I visited these oases as the trustees would have wished, but had continually to leave them for a confusion of streets of which my head could form no clear map. Like most deserts this city is nearly flat and allows no view of a more fertile place. The streets of central Glasgow are also gripped between big buildings but it is always easy to reach a corner where we can see, on a clear day, the hills to the north and to the south. I know I am unfair to London. A normal dweller there has a circle of acquaintance about the size of a small village. Only a stranger feels challenged to judge the place as a whole, which cannot be done, so the stranger feels small and lonely. I visited several publishers with a folder of drawings and a typescript of my poems. I hoped to be asked to illustrate a book, perhaps my own book. I was kindly received and turned away from each place, and although I could not feel angry with the publishers (who would have been out of business if they had not known what was saleable) I turned my disappointment against the city. I grew more asthmatic and walked about refusing to be awed.

The least awesome place I saw was the government church, Westminster Abbey. This once fine Gothic structure is filled with effigies of landlords, company directors and administrators who got rich by doing exactly what was expected of them, and now stand as solid in their marble wigs, boots and waistcoats as the Catholic saints and martyrs they have replaced. Among them is an occasional stone carved with the name of someone who has been creative or courageous. A less pretentious but nastier place is the Tower of London. Built by the Normans for the enslavement of the English natives (who before this had been a comparatively democratic and even artistic people, judging by their export of illuminated manuscripts to the continent) this fort was used by later governments as an arsenal, jail and bloody police station. Nobody pretends otherwise. The stands of weapons and the pathetic scratchings of the political prisoners on their cell-walls are clearly labelled, and folk who would feel discomfort at a rack of police batons or the barbed fence of a concentration camp feel thrilled because these are supposed to be part of a *splendid* past. The tower also holds the Crown jewels. There were more of them than I had imagined, twelve or fifteen huge display cabinets of crowns, orbs, maces, swords and ceremonial salt-cellars. Most of it dates from the eighteenth century – I recall nothing as old as the regalia of the sixth Jamie Stewart in Edinburgh castle. I noticed that the less the monarchs were working politicians the more money was spent ornamenting them. The culmination of this development is the huge Crown Imperial, an art nouveau job created for the coronation of Edward the Fat in 1901, when the Archbishop of Canterbury placed the world's most expensively useless hat on the world's most expensively useless head.

Did anything in London please me? Yes: the work of the great cockneys, the Williams Blake and Turner. Also Saint Paul's Cathedral. Also the underground rail system. I found this last, with the H.G. Wellsian sweep of its triple escalators and lines of framed, glazed advertisements for films and women's underwear, and tunnels beneath tunnels bridging tunnels, and tickets which allow those who take the wrong train to find their way to the right station without paying extra, a very great comfort.

But I was glad one morning to get on a boat-train at Liverpool Street Station and begin the second part of the journey to Spain. I was in the company of Ian McCulloch, who had arrived from Glasgow that morning. He is an artist who received his painting diploma at the same time as myself. He also wanted to visit Spain, and had saved the money to do so by working as a gas lamplighter near Parkhead Forge, Shettleston. We had arranged to travel together and

meant to share the rent of a small place in south Spain.
The boat-train ran along embankments above the usual streets of small houses, then came to a place where towering structures, part warehouse and part machine, stood among labyrinths of railway-siding. The little brick homes were here also, but the surrounding machinery gave them the dignity of outposts. We arrived at the docks.

The ship was called the *Kenya Castle* and long before it unmoored we found it a floating version of the sort of hotel we had never been in before. Our cabin was small but compact. It held two bunks the size of coffins, each with a reading lamp and adjustable ventilator. There was a very small sink with hot and cold water, towels, facecloths, soap, a locker with coat-hangers, a knob to ring for the steward, another for the stewardess. In the lavatories each closet contained, beside the roll of toilet paper, a clean towel, presumably to wipe the lingers-on after using the roll, although there were washbasins and towels in the vestibule outside. (It has just struck me that perhaps the extra towel was for polishing the lavatory seat before use.) The menus in the dining room embarrassed us. They were printed on glazed-surface card and decorated at every meal with a different photograph of some nook of Britain's African empire – *The Governor's Summer Residence, Balihoo Protectorate, The District Vice-Commissioner's Bungalow, Janziboola*, etc. The food, however, was listed in French. Obviously some foods were alternatives to others, while some could, and perhaps should, be asked for on the same plate. We wanted to eat as much as possible to get the full value of the money we had paid; at the same time we feared we would be charged extra if we ate more than a certain amount. We also feared we would be despised if we asked the waiter for information on these matters. Our table was shared with two priests, Catholic and Anglican. Ian and I were near acquaintances rather than friends. With only our nationality, profession and destination in common we left conversation to the priests. They mainly talked about an audience the Anglican had had with the Pope. He addressed the Catholic with the deference a polite salesman might show to the representative of a more powerful firm. He said the Pope's hands were beautifully shaped, he had the fingers of an artist, a painter. Ian and I glanced down at our own fingers. Mine had flecks of paint on the nails that I hadn't managed to clean off for the previous fortnight.

After this meal coffee was served in the lounge. The cups were very small with frilled paper discs between themselves and the saucers to absorb the drips. There were many people in the lounge but it was big enough not to seem crowded. Darkness had fallen and we were moving slowly down the Thames. There were magazines on small tables: *Vogue, House and Garden, John O'London's, Punch*, the magazines found in expensive dentists' waiting rooms, nothing to stimulate thought. I played a bad game of chess with Ian and ordered two whiskies, which were cheap now we were afloat. I took mine chiefly to anaesthetize the asthma, but Ian felt bound to respond by ordering another two, and resented this. He had less money

than I and he thought we were starting the trip
extravagantly. The ship was leaving the estuary for the sea. I felt the floor of that opulent lounge, till now only troubled by a buried throbbing, take on a quality of sway. I was distracted from the weight on my chest by an uneasy, flickering sensation in my stomach. I therefore left the lounge and went to bed after vomiting into the cabin sink.

While eating breakfast next morning I watched the portholes in the walls of the saloon. The horizon was moving up and down each of them like the bottom edge of a blind. When the horizon was down nothing could be seen outside but pale grey sky. After a few seconds it would be pulled up and the holes would look on nothing but dark grey water. The priests' conversation seemed unforgivably banal. I felt homesick, seasick and asthmatic. I went back to bed and used my inhaler but it had stopped having effect. I took a big adrenaline jag. That night breathing became very difficult indeed, I could not sleep and injections did not help much. The impossibility of sitting up in the bunk, the narrowness of the cabin and the movement of the floor increased my sense of suffocation. I lost all memory of normal breathing, and so lost hope of it. However, I could clearly imagine how it would feel to be worse, so fear arrived. Fear lessened the ability to face pain, which therefore increased. At this stage it was hard to stop the fear swelling into panic, because the more pain I felt the more I could imagine. The only way to divert my imagination from its capital accumulation of fear was to think about something else and only erotic images

were strong enough to be diverting. Having no
experience of sexual satisfaction I recalled women in
the London underground advertisements.

Next morning I asked Ian to call the ship's
doctor, who entered the cabin and sat beside the bunk.
He was an elderly friendly Scotsman, straight-spined,
red-faced and silver-moustached. His uniform had
several rings of braid round the cuffs. His speech was
all sudden, decided statements interrupted by abrupt
silences in which he sat erect, gripping his knees with
his hands and looking at the air in front of his eyes. He
felt my pulse, touched me with a stethoscope, agreed
that I was asthmatic and went away. After a while a
nurse came and gave me an intravenous injection
which made me slightly better. Later that day Ian told
me it was quite warm on deck and a whale had been
sighted. The following day the doctor came back, sat
erect beside me and asked how I felt. I said a bit better,
I hoped to get up soon. He said abruptly, "How are
your bowels?" I said I had no trouble with them. He
sat in a tranced rigid silence for a while, then said
suddenly, "Buy a tin of Eno's salts from the ship's store.
Use them regularly," and left.

That night I developed an obstruction of the
throat which coughing could not shift nor spitting
reduce. Erotic images brought no relief though I tried
to remember the most shameful parts of all the
obscene things I had ever heard or read. Next day I
asked again to see the doctor. He told me I had
pneumonia and must be taken to the ship's hospital.
He left and then the medical orderly came with a
wooden wheeled chair. I panicked while being put in

it, my mind crumbled for a few moments and I became
quite babyish. I was not slapped but I was shouted at.
Then I made my body as tense in the chair as possible
in order to hold the mind in one piece. I was trundled
along narrow corridors into the hospital where the
nurse and orderly put me in a real bed. I was able to
be calmer there. The hospital was a neat, bright little
room with four beds and small flower-patterned
curtains round the portholes. I asked for an intravenous
injection of adrenaline. The nurse explained that this
would not help pneumonia. She tied a small oxygen
cylinder to the head of the bed and gave me a mask
connected to it by a rubber tube. This helped a little.
The orderly brought a form, asked several questions
and filled it in. My religion puzzled him. I said I was
agnostic and his pencil dithered uncertainly above a
blank space. I spelled the word out but he wrote down
"agnoist". Ian came and I dictated a letter to my father
to be posted from Gibraltar. A radio telegram had been
sent to him and I wanted to mitigate any worry it might
cause. I noticed nothing special in Ian's manner but
later he told me he had difficulty restraining his tears.
The doctor had diagnosed pneumonia with probable
tuberculosis, and said it would be a miracle if I reached
Gibraltar alive. While we were at work on the letter
the doctor entered with a man wearing a uniform like
his own. This stranger looked on with a faint
embarrassed smile while the doctor spoke to me in a
loud and cheery bonhomous Scottish way. "Aye,
Alasdair, keep your heart up!" he cried, "Remember
the words of Burns: 'The heart's aye the part aye that
maks us richt or wrang'."

"Just so, Doctor, just so," I said, playing up to him. He told me that I would be shifted to a land-hospital next morning when the ship reached Gibraltar, meanwhile (and here he looked at the dial on my oxygen cylinder) I'd better go easy on the oxygen, I'd used up half a tube already and there was only one left in the store. The two visitors went away and the nurse told me the other man was the captain.

After that life was hard for a while. I finished one oxygen cylinder and started on the last, which had forty minutes of comfortable breathing in it. It was difficult to disperse these forty minutes through the eighteen hours before we reached Gibraltar, sleep was impossible and I was afraid of becoming too tired to make myself breathe. During this time I was well cared for by the nurse and the orderly. She was a plain, slightly gawky, serious, very pleasant young woman. She gave me penicillin injections and clean towels to wipe away my sweat. The orderly was a blockily built smallish sturdy man with a clumsy amiable face. He gave me a large brandy at nine in the evening and another at midnight. I felt these two were completely dependable people. At one in the morning the doctor came in wearing dress uniform. I had never seen a celluloid shirt front before. He leant over the bed, breathed some fumes in my face and asked, with an effort at cheeriness, how I felt. I said I was afraid, and in pain. He indicated the oxygen mask, told me to use it if I got worse and hurried out. The cylinder was almost empty. When it was completely empty I rang the bell behind my bed. The orderly ran in at once in his pyjamas. I asked for more brandy, and got it. This did not lessen the pain but made me unable to think clearly about it. I may or may not have rung the bell for other brandies, my subsequent memories are muddled. I remember just one incident very clearly. The nurse entered wearing a flower-patterned long dressing-gown and seeming very beautiful. She looked at the empty cylinder, felt my brow then went away and brought in another cylinder. I laughed and shook her hand and I am sure she smiled. I felt an understanding between us: she and I were in alliance against something dismal. I don't know if she had disobeyed the doctor in giving me the third cylinder. Maybe he had very few and wanted to keep a certain number in case someone else needed them later on the voyage.

Later the ship's engine stopped and I knew we were at Gibraltar. I think this was about five in the morning. I don't recall who did it but I was shifted to a stretcher, wrapped up as snugly and tightly as an Egyptian mummy, carried into a bare kind of cabin and left on the floor. The stretcher had little legs which kept it above the planks. My breathing was easier now and I was beginning to feel comfortable. The doctor, in ordinary uniform, stood nearby looking out of a porthole. He was less drunk than when he had visited me in the night but mellow and communicative. I saw now that his erect abrupt manner disguised a wonderfully controlled, almost continual intoxication. I felt very friendly toward him and he toward me. He sighed and said, "There she is – Gibraltar – under the moon. I never thought to see her again, Alasdair, I forget how many years it is since I last saw her."

"Were you in practice ashore?"

"This National Health Service is rotten Alasdair. Forms to be filled, paperwork, the pen never out of your hand. In the old days the doctor worked with a stethoscope in one hand and a s,s,s, a *scalpel* in the other. How do you feel?"

"A lot better."

"You've come through a bad time, Alasdair, a very bad time .... a Catholic priest told me I was a lost soul last night."

He looked out of the porthole again then said, "I was married once. The girl died a month after the wedding."

"Do you think I could have another brandy?"

"Would ye not like a whisky? I can give ye a good Glenlivet."

I won't pretend the doctor used these exact words but he referred to these things in the order I have recorded them, and stuttered on the s of scalpel, making me imagine a surgical knife vibrating in a trembling fist. Later we heard the chugging of a small boat. He said, "That's the lighter," and went out and came in again with three seamen and a Spanish doctor, a broad, duffle-coated, rimless-spectacled, crew-cut, laconic man. He spoke quietly to the ship's doctor, tested me with a stethoscope then left, refusing the offer of a drink. I heard the chugging of the boat going away.

I was shifted into hospital later that morning in bright sunshine. I was still wrapped tightly on the stretcher with only my face exposed. I felt comfortable, privileged and so incurious I did not try to see anything not directly above my eyes. I saw a section of the high side of the ship against a pale blue sky. I heard a babble of voices and felt a hard cold breeze on my cheek. I think I recall the top of a white mast or flagstaff with a wind-taut flag on it. This must have been aboard the lighter. Sometimes my upward view was irregularly framed by downward-staring faces: the doctor, Ian, customs officers and strangers. Once the lined dry face of a middle-aged lady looked down for a moment, smiled and said, "I say, you hev hed a bit of bed luck, you've come rathah a croppah, heven't you," and some other terse kindly things full of English-hunting-field stoicism. I liked her for her kindness, and for being so easy to classify. I saw the wooden ceiling of a customs shed, the low steel ceiling of an ambulance, and then, after a ten-minute sound of fast uphill car travel, the cream ceiling of a hospital vestibule. In this way I arrived in Gibraltar without seeing the rock. Indeed, since leaving London, I had only once seen the sea, through portholes, during the first breakfast afloat. I was now put to bed under a suspended bottle of cortisone solution, which dripped down through a rubber tube into my arm. I was visited by the hospital chief, the laconic doctor who had examined me on board the ship. He said, "You are suffering, of course, from a bad but perfectly ordinary asthma attack. I was sure of that as soon as I saw you this morning, but could not say so. You understand, of course, that it is against professional etiquette to question the decision of a colleague."

The ward was three times longer than broad with eight beds to each long wall. The wall facing me was all window from pillow-level to ceiling. I saw through it a glassed-in veranda containing a few beds and beyond that the water of a wide bay. The hospital stood high up so steep a slope that I could see only the top of the building in front, two elegant towers faced with biscuit-coloured plaster. Far beyond and below these the bay had several sorts of ship moored in it, protected by long breakwaters with cranes on them. Distance made the ships look too small even to be useful toys while the breakwaters, exceptional bits of engineering to surround such a great body of water, seemed a few lines of forlorn geometry drawn upon it. The far side of the bay was all hills and small mountains with the whitish jumble of a town along the coast at their foot. This was Spain.

Although the head doctor was Spanish the routine and discipline of the hospital was British, the matron was a Scot, and of the three sisters two were English and one Welsh. The nurses were small plump Spanish or Gibraltarian girls, and most of the patients were Gibraltarian: that is, bilingual Spaniards who lived on the rock. They were inclined to be middle-aged and gaunt. There was a Velazquez-type dwarf called Paco with a calm, smooth, dignified face and slightly amused mouth. He would stand beside a bed resting his folded arms on it and talking quietly to the occupant in Spanish, or just leaning his brow on his folded arms. To my right was Major Mellors, elderly, gaunt and hawk-nosed. Facing me across the ward was Sigurdson, a taciturn humorous ship's mate from Lancashire. I learned the names and manners of these people gradually. The inmates of a hospital ward observe their neighbours closely but avoid, at first, contacting them, for each is too engrossed by their own illness to want the burden of sympathizing with someone else.

During my first week in hospital I was visited regularly by Ian, who had taken lodgings in Gibraltar, but after finding I was out of danger he set off into Spain. He was going to the village of Estepona a few hours journey up the coast, for he had heard good reports of it. He meant to find decent rooms there, settle in, and I would join him when I left the hospital. I made him take two pounds to compensate him for some of the money he had lost by the delay. The day after he left for Spain I was surprised to see him enter the ward. He sat by my bed and explained that he did not like Spain.

"It's so unhygienic, Alasdair. I got off the bus at Estepona and set out to find a place to stay, but the flies! I travelled everywhere inside this cloud of flies. I mean, it was ridiculous. And the children who kept following me, begging, were almost as hard to shake off. And everybody stared. I mean, they didn't do it sideways or behind your back, they stood still in the street and really looked at you. I found a place. I won't describe the sanitation because there wasn't any. I went out for a drink with a bloke I had met in the bus. We went into a bar and ordered wine at the counter. Before pouring it out the barman put down two wee plates each with a wee dirty bit of fish on it. I mean, we were expected to eat that. The counter was filthy – nothing was properly clean. I mean, outside the village you get these farm buildings with nice white walls, very picturesque. And when you go near you see the ground covered with little heaps of shit. They must just have squatted in the shadow to get rid of it."

"What was the countryside like?" I asked.

"Oh, it's picturesque all right. I mean, it's beautiful in a queer way. You get these low brownish hills in the dusk with a line of donkeys and their riders going along the top against a fantastic sunset. I mean it might grow on you. But I realize now that what I want to paint is in Scotland. I don't think I've wasted my money if I've discovered that. I think I'll use what's left to do some painting up the East coast, in Fife or Angus. Maybe I'll call in at Paris on the way home."

I won't pretend I used these exact words but he talked in that style and mentioned these things. Three days later he got on a boat which took him to France.

I was not unhappy in that hospital. The staff kept pain out of me with doses and injections. I was nursed, fed and allowed to live completely to myself. The homesickness seemed to have been burned out by my experience aboard ship. Sometimes a faint "Over the graves of the martyrs the whaups are crying, my heart remembers how" feeling drifted through my mind like faint smoke, but that was romantic nostalgia, nothing like the earlier sick hunger for Glasgow and those I knew there. This new equanimity came partly from the routine of hospital, which was familiar to me, but there was another reason.

A few years earlier I had begun work on a tragicomical novel and meant to write some more of it in Spain. In my luggage was a Cantablue Expanding Wallet, a portable cardboard filing cabinet shaped like an accordion and holding two complete chapters and the notebooks and diaries from which I meant to make

the rest. I put this on my bedside locker and began
working. I was slightly ashamed of this activity, which struck me as presumptuous and banal: presumptuous because, like Scott Fitzgerald, I believed the novel was the strongest and supplest medium for conveying thought and emotion from one human being to another, which meant that a novelist needed to understand great states of feeling, and although twenty-three years old I had never known carnal love and feared I never would; banal because one or two friends had also started writing a novel, and the rest had thought of writing one. So when the nurses asked what I was doing I lied and told them I was writing this report. But actually I was in Glasgow, the Glasgow of my childhood and adolescence and studenthood, and far more at home there than when I underwent these painful states, for now my mind hovered above the person I had been in perfect safety, without affection but with great curiosity. I found that person unpleasant but comic and was fascinated by the things and people it knew. My world was confused, shabby and sad, but had as much order, variety, good feeling and potency as any other. I tried to write an ordinary, easily-read language which showed the sadness and shabbiness but made the other things (which keep us alive) equally evident. While I worked at this writing I enjoyed the best happiness of all, the happiness which does not notice itself, until, stopping, we feel tired and see that an hour has passed like a minute, and know we have done as well as we can, and perhaps one day someone will be glad. I am sure this happiness is not rare. Everyone feels a little of it who makes or keeps

something useful in the world, and does not just work for money and promotion. I suspect there is more of this happiness among skilled manual workers than in higher income groups, who have other satisfactions.

I was not shut completely into my head. I often looked out across the bay. Hospitals are generous with pillows to their asthmatic patients and I could see the coast of Spain without raising my head. On bright afternoons a few long wisps of white vapour would trickle up into the sky from wide-apart points on the sides of the mountains. Perhaps it was a memory of old fairy-tales that made me think this smoke came from the huts of charcoal-burners. I tried to imagine myself wandering there and totally failed. Gibraltar has one of the Mediterranean's moister climates and the view was often blotted out by low cloud. I also had an understanding with Major Mellors based upon definite but minimum communication. During the morning I might say, "Was it all right to tip the barber?"
"Yes. How much did you give him?"
"Ninepence."
"That was too much."
In the afternoon he might remark, on a wistful note, "I wonder how my garden's getting on."
"Is there nobody looking after it?"
"Oh yes, my servant Ali."
"Won't he look after it properly?"
"Oh yes, he's very good with flowers."

But the most sociable time was between the half-past-five cup of tea and the seven o'clock breakfast when Sister Price sat at a table at our end of the ward. She was bright and talkative, and Sigurdson and the

Major and I would interject and pass comments which
seemed to us all increasingly witty and humorous. Yet I cannot now recall a single thing we said. The base of the conversation was four very different people wanting to enjoy and please each other and succeeding. For the rest of the day we were friendly in a quiet way which later struck me as British, or even European, when Mr Sweeney arrived.

He was the first mate of a big American ship and was put in an empty bed beside Sigurdson. Had his flesh been firm he would have been a broad tough middle-aged man, but his cheeks were pouchy, he had a pouch under each eye, when not talking his mouth drooped to the left as if his muscles only kept hold of the right-hand corner. But he was usually talking because he could only think aloud. We learned he had a wife in America he seemed not to like much, and a daughter called Baby, living with the wife, whom he liked a great deal. "She's well over forty, she's twice divorced, but she'll always be my Baby."

He was a Christian Scientist and said he had only come to hospital because the company he served could take away his pension if he refused. When disease or death was mentioned he would shrug and say, "After all, what is the body? Just fifty cents-worth of chemicalization."

If a silence lasted too long for him he sometimes broke it by remarking, at random, "After all, the only realities are spiritual realities."

Beneath his bed were three large cases from which he got the hospital porter to produce, at various times, many electrical gadgets connected with hygiene and grooming, cigars, tissues, a radio, three ball-pens which wrote in different colours, and a steel-barrelled pen filled with spirit ink to which could be fixed several thicknesses of felt nib. He did not converse. He might call one of us by name, but his loud, even voice was clearly addressing our entire half of the ward. Once he called out, "Say, Major! Could you lend me just a small spoonful of that toothpowder of yours and tomorrow I'll give you back a whole tin of it?"

"What's that, old man?" said the Major, maybe playing for time.

"Could you lend me one little spoonful of that toothpowder of yours and tomorrow I'll repay you with a whole big new tin of it? I got one in the case."

"Oh you mustn't give away all your pretty things like that," said the Major, gently.

"Major, when I'm tired of giving I'll be tired of living. If people are grateful, well and good. If not..."

He frowned, his mouth sagged into its expression of slightly puzzled vacuity and for some minutes his eyes searched the ward uneasily for something to think about. At last they focused on a point beneath the table where the sister wrote her reports. "Say!" he said, brightening, "That's the saddest waste-paper basket I ever did see! It's twisted, it's all to cock, it needs a new coat of paint ..." and then he ran out of thoughts again and eventually muttered that the only realities were spiritual realities.

We were fascinated by Sweeney because he continually presented himself, which none of us did. At first meeting our accents had shown each other that Sigurdson was a Lancashire seaman, the Major an

English army officer and I a well-read lowland Scot.
The humorous pre-breakfast chats had confirmed this
without adding detail. I knew the Major had
commanded the household troops of some Moroccan
or Algerian ruler, but had not heard it from his lips. He
must have noticed that I was writing something larger
than this report but my privacy did not disturb him. Mr
Sweeney gave us his whole childhood in half a minute.
"For the first twelve years of my life I was reared by my
mother and wow, you should have seen me. Blue
velvet suit. Satin shirt and necktie. Curly hair down to
my shoulders. She had just about made a little girl of
me when my pa came and took me to sea with him.
She didn't want it, I didn't want it, but he said, 'You're
gonna cry your eyes out but one day you'll be grateful.'
And I cried. I guess I cried myself to sleep almost every
night for six whole months. But after a year I was
tough, I was a man, and I was grateful."
He was not embarrassed by his sexuality. One day the
Major asked what he thought of the Japanese.
"I like 'em. Collectively they're skunks but individually
I like 'em. I remember my ship putting into Yokohama
in thirty-six. The Mayor entertained a few of us. I like
Japanese homes. They're clean. No furniture; you sit
on mats on the floor. Nothing like that – " he pointed
to the top of his locker which, like our lockers, was
littered with many more or less useful objects – "All
that stuff is kept in a smooth box in the corner of the
room. And there's not much decoration either. But the
room is built round an almond tree that comes out of
a hole in the floor and goes out through one in the
ceiling and the trunk and branches in the room have

been given a coat of clear .... not varnish, but like varnish .... "

"Lacquer?" I suggested.

"Yeah. They're lacquered. Well, nothing was too good for us. They saw we didn't like their drink so without even asking they sent out for whisky. And when I went to bed, there she was. In a kimono. There are over fifty yards of silk in those kimonos. By the time she'd unwrapped herself I had almost lost my courage."

One day it was announced on the wireless that President Eisenhower had burst a small blood-vessel in his brain, his speech was impaired and he was confined to bed. Sweeney heard this with unusual gravity. He said, "He's sixty-two. My age." and was silent for a long time.

"After all," he said suddenly, "He's an old man. What can you expect?"

He complained of headache. The nurse on duty told him it would go away. "But what's causing it?"

He called the sister, then the matron, who both told him a codeine tablet would cure it. "I won't take dope!" he cried, "You aren't going to dope me!"

He huddled silently under the bedclothes for over an hour. "After all," he said suddenly, "He's old. He's not indispensable, even if he is the president. He'll be replaced one day, just like the rest of us."

He clearly wanted to be persuaded that what he said was untrue. The Major and I kept glancing at each other with furtive, delighted grins, but we were glad when Eisenhower got well enough to make a speech and Mr Sweeney felt better. He was more entertaining when he was confident.

The trustees may wonder why I have spent so many words describing this man. I do so for reasons that would have made me describe Toledo, had I reached Toledo. He displayed a coherent kind of life. I admired his language, which was terse, rapid, and full of concrete detail. I realized this was part of his national culture and found an impure form of it in an American magazine he read each week with great seriousness. "Everything in this is *fact*," he explained, "It prints nothing but the bare facts. Other magazines give you opinions. Not this one."

I borrowed it and read a report of the British Labour Party conference. One of the leaders had tried to persuade the Party that bits of Britain should not be leased to the U.S.A. as bases for their nuclear weapons. Under a photograph of him looking pugnacious were the words "Number one American-hater, rabble-rousing Aneurin Bevan".

But I admired Mr Sweeney quite apart from his national style. With energy, skill, and a total absence of what I thought of as intellectual reserves (a developed imagination, analytical subtlety, wide reading) he had managed ships and men in two world wars and the Korean war. He had worked and enjoyed himself and taken knocks among the solid weights and wide gaps of the world I would not face. Death worried him now that his body was failing, but since the age of twelve he had never been embarrassed by life. And by wrestling with the fear of death openly and aloud he made it a public comedy instead of a private terror. Aboard the *Kenya Castle*, when I was afraid of dying, my fear did nobody any good.

Of course, I had to face the world in the end. Only everlasting money can keep us from doing that, and mine was being used up. Each day in hospital cost me twenty-one shillings and I had been over three weeks there. When to that was added the train fare to London, and cost of lodgings there, boat fare to Gibraltar, ship's hospital fee, the price of the ambulance journey and being X-rayed for tuberculosis, and the small sum I had forced upon Ian, I found I had spent, or else owed, more than half the scholarship money. I recalled, too, that I had never been discharged from hospital feeling perfectly well. It was possible that something in the nature of hospitals pandered to my asthma after the worst of an attack had been cured by them. I asked to see the head doctor and explained that, for financial reasons, I must leave next morning. He shrugged and said, "It cannot be helped." He advised me, though, not to leave Gibraltar until I felt healthier, and even so not to go far into Spain in case I had another attack, as in Spain the hospital charges were extortionate, especially to tourists, and the medical standards were not high. This seemed sensible advice. I asked the nurses for the name of a lodging which was cheap, plain and good. I heard there was an armed-forces leave centre in the south bastion which usually had spare beds, was run by a retired Scottish soldier, and easy to reach. Next morning I dressed, collected my rucksack, left the hospital doorstep and struck with my feet the first earth I had touched since the port of London.

I was on a road slanting up from the town of Gibraltar to the rock's outermost point. The day must have been clear because across the sea to the south I saw the African coast looking exactly as Africa ought to look: a dark line of crowded-together rock pinnacles, domes and turrets with beyond them, when the eye had grown used to the distance, the snowy range of Atlas holding up the sky. The modern hospital behind me, the elegantly towered building in front (a lunatic asylum) stood on a great slant of white limestone rock interspersed with small tough twisted trees. I turned right and walked to the town, breathing easily because I was going downhill. I came to a wall with an arch in it just wide enough to take two cars, and beyond this the road became the main street of Gibraltar. A small lane leading to the left brought me almost at once to the south bastion.

This was a stone-built cliff protecting the town from the sea. The townward side was pierced by vaulted chambers. The lower ones, which had been barracks, were entered from a narrow piazza; the upper, which had been munition storerooms and gun emplacements, were entered from a balcony. All windows faced the town. High tides had once lapped the other side of this bastion but now a broad road ran here with docks on the far side. The guns and gunners had shifted elsewhere long ago and the chambers were used as a guest-house by the Toc H. The Toc H (I never learned the reason for that name) developed in France during the First World War, among British soldiers who wanted spiritual communion and found the official army priests too sectarian and not always near when things got tough. The only communion service was to light a brass oil-lamp in a dark place and pray that human pain would one day produce happiness and peace. Apart from that the organization existed to share extra food, clothing and shelter with whoever seemed in need. Jock Brown, formerly of the Highland Light Infantry in Flanders, was the Toc H man in south bastion. He was small, balding, mild-faced and wore a blazer with a white cross badge on the breast pocket and flannel trousers with bicycle clips at the ankles. His instincts were all turned to being mildly helpful. He believed that youth was a beautiful and noble state but was not surprised when young soldiers brawled, contracted venereal diseases and stole. He liked lending them cameras, books and records in the hope that they would come to enjoy using these instead. With the help of Isabel, a Spanish maid, he kept the hostel tidy and clean, the meals plain yet tasty, the general air of the place as mild as himself. I once heard him called "an old woman" by somebody who thought that a term of abuse. The critic was a man of Jock's age who had not been very useful to other people, so wanted to believe that everyday kindness was an unimportant virtue.

On that first morning Jock led me up a ramp to the balcony and into the common room, a former gun emplacement with a triangular floorplan. A hearth was built into the angle facing the door so that smoke left by the hole through which shells had been fired. The interior stonework was massively rough except for seven feet of smooth wall on each side of the hearth, and later I painted mural decorations here. Jock showed me to a dormitory next door holding four beds and introduced me to room-mates who had not yet risen. These were a private on leave from the Royal Surrey regiment, and an Australian and a German who would both be departing by ship next morning. I unpacked my things into a locker beside my bed then visited a bank in town where I uplifted the second part of the Bellahouston Scholarship money, the first having been received in Glasgow. I pocketed a few pounds and hid the rest in a plastic envelope containing my shaving-kit.

That night, to obtain sound sleep in a strange bed, I decided to become drunk and found a big crowded bar nearby where I would not be conspicuous. The customers were mostly soldiers and sailors but there were women among them. A small plump one approached and asked if I would like a companera? I said I would. She sat beside me, called a waiter and ordered a glass of pale green liquid, for which I paid. She was Spanish and her English was too poor to tell me much else. She tried to be entertaining by folding a handkerchief into the shape of what she called pantalones and unfastening the flies, but I did not find this exciting or feel she wished to seduce me. With each green drink I bought, the waiter handed her a small brass disc. When she went to the lavatory I tasted what was in her glass and found it to be coloured water. I got the waiter to refill the glass with green chartreuse but when she returned and sipped this she grew thoughtful and depressed, then left me. Clearly the management paid her no commission on the real drinks I purchased. So I drank by myself and listened to a small, very noisy band. It played a round of tunes chosen to cause nostalgia in as many customers as possible: *Maybe It's Because I'm a Londoner, Men of Harlech, Galway Bay*, etc. The Scottish number, *I Belong to Glasgow*, was repeated every ten minutes. It is not a tune I normally like but in this place it induced an emotion so heartrending that I had to grapple with it as if it were a disease. However, I stayed drinking until I was sure my head would lose consciousness as soon as it touched a pillow, then returned to the dormitory (which was in darkness), undressed, put the shaving-kit under the pillow, my head on top of it, and did indeed lose consciousness.

I wakened late next morning feeling brighter and healthier than I had done for many weeks. I also felt guilty (the straw mat beside my bed was crusted with vomit) but I knew that a day of brisk sketching or writing would cure that. The English private remained curled below his blankets, the Australian and German had already left to catch their boat. I took my toilet things and the straw mat to the lavatory and washed the mat and myself perfectly clean. Then I dressed and breakfasted, then climbed by an iron ladder to the esplanade on top of the bastion and sat on a shaded bench planning what to do. I still owed money to the hospital. I took my wad of notes from the shaving-kit and found it contained twenty pounds. The rest had been removed.

My instinctive reaction to a painful event is to sit quiet for a very long time, and as I brooded on my position this struck me as an intelligent thing to do. The thief must be one of three people, two of whom were at sea. If I could persuade the police to act for me, which was unlikely, they could do little but spread to others a nasty feeling I had better keep to myself. The thief had left me enough to live on for a while. Although my father was not rich he had some money banked. I wrote him a letter explaining all the circumstances except my intoxication and asking for a loan of the stolen amount, which I promised to repay by taking a regular job when I returned home. He posted the money to me as quickly as he could. The asthma returned. It worsened and improved, then worsened and improved. I remained in the hostel for my twenty-fourth birthday, and the New Year of 1958, and another two months. I wrote five chapters of my book and painted a *Triumph of Neptune* on the common room walls.

And I made friends with other rootless people who used the hostel: a student from the Midlands who had left Britain to avoid national military service and seemed to live by petty smuggling; a tall stooping bronchial man, also from the Midlands, who hovered around the Mediterranean for health reasons; and a middle-aged American with a sore back who had been refused entry into England where he had gone to consult an osteopath of whom he had heard great things. He kept discussing the reasons for the refusal and asking if a slight tampering with the datestamp on his passport would make entry easier if he tried again. There was Cyril Hume, an unemployed able seaman with a photograph of a cheerful, attractive-looking wife in Portsmouth who "realized he needed to wander about a bit". I think it was Cyril Hume who learned that a ship would be sailing to the Canary Isles from a port on the African coast just opposite. Apparently the fare was cheap and the cost of living in the Canary Isles even less than the cost of living in Spain. My health was improving at the time so we all decided to go together. We took a ferry across the bay to Algeciras in Spain, and another ferry from Algeciras to Africa. There was a bright sun, a strong wind, waves ran fast with glittering foamy crests. The jumbled rocky African coast, a steep headland with a medieval fortress on top looked theatrical but convincing. Cyril Hume had bought us cheese, celery, bread. Standing in the prow of the ship it suddenly struck me that cheese, celery and exactly this chalky white bread was the best lunch I ever tasted. Slightly breathless, I produced and used my asthma hand-pump inhaler. The surrounding crowd turned and watched me with that direct, open interest Ian McCulloch had found upsetting. I enjoyed being a stranger who provoked interest without even trying.

The port we reached was Ceuta, a Spanish possession. It looked just like Algeciras: whitewalled buildings and streets bordered by orange trees with real fruit among the leaves. The ship we wanted had left for the Canary Isles the day before so we returned to Algeciras and took lodgings there. Next morning, having slept badly, I decided to stay in bed. After my friends had left a maid entered the room and began making the other beds by shaking up the feather quilts and mattresses. I am allergic to feathers and started suffocating. I cried out to her but had no Spanish and she no English. In my notebook I hastily sketched a feather and told her it was *mal* – I hoped that the Latin root for evil was part of her language too. She smiled and repeated the word with what seemed perfect comprehension and then, when I lay back, relieved, she returned to violently plumping out the quilts. I gripped my hypodermic needle to give myself a big adrenaline injection but my hand trembled and the needle broke short in my flesh. The maid and I both panicked. She screamed and a lot of women ran in and surrounded me, jabbering loudly as I pissed, shat, and grew unconscious.

I wakened in a hospital managed by dark-robed, white-wimpled brides of Christ. A doctor came, gave me pills of a sort that can be bought cheap from any chemist, and charged dear for them. My friends arrived, discharged me, and escorted me back across the bay to Gibraltar and the Toc H hostel, where I stayed in bed for a week. I now had slightly more than ten pounds of money left: enough to buy a cheap boat fare back to London.

One day Jock Brown came to me and said that if I gave him my passport he would get me a ticket for an aeroplane going to London that evening. The ticket cost thirty pounds. Jock did not offer to lend me money. He took my passport, returned with a ticket and helped me to the airport. I crossed Spain at twice the altitude of Everest. It looked brown and as flat as a map. The only memorable feature was the white circle of the bullring in the middle of each town. London was foggy. I went to the University hospital and was given an intravenous adrenaline injection to help me reach Glasgow by overnight train. At Glasgow Central Station I took a taxi to the Royal Infirmary where I was drugged and sent home by ambulance. The morning was fresh and springlike but I felt no joy in homecoming. Glasgow was as I expected.

To sum up, what good was the tour? What did it teach me? Not much about the world, a lot about myself. That I fear to change is evident. Of course we must always change, since the moment of birth starts the alterations and adaptions called *growth*, which is often gradual and foreseeable. If our surroundings don't change much, neither do we. But surroundings can change radically and suddenly. A war began and I hid with neighbours in a dark shelter, queer noises outside. My mother died, I left school, found another, was awarded a scholarship, went to a foreign land in the belly of a posh liner. These events should have made me more independent, but I feared losing the habits by which I knew myself, so withdrew into asthma. My tour was spent in an effort to avoid maturity gained by new experience. Yet in spite of the protective clutter of doctors in which I ended the trip that effort failed. Maturity is either bravely accepted or kicked against, but events always impose some of it. Before going abroad the idea of teaching art to children appalled me. I have now done it for five months, and compared with partial suffocation it is almost painless. I will soon have paid Jock Brown what I owe him, and will then pay my father. Since coming home I have had no more bad asthma attacks, and no longer fear them. The Bellahouston Travelling Scholarship has done me good.

*11 Findhorn Street*
*Riddrie, Glasgow C3*
*April 1959*

POSTSCRIPT. Wishing to attach to this report photographs of my *Triumph of Neptune* I wrote to Jock Brown asking if he would take and send me some. He answered that this was impossible. Soon after I left the hostel it was visited by the wife of Gibraltar's governor. She felt the naked mermaids and the nereids in the commonroom were a bad moral influence upon the soldiers using the place, so her husband asked Jock to paint them out. Jock, who liked my mural, wrote to the Secretary of State for War, Mr Jack Profumo, asking if he need obey the governor's request. Mr Profumo replied that "the man on the spot knows best", by whom he meant, not Jock Brown, but the governor's wife. So Jock, with rage in his heart, covered my mermaids in a coat of khaki paint. It is pleasent to imagine a more liberal age one day restoring them to light. However, the town of Gibraltar needs room to expand, and in a year or two the south bastion will be demolished.

# The World
# of Four to Seven

UP TO THE AGE OF FOUR YEARS most children are action painters – they enjoy paint as they enjoy mud and sand, painting is a business of making sploshy marks. Beyond the age of four years, their painting becomes articulate. They start to make images of things in the world they inhabit. It is a strange world, at once more limited and more arbitrary than ours. This thesis attempts to describe the stages by which that world evolves into the world that we adults inhabit.

It has been said that infants paint in symbols. I think this untrue. *The Everyday English Dictionary* calls a symbol: "That which represents something else", while *The Westminster Dictionary* calls it "The sign or representation of something moral or intellectual". By these definitions no infant art and hardly any child art is symbolic. In the adult world a wig, a flag, a cross and boy archer represent respectively justice, a nation and a religion and love; but up to the age of five infants know none of these things, and therefore do not need to symbolize them. Infants love and are loved, but do not know love,

After art school I earned money by part-time art teaching without a truly qualified certificate, for I lacked a pass in maths & another language then needed to enter a teacher training college. Shortage of teachers led to entrance being granted to folk with only my art school diploma. It was wonderful to again live on a State bursary and be **trained** to teach. This was much easier than being a teacher. Scots Education needed another thesis from me. I liked putting this one together in 1960 for the teachers training college of old Jordanhill, now merged with the Strathclyde University campus. I illustrated it with orginal pictures in poster-colour by infants of Wellshot Road Primary School, close to Tollcross Park, and what was Parkhead Forge.

fear punishment but have no theory of justice to assure them that it is deserved. As a result they are thorough materialists, and more objective about the things they experience than they can ever be again. They have no sense of tragedy or reverence, as any teacher knows who has heard an infant speak of a family disaster.

To sum up, the infant world has facts in it, but no truths. The only things they paint, therefore, are facts; such unarguable facts as their mummy, daddy, house, dinner, bed, and (of course) selves. These are usually depicted in a spaceless world – space, after all, is not a thing, its existence has to be deduced by refering to things, and this deduction comes gradually to children over several years. The infant world has no space in it because the things in that world are not much thought of as being related to each other, but only to the infant.

When Margaret Carson made the painting of things at home, she painted mummy, television, door, bath, cooker, pot, bed and me with mummy biggest and herself not much bigger than anything else, nor does she consider the relation of these things to the rooms they are in though they are shown the right way up. Ann Anderson who is also five paints some of the same things when showing visitors coming for a meal. She does this in a plan view of the table with six chairs round it, and finding it hard to paint visitors on the chairs she has painted a separate table to one side with somebody on it – probably herself. In the anonymous painting above Ann's there is not the same attempt to show an event – but the things and people are all seen from in front on a kitchen floor and only a fork and spoon above are shown in plan.

I insist that there is no symbolism in these paintings. In the picture of a family out walking the father is shown with everything the artist remembers as important about his father – long legs, pipe with smoke coming out and a hat. If he had remembered arms he would have included them too.

I said earlier that the young infant does not know love or justice. This is because knowledge of a thing depends on the power to see it in other people. Infants are too self-centred to recognize love in other people, therefore they cannot recognize it in themselves. Gradually, through experience, they recognize that the things of this world are related to each other in an order which does not depend upon them. A little later than this they come to recognize that other people do not exist purely to help them, but sometimes also need help. Thus they discover sympathy. Not surprisingly the first manifestations of sympathy are towards things weaker than the child itself, often a pet animal.

Most children sense that animals, like themselves, are small and dependant. These pictures show that fellow feeling goes to the lengths of giving it a human size. Of course in lonely or neglected children the discovery of the space which cuts people off from each other will be resisted, and they will continue to inhabit a self-centred world which their companions have grown away from. Such children develop with some defect of the sympathetic emotion; either it is suppressed and replaced by coldness or even cruelty, or exhibited in an excessive form towards something unworthy of it. At best the child of five and six is beginning to live in a larger and less arbitrary world –> physically larger and morally less arbitrary.

Here are pictures of this world, mostly by boys. Everything happens between earth and sky. Mummy & Daddy, figures who occurred all the time in earlier pictures, are nowhere to be seen. The subject for all six was "a game in the park". Everybody has included some non-human living thing though this was not insisted upon. Aeroplanes are popular – suggesting liberty and manliness. One boy has gone to the length of differentiating himself by painting a woollen helmet of which he is particularly proud. Note that this boy is the only one to recognize that the sky is not like a ceiling, but actually begins at ground level.  These children of seven are aware of space, though they may not have accepted the limitlessness of space. They will be found to have a sense of what is "fair", even if they depart from it, and will have some kind of code of what is due to one's companions and oneself. In short, they have started to use truths (justice, honour) to guide them through the wilderness
of mere facts.

# An Apology for my Recent Death

IN LAST WEEK'S RADIO TIMES was a photograph of me looking sombre, beside an article which began: 'I first met the late Alasdair Gray ten years ago on New Year's Eve in Glasgow...' It was signed 'Robert Kitts'. I was only slightly surprised (I had expected something similar) but I was still depressed and uneasy. The mistake came from several discussions and compromises which began last summer when the BBC started making a documentary television film about my work. I must apologise to those who were upset by that mistake which, as printed in the *Radio Times*, is an outright lie. I can do that best by telling how it happened.

I first met Bob Kitts ten years ago on New Year's Eve in Glasgow outside the State Bar in Holland Street. We were both studying to be painters, I in Glasgow School of Art, he in the London Slade. Both were just out of our teens or nearly so, both of us spoke vigorously with local accents (I Glaswegian, he Cockney), both had been drinking but I was the least sober. We began a conversation that lasted through a succession of parties, thus learning that as

*On 18th January 1965 this article was sent to the Glasgow Herald which did not use it, but the making of the film led to London visits and meeting TV producers. These gave ideas for* **The Fall of Kelvin Walker**, *a play broadcast by London BBC TV in 1968. This led to Stewart Conn, head of Scots BBC radio drama, over the next 10 years commissioning & broadcasting half a dozen of my radio plays. Combined with income from a few TV works & lecturing on art appreciation for the extra mural department of The University of Glasgow, I earned enough to live without school teaching & hardly ever getting Social Security help. Despite mixed feelings at the time, I now think this a worthwhile film.*

working class children our lives had both been re-
shaped by World War II evacuations from the cities of our birth, and that we were now beneficiaries of the welfare state created after it, especially the education grants. We were both writing long novels based on our experiences, novels showing what was good and bad in the nation that had given birth to such remarkable geniuses as ourselves.

Thus began a lasting friendship kept up by his occasional visits to Glasgow and mine to London, and an exchange of letters between these. On our first night together we agreed that our equal interests in both pictorial and literary art must one day come together in the art of film-making. This never happened with me, but before leaving the Slade Bob went into film studies and after early struggles became first an ITV film director, then a director for the BBC second channel under Hugh Wheldon, producer of Monitor, the arts programme catering for what Wheldon calls "the large minority" – viewers not only interested in classical music and drama, but in avant-garde forms, or both. Wheldon is open to new ideas.

On leaving art school I tried to go on painting and writing while earning money, first as a part-time art teacher, then for a short spell as a cabaret performer. Then I married and became a full-time art teacher to support my family. Perhaps I found teaching more frustrating than many, because it left so little time for making things I felt would one day please people more. I remember writing to Bob, saying I felt like a stoker of a locomotive engine, compelled to fuel a train travelling in the opposite direction to my talent.

Luckily I got the chance of becoming a painter of scenery for *Dick Whittington*, the Pavilion Theatre pantomime. The wage was less than for teaching but the work far more agreeable. At Christmas when the pantomime opened the Pavilion management decided that in future it would rent all scenery from an English firm of theatrical suppliers. The set painting department where I was designer and painter closed and for a month I became assistant set painter at Glasgow Citizens Theatre, but did not last because I failed to satisfy the head designer. This led to a spell of unemployment and life on the dole, not my first. Between one school and another, one job and another, I had been often unemployed. This was my first spell as a married man. My wife did not complain – she had just borne our son and liked having me to help at home. Sale of a drawing or painting sometimes brought in a little money which I admit I did not declare to The Authorities.

This spell of unemployment lasted into the summer of 1964 when I received a letter from Bob saying that at last he was being paid to make films on themes of his own choosing. He wanted to make a film about me and would I phone him at BBC London, reversing the charges? I did: and after hiding my exhilaration at his proposal under a few words of modest acceptance we discussed the film.

All documentary films I had seen about living artists had struck me as false. I remember one where Graham Sutherland walked down a lane looking for something to sketch, pretending not to notice a van with a camera which must have been travelling slowly

in front of him. I knew from Sutherland's paintings he
must often walk through the countryside looking for things to sketch, but knew too that when the film was being made he *could not* be really doing that – he must be acting the part. That he was acting himself seemed even more false than pretending to be someone else. In Bob's film I did not want to be shown in my studio pretending to paint, while my wife came in with the baby and a cup of coffee pretending to be my wife. An artist's person adds nothing to true enjoyment of art, though I suspect that Van Gogh cut off his ear has given simple pleasure to more than enjoy his sunflowers. Interest in artists as people degrades art into excuses for gossip. I wanted Bob to film my paintings and record my voice, and leave my private life private.

We discussed this through telephone calls and a weekend when he came north to stay with us. He explained that the sort of art-film I wanted would be switched off at once by most viewers who cared nothing for the pictures and words of an obscure Scotsman unless, like trout, they were first attracted by the worm of my person into biting the hook of the arty stuff behind. Then Bob came up with an idea which would let me appear on the screen as little as I wished, yet still arouse interest. He would have me talking straight to the camera at the start of the film, then with melancholy music and a commentator speaking in the past tense would imply that I had died soon after. He would go on to present my personality through the words of people who had known me, then have a long sequence about the works themselves, with my voice talking over them reading my relevant verse.

The film would end in a Glasgow BBC television control room where I would be filmed along with himself, discussing reasons for the deception.

He persuaded me that this was a good idea whenever we talked about it, but when talking of it to others I felt uneasy. He said 'I'll write a piece about it for the Radio Times leaving readers unsure if you're alive or dead, so they'll switch on the TV to find out.'

Five weeks after filming in Glasgow Bob had me come to London to record material for the soundtrack, I saw the film nearly completed and was shocked by two things. My appearance was not as firm and manly as I wished, and though everyone I knew in the film spoke kindly, some exaggerations and omissions made me seem that harmless comic, The Mad Artist.

Mr Young, Session Clerk of Greenhead Church, said that when working on my mural I said I would finish it in a week, yet completed it three years later. True; but this omits that in a week, I brought the mural to an acceptable state from the congregation's point of view, but not from my own. Mr Hart, the Minister, saw I was unhappy to leave it and told me to complete it when I liked. I was painting for nothing but the cost of the materials, was delayed by my need to earn money, so in my free time I felt justified in making every alteration that would improve the mural. Mr Young may have explained this to the camera, but it was left out in the editing. No film about a real subject can record every relevant fact so I am foolish to quarrel with how I came to seem. But Mr Bovey, I was not carried out of the McLellan Galleries on a stepladder. Mr McAllister, in the Scotland USSR Friendship Society

I did not use four dozen teacups to mix my paint.

Before the film appeared, the Radio Times had an article calling me "the late Alasdair Gray" and conveying that I was very dead indeed. Bob tells me (I believe him) that the word "late" was added by a Radio Times sub-editor who, sure I must be dead, had made alterations to leave no doubt. Only viewers can say if they enjoyed the film but I know some who felt annoyed and cheated. I am to blame for that. By preventing the film being made to show normal kinds of falseness it showed a
larger kind.

# Instead of An Apology

FOUR WEEKS AGO I ended a job that left me feeling slightly guilty, a play about a modern love affair. The setting was any town with an adult education college. I am Scottish but set it in England. Most authors set their fictions on their native soil because the familiar is often more easily imagined by them and their audiences, but Shakespeare set good plays in Scotland, Denmark and Italy, Brecht some others in England, Italy, the U.S.A. and China. My guilt derived from a meeting last November with a London BBC television producer.

I wanted him to commission a play from me. I knew the main characters and how they would interact, but not much more when the producer asked where I would locate the play, since the actor's accents would largly indicate that. I thought a little; then said that, like *Miss Julie* by Strindberg, it was a play about tension between social classes. My heroine could be posh English, but the accents of the hero and his father should be from an exact British location. The producer said the BBC would commission my play if the location was English. This was because

This swipe at London BBC's anti-Scots ideas still holds good. Unlike the last apology, this one appeared in the 1969 **Glasgow Herald**, when TV commissions had begun to come from the London BBC & Granada, so I expected a secure future in television. I was paid for this play but it was finally turned down by someone senior to the producer who had wanted it. A year or two later I acquired an excellent literary agent in London, Francis Head, who sold it to Granada. It was broadcast titled **Triangles**. When in later years my I had succeeded as a novelist but lacked ideas for more, this was one of my forgotten plays that I turned into prose fiction. In 1996 Bloomsbury published it with the title **Mavis Belfrage: with 5 Shorter Tales**.

most British viewers live in the south around London, where it has been found that Scottish voices in a play inclines them to switch their channel. But some recent books and films (*Room at the Top, Billy Liar, A Taste of Honey*) had shown that even Londoners could enjoy other English settings, so my play could be located in Yorkshire or anywhere south of the Scottish border.

Did I say that for South Britain to declare itself the only area of dramatically useable life was despotic provincialism at its smuggest? Did I say that attitude led to the neglect and depression of life in all but the wealthiest part of the British archipelago? No. I said that as a child I had lived for three years in Yorkshire so would set my play there if the BBC would commission it. A contract was signed, the play written and the script posted to the Shepherd's Bush TV centre.

Scotland has only two training colleges of the sort where a love affair between my hero teacher and heroine student could happen. Such affairs are frequent, and those who like to believe plays are based on real events will have less room to speculate with the English location. To avoid the distraction of such speculations James Joyce lived thirty years in Trieste, Switzerland and Paris while writing four books set in his native Dublin. That has nothing to do with my guilt. To explain it I must first say what drama is and does.

It is a public performance exciting onlookers. Defined thus, theatre, film and television provide a small fraction of a dramatic world containing football and every other sport. Weddings and funerals are drama, especially the church kind, which is why many non-christians prefer them. So are ship launchings, all processions, strikes, protests meetings, trials and everything else reported upon or broadcast as news, including crimes, fires, floods, plagues, earthquakes, wars and other disasters.

Am I stretching the word too far? A play succeeds by amusing the audience. A strike can interest many but succeeds for the strikers if they win higher wages, for the employers if the strikers are defeated. The climax of *Hamlet* and a stabbing in a dance hall may enthral onlookers for similar reasons, but murder in a stage play kills nobody. My definition lumps the real with the imaginary in a manner unfair to both. True, but I am not considering events from the viewpoint of those enacting them, but from the bystanders viewpoint, which in real life is mostly irresponsible. Television has increased irresponsible viewing. For almost everyone the difference between the speeches of King Lear and Harold Wilson is a difference of dramatic quality. Both are nominal rulers of Britain who find themselves impotent in the face of events. Lear has the advantage of a superior script writer but Harold's drama has the advantage of suspense. We don't yet know the end.

This may sound like a metaphor but in the ancient Greek democracies it was a reality. Parliament was held in the civic theatre. Everyone not a slave, child or woman could speak and vote there. If a fishmonger thought of a fairer way to collect taxes he could take the stage and explain it. If a majority liked the scheme he would be put in charge of tax-collecting and would take the rap if his method failed. In more sophisticated societies it takes revolutions to put the population on the stage, a process so strenuous that few nations have more than one big revolution per century. No matter how costly the seats and poor the play, most of us, most of the time, want to be just audience.

But onlooking is not simple escapism. Our stage is the world, the plot is history whose drama is the sum of our lives, and we want to see our own place in it. We are partly at the mercy of mysterious forces like the American defence-policy, and the ownership of oil wells, but are also affected by much nearer things – local council meetings, the structure of multi-storey flats, and much else not always reported in the daily news. In democracies these public matters exist for the audience, not vice-versa. Politicians can seldom do more than their supporters will let them. Even the most conspicuous events depend on such intimate private things as how people earn their livings, love their wives and children, what they think about their bosses and neighbours.

The essential details of our lives only convincingly appear in good novels and dramas especially written for the stage or broadcasting networks. An adequate reporter deals with public events, an adequate author deals with what mostly happens in private because here are roots of everything eventually accepted as history.

I say 'adequate' rather than 'great' because art does not always need genius to make it effective. Over twelve years ago a play and two novels made a considerable stir in Britain. *Look Back in Anger, Lucky Jim* and *Room at the Top*. These were not great literature but they were important, esepcially when turned into films. Government grants to education at the end of World War II had let an unprecedentedly large number of working-class boys and girls achieve professional qualifications. This multitude was in a historically unique position, a position which had been planned by a government and could be demonstrated statistically. Yet this multitude was a dispersed crowd of individuals until the rant of Jimmy Porter and the funny faces of Jim Dixon made them known as a class and gave them confidence. This is the best thing plays can do: show people they are parts of a larger society and excite them into confidence.

Which returns me to the play I set in an English rather than Scottish suburb, and to guilt about this which still haunts me. I don't blame the producer. He was English, and spoke for an English majority who wanted the excitement of viewing themselves. Maybe a Scottish majority also prefer watching the English. Perhaps (outside football matches and historical serials) we feel too commonplace to be interesting. If my play had been set in Scotland, and been transmitted, and been good, it would have shown this was not the case. Even if it had been only partly good it would have shown some vitality in a depressed area. As Hugh MacDiarmid has written

*Inadequate maps are better than no maps*
*At least they show that the land exists,*
*that there's more than one possible route from*
*the womb to the coffin.*\*

\**These words are not by MacDiarmid. I foisted them on him as a way of getting a piece of my own verse in print. MacDiarmid was still alive then but I knew he would never deny they were his, as he admitted having published so much that he could not remember it all, including lines he had taken from others.*

# Of Bill Skinner: A Small Thistle*

THE DECLARATION OF INDEPENDENCE by the United States' representatives in 1781 put the American episcopal church into great difficulty. It had no bishops, yet believed that bishops were essential to the making of new priests. Hitherto English bishops had consecrated American priests, but now the two countries were at war. The Church of England was headed by King George, who thought the U.S.A. an illegal organization. It seemed that the American episcopal priesthood might dwindle through senility into extinction, or turn itself into a wholly new kind of protestant sect. However, a third way was found. Although England's government had absorbed the Scottish one seventy-five years earlier, Scotland's legal system and churches had stayed independent and intact. A leading light in the tiny Scottish Episcopal Church was the Rev. James Skinner, a poet whose *Reel of Tullochgorum* and *The Ewie wi' the Crookit Horn* are still found in anthologies. His son, William Skinner, was a man of liberal sentiments, and Bishop of Aberdeen, and would soon be episcopal Primate of Scotland. So in 1784 William Skinner and two other Scottish bishops laid their right hands on the head of Dr. Seabury, a Connecticut Yankee, thus turning him into a

* Most of this was in an obituary I wrote for a 1973 **Glasgow West End News**, then it became an entry in the 1984 **Glasgow Diary** published by Polygon Books, Edinburgh, edited by Donald Goodbrand Saunders, and was finally enlarged for publication in **Lean Tales**, 1985, published by Jonathan Cape, London: a collection of short stories by Agnes Owens, James Kelman and me, who made three of mine factual, like this.

bishop too. The blessing which Jesus once bestowed on Saint Peter could now be carried across the Atlantic in a contagious form.

On Monday morning the 24th May 1973 Bill Skinner, a last descendant of the episcopal Skinners, died of heart failure in Gartnavel General Hospital, Glasgow, at the age of sixty-nine. The family fortune had trickled very thin by the time it reached Bill. His father, a robust but feckless man, had been educated at Heidelberg University and then lumberjacked and bummed his way across America before ending his days in the Town Clerk's office of Glasgow Corporation. When Bill left school he entered the shipyards as a maker-off, chalking points on steel plates where the rivet holes were to be cut. Retiring with heart-disease in the 1940s he worked thereafter as a part-time laboratory assistant in a private college which crammed people for the University entrance exams. When that closed in the mid sixties he lived frugally on his National Insurance pension. He never married, spending most of his life with his widowed mother at their home in Otago Street, in what was surely the last gas-lit tenement flat in Glasgow. He had no children. His only surviving relative had been a distant cousin in America.

These are the bare statistical bones of Skinner's life, and one could be excused for thinking them bleak. The living reality was wonderfully different. Bill filled his life with such various imaginative activities – political, artistic, scientific, alchemical – that he became a source of delight and satisfaction to an unusually wide circle of friends. He was a member of the Andersonian Society, the Connolly Association, the

CND, an American scientific correspondence society, and the Scottish-USSR Friendship Society.

His Otago Street home had a small laboratory where he did research into Particle Compression and the Origins of Life, printing (at his own expense) a small pamphlet setting out his views on these subjects. Anyone who cared to make an appointment would be shown over the small museum he had constructed in his mother's front parlour, with its fossils, pressed plants, the headphones powered by body electricity, the transparent seagull's skull and his exhibition of paintings. On average he produced two paintings a year: clear-edged, mysteriously coloured little symbolic works with names like *Scotia Aspires*, *Tyro Wizard Town* and *Death of Death*. I once heard him grow highly indignant with a critic who called him a Primitive. He thought this was a slur on his meticulous technique. Even in his last years, when badly crippled with arthritis, he produced, with the help of friends, two editions of the magazine *Anvil Sparks*, in which he wrote science, art and political notes, advertised the exhibitions of friends, and serialized the career of Henbane Dwining, the alchemist in Scott's novel *The Fair Maid of Perth*, a character with whom he felt great sympathy.

Before illness confined him to the house he was an alert, quick, small boyish man with nutcracker nose and chin, and a mop of pale nicotine-coloured hair. Apparently it had once been bright red. When this faded he tried reviving the colour with a concoction of his own, but without much success. His pubs were the State Bar, the Blythswood Bar and the Pewter Pot before they were modernised. His favourite drinks were vodka with lime and High-Ho, another invention of his which he distilled from pharmaceutical alcohol. It was only brought out at Hogmanay, and a small glass of it diluted by three parts of water to one and flung in the fire could still produce dangerous explosions. He was cheerful, utterly independent, had many friends of both sexes and all ages, and not one enemy. He *succeeded* in life.

Some time in 1940, when working in the yards, he became a founder of a political party which drew its members mainly from the Anarchist, Trotskyite and Nationalist blocs. At the end of his life he was its only member, and he advanced its principles by fixing (with immense caution) small stickers to trees and lamp-posts in quiet streets near his home. The slogan on these stickers should be his epitaph:

SCOTTISH
SOCIALIST
REPUBLIC
NEUTRALITY

Beside these words is a small thistle.

# Catalogue
# Introduction*

ONLY UNLUCKY PAINTERS have more than a few finished pictures in their studio at one time, so for a big show most of us borrow back work from patrons. Andrew Sykes, the Strathclyde Professor of Sociology, has bought from me steadily for fifteen years. When visiting him Stephen Ellson, curator of the Collins Exhibition Hall, saw my paintings and suggested this show. Mr. Ellson and I felt that the best order was chronological, to show the growth of my talent. I am therefore showing pictures from seconday school days and art school days, some of them unsuccessful like *The Fall of the Star Wormwood*, which tackled a problem too big for my talent, or unfinished, like my biggest canvas *The North Glasgow Skyline*, which I may live to finish.

I was born in Glasgow, late December 1943. Like other artists, picture-making obsessed me so a normal education was unable to stop it. Miss Jean Irwin's Saturday painting class for children in Glasgow Art Galleries greatly encouraged me. The muddled style of the early work is caused by trying to blend the colour and figurative grandeur of Blake with the clean elegance of Beardsley, the social paradises and Hells of Bosch and the realism (not expressionism) of Munch. The results of that effort are raw and harsh, interesting but ugly. I was also influenced by Gulley Jimson, to me, the greatest of modern English painters.

*Catalogue published 28 March 1974 by Strathclyde University.*

# Of Gable-End Murals 1975<sup>*</sup>

DEAR CHARLOTTE RIORDAN, most of your questions about the 1970s tenement gables mural scheme do not apply to me. Like other artists commissioned for a design I drew one up, and perhaps it was too ambitious. It was a scheme for the four adjacent gables along the profile of Garnethill. From the western pavement of St George's Road three tenement and a two storey house gable are visible above the embankment sloping down to the trench containing the motorway to the Kingston Bridge. Designs for these gables, a panorama of them on the hillside, plan of the area, typed essay explaining the idea were mounted on card and, as required, delivered to the Third Eye Centre. Tom McGrath was then boss, and may have been partly responsible for the scheme. I was paid for my plans but not employed to carry them out. Several months later, realising they would not be used, I asked for them back and was told nobody knew what had become of them. I assume they were abandoned at the back of some cupboard and have long been destroyed. I have a dyeline print of the whole panorama – nothing else – but can give you a rough précis of my general idea.

Big mural paintings on outside walls in working class districts seem to have originated in North America as a way of making dull, unbeautifully designed brick

* *This letter replied to a lady who wrote asking me about the scheme, I forget why.*

and concrete buildings look cheerful and interesting.
But Glasgow tenements, even in poor districts, were of well-built stone and had well-designed architectural completeness – even the street plans had usually been designed on a dignified grid pattern. Industrial depression between the wars had turned many into overcrowded slums without decent plumbing. These tenements were mainly thought ugly by visitors from England who thought brick terraces the only civilised urban architecture, so among Glasgow town planners and councillors after the Second World War there was a general opinion that all old Glasgow tenements should be demolished and the town centre completely rebuilt with sweeping motorways, multi-storey tenements and office blocks. A plan for this was commissioned from an architect called Bruce in the fifties. A model of it exhibited in the Kelvin Hall showed a future Glasgow where the Civic Chambers, the Cathedral, Kelvingrove Art Galleries and University were all that remained from the past. The amount of demolition proposed was impractical, but some of the scheme was carried through and explains why Glasgow acquired many more miles of motorway round the centre than London, why multi-storey schemes were built that have since been demolished, why so many Glasgow tenements had blank gables because they had been half or a quarter demolished. So why not brighten them with murals by professional artists, big and bright enough to put graffiti artists to shame?

I thought that designs for a big new mural in a conspicuous public site where people lived should be submitted to them for approval. Better still, artists should first meet them, propose several designs, and after discussion, chose one a majority of residents preferred. This was not done because democracy gives officials more trouble than they like. A committee of folk from outside a district find it easier choosing a mural for it by an artist who also lives elsewhere. And since I thought Glasgow tenements better architecture than the industrial housing areas of North America, I felt some sorts of mural would demean them almost as much as a gigantic commercial advertisement. I do not know if John Byrne's gable end near Duke Street survives – I hope so – it filled the space amusingly with a Wally Dug three storeys high – but it demeaned the scale of the tenement. Certainly it was better than nothing, and cheaper than covering a concrete skim-coat with new stonework and windows that harmonised with the tenements front and back.

I thought my design for the four gables between the western ends of Carnarvon and Renfrew Street could easily be approved by those living behind them, as their gables overhung a steep hillside abandoned to shrubbery, ending in the gulley containing the new motorway. They would only be seen from the other side of St George's Road. The huge trees I wished to paint on these gables, would appear to grow from the bushes at the foot of them, trees with spreading branches. Behind these I would have trompe l'oeil painting of the original gables, which have been demolished when the west end of Garnethill was cut back to let the motorway through. I hope that answers your questions. Yours truly,
Alasdair Gray.

# New Lanark Craft Community

THE AREA:– The Royal Burgh of Lanark is famous for several reasons. The first recorded Scottish Parliament met here in 978, William Wallace began the war of independence here by killing the English sheriff, and for two centuries the town was trusted with the keeping of the nation's weights and measures. In the 18th century, like many Scottish market towns, it owed its prosperity to the weavers in the back-close sheds. Beyond the county it was chiefly known for the nearby Falls of Clyde. Tourists had always visited the rich cities of Italy and France, but a new taste was developing for wild, wet, craggy places, and from the days of Sam Johnson to Felix Mendelssohn the Scottish tour included a visit to Lanark and a stroll up the wooded glen to the great cataracts of Corra and Bonnington Linn. The tiny cave where Wallace is said to have hidden so impressed William Wordsworth that he wrote a bad poem linking love of liberty with the untamed beauty of the scene. The free powers of nature are more usually admired where it is known how to harness them commercially.

*In 1975 I was a friend & lodger of Gordon and Pat Lennox, art students. They, a few artist friends and I tried to form this craft community. The article does not tell all the reasons why. The idea of this community came from a Tory councillor with a small craft shop in New Lanark. She thought her shop could sell the community's products. I and a majority thought nothing wrong with her being a member of the scheme she had imagined. So a Labour councillor encouraged us to write a constitution and generously had it both typed and photocopied for us. There we found* **Rule 1** *was:* **Only crafts-people can be members.** *Thus rid of the Tory conceiver of the community, in less than a year Lanark's Labour council dropped it completely.*

THE VILLAGE:– In 1784 David Dale took Richard Arkwright to Dundaff Linn where the Clyde spilled from a ravine into a marshy place enclosed by steep, wooded hills. Dale had begun his career with a packhorse peddling cotton to the spinners cottages and yarn to the weavers sheds. As Glasgow grew rich by trade with America, he too became rich as cotton importer and merchant banker. Arkwright's new spinning frames made the world's fastest thread. His invention and Dale's capital could use a Clyde fall to twist American cotton. This is why New Lanark was built. With the Clyde embanked, and a mill-lade tunneled through 300 feet of rock, then mills and a village were built and built well, in elegant, austere Georgian terraces.

Arkwright was the foremost designer of those dark, satanic mills which throughout the 19th Century showed the factory system at its worst, in England and the west of Scotland. Dale, however, was a kindly man, with a home both in Glasgow and in the factory village where he lived beside his workforce. Many of these were Highlanders expelled from their homes by landlords who found sheep more profitable – this is why one block of houses is called Caithness Row. As was customary, Dale employed child labour, orphans sent to him by local governments who avoided responsibility for them, in return for a promise that they would be fed and housed. These slept in the mill where they laboured, but unlike most employers Dale gave them time and teachers so that they learned reading and writing, singing and the dance.

By 1800, New Lanark was nearly finished and

the mills were the biggest and most productive in
Scotland. In that same year Dale, wishing to retire,
took his son-in-law Robert Owen into partnership and
made him manager.

M R TOOGOOD:– Owen was a Welshman and an
atheist. Hard, determined work changed him
from a poor shop assistant to manager, at nineteen, of
the Chorlton Twist Mill near Manchester. He had
noticed that people work better when not starved or
driven to the point of exhaustion, and were usually
more trustworthy when less demoralized. From this he
drew conclusions which contradicted the religious and
economic theory of his day. He thought more
happiness would make people behave better towards
one another, perhaps even towards their employers;
and that basing the prosperity of some on the
deprivation of the rest was not only wrong but
unnecessary. Thomas Peacock caricatured Owen as
Mr. Toogood in the novel *Crotchet Castle*.
*"Mr Toogood the co-operationist, who will have
neither fighting nor praying; but wants to parcel out
the world into squares like a chessboard, with a
community on each, raising everything for one
another, with a great steam engine to serve them in
common for tailor and hosier, kitchen and cook."*
Owen thought employers should spend profits
over 5% on the welfare and education of their
workers. He built a nursery, a school and an Institute
for the Formation of Character. This last was less
frightening than its name. It held a dance-hall, church,
adult lecture-theatre and infant school. Like most kind-

hearted dictators Owen got on well with the very young, and he angered the churchgoers of Lanark up the hill by making the mill-children's Sabbath a day of recreation. He organized dancing in the open air and took them on nature-study rambles in the glen. The adults disliked him at first. Working mothers were glad to buy cheap food from the village store and liked having family lunches cooked in the communal kitchen, but they hated having their homes examined for cleanliness, and the men found Owen a stricter manager than Dale. Nevertheless, he gained their respect.

Owen left New Lanark in 1825 and went to America, where for four years he vainly strove to establish a socialist community at New Harmony, Indiana. When he died, at the ripe old age of 87, having had several fortunes pass through his hands, Mr. Toogood had clearly found the life-struggle more rewarding than most.

TILL THE ROPEWORKS SHUT:– The village was preserved by less idealistic owners, the only addition being a little Victorian church in 1889. New Lanark was lit by electricity when few other villages had gas. Perhaps to economize on a small generator, perhaps as a relic of Owen's paternalism, the manager operated the only switch in the village, turning all the lights on at nightfall and off at a reasonable bedtime. This was no hardship to folk who still had the use of oil-lamps and candles, but if a doctor attending a birth in the early hours demanded light, the manager had to be knocked-up and every home flooded with brilliance.

In 1914 mills and village were acquired by the Gourock Ropeworks. After the Great War the Clyde falls were put in the pipes of a power station, and a historic beauty-spot became a line of pools linked by a thin trickle, but visitors still come down the hill to see New Lanark. A suburb of Lanark reached a hilltop overlooking it, but though only a mile and a half from Lanark's High Street (as close as many housing schemes to their shopping centre) the village seemed and still seems isolated.

By 1960 most of the houses in the village had fallen below a tolerable standard. The New Lanark Association was formed and by dint of their hard work and financial aid from interested bodies, Caithness Row and the Nursery Buildings underwent a highly successful renovation. But in 1968, Gourock Ropeworks moved out and the mills were shut at last.

NOWADAYS:– Families still live in Caithness Row, but most other buildings stand empty. The store still opens and a mail-ordering firm dealing in Scottish crafts is housed in part of the Nursery Buildings. The mill area is used by a scrap metal firm with a handful of local employees. The school roof has fallen in, and the unoccupied buildings are threatened with dilapidation.

Due to a financial crisis the work of the New Lanark Association came to a halt. Their modernization of the Nursery Buildings received a well-deserved Civic Trust Award. In 1972 the New Lanark Working Party was formed and Provost H. Smith of Lanark was appointed chairman. Their first action was to commission a feasibility study. This decided that every effort must be made to restore the village to life and its essential character must be maintained. Existing buildings without external alteration can be adapted for various uses. Suggestions include a youth hostel, a field study centre for sixth-form and university students, a training centre for young engineers and an industrial museum for Scotland's most industrialised county. To encourage visitors, a tea-room or restaurant is very necessary.

The working population would be involved in small home-based industries and much of the residential property could readily become studio-workshops where craftsmen could live and work. Products could be sold direct to visitors, exhibited at The Present Gallery in Lanark, or, if produced in great enough quantity, marketed through Scotland Direct, the mail-order company. Summer schools staffed by the resident craftspeople would attract visitors who would find accommodation in the youth hostel or in Lanark hotels.

These activities can only stimulate growth and life, encouraging as they must, an influx of new people and new ideas.

THE CRAFT COMMUNITY:– Now numbering about thirty members this community was formed by artists and craftsmen coming together with one common aim – to live and work in New Lanark. When premises become available these will be allocated by ballot arranged such that a wide variety of crafts will be represented.

To become a full member of the community the applicant must be actively practicing his craft in a professional manner or have recently completed a professional training. We are not a commune. Each member is responsible for marketing their own work and payment of their own rents. There will, of course, be regular group exhibitions. Anyone interested in joining should contact the secretary, Miss Sandra Ewing, The Present Gallery, Broomgate, Lanark.

THIS EXHIBITION:– The purpose of this exhibition is to give the people of Lanark a look at the sort of folk who want to be their neighbours and at the kind of things these neighbours are going to make. We are weavers, embroiderers, silk-screen printers and dressmakers and a painter. We hope to be joined by other craftsmen. The future of New Lanark in the glen and Old Lanark on the hill are now linked, and we newcomers wish to
be part of it.

# Writers Groups

MOST WRITERS GROUPS HAVE members who like talking about writing more than doing it, but usually the members have written one poem or story or essay about something they deeply feel. Each wants to share that work, that feeling, and in return for some attention will often attend to the work and feeling of others. A writers' group can thus be an undemanding friendly society, but since clever writers seek ways to improve their work, and nearly all can see flaws in the work of the rest, most groups contain intelligent life. In Britain the most famous groups started casually in public drinking houses; the Mermaid Tavern on the first Friday of every month, and more often, though less regularly, in the Mitre coffee house, Fleet Street. In Italy the groups (called academies) were founded by noblemen, and had written constitutions. Every fine city had one presided over by eminences of church and state. They improved the manners and conversation of people who wanted polite societies, they lasted for centuries and gave dinners to heretical tourists like Milton, but they produced less interesting work than

Here follows 2 essays on one subject: being a staff member in The University of Glasgow. The 1st was written in 1974 when I became Writer in Residence, for though I had enjoyed months of being the artist-recorder of Glasgow for its own museum of local history, the wage (paid by Harold Wilson's Jobs Creation Scheme) was not enough to pay my sons boarding school fees. This new job did. I much enjoyed having a steady wage in return for the easy teaching of willing pupils for only 2 1/2 days a week, letting me work at what I wished for the rest. The second essay was written 6 months after. Some of my later experiences of Glasgow's great University are described in the introduction to **The Knuckle End** starting page 364.

the fleeting English groups, and some French ones which met later in Parisian cafés.

In that high noon of the British welfare state, the nineteen-sixties, local governments and educational bodies created writers groups by advertising courses of meetings open to all. They also provided a room for them, and paid an usher to open the room, collect fees, arrange readings of members' work, and conduct discussions. Such groups still exist, with or without an usher, for the usher's qualification is seldom more than a degree in English or some work in print, so an efficient member can sometimes do that job as well as anybody employed by a local government. The best organizers get copies of work distributed to members a week before the meeting where it is read and discussed. They do this for four reasons.

**1** – It lets work be read more than once, and on a second reading some work seems finer, some poorer.

**2** – It lets each member form an opinion, and find reasons and words for it, apart from members whose opinions might distort or silence theirs.

**3** – It warns away members whose response to a work, even on a second reading, is mere revulsion.

**4** – It is a small form of publication, and so pleases the writer.

Those who conduct a critical discussion can keep it helpful, and prevent damage to the writer's self-esteem, by leading the discussion of the work as fulfilment of the writer's idea. A poem written to convey horror of artificial abortion is not criticized by arguing that most abortions are painless and prevent worse evils. The group should discuss which words and sentences serve the writer's intention, which contradict it or are superfluous. If it presents logical argument the group should discuss its terms, and discover where they hold together or fall apart. If it presents a description, the group should discuss where and how it convinces, and if not, why not. The discussion should sound like carpenters discussing a table one of them has made: carpenters who feel table-making is important and enjoyable, and that most tables can be made better. If the table is not intended for children, and someone shows the surface is too low for people of normal height, a discussion on how to lengthen the legs need not sound like the reaction of jealous or stupid colleagues, even if the maker wants users to sit cross-legged on floor cushions. The trouble is that writers seldom see their earliest poems and stories as things made out of cheap, easily replaced words, but as small bodies they have given birth to and animated with their blood. The more easily they wrote a thing the more they feel nature or a divine spirit inspired it, and think alteration can only damage. But written work is not natural growth. If we take words from a poem and dislike the result we can restore words and poem exactly to their original state, which cannot be done when petals are taken from a flower or toes from a foot.

The best writing class I ever attended was run by Philip Hobsbaum on lines I have just described. He began it a year after arriving in Glasgow to work at its oldest university. He did not advertise, but invited local writers who interested him to it, starting with a small core of students, mostly mature ones. He used

university facilities to copy and post out the members'
work, but got no pay for what he did, and few thanks, for the Scots are not good at showing gratitude and Philip never invited it. The meetings were in his home. This was fifteen years ago, and there I met many good local writers I had never met before, some of them now my closest friends, and several who (though unpublished then) are not only published now but are well known. One reason why Philip got few thanks was, that though he connected us, we were more consciously influenced by each other than by him, who chiefly functioned as a good chairman: though he sometimes presented his own poetry, and accepted strictures on it as thoughtfully as we came to accept strictures on our writing. We knew we could have met and shared work at the constructive level without him, so forgot that we never would have done. Much later I read an article by Seamus Heaney which dated Ulster as a district of self-aware, self-confident literary production from the arrival of Philip Hobsbaum in Belfast and the writers' group he created there.

Most groups exist without a unique person to form them. The members continue learning in these what schools and colleges start to teach and sometimes prevent: how to recognise our thoughts and feelings, and express them, and share them. The value of a writers' group is in more than the few members who get published and famous. Even
Italian academies
knew this.

## POSTSCRIPT: FEBRUARY 1974
### A Writer In Residence Reports

I AM GLAD of this chance to report upon my first six months at Glasgow University. If I do it cunningly I may get new customers. But I will start with a warning and an excuse. The job of creative writer-in-residence is temporary for a good reason. Three of us in Scotland are paid to help students make poems, plays, stories – kinds of fiction their lecturers are paid to explain. Being professional writers we must prefer the literary virtues we want in our own work, so without intending, must be unfair to folk prefering other virtues. I try to make my writing clear and definite, with a smooth and ordinary grammar. Yes, part of the meaning of words is their sound, so I enjoy the moan of doves in immemorial elms, good strong, thick, stupefying incense smoke and jellies soother than the creamy curd. But I agree first with the duchess in *Alice in Wonderland*: 'Take care of the sense and the sounds will take care of themselves'. I have a cloth ear for the mainly sonorous, so can miss nuances which depend on it. Some student writers will inevitably find my advice discouraging because their talents are struggling in a different direction.

But a university course lasts four years, no resident writer lasts longer than two, so a student has the chance of more than one professional opinion. And the conditions of my job stop me doing much damage. I have no register and make no official reports. Those who dislike my advice stop seeing me. But since last October I have had over forty student writers, two thirds calling three or four times and a few coming steadily, so I am not too forbidding. I have had writers from the staff as well as students, from the sciences as well as the arts. Some of the best writing is from the science side. On weekdays I am available all Tuesdays, Wednesdays, and the morning of Thursdays. My rooms are on the fourth floor of Humanities, in the south-west corner of the west quadrangle. The outer room has two doors on different corridors, 65 and 67 which are not locked. The inner room is my office. Outside its door hangs a timetable and pencil on a string. Visitors make an appointment by writing their names opposite a blank hour convenient for them. I like to read new work two or three days before discussing it, so slide work under the office door if I'm not in when you call.

On Wednesday evening I hold a writing seminar where the work of one student is discussed, copies of the work being distributed to the other members the week before, so that they can judge it privately. At the seminar it is read aloud by the author, then discussed with a view to improving what some may dislike. Most writers of stories or poems start without encouragement of parents and friends, so feel that having made one is a solitary achievement they must protect. But though writing must be done in a shell of privacy its purpose is to break that shell. The assumption behind our most intimate works is that our strongest feelings and thoughts may be told in public language. The Wednesday seminars, like the tutorials, are for those who (of course) want approval for their work, but also useful criticism.

I am sorry that nobody, so far, has asked my advice on the prose of their theses or scientific reports.

I believe most writing nowadays is more obscure than it should be, and this is as true in the sciences as in poetry, especially in the indefinite sciences of philosophy, psychology and sociology, which were regarded as branches of literature until the middle of the last century. This obscurity, I think, is not caused by the unavoidable increase of technical terms, but by a general habit of using many-syllabled phrases instead of ordinary words. This inflation (too many syllables chasing too little meaning) comes from the old error that because educated people know more long words than others they should use them as often as possible. The odd result is that in universities most people speak clearer prose than they write.

There are several things I have failed to do. When I started in October I intended (having written more plays than anything else) to see a lot of the Student Theatre Group. Tuition and my own private work prevented this, in spite of Robert Paterson producing an effective lunch-hour performance of my play *The Loss of the Golden Silence*. Nor have I contacted the university TV service about the possibility of recording presentations of student work. Nor have I continued the lunch-time readings by well-known authors started by my predecessor, Alan Spence. I will start repairing the last omission in May, when the Irish poet Seamus Heaney will come and read to us.

Look out for posters.

# Of Joan Ure: Playwright*

W HEN JOAN URE was born in 1919 she was christened Elizabeth Carswell. Her father was an engineer with Vickers-Armstrong. Both parents came from three generations of small Clydeside shipbuilders and engineers, folk who had managed by hard work, thrift and steady, conventional behaviour to get free of the unemployment and poverty which threatened all parts, but especially the less skilled or more reckless part, of the Scottish work-force. An anecdote. Betty Carswell's grandfather, a foreman, often spent an evening seated alone in the best parlour of his house, consuming a bottle of whisky in perfectly orderly silence. Had he drunk in a pub with fellow-workers he would have lessened his authority over them and perhaps lost the confidence of his employer. Had he drunk with his wife and family he would have lessened his authority over them and lost their respect. Betty was born into a culture which gave her good food, good clothing and a well-furnished home in return for self-suppression. In the nineteen-twenties bottle-parties and sexual daring were fashionable among wealthy people, but the lower-middle classes or respectable working classes (call them what you like) maintained a code of careful manners which recalled the world of Jane Austen.

✱ *This biographical sketch was one of the three I had in the* **Lean Tales** *anthology published by Jonathan Cape in 1985. It was based on a Scottish BBC radio documentary about her life commissioned from me and broadcast in 1978 or 79.*

Betty then had a younger sister, Joan, and younger brother, John. They went to family gatherings where their mother presented them to her mother for a clothes-inspection, and reported their behaviour in the previous week, and got approval and reinforcement for the rewards and punishments she had meted out. After a meal the men conversed on one side of the room, the women on the other, and the children by turns gave little recitations in the middle.

When Betty was twelve her mother entered hospital with tuberculosis, and Betty became her father's house-wife and working mother to her sister and brother. Mrs Carswell came home after two years and thereafter managed the house from her bedroom. It was important for Betty to keep looking happy. Depression was construed as ingratitude to the mother who bore her, the father who nourished. How did she avoid becoming a neurotic drudge or empty-headed puppet? By imagination. By developing an inner world where, for a change, she had authority. It was not an exclusive world. When seven she had written a thirteen-page story and given it to her mother, thinking it beautiful. Mrs Carswell punished her for a misdeed by burning it, and was surprised by how much she cried. Before the days of television there were no university grants, there was no national health service and an invalid in the family was a financial burden. Betty wanted to be a teacher, she would have been a splendid teacher, but she left school at fifteen then became a typist in Glasgow Corporation housing department. Two years later she met and married a businessman and became Mrs Betty Clark. The Second

World War began. Mr Clark was posted overseas and for five years she lived alone in Glasgow bringing up her young daughter.

By this time she must have appeared as she did in the last twenty years of her life when I came to know her; small, slender, fair-haired, with beautifully clear-cut features and always very young-looking, though a little too bony – her guilt about being supported by someone else, implanted in childhood, lasted through marriage and led her to eat too little. She made her own clothes and dressed very well. She was eye-catching in a way that was too individual to be merely fashionable, too smart to be eccentric. Her manner upset some people at first, she was so ladylike, and polite, and anxious to be helpful and understanding in every possible way. And within this gushing manner was a gleam of desperate amusement amounting to laughter, because her intelligence was saying, "Yes, we must help and understand each other in every possible way all the time, which can't be done. Yet it must be done." In later years this manner greatly disturbed directors of her plays. She was not afraid of authority but she knew people in authority have delicate egos, and it distressed her to hurt them by explaining how her work should be performed, and why bits should not be cut out and others grafted in. It also distressed them to find that, in spite of her eagerly submissive manner, she could not be brushed aside.

But at the end of the war Betty had not committed herself to being anyone but Mrs Clark. Her life so far, though sad, and providing all the insights a writer needs, had not been unusual for a woman. Then two extra hard things happened. Her young sister Joan returned from the Women's Auxiliary Air Force to live with her parents, and entered a religious melancholy, though the family was not particularly religious. Joan was found dead under a bridge with her face in a stream, perhaps by misadventure, perhaps not. Then Betty entered hospital with tuberculosis. Lung-scars showed she contracted it while nursing her mother.

Much later she wrote a story about a woman with a talent. Thinking it too small to matter, she suppresses it, and faints. She is pleased, for that suggests the talent is genuine. To be absolutely certain she hides it again. "Very soon she coughed up the first gobbets of blood. And there she saw, brilliant at last, the brightness of the tiny talent she had." The woman dies rejoicing. She knows her talent is genuine, for it was death to hide it.

Betty used the materials of her life as much as any writer, but was seldom autobiographical. The people she presents are alternative forms of herself, the ends of roads she had walked short distance along. She did not to hide her talent. She signed herself out of hospital against medical advice and lived another thirty years. To become a writer she took a pen-name: Joan Ure. It is a Scottish tradition. The authors of *Waverley*, *The House with the Green Shutters*, *A Drunk Man Looks at the Thistle* and *Sunset Song* did it, mainly to avoid embarrassing their relations. The lowland Scots suspect the creative imagination. John Knox, the man we love to hate, is usually blamed but poverty is the cause. English inheriting classes know that imagination can be a way of managing things.

Artistic wives and offspring can get jobs connected with publishing, television or education. Where there is little wealth even those who have some fear the future and are sure that only carefulness will help them survive it. They know imagination can excite passions, especially sexual ones, and lead to discontent and extravagant action. For those with low salaries and positions, unimaginative carefulness often is a way to avoid pain in the short run. In the long run it makes us the easy tools of people with high salaries and positions, and when they have no use for us they drop us in the shit. As in 1985 Britain. So an active imagination, though painful, is our only hope, and by imagination I do not mean fantasy. In Joan Ure's play *Something In It For Ophelia*, a young, energetic, slightly stupid girl has been to a performance of *Hamlet* and recognized in Ophelia (exploited and abused by a father and boyfriend who have no real interest in her) a form of herself. Appalled, she feels such things should not be shown on stage, and people certainly should not be applauded. She has read in the *Scotsman* that the Scottish suicide rate is as high as the Swedish, but most of our suicides are women.

So Joan Ure became an imaginative intelligence pointing us to passionate self-knowledge, the only knowledge able to make us so self-governing and tough that we cannot be managed and dropped by others. I am not particularly speaking of women when I say 'us' and 'we'. Of course she wanted women's liberation, but liked men too much to wish the sexes divorced. I doubt if matriarchy attracted her. As a child she had lived under one. Her plays handle the common-place facts: that hard housework, factory-work, office-work are unavoidable but we wither without freedom; that all could have more freedom with a fair sharing of power, but are everywhere in chains because we live unfairly, our love twisted by exploitation and warfare, men oppressing women and other men with their greater economic strength, women exploiting men and other women with their greater emotional insight. Yet Joan's plays are not dour, but witty, moving, and usually short. I'll speak of those I like most.

## I SEE MYSELF AS THIS YOUNG GIRL
### 40 minutes, 3 actors

A middle-aged woman, left to mind a baby by her brisk student daughter, encounters a lonely sales-clerk who has "adventured out in his shorts". Each reveals the fantasies that keep them going. She imagines herself a young girl – not the actual daughter who exploits her, but someone more sentimental with nobody to help her. This is the one way she can allow herself the luxury of self-pity. The play is about the need to soar above our responsibilities without abandoning them. The tone of it is funny and melancholy.

## SOMETHING IN IT FOR OPHELIA
### 40 minutes, 2 actors

A Scottish Hamlet and Ophelia meet on Waverley Station platform while waiting for a train and reveal themselves as incapable of love. Ophelia is the tougher of the two but less admirable. She leaves the more sensitive Hamlet prostrate. Funny and harsh.

## THE HARD CASE
### 40 minutes, 1 actor

A football fan, a small Glasgow businessman, is so
appalled by the death of the children crushed at the end of that disastrous Rangers-Celtic game of 1970 that he deliberately smashes a shop window to get the chance of making a public statement about it. In the course of that statement he becomes his own judge, and binds himself over to keep the peace. At the time of writing it looked as if a new period of decency for Scottish football was beginning because the managers of both Rangers and Celtic had promised to abandon the policies which increased their gate money along with insensitive violence leading to stampede and killing. This is now forgotten. Rangers still refuse to employ Catholic players. Nowadays only Joan's play deals with Scottish football, and injustice, and that disaster, so openly yet delicately. No other writers have dared tackle it. Too big for them.

### THE LECTURER AND THE LADY
#### 40 minutes, 2 actors

In this play Joan Ure is confronted by Betty Clark. An ageing, conventional housewife approaches a young adventurous thinker, hoping she will receive the inspiration to leave the very dull husband she loves. She does not get it. The thinker who has abandoned her child and husband – "Two terrible things! And not been struck down dead!" – will not advise everyone to do as she did. When they part the brave thinker is sadder for having met the lady, the lady is a little braver for having met the lecturer.

### CONDEMNED FOR ECSTASY
#### 75 minutes, 7 or 8 actors

This is a play about oppression and liberation, and is

based on two peculiar historical events. In the late 17th century a pious, dutiful young woman, who kept house for her widowed father and bachelor brothers, found such consolation in reading about the sufferings of Jesus that she entered ecstatic states and coughed blood. She was tried for this by the local kirk session and told that her ecstasy was the work of the devil, and she should not submit to it. A hundred years later, at the time of the French Revolution, a remarkable Ayrshire woman got such ascendancy over her minister that he helped her found a matriarchal commune with herself as the Holy Mother. The stories of these women are introduced by a late 19th century "New Woman" of the Beatrice Webb type, who realizes that the outlandish failure and success of the earlier women is a form of her own.

The foregoing is a partial list and only includes her plays which I have seen well acted. *Take Your Old Rib Back Then* is a play I cannot read with pleasure – the words on the page recall the gabbling of the actress I heard say them. The long speeches embarrassed so she spoke too fast. Joan's plays had very few decent productions because: she worked in Scotland where hardly any theatres used local writing. All but a few of her plays are short, a two hour performance would require more than one and the public aren't thought to like that. Her plays were clever, and managements are uneasy with unfamiliar work which is cleverer than them – they think it may be stupid. Joan's characters hardly ever shout and always converse in clear, formal language. Restoration dramatists, great Irishmen and Noél Coward can do that, but surely not the Scots! We are a tough, violent people. O.K.?

To get her work seen Joan directed small productions performed by friends wherever she could, and sometimes acted in them. She worked hard, usually unpaid with amateurs and companies trying to change things, like the abortive Scottish Stage Company and the Scottish Society of Play Wrights, which survives. She is partly responsible for a few things being slightly better for playwrights in Scotland today, but the wear on her highly-strung nature was punishing. Most writers grow a surface to protect their nerves, rhinoceros hide or porcupine bristles or slippery suavity or facetious jollity. Joan Ure never did. What you saw of her at any time was all there was, so even the company of close friends exhausted her after an hour or two. Apart from a year when she got a Scottish Arts Council grant she had always too little money. Her intense drive and intense fragility led some to call her "the iron butterfly". Intellectually she was no butterfly, physically she was not iron. She did not rust and corrode like many but drove to breaking point. Her last months were painful and lonely. She refused to depend on friends, loathed hospitals, but had to enter them before her lungs completely failed.

The value of a life is not in its end but in what it has given the world before. I admire Joan Ure's art so find much in her life to mourn, nothing to wish undone. She left several poems, an uncounted number of short stories and essays, over twenty-four plays and play fragments. Manuscripts and typescripts of these are now owned by Glasgow University Library. The Scottish Society of Playwrights has acting copies of most completed plays, and has published *Five Short Plays* by Joan Ure, with an introduction by Christopher Small. Joan's bad luck still pursues her art. The book, though readable, is unevenly inked, has irritating typographical errors, and contains *The Hard Case* in a mutilated radio version. But in the University and S.S.P. libraries her work is where directors, actors and scholars who enjoy good writing can always obtain copies with out much fuss or great expense. Her daughter, a doctor in Canada, and her brother John Carswell, in Newton Mearns, have her personal letters, diaries and tape-recordings. I hope one day to see a complete volume of all her plays, and of her poems and prose pieces.

At her funeral in 1978 the writers and theatre folk who knew Joan Ure met Betty Clark's family for the first time, and made a surprising discovery. We had thought Joan a woman in her late forties who looked much younger, when she was on the verge of sixty. In this matter our friend, whose life and art expressed more truth than most, had let us deceive ourselves. I
don't know why this cheered
me, a little.

# Epilogue to Lanark

H E ENTERED A ROOM with no architectural similarity to the building he had left. The door on this side had deeply moulded panels and a knob, the ceiling was bordered by an elaborate cornis of acanthus sprays. There was a tall bay window with the upper foliage of a chestnut tree outside and an old stone tenement beyond. The rest of the room was hidden by easels holding large paintings of the room. The pictures seemed brighter and cleaner than the reality and the tall beautiful girl with long blonde hair reclined in them, sometimes nude and sometimes clothed. The girl herself, more worried and untidy than in her portraits, stood near the window wearing a paint-stained butchers apron. With a very small brush she was adding leaves to a view of the tree outside the window, but she paused, pointed round the edge of the picture and told Lanark, "He's there."

A voice said, "Yes, come round, come round."

Lanark went behind the picture and found a stout man leaning against a pile of pillows on a low bed. His face, framed by wings

*This contains my ideas for writing this, my 1st novel: ideas that well-known writers usually give in their prologues or epilogues. Not being known outside the small world of Scots writing, I put this between chapters 40 and 41, and kept some of the narrative going through it. For 3 years publication was delayed by lucky accidents which gave me time to illustrate the book and add to the Index of Plagiarisms, in a column like this one, in the outer margin of the main text. In alphabetic order it gave names of all the writers I enjoyed & words I had stolen from them, with the pages on which they appeared. This was both a parody of academic criticism & a fair example of that. Reviewers then, & lecturers since liked it, but there is no room to print it here.*

and horns of uncombed hair looked statuesque and noble apart from an apprehensive, rather cowardly expression. He wore a woollen jersey over a pyjama jacket, neither of them clean. The coverlet over his knees was littered with books and papers, and there was a pen in his hand. Glancing at Lanark in a sly, sideways fashion he indicated a chair with the pen and said, "Please sit down."

"Are you the king of this place?"

"The King of Proven, yes. And Unthank too. And that suite of rooms you call the institute and the council."

"Then perhaps you can help me. I am here—"

"Yes, I know roughly what you want and I would like to help. I would even offer you a drink, but there's too much intoxication in this book."

"Book?"

"This world, I meant to say. You see I'm the king, not the government. I have laid out landscapes, and stocked them with people, and I still work an odd miracle, but governing is left to folk like Monboddo and Slodden."

"Why?"

The king closed his eyes, smiled and said, "I brought you here to ask that question."

"Will you answer it?"

"Not yet."

Lanark felt very angry. He stood up and said, "Then talking to you is a waste of time."

"Waste of time!" said the king, opening his eyes. "You clearly don't realise who I am. I have called myself a king – that's a purely symbolic name. I'm far more important. Read this and you'll understand. The critics will accuse me of self-indulgence but I don't care."[1]

With a reckless gesture he handed Lanark a paper from the bed. It was covered with childish handwriting and many words were scored out or inserted with little arrows. Much of it seemed to be dialogue but Lanark's eye was caught by a sentence in italics which said: *Much of it seemed to be dialogue but Lanark's eye was caught by a sentence in italics which said:*

Lanark gave the paper back asking, "What's that supposed to prove?"

"I am your author."

Lanark stared at him. The author said, "Please don't feel embarrased. This isn't an unprecedented situation. Vonnegut has it in *Breakfast of Champions,* Jehovah in the books of *Job and Jonah.*"

"Are you pretending to be God?"

"Not nowadays. I used to be part of him, though. Yes, I am part of a part which was once the whole. But I went bad and was excreted. If I can get well I may be allowed home before I die, so I continually plunge my beak into my rotten liver and swallow and excrete it. But it grows again. Creation festers in me. I am excreting you and your world at the present moment. This arse-wipe" – he stirred the papers on the bed – "is part of the process."

"I am not religious," said Lanark, "but I don't like you mixing religion with excrement. Last night I saw part of the person you are referring to and it was not at all nasty."

"You saw part of God?" cried the author. "How did that happen?"

1. *To have an objection anticipated is no reason for failing to raise.*

Lanark explained. The author was greatly excited. He said, "Say those words again."

"*Is. . . is. . . is. . .* then a pause, then *Is. . . if. . . is. . .* "

"If?" shouted the author sitting upright. "He actually said if? He wasn't simply snarling Is, is, is, is, is all the time?"

Lanark said, "I don't like you saying 'he' like that. What I saw may not have been masculine. It may not have been human. But it certainly wasn't snarling. What's wrong with you?"

The author had covered his mouth with his hands as if to stifle laughter, but his eyes were wet. He gulped and said, "One *if* to five *is*es! That's an incredible amount of freedom. But can I believe you? I've created you honest but can I trust your senses? At a great altitude *is* and *if* must sound very much alike."

"You seem to take words very seriously," said Lanark with a touch of contempt.

"Yes. You don't like me, but that can't be helped. I'm primarily a literary man," said the author with a faintly nasal accent and started chuckling to himself.

The tall blonde girl came round the edge of the painting wiping her brush on her apron. She said defiantly, "I've finished the tree. Can I leave now?"

The author leaned back on his pillows and said sweetly, "Of course, Marion. Leave when you like."

"I need money. I am hungry."

"Why don't you go to the kitchen? I believe there's some cold chicken in the fridge, and I'm sure Pat won't mind you making yourself a snack."

"I don't want a snack, I want a meal with a friend in a restaurant. And I want to go to a film afterward, or to a pub, or to a hairdresser if I feel like it. I'm sorry, but I want money."

"Of course you do, and you've earned it. How much do I owe?"

"Five hours today at fifty pence an hour is two pounds fifty. With yesterday and the day before and the day before is ten pounds, isn't it?"

"I've a poor head for arithmatic but you're probably right," said the author, taking coins from under a pillow and giving them to her. "This is all I have just now, nearly two pounds. Come back tomorrow and I'll see if I can manage a little extra."

The girl scowled at the coins in her hand, then at the author. He was puffing medicinal spray into his mouth from a tiny hand pump. She went abruptly behind the painting again and they heard the door slam.

"A strange girl," murmured the author, sighing. "I do my best to help her but it isn't easy."

Lanark had been sitting with his head propped on his hands. He said, "You say you are creating me."

"I am."

"Then how can I have experiences you don't know about? You were surprised when I told you what I saw from the aircraft."

"The answer to that is unusually interesting; please attend closely. When *Lanark* is finished (I am calling the work after you) it will be roughly two hundred thousand words and forty chapters long, and divided into books three, one, two and four."

"Why not one, two, three and four?"

"I want *Lanark* to be read in one order but eventually thought of in another. It is an old device. Homer, Virgil,

Milton and Scott-Fitzgerald[2] used it. There will be a prologue before book one, an interlude in the centre and this epilogue two or three chapters before the end."

"I thought epilogues came after the end."

"Usually, but mine is too important to go there. Though not essential to the plot it provides comic distraction at a moment when the narrative sorely needs it. And it lets me utter some fine sentiments which I could not trust to a mere character. And it contains critical notes that will save researchers years of toil. In fact my epilogue is so essential that I am working on it with nearly a quarter of the book still unwritten. I am working on it here, now, in this conversation. But you have reached here through chapters I haven't clearly imagined yet, so you know details of the story which I don't. Of course I know the broad general outline. That was planned years ago and musn't be changed. You have come from my city of destruction which is rather like Glasgow, to plead before some sort of world-wide parliament in an ideal city based on Edinburgh, or London, or even Paris if I can wangle a grant from the Scottish Arts Council to go there. Tell me, when you were landing this morning, did you see the Eiffel Tower?[3]

Or Big Ben? Or a rock with a castle on it?"

"No. Proven is very like –"

"Stop! Don't tell me. My fictions often anticipate the

2. *Each of the four authors mentioned above began a large work in* **medias res**, *but none of them numbered their divisions out of logical sequence.*
3. *In 1973, as a result of sponsorship by the poet Edwin Morgan, the author received a grant of £300 from the Scottish Arts Council to help him write his book, but it was never assumed that he would use the money to seek out exotic local colour.*

experiences they're based upon, but no author should rely on that sort of thing."

Lanark was so agitated that he stood and walked to the window to sort out his thoughts. The author struck him as a slippery person, but too vain and garrilous to be impressive. He went back to the bed and said, "How will my story end?"

"Catastrophically. The Thaw narrative shows a man dying because he is bad at loving. It is enclosed by your narrative which shows civilization collapsing for the same reason."

"Listen," said Lanark. "I never tried to be a delegate. I never wanted anything but some sunlight, some love, some very ordinary happiness. And every moment I have been thwarted by organisations pushing me in a different direction, and now I'm nearly an old man and my reasons for living have shrunk to standing up in public and saying a good word for the only people I know. And you tell me that word will be useless! That you have *planned* it to be useless."

"Yes," said the author, nodding eagerly. "Yes. That's right."

Lanark gaped down at the foolishly nodding face and suddenly felt it belonged to a horrible ventriloquist's doll. He raised a clenched fist but could not bring himself to strike. He swung round and punched a painting to an easel and both clattered to the floor. He pushed down the other painting beside the door, went to a tall bookcase and heaved it over. Books cascaded from the upper shelves and it hit the floor with a crash that shook the room. There were long, low shelves round the walls holding books, folders, bottles and tubes of paint. With sweeps of his arm he shoved these to the floor, then turned, breathing deeply, and stared at the bed. The author sat there looking distressed, but the paintings and easels were back in their own places, and glancing around Lanark saw the bookcases had returned quietly to their corner and books, folders, bottles and paint were on shelves again.

"A conjuror!" said Lanark, with loathing. "A damned conjuror!"

"Yes," said the conjuror humbly, "I'm sorry. Please sit down and let me explain why the story has to go like this. You can eat while I talk (I'm sure you're hungry) and afterwards you can tell me how you think I can be better. Please sit down."

The bedside chair was small but comfortably upholstered. A table had appeared beside it with covered dishes on a tray. Lanark felt more exhausted than hungry but after sitting for a while he removed a cover out of curiosity. There was a bowl beneath of dark red oxtail soup, so taking a spoon he began to eat.

"I will start," said the conjuror, "by explaining the physics of the world you live in. Everything you have experienced and are experiencing, from your first glimpse of the elite cafe in chapter one to the metal of the spoon in your fingers now and the taste of soup in your mouth is made of one thing."

"Atoms–" said Lanark.

"No. Print. Some worlds are made of atoms[4] but yours are made of tiny marks marching in neat lines, like

4. **Atoms** and **Print** are a false antithesis. Printed paper has an atomic structure like anything else. **Words** would have been better than **Print**, since less definably concrete.

armies of insects across pages and pages and pages of white paper. I say these lines are marching, but that is a metaphor. They are perfectly static. They are lifeless. How can they reproduce the movement and noises of the Battle of Borodino, the white whale ramming the ship, the fallen angels on the flaming lake?"

"By being read," said Lanark, impatiently.

"Exactly. Your survival as a character and mine as an author depend on us seducing a living soul into our printed words world and trapping it here long enough for us to steal the imaginative energy which gives us life. To cast a spell over this stranger I am doing abominable things. I am prostituting my most sacred memories into the commonest possible words and sentences. When I need more striking sentences or ideas, I steal them from other writers, usually twisting them to blend with my own. Worst of all I am using the great world given to everyone at birth – the world of atoms – as a rag-bag of shapes and colours to make this second-hand entertainment more amusing."

"You seem to be complaining," said Lanark. "I don't know why. Nobody is forcing you to work with print and all work involves some degradation. I want to know why your readers in their world should be entertained by me failing to do any good in mine."

"Because failures are popular. Frankly, Lanark, you are too stolid and commonplace to be entertaining as a successful man. But don't be offended; most heroes end up like you. Consider the Greek book about Troy. To repair a marriage broken by adultery, a civilization spends ten years to smashing another one. The heroes on both sides know the quarrel is futile but they continue it because they think willingness to die fighting is proof of human greatness. There is no suggestion that the war does anything but damage the people who survive it.

Then there is the Roman book about Aeneas. He leads a group of refugees in search of a peaceful home and spreads agony and warfare along the north and south coasts of the Mediterranean. He also visits Hell and gets out of it. The writer of this story is tender towards peaceful homes, he wants Roman success in warfare and government to make the world a peaceful home for everyone, but his last words describe Aeneas, in the heat of battle, revenging himself by killing a helpless enemy.

There is the Jewish book about Moses. It is very like the Roman one about Aeneas, so I'll go on to the Jewish book about Jesus. He is a poor man without home or wife. He says he is God's son and calls all men his brothers. He teaches that love is the one great good, and is spoiled by fighting for things. He is crucified, goes to Hell, then to Heaven which (like Aeneas's peaceful world) is outside the scope of his book. But if, as a hymn says, 'He died to make us good,' he too was a failure. The nations who worshipped him in their churches became the greediest and most successful conquerors the world has known.

Only the Italian book shows a living man in heaven. He gets there by following Aeneas and Jesus through Hell after the first woman he loved married another man and died. His is the only book to show a convincing ascent to the heights of Heaven, from which he sees the whole universe is sublime, but on that journey he learns that all his political hopes for Italian peace and plenty have failed.

There is the French book about the giant babies. Pleasing themselves is their only law, so they drink and excrete in a jolly male family which laughs at everything adults call civilization. Women exist for them, but only as rubbers and ticklers.

There is the Spanish book about the Knight of the Dolorous Countenance. A poor old bachelor is driven mad by reading the sort of books *you* want to be in, with heroes who triumph here and now. He leaves home and fights peasants and innkeepers for the beauty which is *never here and now*, and is mocked and wounded. On his deathbed he grows sane and warns his friends against intoxicating literature.

There is the English book about Adam and Eve. This describes a heroic empire-building Satan, an amoral and ironical but boundlessly creative God, a war in Heaven (but no killing) and all this centres on a married couple and the state of their house and garden. They disobey the great Landlord who evicts them, but promises them accomodation in his own house if they live and die penitently. Once again success is left outside the scope of the book. We are last shown them setting out into our world to raise children they know will murder each other.

There is the German book about a respectable old bachelor doctor who grows young by selling his soul to Satan, who helps him grab everything he wants and abandon all he tires of, including the girl who loves him and Helen of Troy. He becomes Europe's chief banker and, financed by piracy, steals land from peasants to make his own empire. When a hundred years old and blind, he dies believing he has benefited the whole human race and is received into a Heaven like the Italian one because *man must strive and striving he must err*, and because, *he who continually strives can be saved*. Yah! The only striver in this book is the poor Devil who does all the work and is tricked out of his wages by the angelic choir showing him their bums.[5] The writer of this book was depraved by too much luck. He shows the sort of successful man who does indeed dominate the modern world, but only at the start and near the end shows the damage they keep doing. Surely *you* don't want that kind of success?

The honest American book about the whale comes as a relief. A captain wants to kill it because the last time he tried to do that it bit off his leg. He embarks with a cosmopolitan crew who have escaped from home life because they prefer this way of earning money. Brave, skillful and obedient they chase the whale round the world in pursuit of this living oil resource and all drown in the act of destroying it, except for the storyteller. He describes the sea closing over them as if they had never existed. This book has no women or children except for a little black boy whom they accidentally drive mad.

Then there is the Russian book about war and peace. That has fighting in it, but fighting which fills us with astonishment that men can so recklessly, so resolutely

5. **"Von hinten anzusehen – Die Racker sind doch gar zu appetitlich"** *is little more than a line. Louis MacNeice omits it from his Faust translation because it reduces the Devil's dignity. The author's amazing virulence against Goethe is perhaps a smokescreen to distract attention from what he owes him.*

pester themselves to death. The writer, you see, has
fought in real battles and believed some things Jesus taught. This book also contains" – conjuror's face took on an amazed expression – "several believable happy marriages with children who are well cared for. But I have said enough to show that, while men and women would die out if they didn't usually love each other and keep their homes, most of the great stories[6] show them failing spectacularly to do either."

"Which proves," said Lanark, who was eating a salad, "that the world's great stories are mostly a pack of lies." The conjuror sighed and rubbed the side of his face. He said, "Shall I tell you the ending you want? Imagine that when you leave this room and return to the grand salon, you find that the sun has set and outside the great windows a firework display is in progress above the Tuileries garden."

"It's a sports stadium," said Lanark.

"Don't interrupt. A party is in progress, and a lot of informal lobbying is going on among the delegates."

"What is lobbying?"

"Please don't interrupt. You move about discussing the woes of Unthank with whoever will listen. Your untutored eloquence has an effect beyond your expectations, first

6. *The index proves that* **Lanark** *is erected upon an infantile foundation of Victorian nursery tales, though the final shape derives from English language fiction printed between the 40s and the 60s of the last century. The hero's biography after the death occurs in Wyndham Lewis' trilogy* **The Human Age***, Flann O'Brien's* **The Third Policeman** *and Golding's* **Pincher Martin***. Modern afterworlds are always infernos, never paradisos, presumably because the modern secular imagination is more capable of debasement than exaltation. In almost every chapter of the book there is a dialogue between the hero (Thaw or Lanark) and a social superior (parent, more experienced friend or prospective employer) about morality, society or art. This is mainly a device to let a self-educated Scot (to whom "the dominie" is the highest form of social life) tell the world what he thinks of it: but the glum flavour of these episodes recalls three books by disappointed socialists which appeared after the second world war and*

on women, then on men. Many delegates see that their own lands are threatened by the multinational companies and realize that if something isn't quickly done the council won't be able to help them either. So tomorrow when you stand up in the great assembly hall to speak for your land or city (I haven't worked out which yet), you are speaking for a majority of lands and cities everywhere. The great corporations, you say, are wasting the earth. They have turned the wealth of nations into weapons and poison, while ignoring mankind's most essential needs. The time has come etcetera etcetera. You sit down amid a silence more significant than the wildest applause and the lord president director himself arises to answer you. He expresses the most full-hearted agreement. He explains that the heads of the council have already prepared plans to curb and harness the power of the creature but dared not announce them until they were sure they had the support of a majority. He announces them now. All work which merely transfers wealth will be abolished, all work which damages or the kills people will be stopped. All profits will belong to the state, no state will be bigger than a Swiss canton, no politician will draw a larger wage than an agricultural labourer. In

6. *(cont.) centred upon what I will call dialogue under threat:* **Darkness at Noon** *by Arthur Koestler,* **1984** *by George Orwell, and* **Barbary Shore** *by Norman Mailer. Having said this, one is compelled to ask why the "conjuror" introduces an apology for his work with a tedious and brief history of world literature, as though summarizing a great tradition which culminates in himself! Of the eleven great epics mentioned, only one has influenced* **Lanark**. *Monboddo's speech in the last part of* **Lanark** *is a dreary parody of the Archangel Michael's history lecture in the last book of* **Paradise Lost** *and fails for the same reason. A property is not always valuable because it is stolen from a rich man. And for this single device thieved (without acknowledgement) from Milton we find a confrontation of fictional character by fictional author from Flann O'Brien; a hero, ignorant of his past, in a subfuse modern Hell, also from Flann O'Brien and, from T. S. Elliot, Nabokov and Flann O'Brien, a parade of irrelevant erudition through grotesquely inflated footnotes.*

fact, all wages will be lowered or raised to the national average, and the later to the international average, thus letting people transfer to the jobs they do best without artificial feelings of prestige or humiliation. Stockbrokers, bankers, accountants, property developers, advertisers, company lawyers and detectives will become schoolteachers if they can find no other useful work, and no teacher will have more than six pupils per class. The navy and air forces will be set to providing children everywhere with free meals. The armies will dig irrigation ditches and plant trees. All human excrement will be returned to the land. I don't know how Monboddo would propose to start this new system, but I could drown the practical details in storms of cheering. At any rate, bliss it is in this dawn to be alive, and massive sums of wealth and technical aid are voted to restore Unthank to healthy working order. You board your aircraft to return home, for you now think of Unthank as home. The sun rises. It precedes you across the sky; you appear with it at noon above the city centre. You descend and are reunited with Rima, who has tired of Sludden. Happy ending. Well?"

Lanark laid down his knife and fork. He said in a low voice, "If you give me an ending like that I will think you a very great man."

"If I give you an ending like that I will be like ten thousand other cheap illusionists! I would be as bad as the late H. G. Wells! I would be worse than Goethĕ. Nobody who knows a thing about life or politics will believe me for a minute!"

Lanark said nothing. The conjuror scratched his hair

7. *This remark is too ludicrous to require comment here.*

furiously with both hands and said querulously, "I understand your resentment. When I was sixteen or seventeen *I* wanted an ending like that. You see, I found Tillyard's study of the epic in Dennistoun public library, and he said an epic was only written when a new society was giving men a greater chance of liberty. I decided that what the *Aeneid* had been to the Roman Empire my epic would be to the Scottish Cooperative Wholesale Republic, one of the many hundreds of small peaceful socialist republics which would emerge (I thought) when all the big empires and corporations crumbled. That was about 1950. Well, I soon abandoned the idea. A conjuror's best trick is to show his audience a moving model of the world as it is with themselves inside of it, and the world is not moving towards greater liberty, equality and fraternity. So I faced the fact that my world model would be a hopeless one. I also knew it would be an industrial-west-of-Scotland-petitbourgeois one, but I didn't think that a disadvantage. If the maker's mind is prepared, the immediate materials are always suitable.

During my first art school summer holiday I wrote chapter 12 and the mad-vision-and-murder part of chapter 29. My first hero was based on myself. I'd have preferred someone less specialized but mine were the only entrails I could lay hands upon. I worked poor Thaw to death, quite cold-bloodedly, because though based on me he was tougher and more honest, so I hated him. Also, his death gave me a chance to shift him into a wider social context. You are Thaw with the neurotic imagination trimmed off and built in to the furniture of the world you occupy. This makes you much more capable of action and slightly more capable of love.[8] The time is now" – the conjuror glanced at his wristwatch, yawned and lay back on the pillows – "the time is 1970 and although the work is far from finished I see it will be disappointing in several ways. It has too many conversations and clergymen, too much asthma, frustration, shadow; not enough countryside, kind women, honest toil. Of course not many writers describe honest toil, apart from Tolstoy and Lawrence on haymaking, Tressel on housebuilding and Archie Hind on clerking and slaughtering. I fear that the men of a healthier age will think my story a gafuffle of grotesquely frivolous parasites, like the creatures of Mrs. Radcliffe, Tolkien and Mervyn Peake. Perhaps my model world is too compressed and lacks the quiet moments of inconsiderable ease which are the sustaining part of the most troubled world. Perhaps I began the work when I was too young. In those days I thought light existed to show things, that space was simply a gap between me and the bodies I feared or desired; now it seems that bodies are the stations from which we travel into space and light itself. Perhaps an illusionist's main job is to exhaust his restless audience by a show of marvellously convincing squabbles until they see the simple things we really depend upon: the movement of shadow round a globe turning in space, the corruption of life on its way to death and the spurt of love by which it throws a new life clear. Perhaps the best thing I could do is write a story in which adjectives

8. But the fact remains that the plots of the Thaw and Lanark sections are independent of each other and cemented by typographical contrivances rather than formal necessity. A possible explanation is that the author thinks a heavy book will make a bigger splash than two light ones.

like *commonplace* and *ordinary* have the significance which *glorious* and *divine* carried in earlier comedies. What do you think?"

"I think you're trying to make the readers admire your fine way of talking."

"I'm sorry. But yes. Of course," said the conjuror huffily. "You should know by now that I have to butter[9] them up a bit. I'm like God the Father, you see, and you are my sacrificial Son, and a reader is a Holy Ghost who keeps everything joined together and moving along. It doesn't matter how much you detest this book I am writing, you can't escape it before I let you go. But if the readers detest it they can shut it and forget it; you'll simply vanish and I'll turn into an ordinary man. We mustn't let that happen. So I'm taking this opportunity to get all of us agreeing about the end so that we stay together right up to it."

"You know the end I want and you're not allowing it," said Lanark grimly. "Since you and the readers are the absolute power in this world you need only persuade them. My wishes don't count."

"That *ought* to be the case," said the conjuror, "but unluckily the readers identify with your feelings, not with mine, and if you resent my end too much I am likely to be blamed instead of revered, as I should be. Hence this interview.

And first I want us all to admit that a long life story cannot end happily. Yes, I know that William Blake sang on his deathbed, and that a president of the French Republic died of heart-failure while fornicating

9. *In this context to butter up means to flatter. The expression is based upon the pathetic fallacy that because bread tastes sweeter when it is buttered, bread enjoys being buttered.*

on the office sofa,[10] and that in 1909 a dental patient in Wumbijee, New South Wales, was struck by lighting after receiving a dose of laughing gas.[11] The God of the real world can be believed when such things happen, but no serious entertainer dare conjure them in print. We can fool people in all kinds of elaborate ways, but our most important things must seem likely and the likeliest death is to depart in a 'fiery pain-chariot' (as Carlyle put it), or to drift out in a stupefied daze if there's a doctor handy. But since the dismaying thing about death is loneliness, let us thrill the readers with a description of you ending *in company*. Let the ending be worldwide, for such a calamity is likely nowadays. Indeed, my main fear is that humanity will perish before it has a chance to enjoy my forecast of the event. It will be a metaphorical account, like Saint John's, but nobody will doubt what's happening. Attend!

When you leave this room you will utterly fail to contact any helpful officials or committees. Tomorrow, when you speak to the assembly, you will be applauded but ignored. You will learn that most other regions are as bad or even worse than your own, but that does not make the leaders want to cooperate: moreover, the council itself is maintaining its existence with great difficulty. Monboddo can offer you nothing but a personal invitation to stay in Provan. You refuse and return to Unthank, where the landscape is tilted at a

10. The president in question was Felix Fauré, who died in 1909 upon the conservatory sofa, not office sofa, of the Elysée Palace.
11. The township of Wumbijee is in southern Queensland, not New South Wales, and even at the present moment in time (1976) is too small to support a local dentist. In 1909 it did not exist. The laughing gas incident is therefore probably apocryphal but, even if true, gives a facetious slant to a serious statement of principle. It will leave the readers (whom the author pretends to cherish) uncertain of what to think about his work as a whole.

peculiar angle, rioters are attacking the clock towers and much of the city is in flame. Members of the committee are being lynched, Sludden has fled, you stand with Rima on the height of the Necropolis watching flocks of mouths sweep the streets like the shadows of huge birds, devouring the population as they go. Suddenly there is an earthquake. Suddenly the sea floods the city, pouring down through the mouths into the corridors of council and institute and short-circuiting everything. (That sounds confusing; I haven't worked out the details yet.) Anyway, your eyes finally close upon the sight of John Knox's statue – symbol of the tyranny of the mind, symbol of that protracted male erection which can yield to death but not to tenderness – toppling with its column into the waves, which then roll on as they have rolled for... a very great period. How's that for an ending?"

"Bloody rotten," said Lanark. "I haven't read as much as you have, I never had time, but when I visited public libraries in my twenties *half* the science-fiction stories[12] had scenes like that in them, usually at the end. Banal world destructions prove nothing but the impoverished minds of those who can think of nothing better."

The conjuror's mouth and eyes opened wide and his face grew red. He began speaking in a shrill whisper which swelled to a bellow: "*I am not writing* science-fiction! Science-fiction stories have no real people in them and all my characters are real, real, real people! I may astound my readers by a dazzling deployment of dramatic metaphors designed to accelerate

12. *Had Lanark's cultural equipment been wider, he would have seen that this conclusion owed more to* **Moby Dick** *than to science fiction, and more to Lawrence's essay on* **Moby Dick** *than to either.*

and compress the action but that is not science, it is magic! Magic! As for my ending being banal, wait 'til you're inside it. I warn you my whole imagination has a carefully reined-back catastrophic tendancy: you have no conception of the damage my descriptive powers will wreak when I loose them on a theme like **THE END.**"

"What about Sandy?" asked Lanark coldly.

"Who's Sandy?"

"My son."

The conjuror stared and said, "You have no son."

"I have a son called Alexander who was born in the cathedral."

The conjuror, looking confused, grubbed among the papers on his bed and at last held one up, saying, "Impossible, look here. This is a summary of the nine or ten chapters I haven't written yet. If you read it you will see there's no time for Rima to have a baby in the cathedral. She goes away too quickly with Sludden."

"When you get to the cathedral," said Lanark coldly, "you'll describe her having a son more quickly still."

The conjuror looked unhappy. He said, "I'm sorry. Yes, I see my ending becomes unusually bitter for you. A child. How old is he?"

"I don't know. Your time goes too fast for me to estimate."

After a silence the conjuror said querulously, "I can't change my overall plan now. Why should I be kinder than my century? The millions of children who've been vilely murdered this century is – *don't hit me*!"

Lanark had only tensed his muscles but the conjuror slid down the bed and pulled the covers over his head; they sunk until they lay perfectly flat on the mattress.

Lanark sighed and dropped his face into his hand. A little voice in the air said, "Promise not to be violent." Lanark snorted contemptuously. The bedclothes swelled up in a man-shaped lump but the conjuror did not emerge. A muffled voice under the clothes said, "I didn't need to play that trick. In a single sentence I could have made you my most obsequious admirer, but the reader would have turned against both of us. . . . I wish I could make you like death a little more. It's a great preserver. Without it the loveliest things change slowly into farce, as you will discover if you insist on having much more life. But I refuse to discuss family matters with you. Take them to Monboddo. Please go away."

"Soon after I came here," said Lanark, lifting the briefcase and standing up, "I said talking to you was a waste of time. Was I wrong?"

He walked to the door and heard mumbling under the bedclothes. He said "What?"

". . . know a black man called Multan. . ."

"I've heard his name. Why?"

". . . might be useful. Sudden idea. Probably not."

Lanark walked round the painting of the chestnut tree, opened the door and went out.[13]

13. *As this "Epilogue" has performed the office of an introduction to the work as a whole (the so-called "Prologue" being no prologue but a separate short story) it is saddening to find the "conjuror" omitting the courtesies appropriate to such an addendum. Mrs. Florence Allan typed and re-typed his manuscripts, often waiting many months without payment and without complaining. Professor Andrew Sykes gave him free access to professional copying equipment and secretarial help. He received from James Kelman critical advice which enabled him to make smoother prose of the crucial first chapter. Charles Wylde, Peter Cheiene, Jim Hutcheson, Stephanie Wolfe-Murray engaged in extensive lexical activity to ensure that the resulting volume had a surface consistency. And what of the compositors employed by Kingsport Press of Kingsport, Tennessee, to typeset this bloody book? Yet these are only a few of hundreds whose help has not been acknowledged and names not noted.*

# Two Wee Articles

SIR HUGH CASSON is an architect, designer and member of many royal committees. His activity in the London area has maintained and promoted elegance in the surroundings of prosperous, well educated people. His published diary is a self-consciously light-hearted record of "a full and fascinating year in the service of a great institution, **The Royal Academy**", of which he is president. It gives a slight self-portrait of a busy man travelling the world as a distinguished guest, and recording nothing to stimulate thought or imagination. This diary contains no tension, no malice, no strong encounters or sharp pen-portraits. This is a typical entry:

*Wednesday 11th, London Royal Fine Art Commission all day. Return visit of the Highgate Witanhurst project... How expensive and timewasting these endless indecisions. Some huge shopping complexes of indifferent quality. (Do people really like these air-conditioned malls with their emasculated Calders and potted plastic trees? Perhaps no. Men, as non-shoppers, should perhaps keep quiet.) Dinner at the Stock Exchange. Misprinted*

*In 1982 these reviews of a book and two exhibitions of paintings were written for* **The Sunday Standard**. *It then seemed that the closure of some Scottish daily papers had left room for a new one, & there were now unemployed journalists available to staff it. This new daily paper lasted less than a year. The galleries showing work reviewed here lasted longer. The Third Eye Centre, founded in 1972 by Tom McGrath, was managed after he left by those who came to have little or no contact with local art, so it failed in 1990. The Collins Gallery of Strathclyde University, was for 40 years a fine exhibition space, closing in 2011 as modern economic policy (higher wages for millionaires) mean only some ancient universitys can afford luxuries like art galleries.*

*invitation gets me their half an hour early. Soothed by grovelling apologies.*

Sir Hugh Casson knows that shopping malls are not built because women prefer shopping in them to smaller high street shops and traditional department stores. The Stock Exchange where he dined contains the financial forces that drive women into them, and employ him with other designers to give them a pleasant surface. However, he did not publish this book in order to tell the readers all he knows.

It would be a dull book without many little marginal watercolour sketches of elegant, spacious places Sir Hugh enjoyed visiting. These really do convey his enjoyment. He seems like a waiter handing us a small sample of icing from the top of the national cake, and doing so with the modest yet pleasent air of one who feels it is a very good cake. If, like me you are a jealous, cross-grained Glasgow man who thinks the national cake is in a wormy state and the icing nourishes nobody *he* knows, this sample may leave you feeling slightly sick. If you approve of the present government, buy the book for a female relative. She will probably find it charming. It costs £8.95.

GOOD PAINTING grounded on observant, careful drawing is a rarity nowadays, because the advertising which governs us suggests that good things should be immediately stimulating and gulped down quick. The current Chicago Exhibition at the Third Eye Centre showed paintings of the sixties and the seventies when many painters adopted the vivd colour and simple images of commercial art. These works were inventive and entertaining. The proper reaction to them was and is WOW! After being overwhelmed hardly anyone would find nothing to stand and look at for very long, but if life is a noisy party, these were the decorartions for it.

In the Collins gallery, Strathclyde University, is a show of paintings by James Cowie, who taught art in Bellshill Academy, Lanarkshire, during the 1920s and 30s, then became resident warden of Hospitalfield Artists Retreat. With slow, loving care over these years he made many drawings and a few remarkable paintings of children sitting in corners of an ordinary classroom, with an occasional breath of air entering from a landscape outside the window. Like the Mona Lisa and portraits by Holbein and Raeburn they face us with the mystery of other human beings, each of them as much the centre of their universe as we are.

Abiding contemplation, they nourish parts of the soul some painters cannot reach.

# A Modest Proposal*

LAST NOVEMBER the Edinburgh University Press, Polygon Books, held a conference in the bar of the Traverse theatre club to publicise their reprint of Edwin Muir's book of the thirties, *Scott and Scotland*. The theme of the conference was 'The predicament of the Scottish writer'. On the platform were Iain Crichton Smith and myself and Trevor Royle and Alan Spence. Allan Massie was chairman. I had accepted his invitation to speak as immediately as a dog shuts its jaws on a proffered bone. Talking in public for a fee is much easier than writing sentences of informative prose, unless the talker writes the speech beforehand. It had not occurred to me to do that. I had decided to be spontaneous yet modest. In referring to The Scottish Writer I would make no references to myself, so that the writers and students and theatre people and arts administration people in the audience would know I was speaking for all of them, too. And when I came to The Predicament I would ignore sexual, parental, educational, religious and emotional predicaments, since these vary from person to person. I would stick to poverty and unemployment, of which everyone has, or pretends to have had, considerable experience. In general terms I would explain that 'the predicament of the Scottish writer' is the predicament of the crofter

✱ *This was written for a 1983 number of* **Chapman**, *edited by Joyce Hendry in Edinburgh. It also had my first cover design for this Scots literary magazine.*

and steelworker – the predicament of Scotland itself. What a radical, hardhitting yet humane speech that would be. Since there would be no crofters or steel workers in the audience I would not upset a single soul.

I was first speaker and with a sinking heart saw Tom Leonard in the front row before me. He has a sharp ear for the glibly phoney phrase. However, I managed to forget him, and with vehemence and quirkiness I delivered a speech so essentially bland that I cannot now remember a word I said. Then Iain Crichton Smith spoke sadly about the predicament of writing within, and for, the Gaelic and Lowland Scots language groups; and Trevor Royle spoke embarrassedly about the embarrassment of being born in England before writing in and about this place; and Alan Spence, in his soft, quiet, clear, hypnotic, even-paced, level voice, spoke in terms which were probably as general as my own, for I cannot now remember a word he said, either. Then Allan Massie, who had introduced us with the crisp firmness of a Victorian headmaster, invited questions and comment from the audience.

George Byatt asked why there were no playwrights on the platform. Did the conference organizers think writers for stage and television were negligible? Allan Massie replied that the conference had been organized by book publishers to publicise a book. Several other people made clear and necessary statements which led to no debate or exchange of ideas, because once uttered they seemed obvious. Eventually a troublemaker tried to get a positive expression of personal prejudice from the platform.

He asked why there were no women on it. The chairman said nothing. The questioner asked the other speaker to comment on this and only I was stupid enough to do so. Forgetting that Joan Lingard was in the audience and that she and Muriel Spark and Jessie Kesson and Naomi Mitchison and Ena Lamont Stewart and Elspeth Davie and Ann Smith and Agnes Owens and Marcella Evaristi and Liz Lochhead would constitute a brace of quintets twice as dazzling as our enplatformed one, I stammeringly suggested that the proportion of male to female Scottish writers, statistically calculated, might, er, not, er, perhaps justify, er, the presence of more than half a woman... Like a true friend Tom Leonard interrupted me here. He asked if this did not demonstrate that Scottish writing had a basically homo-erotic foundation? I was able to change the subject by denouncing him for exposing our secret. Whereupon headmaster dismissed the entire class.

So I cannot remember the conference with much pleasure or interest, apart from an extract from Edwin Muir's *Scott and Scotland* which Allan read out at the start as an indication of what 'The Scottish writer's predicament' was. Iain Crichton Smith took account of it at the time. I fudged it over. A few weeks ago I was answering a questionnaire sent by research students, and one of the replies became the speech I would have given at the conference if I had been honest and careful enough to write it out beforehand.

**Question** An important consideration for any writer is the audience he wishes to reach; do you write for a Scottish audience primarily, or for a British audience or international audience? And do you feel that awareness of a potential readership in any way determines what and how you write?

**Answer** Surely no good author considers national boundaries important unless he is explicitly writing about them. Writers who seek to persuade a limited class – commercial writers and propagandists – must think that way, but I'm sure that the stories and poems which the world has not yet allowed to die were written by folk who believed any ordinarily educated, sensible soul would enjoy them if they skilfully uttered what they thought important as best they could.

I want to be read by an English-speaking tribe which extends to California in the West to Bengal in the East, and lies between the latitudes of Capetown in the South and George MacKay Brown in the North, unless the Shetlands and Alaska are further North still. This does not preclude me from using any words of Scots origin that I please – dunt, docken, eerie, canny etcetera, or bunnet, polis, ya prickye, if I feel like being Glaswegian. The Indians have also given words to the English language, though at the moment only shampoo comes to mind. I am sure that Oxford and Cambridge have contributed useful words to the English language, though at present I cannot remember any. Most English words were originally used by illiterate Celts, Germans and Scandinavians. To these an international civil-service of priests added some long Latin words and a clan of bullyboy Norman invaders some posh French ones. In the past century the main additions to our vocabulary have been devised by scientists and technicians.

Words stay alive because we find them useful or entertaining. An element in entertainment is surprise. One of the riches of English is the chance it gives to surprise the reader by putting a plain simple noun or verb, sometimes a strongly local one, into an abstractly posh-sounding sentence, and vice-versa. When a writer is using English dramatically – not necessarily in a play, it can be in a story where several speakers are quoted – the verbal colouring (if his characters are not bound to one social class in one emotional state) will be tinted with idioms which vary from biblical to the Johnsonian, from American film commercial to local cockney, Oxbridge or Glaswegian. And this is simple realism. Any writers in English – if their range of reading is sufficiently wide – can take an exciting but generally unfamiliar word heard in a nearby street and, if it is useful, make the meaning and nuance plain to a reader from a different English idiom through the context in which it is marshalled.

Good writers can also use the main diction of their locality, and if the thought and feeling is sufficiently strong and well expressed, folk from other places who like good writing will teach themselves to understand. Burns demonstrated this two centuries ago. English literature took to him at once - if by Eng. Lit. we mean the acclaim of his fellow poets and every really intelligent reader. Scott and Hogg and Galt came soon after him, Hugh MacDiarmid, Sorley MacLean and Tom Leonard more recently. Their achievements contradict Edwin Muir's most quoted example of the double-bind: *Write Scottishly and you'll be sincere but neglected by the world-as-a-whole, write for the*

*English world-as-a-whole and you must neglect the true speech of your emotional life.* Surely that is nothing but a huge failure of nerve from lack of respect for our best examples.

MacDiarmid was one such example. He spoke of all the things he believed, using all the language he could master: local and historical, scientific-technical, political-polemical. One literary idiom was out with his ken – the dramatic. Burns, Scott, Hogg, Galt could dramatize, find language for people they were not. MacDiarmid had to make poetry from the dialectics of his self-contradictory intelligence. But that intelligence, that poetry, is still big enough for us to have worthwhile adventures inside. It is very queer that a small nation which has bred so many strongly local writers of worldwide scope still bickers and agonizes over the phoney local versus international double-bind.

Why? The fact that Scotland is governed from outside itself, governed against the advice of the three Parliamentary Commissions which looked into the matter, and against the wishes of most Scots who voted on the matter, cannot be used to explain our lack of talent, because at least in literature that lack is no longer evident. Scotland has as many first rate writers as the USA had when Twain wrote *Huckleberry Finn* and a far greater crop of good second-raters, all surveying the universe across a Scottish foreground from the current of their particular Mississippi. There is no evidence that the local experience of Royal Home Counties writers gives them worthier subject matter or more intelligent dictions. Why should it? Does the proximity of a thing called a government allow for a finer class of thought? It might, if the government was fostering peaceful employment and social equality. It doesn't, so all it fosters is the wealth of the rich and a false sense of self-importance. John Braine feels more significant because Michael Foot nods to him in a restaurant, but the best London-based writers show lives as unblessed by government as Scotland is.

The foregoing diatribe is too long an answer to a short question. The short answer is, that since I resemble other people I can entertain and inform them if I entertain and inform myself with matter and language which do it best. This is a partial truth, but saves wasting time on market-surveys and public-relations work.

# 1982 Janine

EPILOGUE FOR DISCERNING CRITICS. You have noticed lines in this book taken from Chaucer Shakespeare Jonson *The Book of Common Prayer* Goldsmith Cowper Anon Mordaunt Burns Blake Scott Byron Shelley Campbell Wordsworth Coleridge Keats Browning Tennyson Newman Henley Stevenson Hardy Yeats Brooke Owens Hasek (in Parrott's translation, shortened) Kafka Pritchett Auden Cummings Lee and Jackson, so I will list writers who gave ideas for bigger bits.

The matter of Scotland refracted through alcoholic reverie is from MacDiarmid's *A Drunk Man Looks at the Thistle*. The narrator without self-respect is from Dostoyevsky's *Notes from Underground,* Celine's *Journey to the End of the Night,* the first-person novels of Flann O'Brien and from Camus's *The Fall*. An elaborate fantasy within a plausible everyday fiction is from O'Brien's *At Swim-Two-Birds,* Nabokov's *Pale Fire,* Vonnegut's *Slaughterhouse-Five*. Making the fantasy pornographic is from Buñuel's film *Belle de Jour* and from *The Nightcloak*, a novel by someone whom I forget. The character of

*I had planned* **Lanark** *to be my novel, followed by one book of short stories, then a collection of my poems, then my book of plays then a collection of prose essays such as this one. Then I would work all the time as a visual artist. When Resident Writer at the University of Glasgow, from 1977-79, I heard* **Lanark** *was to be published and I now had leisure to complete my short story book* **Unlikely Stories, Mostly,** *so called as it was going to contain a few realistic tales. At the last moment these were left out. In 1981 I began finishing one of the realistic tales. It started by using the politics of the day & my hero's erotic fantasies. It grew fast into my best novel. It was finished in 1982 (hence the title) and published by Jonathan Cape of London in 1984.*

Mad Hislop is taken from Mr Johnstone in Tom Leonard's poem *Four of the Belt*, which he here allows me to reprint:

*Jenkins, all too clearly it is time*
*for some ritual physical humiliation;*
*and if you cry, boy, you will prove*
*what I suspect – you are not a man.*

*As they say, Jenkins, this hurts me*
*more than it hurts you. But I show you*
*I am a man, by doing this, to you.*

*When you are a man, Jenkins, you may hear*
*that physical humiliation and ritual*
*are concerned with strange adult matters*
*– like rape, or masochist fantasies.*

*You will not accept such stories:*
*rather, you will recall with pride,*
*perhaps even affection, that day when I,*
*Mr Johnstone, summoned you before me,*
*and gave you four of the belt*

*like this. And this. And this. And this.*

Brian McCabe's *Feathered Choristers* in the Collins Scottish short-story collection of 1979 showed how all these things could combine in one.

The most beholden chapter is the eleventh. The plot is from the programme to Berlioz's *Symphonie Fantastique*; rhythms and voices are from the

Blocksberg scenes in Goethe's *Faust* and night town
scenes in Joyce's *Ulysses*; the self-inciting vocative is
from Jim Kelman's novel *The Bus-Conductor Hines*; the
voice of my nontranscendent god from E. E. Cummings.
The political part of Jock's vomiting fit is from *The
Spendthrifts*, a great Spanish novel in which Benito
Pérez Galdós puts a social revolution into the stomach
and imagination of a sick little girl. The graphic use of
typeface is from Sterne's *Tristram Shandy* and poems
by Ian Hamilton Finlay and Edwin Morgan.

Though too busy to be aware of the foregoing
influences while writing under them I consciously took
information and ideas (which she would disown) from
a correspondence with Tina Reid, also anecdotes from
conversations with Andrew Sykes, Jimmy Guy and Tom
Lamb, also three original phrases of Glasgow invective
from Jim Caldwell. Richard Fletcher informed and
improved the book's electrical and mechanical parts.
The fanciful use of light and space technology comes
partly from conversations with Chris Boyce and partly
from his book, *Extraterrestrial Encounters*.

Flo Allan typed all perfectly with help from Scott
Pearson in the denser pages of chapter 11. Ian Craig
the art director, Judy Linard the designer, Jane Hill the
editor, Bunge, Will, Phil and Tom the typesetters, Peva
Keane the proofreader, worked uncommonly hard to
make this book exactly as it should be.

And now a personal remark which purely
literary minds will ignore. Though John Mcleish is an
invention of mine I disagree with him. In chapter 4, for
example, he says of Scotland "We are a poor little
country, always have been, always will be." In fact

Scotland's natural resources are as variedly rich as those of any other land. Her ground area is greater than Denmark, Holland, Belgium or Switzerland, her population higher than Denmark, Norway or Finland. Our present ignorance and bad social organization make Scots poorer than other north Europeans, but even bad human states are not everlasting.

Finally, I acknowledge the support of Mad Toad, Crazy Shuggy, Tam the Bam and Razor King, literature-loving friends in the Glasgow Mafia who will go any length to reason with editors, critics and judges who fail to celebrate the shining merit of the foregoing volume.

# Of Alasdair Taylor: Painter*

THE ART OF PAINTING IS IN A POOR WAY. The ambitious pictorial talents try for film and television while decent second-raters (the backbone of any industry) are lost to advertising. We needn't regret this. As Peggy Guggenheim said, the 20th century has already enjoyed more than its share of great painters. In the first fifty years of it Bonnard, Braque, Burra, Chagall, Kandinsky, Klee, Léger, Matisse, Mondrian, Munch, Nash, Picasso, Rivera, Rouault, Schwitters, Sickert, Soutine, Spencer and a dozen other fine artists were working contemporaries. If no such list of painters can be made today we can balance it with a list of creative film-makers. Paintings, of course, are still produced and sold for big sums. As a means of non-taxable banking, painting lags far behind the diamond industry, but it is still ahead of secondhand postage stamps. Our monetary system still has a use for an occupation which, since the big studio-workshops of Medieval and Renaissance times, has dwindled to a cottage industry. The galleries of the large dealers are close to the major stock-exchanges, and if such a dealer decides some new canvases can be propagated as sound investments, the maker of them has a chance of working in comfortable conditions.

Scotland, however, is a notorious low-investment

*This essay was first printed in a 1973 **Scottish International** magazine and also was one of the three biographical sketches in the **Lean Tales** anthology beside work by Agnes Owens and James Kelman, published by Jonathan Cape in 1985.

area and pictorially speaking we have never recovered from the depression of the thirties. From 1880 to 1925 Scotland supported a large population of full-time professional painters, the bulk of them living in the west. It is not coincidence that the Glasgow School of Painting throve when Glasgow was the second biggest city in Britain and the main supplier of the world's shipping. Dealers like Reid and Annan were not only exporting local painting to England and France, they were importing continental masterpieces for the collections of magnates like Cargill and Burrell. Scotland's art schools and municipal galleries were built in this period, and built well. Things is nut whit they wur. In 1944 Sir William Burrell gave Glasgow Corporation the best private collection of French, German, Italian and oriental artifacts in Europe. The cost of housing this and employing a sufficient staff of administrators, conservators and security guards ensures that in the Scottish middle-west little public money will be spent on local painting for the foreseeable future. The Scottish dealers making a sure profit nowadays are handling paintings of the 1830-1925 period, mainly for the London market where not only Hornels and Laveries, but Houstons and Docherties have become sound investments. Annan's lovely gallery in Sauchiehall Street became an army recruiting office in the sixties around the time that Upper Clyde Shipyards went into liquidation. The Scottish export of machines, coal and paintings has shrunk to a trickle.

It is not flippant to couple the health of a nation's art with the health of its bigger industries. The drop in the sale of newly made Scottish paintings since the start of the century is sometimes explained by saying that photography has ousted the portrait, that today's homes are too small for big canvases, that modern art is so peculiar that only very sophisticated people like it. All these explanations are contained by the statement, "Most people can't afford to buy paintings." Quite true. Fine paintings always belong to rich private or public bodies, so the sales are happening where our prosperity moved to, near London. The number of commercial London galleries has multiplied by five or six since the start of the century. Prosperity is treating art as it treats other special skills, and drawing it south by feeding it best there.

Now, when prosperity (which is called Capital in the Free West) sailed south in the thirties it left Scottish painters clinging to their art-schools like drowning seamen to rafts. It is strange to think how unimportant the Scottish schools were to earlier masters. At the turn of the century art teachers were few, often foreign, and most Royal Scottish Academicians and members of the Glasgow Institute had nothing to do with them. Nowadays the greatest part of those who exhibit in the Royal Scottish Academy and Royal Glasgow Institute are dominies. Three-quarters of our painters work in the time left from educating people, so the dominie is our most obvious kind of artistic life. This may be a pity. In the present state of money-sharing it is inevitable.

I am sorry to spend so many words upon money when writing of an art-form. Nobody has more respect than the Scots for what can be measured by weight, volume and cash, but in softer moods we prefer to believe in the superior virtues of love, friendship, home, the church, a football team, the Orange Order and (if educated to it) Art. All the same, half the story of art is the story of who pays money for it. In Medieval days abbots and bishops hired stone-carvers and painters to do jobs as quickly as they hired weavers and builders, and a genius was one who did his work well enough to set a famous example. The city rulers of the Italian Renaissance spent new wealth raising and decorating public buildings with a competitive exuberance which our own rulers keep for weapon research: artists of extra skill and imagination were given marble and gold to work with, teams of assistants to direct, were bargained for by competing governments. Painting became an unstable industry when the rich stopped ordering art for their community and started wanting it mainly for themselves. They began searching for completed work by guaranteed, rock-bottom, gilt-edged geniuses, preferably dead ones who couldn't spoil the market by flooding in new pictures. However, despite the instability of their profession nowadays, few painters kill themselves. Those who can neither live by painting nor bear to lose touch with it rarely put bullets into their skulls as Van Gogh did. In Scotland, as I said, they become dominies.

Now, while it is possible for a good painter to teach (Klee, Kandinsky and Cowie did it) there occur, even in Scotland, painters who are unable to be anything else, and unless, like Joan Eardley, they have an unearned income, they need unusual toughness to survive. Modern artists' early years are always a struggle because they are usually in their thirties before they have hammered out a mature style. But where Matisse, Braque, Bacon, Pollock finally matured their style there were galleries to show it and a public to buy. Where Angus Neil, Pierre Lavalle, Tom McDonald, Bet Low and Carole Gibbons matured their styles hardly anyone noticed. In public exhibitions their work was swamped by the products of the dominies, and there was no critical journalism to take note, no local dealer to persuade wealthy citizens or the municipal gallery that here was good new work. Moreover, exhibiting costs money which full-time painters can't always afford, so they struggle to paint through thickening loneliness. They grow touchy with prosperous friends, resentful of the dominies, who can treat their touchiness as a joke.

Unluckily this resentment is not the healthy distrust expressed between Scottish writers, a robust gregarious activity, a way of drawing attention to ourselves when we have nothing useful to say. The full-time painters' resentment is isolating, self-hurtful, and can lead to that rigid despair which unintelligent doctors try to clear from the brain with electric currents. They become hermits, and nobody is to blame: not the art schools, the Arts Council, the R.S.A. or the Scottish public. The force which turns artists into teachers or hermits is the force which shut Denny's shipyard in Dumbarton, which developed the hovercraft. As a friendly member of the Arts Council once said to John Connolly, the sculptor, "You must be mad to do this kind of thing in Scotland." No no no no no! Not mad, just bloody unlucky. For in spite of the depressed state of local industry there are skilled workers among these part-timers and full-timers, these dominies and hermits. Why don't they take their skill south if they're any good? That's what the best Scottish tradesmen and technicians do.

Artists do go south of course, but if there is more talent in Scottish painting and writing than in our other professions it is because nowadays workers in imaginative industries take longer to teach themselves their jobs, and when they've done it they sometimes find they've made unbreakable connections with a few houses and people, with a kind of life and kind of landscape. They have become natives.

Alasdair Taylor is a native artist, a full-time painter, and something of a hermit.

He was born in 1936 in the village of Edderton, Ross-Shire, where his father was station-master. His first profession was musical, for his mother was pianist in a small dance-band entertaining the Forces on leave, and at seven he began accompanying her on the drums. "When I felt tired they rolled me in a curtain at the side of the stage, I fell asleep and my father took over the drums. But he wasn't much good." In 1946 the family moved to Coalburn in Lanarkshire. He attended Larkhall Academy and Lesmahagow High School, grew keen on painting, but still drummed with small bands at balls and farmers' weddings. And at Glasgow School of Art he played with a student jazz group. He was also in the Student Christian Movement, where a meeting with a Franciscan inspired him to visit a monastery in England with thoughts of becoming a monk.

I mention this because Alasdair Taylor is a lyrical painter: a painter whose colour, like a musician's sound, makes sombre and radiant feelings without showing (as many painters do and all good writers must) details of the social life causing them. Such an artist knows very well the feelings of hell, purgatory and heaven which were the material of religion before clergymen grew embarrassed by them. Alasdair Taylor rejected the Franciscans for the Presbyterian reason that he hated ritual. Since then he has experienced several religions and spiritualisms, but without desiring that fixed state of mind called belief. Belief in one system would put too narrow a box round his feelings.

In the third art-school year he came to London to look at Rembrandt etchings, and visiting an almost empty cinema one afternoon saw a beautiful girl some rows ahead. He spoke to her. She was a Danish au pair girl. They met several times and became firm friends. She returned to Denmark. On leaving art school he received a £50 painting prize, sold his drums, used the money to follow her to Silkeborg, and they were married. I give these details to show his jazzman's power: the power of acting spontaneously then building soundly on the result. Annelise is remarkable. She has calmness, strength, intelligence, and the love of painting not to nag her husband out of it when life is hard. She has prevented the usual despair and become the foundation of his art. One rare strong person who loves and supports your talent can outweigh a society which does not give a damn for you.

They returned to Scotland. He taught art for three days in a Dumbarton school then handed in his notice and got work as a midden man with Glasgow Cleansing Department while Annelise bore their first daughter. Six months later the Church of Scotland minister of Glasgow University made him caretaker of the Chaplaincy Centre. It was a busy place but for nearly five years it gave him room, time and security to work, and it was here I first saw his paintings.

He had two main sorts in that period, and the sort I preferred were the figures and portraits. The touches of pen and brush he used to show faces and bodies were amazingly free. An encounter with the Danish artist Asger Jorn had excited him to use paint richly and thickly. Rembrandt is said to have once painted a portrait so thick that, laid flat on the floor, it could be lifted by the nose. Sometimes Alasdair worked like that, building up the paint in jewel-like flakes. Yet he could still show whole characters and forms with a few quick nervous pen-strokes on paper. I was baffled and stunned by other works which art jargon might describe as abstract-expressionist-dadaism with bits of pop-collage. Their outraged energy that sometimes incorporated swear-words. Why?

My answer is banal. Urban life, like the art of painting, is in a poor way. Commerce and government, always selfishly greedy, are now greedy in more versatile and quickly changing ways. In the prosperous sixties a work of popular sociology announced that modern happiness meant learning to accept, not only disposable furnishings, clothes, cars, but disposable homes, friendships, marriages. Painters are forced by their eccentric position to look hard at the life round about them, and their products show it. Some see the communal world reshaped by advertising and have made art out of commercial pornography, soupcan labels, popstar photographs. Some, excited by the impossibility of seeing exactly what our highly calculating technology is doing to us, have painted unsensual abstracts intricately calculated to stop the eye of the viewer focusing on them. Others, who feel the world at its best is a succession of exciting shocks, make works which are quaintly or vividly shocking, but have little other content.

In England a recent group of painters called The Ruralists find modern their world so distasteful that they paint rural fairylands of little girls, flowers, rich country gardens, topiary lawns, parasols and Edwardian ballgames. But the two best-known British artists still paint modern people. Hockney makes his eye very cold and shows people as chalky-surfaced additions to modern furniture, bathroom fittings, swimming pools and glass-fronted banks. Bacon looks under the skin at our twisted loneliness and capacity for pain. And Alasdair Taylor, living in Glasgow, crucified an umbrella on a canvas and wrote swear-words under it, because his artistic gift was lyrical and nothing around him fed it.

In 1965 the job of Chaplaincy caretaker ended and the Taylors moved to Northbank Cottage, a small farmhouse near the tip of the Hunterston promontory. Behind it rises a high red cliff with a strip of ancient

1. Disposable *used to mean nothing but* easily positioned. *The rapid manufacture and marketing of the sixties and seventies brought it to mean also* replaced *and, in addition, rejected after use. Then military logicians started using it to denote the part of a fighting force or population whose death will prevent victory and perhaps assist it.* Disposable *thus came to mean* dispensable *and, in the eyes of authority, useless and unnecessary.*

tangled woodland at the foot. The front faces the Firth of Clyde across a narrow field usually given to potatoes, and the view embraces three islands: Millport (a seaside village under a serrated green hill) the Wee Cumbrae (rocky terraces of golden bracken and heather) and Arran (a blue-grey mountainous silhouette). The nearest building is the atomic power station, half a mile along the coast to the north and partly hidden by a bend in the cliff. To the south the clachan of Portencross is hidden by a fault-dyke with an opening cut in it to let the track through. The cottage has an outhouse with a skylight which was once the studio of the landscape painter Houston, but is now used to store seed-potatoes. Alasdair's studio is in the main building, entered from a separate door at the back. The cottage, whitewashed and lit by oil-lamps, was the scene of a famous unsolved murder in the thirties. It has a plain, friendly feeling about it which is not purely why the Taylors moved there. The promontory is good farming ground, the landowners wanted an eye kept on the fields hidden by the cliff, so the cottage rent was a few shillings a week.

When Alasdair left Glasgow many people thought he would soon return. He had poured out such streams of conversation in their company that they thought him a mainly social animal. They forgot he had grown up in mainly country districts, and that social animals spend hours together without talking at all. The drummer in Alasdair felt that company should be stimulated and stimulating, so his conversation was always very quick, intense, crammed with insights and therefore exhausting. It drew off energy he needed for work, work which was best fed by reflections in the country near the wife and daughters who loved him and took him for granted. On coming to Northbank he collected small boulders and driftwood from the beach, weathered roots from old trees by the cottage. The stones moved him to mark them with enamel hieroglyphs. He sculpted the wood into shapes suggested by its shape and grain. Wood, even flat slabs of it, can be got more cheaply than canvas, especially by a trained midden man, so his next paintings were on wood. Abstractions based on the life of Christ were painted on polished and varnished slices of a railway sleeper which was floated in by the tide. The colour had a richness he had once used mainly in portraiture.

Later a friend brought down in a lorry some backdrops a theatre-group had thrown out, because they were a fire risk. Alasdair cut them down, stretched them, took them into Houston's old studio, empty at the time. He now had nearly forty big canvases, each stained with blues, buffs, dull greens and pinks which had once, across the footlights, seemed like skies, trees and mountains. These shapes began to suggest pictures to him, as the tree-roots had suggested sculpture. Money was short; these were his first canvases for many years; he decided nothing must be wasted. He touched them only when feeling exactly what strokes of colour to apply, working with brushes, oil colour and spray-paint cans. These cans are a popular medium with amateur muralists in the poorer parts of Glasgow, but cost nearly a pound each. Annelise, now working in an Ardrossan youth centre, bought more when she saw the supply run low. He left the choice of colours to her. He expected the canvases to last a year or two, but they were completed in a few weeks.

This was the first work of his artistic maturity. The surfaces were as energetic as before but with new variety, depth and harmony. They hold many kinds of light and colour; light in cloud, water and leaves, colour in seaweed, pebbles, moss and rusty iron. Only the works themselves can show the coolness and warmth, nearness and remoteness they contain, but I have said enough to indicate that Alasdair Taylor is an abstract expressionist, one of the school containing most Kandinsky, much of Klee, all of Jackson Pollock, and in present-day England, Albert Irvin. This kind of painting, since it gives the beholder a shock which is not a shock of recognition, strikes most people as a chaos, a mere explosion of paint. Many abstract expressionist works strike me that way too. After a pleasurable shock at an obvious explosion of energy, many strike me as duller with each glance because they lack the variety of compostion, contrast and harmony which make a picture worth contemplating. But Alasdair's pictures abide contemplation. The shock of seeing one as a whole, at a distance, becomes at close range a pleasure in those strongly, subtly varied colours which are a main part of my sensual, visual delight in the airy, watery, rocky and growing world outside his studio.

From that time to this an abstract expressionist has lived and worked in a cottage on the Ayrshire coast, steadily painting, brooding, and painting again; sometimes visited by friends, a few of whom buy a picture from time to time; and partly unknown to, and

partly ignored by, the official art world. For in
Scotland, as elsewhere in Britain, a new official art
world has come to exist, a separate one from art
schools, institutes and academies.

In the early seventies, by Arts Council subsidy
and local government donation, new arts centres with
exhibition galleries and salaried administrators came
to most of the Scottish cities. The administrators are
usually strangers to the cities where they work and are
often English, because there are more highly qualified
English than Scots looking for work in modern Britain.
The administrators honestly wish to show the best in
modern art, including local Scottish art, but how do
they know what that is? By repute, and by experience.
If artists exhibit once or twice a year with other artists,
and have a single show of their own from time to time,
administrators get to know them almost unconsciously,
through an accumulation of tiny repetitions of names
in conversations, invitation-cards and posters. They
can also see the artists' product in galleries, in their
absence, in a context of acceptance and appreciation,
and can decide to exhibit it without meeting and
judging a peculiar human being. Administrators,
therefore, hardly[2] ever meet the Scottish hermit painter,
and only do so with discomfort on both sides. And
nobody can help by approaching an administrator,
pointing to a distant figure and saying, "See him! Show
him! He's great!" Those who do are the artist's friend,
and prejudiced.

So in 1985 Alasdair is one of over 350,000 Scots

2. *When this article was written and Mrs. Thatcher's government had only started to
privatise Britain in the big way continued ever since. The state of art in Scotland, for
better or worse, is different in 2014.*

whose work is not wanted and whose artistic activity embarrasses well qualified, highly salaried officials who administer arts centres and galleries.

His wife has stopped him being a tragic soul by becoming the family's breadwinner, so he is not on the dole, and continually works hard at what he does best. He often feels lonely and useless, but we all have our troubles. Hardworking, salaried arts administrators and teachers have quite different troubles, and can dismiss him with a touch of envy. He creates what they are paid to promote. His work accumulates. I would like to think that one day more than a few people will see and love it.

# Of R. D. Laing

AFTER *THE DIVIDED SELF* was published in 1960 and *The Politics of Experience* and *The Bird of Paradise* in 1967 Ronald Laing's thoughts about the nature of madness appealed to many educated minds, including mine. In 1985 he came to Glasgow to publicise his biography *The Making of a Psychologist* and Peter Kravitz, editor of *The Edinburgh Review,* arranged for him to meet James Kelman, Tom Leonard and me in a Byres Road pub after a talk he was giving in Gartnavel Royal Hospital, where he had first worked as a psychologist. We attended the talk. I was embarrassed at first by his slow, careful speech with long pauses between sentences, and (worse still) between words within a sentence. These disconcerting pauses did not distract from an important argument.

He announced that he would amuse us by reading from a manual published by the pharmaceutical industry, for the guidance of medical practitioners in the U.S.A. and Britain. It advised which drugs should be used to treat mental illness, and had a lot to say about those whose behaviour has been described under many names since the end of the 19th century, but is now widely known as schizophrenia. It said schizophrenics were all manipulative, sometimes aggressively so, but also sometimes managed others by acting passive to the point of extreme shyness. They could be highly sexed and erotically demanding, but also totally frigid, or cunning enough to appear completely normal. As Laing read from the manual it became clear that doctors could use it to find almost any patient's behaviour clinically suspect and use it as an excuse for drugging them. He ended by saying, "Why are we using this fucking thing?" and flung it on the floor.*

As we left he was talking to former colleagues by the doorway, so on the way past I mentioned my name, saying I hoped to see him later. He asked for the name again, then embraced me and kissed me long and hard on the lips. I knew this was a kind of test so did not struggle, and left smartly when released.

On meeting him later in the pub there was nothing in his speech which, earlier, had made me think him drunk. At that time I had not seen a dentist for many years. He said, "I see you've lost even more teeth than me," and smiled showing a set of strong white upper dentures with one obvious gap. I asked how that had happened. He said, "I was punched in the mouth by a Buddhist monk." I asked why. He said, "I called him a stupid fucking yellow cowardly bastard." He said also he was glad I had written *Lanark* because it accurately described the link between asthma and guilty feelings about masturbation. He said he had wanted to write about that, but could not, and now need not because I had done it.

In later years I met him in the home of John Duthie, with whom he stayed when visiting Glasgow, where his seperated first wife and children lived. He

*2014 Postscript. In the most recent addition of the pharmaceutical handbook Ronnie denounced, grief for the death of a loved one that persists for more than a fortnight is defined as a mental illness of a sort to be treated with named drugs.

told me that his friend Sean Connery was keen to play the part of King Pentheus in *The Bachae of Euripedes* and had asked him to consider writing the script, a job he felt I was more equipped to do. He dictated a short letter to the actor in a familiar, easy style offering my services, which he thought had the right tone. I wrote, signed and posted it with no great expectations of a reply so was not disappointed.

He died in 1989, and two years ago his daughter asked me to say a few words and unveil a plaque commemorating him over the close of the tenement where he was born and had grown up. The tenement was like those in Riddrie, the housing scheme where we all thought ourselves middle class though Marx would have called petit bourgeoisie. Laing's dad had worked in a civil engineering firm. The gathering was a small one with no reporters from radio, television and the local press. I praised Laing as a psychologist with the patience to listen carefully to his patients, even some who did not pay him big money. I knew he was not a good family man – a pity, but perhaps slightly damaged folk can most intelligently sympathize with others of that sort. I gathered that more doctors were finding drugs the most convenient treatment of mental problems. Laing, of course, would have hated that, I thought with good reason.

I told his daughter that an article in an English paper had implied that her father had grown up in a tough Glasgow slum, and supposed this was because in London the words *Glasgow tenement* suggested thugs fighting with razors. She smiled and said, "Dad liked to dramatize himself."

# Of Scottie Wilson*

IN LATE NINETEENTH CENTURY Glasgow, Louis Freeman, the son of Lithuanian Jews, learnt to talk with a Scottish voice. His first forty years of life were harsh but richly varied. He was a street-trader in Glasgow and London between soldiering in Africa, India and the Flanders trenches. Perhaps he deserted from the Black-and-Tans in Ireland but certainly, calling himself Robert Wilson, he got to Canada, where he was nicknamed Scottie. One day in the midst of middle-age he sat at the back of his junkshop in Toronto, picked up an old fountain pen collected for the gold in the nib, started doodling with it and didn't want to stop. Pictures began flowing from him. This is explicable. Imagine a man with a strong inbred shaping skill, an intuitive sculptor who has never touched the tools of his craft and has found no joy in life before, at the age of forty, he starts accidentally whittling a stick.

Wilson was an instinctive designer, which is why his later work translated so well into textile, ceramic and Unicef greeting cards. Using pen and crayon like an embroiderer, each stroke a coloured stitch, for over forty years he made spooky, colourful, mainly symmetrical designs blending shapes of bird, fish, tree, house and his own knubbly face. He made so many

*A **Times Literary Supplement** *review, 14.03.1986, of* **It's All Writ Out for You**, *the art of Scottie Wilson chosen and introduced by George Melly.*

that fourteen years after his death dealers still have stores of them, and have combined with the publishers of George Melly's book to exhibit and promote them.

It's All Writ Out For You contains forty-eight colour plates showing the variety and growth of Wilson's talent: the scratchy earlier work which shows its origin in the automatic doodle, the densely organized and ominous compositions of his middle period, and the garden-like later tapestries which are as beautiful as fine Persian carpets, and for the same reasons. The colour reproduction is good, except of the larger works, which are given a shrunken postcard look by the broad white surrounding margins. Only the jacket reproduces detail on a scale showing the texture of a surface.

George Melly's text was written at the wish of Victor Musgrave, Wilson's main friend and dealer who died before he could write it himself. Inevitably, given Wilson's history, the result is a commentary on hearsay, but the commentary shows how hard it is for a cultured Englishman to believe that someone of a different culture is equally intelligent. In his autobiographies Mr Melly writes wise and entertaining prose; he is a good, popular jazz singer so no snob; he has liked and promoted Wilson's art for nearly forty years, yet discusses him like a liberal Victorian ethnographer discussing a Maori. Wilson spoke highly of Blake, having heard his poems on the radio and having been shown his pictures by Swiss collectors. Says Melly, 'The lovers of primitive painting seem unable to resist this sort of thing. It's a dangerous activity, exactly threatening the self-taught spontaneity *which...'* etc. In other words, these foreign agitators could upset the frail culture of our natives by giving them new *ideas.*

Melly knows Wilson was a conscious comic who also told tall tales, but doubts if he knew exactly where reality stopped and fiction began, and to many in the professional classes the British working class is indeed an aboriginal tribe, more so if it is also Scottish. And were the many small strokes Wilson put into his work a substitute for masturbation? Was he schizophrenic? Did painting, on the contrary, stop him going insane? The book asks these impertinent, clinical questions (which could be asked of Francis Bacon or any original artist) and of course cannot answer them. They are phrases to disguise bafflement.

The bafflement is understandable. Like *Ulysses*, and *Huckleberry Finn*, and other globetrotters who had to live by their wits among strangers, Wilson used false names and gave enquirers versions of his past which would best please them, becoming Jewish among Jews, a Scot amongst the British. The Glasgow Third Eye Centre exhibition displays a photograph of him promoting his work in Canada. His crisp waistcoat, collar and tie and impressive owl-like glasses make him look like the present head of a northern Arts Council. Europeans preferred the working-class eccentric and it was easy to oblige them. The Thames and Hudson press handout says, 'he remained steadfastly outside the modish art world', which only means that he dressed like the street-trader he had been, and therefore looked like an ordinary part of the London where he lodged and worked. He disliked selling his pictures, yet (according to Musgrave) sold them cheaply, preferably in bulk. And he worked hard. But the modish art world was his meat and drink, it let him live by the creations of his vision, so he clung to it, although (says Roger Cardinal) 'he always knew that his attendance at cocktail parties in the galleries was by way of decoration'. Cardinal means that the presence of folk who bought and sold art were essential to gallery shows – not the artist Wilson. Lucian Freud, Francis Bacon, any English artist educated at an expensive boarding school was essential but Scottie Wilson was decoration. What a queer country Britain is! No wonder Wilson half-hated the art-dealing folk he needed to earn a living by sale of his work.

The travelling exhibition which has started at the Glasgow Third Eye Centre shows the widest range of Wilson's pictures. These are not for sale. The Mayor Gallery, Cork Street, exhibits work exclusively from the 1950s and is already half sold out. The Gillian Jason Gallery shows work from the 1960s too. The exhibition in the Arthouse, Lambeth, though small, is the most attractively grouped and mounted. The overall prices seem right for the works of one who is minor, but a definite, and definitely enjoyable master.

# Five
# Glasgow Artists Show*

ORGANIZER TELLS EVERYTHING. Astonishing news! Last year the British publicity machines broadcast a new and astonishing fact: four recent graduates of Glasgow Art School are making enough money from the sale of their paintings to live by painting alone. Their work was admired by a Glasgow Art School director with the enthusiasm, knowledge and contacts to promote it in New York and therefore also in London, and thus in Scotland too.

So painting in Glasgow is now news: news flowing through catalogues, television documentaries, Edinburgh literary magazines, English quality papers and the *Glasgow Herald*. Some local history is needed to explain why this news induces a mixture of anger, envy and hope in other Glasgow artists: especially in us old ones who grew up in the Dark Age between the emigration of Rennie Mackintosh in 1914 and the coming of the Glasgow Pups seventy years later.

**WHAT JACK SAID**

Recently Jack Maclean, our urban Voltaire, a Glasgow art teacher with a journalist's gift of the gab, said the arts in Glasgow reminded him of a diamante brooch on a boiler suit. He knew, of course, he was saying what most people in Glasgow, Edinburgh and England take for granted. Once they thought differently.

*1986 catalogue introduction to five retrospective shows in Glasgow McLellan Gallery, which transferred to the Talbot Rice Gallery, Edinburgh, then to the municipal art gallery of Aberdeen.

## THE GOLDEN AGE

Around 1900 Glasgow had schools of painting and design with international reputations. Like their contemporaries, the French impressionists, the artists of the Scottish middle-west were mostly from prosperous families, yet maintained themselves by their talent. Their products were imported and acclaimed by galleries in Vienna, Munich and London, yet they were respected by an informed Glasgow public before, not after they got famous abroad. Dying Whistler by-passed all the English art galleries and willed his unsold work to the Hunterian Museum because of Glasgow's reputation as a cultural capital.

## SIXTY YEARS HARD

Yet after the First World War all young Scots who showed artistic talent were told by their teachers, 'Of course, you'll never make a living by your art in Scotland', and for over sixty years this was an almost absolute truth. Talented moderns like Colquhoun and McBride emigrated. The artists who remained became dominies or hermits. The dominies painted between teaching. Some of them, like Cowie, kept their talent bright and effective but produced a fraction of their potential, while the art of the rest became stale and dated, though they dominated the art schools and the official exhibitions. The hermits shrank into eccentric seclusion. Only one of them – Joan Eardley – had a small private income, so developed as she should have done. Most hermits were poor, like Joan's friend Angus Neil, so their talents afflicted them like incurable diseases. In the late sixties a sort of artist appeared who was neither emigre, dominie or hermit, but supported his pictorial art by a share-time literary job. I say 'his' pictorial art because the only artists of this sort I know are John Byrne and me. But an informed Scottish public for modern Scottish art – or any kind of modern art – had almost vanished. Why?

**THE CATASTROPHE**

What had befallen Scottish art had befallen other industries. The industrial boom years before 1914 happened when the British Admiralty had most of its battleships built on Clydeside. The later managers of British capital decided they could save money by concentrating it in South Britain or by investing abroad, so Scottish investors lost confidence in their homeland as a place where good modern things could be originated.

This explanation is insufficient. The recent good fortune of the so-called *Glasgow Pups* shows that the widespread neglect of local Scottish art this century was not made inevitable by John Knox or Economic Necessity. An informed, imaginative promotion of it by Glasgow dealers with international connections could have maintained confidence. Before 1914 Glasgow had several dealers of that calibre who promoted modern Scottish painting at home and overseas. Such dealers as Annan and Reid were still there in 1919. Why was their work for Scottish art not resumed?

**THE CURSE OF THE BURRELL**

Because they were too busy. Sir William Burrell, ship owner, had sold his merchant shipping fleet to the Australian Government, become a multi-millionaire, retired from business, and decided to give Glasgow the biggest private art collection in Europe. He had very little interest in modern art and none in contemporary Scottish art. Scotland's best private dealers – the ones with international connections – made so much money helping Sir William to acquire foreign antiques that modern Scottish painting became one of their less profitable sidelines.

Burrell was not the only Glasgow millionaire collector, but the other (Cargill) was equally uninterested in local products. When Burrell and Cargill died after World War Two the old Scottish dealing firms had lost contact with contemporary painting at home and abroad and dwindled to insignificance. Annan's splendid gallery in Sauchiehall Street became a recruiting office. To get any attention at all Glasgow artists had to appear in self-help organisations like the Royal Glasgow Institute, the Arts Club and the Glasgow Group, which were unable to sustain a general public for themselves or start a controversy interesting enough to be important news. And this was hardly the organisations' fault. A vital idea embodied in a work of art would not have been news to our local press and broadcasters. We had become provincial, by which I mean a people who expect news and initiatives to come from elsewhere.

**A SOURER NOTE**

So when a Glasgow baillie refers to the culture of Glasgow he is probably thinking of The Burrell Collection. This splendid modern building contains tapestries, church furniture and antiques from France, Italy, Germany, Spain, Egypt, China, Japan, chiefly maintained by English art specialists, and visited by thousands of tourists from France, Italy, Germany etceteras who are able to enjoy the art of their own lands in a South Glasgow setting. If their feet get tired they visit the restaurant and sit on expensive chairs of tooled hide and polished timber bought from Denmark. Nobody recalls that between the wars Glasgow firms furnished the interiors of luxury liners and State Capitals. But Glaswegians have the consolation of knowing that, though the money which originally paid for all this was Australian, it was raised by a sale of ships built by some of their ancestors. Though nothing of Scottish make appears in it, the whole thing belongs to them through the agency of the Labour councillors most of them have elected.

It is also likely that recent wide acceptance of Charles Rennie Mackintosh as a great architect and designer have led our councillors to think of his buildings as a cultural addition to the Burrell.

**DISCLAIMER**

This monologue is not another lament for puir auld Glasgow. I believe that, even off the football pitch, Glasgow art exists, but in such broken patchy ways that most folk think it is not there at all, or mistake something else for it, or believe, with Jack MacLean, that it is the pretentious hobby of wealthy snobs. He may be right. I will stop talking historically about Glasgow art and explain how I started trying to make the stuff, and met others with the same obsession.

**PERSONAL NOTE**

I grew up in Riddrie, a corporation housing scheme in East Glasgow where the Edinburgh and Cumbernauld roads diverge. Our tenements were fronted with red sandstone, and the green at the back was all grass with no bare earthy bits. ✶✶✶✶✶✶✶✶✶✶✶✶✶✶✶✶✶✶ ✶✶✶✶✶✶✶✶✶✶✶✶✶✶✶✶✶✶✶✶✶✶✶✶✶✶✶✶✶✶ ✶✶ *Deleted here is information given in replies* ✶✶ ✶✶ *to a questionnaire starting on page 21.* ✶✶ ✶✶✶✶✶✶✶✶✶✶✶✶✶✶✶✶✶✶✶✶✶✶✶✶✶✶✶✶✶✶ ✶✶✶✶✶✶✶✶✶✶✶✶✶✶✶✶✶✶✶✶✶✶Luckily from early childhood my painting and writing had been encouraged as a hobby by parents and teachers, who also said 'Of course you'll never make a living by your art in Scotland'. But when 17 this hobby got me accepted as a student with a Welfare State bursary by –

**GLASGOW ART SCHOOL**

The money which created this school had been raised in the last century by wealthy manufacturers who needed designers for their buildings, furniture and vehicles. Since a designer's basic training requires drawing and painting they did not mind producing some professional artists too. When our Golden Age ended most students looked forward to careers in teaching. I attended art school in a boom period for potential teachers. The increased birth-rate following the war had made more teachers necessary, and the new welfare state was paying for the further education of people like me whose parents could not have afforded it. So for four or five years a lot of us were able to feel we were entering the profession of Michelangelo and Rembrandt, while knowing that after receiving our diplomas there would be none to commission work from us, no dealers to handle it, and hardly any firms who wanted our skill as designers.

It is not strange, in such circumstances, that few teachers in the art school excited their students' imaginations. There had been a fine head of the painting deaprtment in the school during the war – Colquhoun, McBride and Eardley were trained by him – but the Art School governors thought him a bad influence and got the Director to dismiss him. So our teachers painted in what was then called 'the academic tradition'. They painted as they thought Van Dyke or Corot would have painted had these great men been forced to work in Glasgow. They warned us against Post Impressionism, though one said Cezanne would have painted perfectly well if his eyesight had been repaired by decent spectacles. Students who wanted to make new, exciting art had to learn from each other. Luckily Alan Fletcher was among us.

## ALAN FLETCHER

There is no such thing as an artistic type. Artists have been henpecked husbands, Don Juans, cautious bachelors and reckless homosexuals. They have been orthodox diplomats working for catholic monarchs (Rubens), fanatical agents of revolutionary republics (David), and comfortable bourgeois Hedonists (Renoir). Alan Fletcher is the only artist I know who naturally looked like the Bohemian artist of legend. He was the free-est soul I ever met, and impressed me so mightily that a diminished version of him has been a character in all the novels I ever wrote. He had to be diminished, or he would have stolen attention from my main characters, who were versions of me. Alan was more mature than most of his contemporaries, having come to art school after serving his national military service. His father was an engineer who maintained the heating in the Grand Hotel at Charing Cross. Alan had taught himself to build up a painting in broad, simple strokes by studying the Whistlers in the Hunterian museum. From reproductions in books and magazines he absorbed essential lessons from contemporary artists like De Stael and Giacometti. He could talk easily to anyone, looked with interest on everything, but laid aside all that was not practically useful to his own vision, his own soul or self. Like a true teacher he did not move others to act or work like him, his example helped us grow more like ourselves. It is not a coincidence that his closest friends (John Glashan, Douglas Abercrombie and Carole Gibbons especially) went on to become professional artists of very different sorts.

I believe that Scottish painting, especially in the Scottish middle west, would have been a healthier, more public growth had Alan lived. Even without the machinery of art-dealing and patronage his existence as a strong creative intelligence would have drawn attention to his native city and given more courage to the rest of us. But he died.

## MORE PERSONAL NOTES

Alan and I had only one thing in common: we both loved painting, but the painting teachers did not want us in their classes. He was directed into sculpture and I into mural decoration. Neither of us minded. Alan could master any medium and I was intrigued by the thought of painting on a public scale. Like many artists since the days when most art was commissioned to decorate public buildings, I often regretted that most of my work, if sold, would become just private property. At the age of thirteen I had read *The Horse's*

*Mouth* by Joyce Cary, which made me want to paint the murals I imagined Gulley Jimson painting. It also described accurately how this would be. The greatest act of intelligent heroism I could clearly imagine was making a great art work for folk who could not like it. It would be nobler still to die in the attempt. I had no intention of dying, but readers of my first novel will notice that I was looking for the raw materials for it in my own life.

So in the autumn of 1957 I was given my Scottish Education Department Diploma of Design and Mural Decoration, and left Art School for the wilderness of the world. Though not inspiring, the staff were tolerant. They had not stopped me learning what I most wanted to do, and I was grateful.

I worked as a part-time dominie from 1958 to 1962, while painting, in a Church near Bridgeton Cross, a mural I hoped would make me famous. It didn't, but this is not a hard luck story. I stopped teaching and some plays I wrote were bought by television: not enough to support me, but enough to comfortably support half of me while the other half was supported by occasional portrait or mural jobs. I got friendly with Alasdair Taylor and John Connolly, whose addiction to painting and sculpture would have made them very lonely hermits, had they not had good wives who loved their art too. They lacked the means to exhibit it however. When I first met them Alasdair was a dustman and John an electrical engineer. I was luckier. By the sixties the private galleries which had flourished when Glasgow was an industrial and artistic force had dwindled to nothing very useful. They could be rented,

but were dear, so from 1959 to 1974 I put on at least
one exhibition a year in places which could be rented more cheaply, such as the R G I Gallery (later called the Kelly Gallery) and places which would cost me nothing: in foyers of the Cosmo Cinema and Citizen's Theatre, in Glasgow University Research Club, Strathclyde University Staff Club, and once (to coincide with my first TV play) in a colour television showroom in Cuthbertson's music shop on Cambridge Street. I also showed in the Edinburgh Traverse Theatre Gallery, which was run for a few years by Sheila Ross. At none of these shows did I sell enough to pay for the framing and publicity costs, but they proved I was an artist. When the *Herald* or *Scotsman* printed a few inches of criticism by Martin Bailie or Cordelia Oliver my heart would leap and I would think "I exist! I exist!".

And some folk bought my work. Andrew Sykes, an eccentric curmudgeon who will not bring a libel action against me for saying so, bought steadily from the time he was a mature student at Glasgow University to the time he became a Professor at Strathclyde. In 1974 Mr Steven Elson of the Collins Gallery visited Professor Sykes, saw his collection of Grays, and offered me a large retrospective show for which I did not have to pay. It went well. I sold three pictures, which was all sheer profit. And the three usual Scottish art critics were quite kind, though Emilio Coia was a little surprised that such a big show had been offered to one so unvenerable. (I was only 40).

## A GOOD RESOLUTION

But I decided never again to pay for an exhibition of my art, or display it unless someone else asked me so.

## WESTMINSTER DOES IT BEST

Now, the government in South Britain had noticed Scotland was now a depressed province. Within fifteen years it appointed three Royal Commissions to investigate the problem, but since all three had advised that Scotland be given government of its own affairs, their findings had to be ignored. So while our main industries were acquired by outside companies which pulled them out or closed them down, some organizations were created to promote activities which might help us to feel something better was happening. Various Boards were set up, and we got our very own Arts Council. And the Arts Council helped to create new galleries and art centres, so by the late seventies we had many more salaried modern art administrators than self-supporting modern artists.

The new galleries presented travelling shows of work from South Britain and also art by our own locals, though few of these left the place where they started. So I was delighted when Chris Carrell, director of Glasgow's Third Eye Centre, offered me a big new retrospective which he wished to take to other cities. So he posted advertisements for this show to other British galleries, asking if they would like to take it. Hardly any answered, and those who did said "No".

## A RESOLUTION SHATTERED

Hell hath no fury like the neglected egoist. I was now really keen on a travelling show of my work, a big one which would appear in cities with perhaps more ardent publics. Since the Third Eye could not arrange this I decided to do it for myself, but to do it successfully I needed company. Galleries which had ignored the Third Eye offer of my work might accept me if I hid among Fletcher, Gibbons, Connolly and Taylor who are a very important, but hardly ever visible, part of Scottish painting. Most art students have never heard of them.

The ploy worked, though it detached me from the Third Eye Centre which lacked the space to put on such an ambitious show in Glasgow. So my first act was to rent the greater part of the McLellan galleries for the December of 1986, and seek venues for my work elsewhere in galleries which would pay the costs of transport, hanging and publicity.

I was lucky in Edinburgh. Dr Duncan MacMillan offered the Talbot Rice Centre in Edinburgh University's Old College. So did Andrew Brown in his Cowgate 369 Gallery. Neither has space to show all our work, but in January the Talbot Rice will show Alasdair Taylor, John Connolly and me, the 369 Carole Gibbons and Alan Fletcher. In February 1987 we are recombining in the splendid municipal gallery of Aberdeen. I failed to get shows in England, but nearly got an Irish show through the friendship of Ted Hickey, curator of Belfast municipal art gallery. Something may still come of this. The show in its present form will not leave Scotland, so will be a financial loss to me, although I dearly hope, perhaps, an imaginative victory.

## ACKNOWLEDGEMENTS

The Scottish Arts Council helped us by lending us our work in their collection, and serving as a forwarding address when I advertised for information about works whose present ownership is not known. The Scottish Arts Council did not help us under their scheme of partial guarantee against loss. Their letter of refusal said this was because they 'were particularly concerned about the basic concept of the exhibition'. I do not know what that meant, apart from being a refusal, but it was certainly final. The panel also felt the rent of the McLellan Galleries was too high for it to help me.

I tried to do something about that. The gallery is owned by Glasgow District Council, so I asked for advice from one of the few Glasgow baillies who has helped the living arts as much as the antique ones. He said there were a couple of committees with the power to reduce the galleries' rent, and if I sent him some copies of an information sheet about the show he would give them to the relevant people. I did so. A few months later we met by accident and he was not surprised to hear I had had no response. Many decision makers who don't say yes to a request prefer to reply with silence, since refusals often offend. But I suspect the fault may have been mine. My information sheet was seven pages of factual detail and politicians, whether local or national, have no time for a lot of reading.*

*The friendly Glasgow Labour town councillor, Johnny Ross, was once the city's treasurer, and one of our few baillies interested in Glasgow's arts. He was the practical founder of the Tron Theatre in Glasgow's oldest kirk, if we exclude the cathedral. Two or three months after McLellan gallery show ended, through him I received a cheque for the money I had paid to rent the McLellan gallery for this exhibition.

# Of John Glashan

To the Department of German Literature,
Edinburgh University,
10 February 1986

Dear Dr Manfred Malzahn

Stephanie Wolfe-Murray tells me you would like any information I can give about John Glashan. All I can give you is gossip I have picked up about this great graphic artist whose verbal subtleties fit the eccentric character of his drawings. His father, Archie McGlashan, was a portrait painter and, I think, a Royal Scottish Acadamecian of Edinburgh, though living in Glasgow. I remember portraits of children he painted vigorously in an early 20th century realist style that would please parents, yet without the falsehood of flattery. John dropped the Mc from his second name after going to London in the late 1940s.

John attended Woodside Secondary, a non fee-paying school for the children of manual workers, tradesmen, clerks and professional folk living near Woodlands Road. This runs from Sauchiehall Street toward Glasgow University, so this district had a wide social mixture, and local children from richer families in those pre-comprehensive school days, mostly went to Hillhead Secondary or Glasgow Academy, so although John's dad was a professional artist his son, while perfectly self assured, did not feel he belonged to a superior class. In adolescence he was sometimes what in the first half of the 20th century Glasgow called a corner boy. These youths had not enough pocket-money to sit for long in cafes, so stood talking and smoking cigarettes at street corners near their homes, while also exchanging comments on the passing scene. After leaving school John, like all fit youths in those days, did two years National Service in the army. A younger Woodside School pupil saw him when home on leave, at a street corner eating chips from a paper bag. Whenever an attractive girl passed Glashan was heard to say, "Gad! A white woman!" which made his young contemporary think John was on leave from Africa.

This contemporary, Alan Fletcher, told me nearly all I am telling you about John Glashan, for they became close friends when both were students at Glasgow Art School. The age difference meant that Glashan was in his final years when Fletcher was in his first, but they influenced each other in a way that I can only explain by describing Alan Fletcher himself. He was over six feet tall with a dark complexion, thick black hair, thick eyebrows, huge arching nose, large white teeth and pointed beard – he resembled, in fact, popular notions of a devil. Without being a deliberate rebel he had no instinctive reverence for authority, so teachers and heads of department found him disturbing. But he was so remarkably talented and polite that they were afraid to become ridiculous by reprehending him. He twice repeated a year at art school, first for poor attendance (he worked hardest at night, so almost always slept late in the morning), the second time because a visiting assessor, faced by a studio of his sculpture, refused to assess it. Saying "I'm not going to say anything about this," the judge left without passing judgement. This meant Alan repeated his last year, at the end of which a new judge declared Alan's work excellent, and he was awarded a travelling scholarship – unfortunately. He travelled to Italy and in 1958 died in an accident outside the grounds of Milan youth hostel.

I have described Alan Fletcher's appearance because people in nearly all John Glashan's cartoons are partly based on Alan. The bohemians, alcoholics and geniuses of Glashan's world have John Glashan's less than average height, his eyes and his spectacles, with Alan Fletcher's nose, beard and hair. This visual hybrid stems from an intellectual amalgamation which happened at Glasgow Art School in the early 50s. Both brought that high degree of intelligence to their work which gets folk labelled geniuses. Both knew it and discovered together, or forged together, their own sort of verbal and visual irony. Glashan's wit is so like Alan Fletcher's that his cartoons give me the feeling that part of Alan is as alive, creative and funny as ever. I am prejudiced. Three of my novels have a main character based on Alan Fletcher. I first knew Alan after John left for London in 1951. Alan was a collector of discarded oddments, salvaging anything well-made, however useless, including fashion magazines of the *Vogue* and *Tatler* sort. The tall, rich, elegant looking models posturing like prostitutes in clothing adverts amused him – also Glashan who, visiting Alan, would draw additions to these in ballpoint pen. After making these additions John would scribble over it, like a cat scratching dirt over a spot where it has urinated. Alan showed me one he had with difficulty preserved. It was a double-page spread swimwear advert in which three beach beauties in bathing costumes smiled tenderly at a child holding a small pail above a sandcastle. John's additions had turned the child into an adult dwarf with a clerical collar urinating into the pail. He had not touched the women, yet their smiles had gained a wide range of ambiguous meanings.

Like most who go to London without much money John survived there with difficulty for years before his work earned him a secure living, hence his cartoons deal with the ironies of great poverty and wealth. I heard that, when forced to spend a night with friends who lacked spare beds, he could sleep on a chair without his garments next day looking very crumpled or grubby – so a calm sleeper who did not sweat much, a self-contained, phlegmatic man. In 1956 I briefly met him in Alan Fletcher's kitchen. We exchanged no words but I probably tried to impress him. When Alan referred to me on a later occasion, John said, "Alasdair Gray? That funny boy who sat by the fire saying wise things about nothing like an old Scottish shepherd?"

POSTSCRIPT

In the 1960s I taught art beside Connie Cochran, a lady with a sense of humour who had also been a friend of John and sometimes walked out with him. They would stop at a shop where John would order cigarettes, adding "...and a comic for the girl," tossing her a Beano or Dandy, strip cartoon weeklys for the under twelves. She was a head and neck taller than him.

# Of Ian Hamilton Finlay

SIR, WHEN NOT INSIDE THEIR own small mutual aid groups most British artists ignore each other. No wonder. A minority of us live by our work, so most feel miserable about it. Why enlarge our misery by envying the achievement of others or caring for their troubles? Even cheerfully comfortable artists can be envious. I took a sneaking pleasure in the news that Ian Hamilton Finlay, Scotland's only landscape poet, had lost a big commission because a clique of critics told the French Government he was a fascist. It made me feel right not to have seen or thought much about his work. Then I remembered I had three times seen a great part of his work, and had thought it beautiful and good. I want to tell your readers this, before current publicity makes me feel I am a fascist because I enjoyed the flowerbeds, pools, twining paths and sculptures of Little Sparta, Mr Finlay's home near Biggar.

Mr Finlay's garden shows that, like half the male sex, and all governments, and most folk born just before the second world war, he is fascinated by tanks,

This letter was printed by **The Times**, **Scotsman** and **Herald** 12 April 1988, in support of Finlay on withdrawal of a commission by the government of France as a memorial to the 1789 Revolution's 2nd centenary. A critic who had been keen on Finlay's work had come to feel Finlay had not acknowledged his support, so began writing that Finlay's love of weapon imagery from the Panzer tanks to nuclear submarines, plus his use twice or thrice of the Fascist lightning flash, showed he was one. In reply to this letter I got one from Finlay saying enemies were preferable to friends like me; he had read no books of mine, but that I was thought a writer of importance was added proof of how rotten Scots culture had become. He may have been right.

submarines and aeroplanes. A small lily pond holds a much smaller stone bird table shaped like an aircraft carrier, on whose flight deck finches land and feed. Other carvings recall equally threatening weapons, all ironically diminished and made into elegant, playful parts of a fine garden, itself an arrangement of small, intimate spaces. The effect is the reverse of that Great British chamber of horrors, the Imperial War Museum. No child exploring Little Sparta will feel a thrilling urge to join an army or privately attack those of another race, political party or religion.

Only one detail of Mr Finlay's work has been construed as antisemitic. A stone was carved with a double zigzag, the old Roman thunderbolt sign, which is now notorious as an SS badge. That sign was dreadful to millions the Nazis killed and wished to kill between 1933 and 45, as the crucifix was dreadful to millions crusaders, inquisitions and pogroms killed. But the cross has several meanings. By putting his double thunderbolt between two circles Mr Finlay made the Italian word for bone, clearly reminding us that the Nazis and Romans turned people into bones in horrible ways. Mr Finlay says for him the sign means the destructive force of unreasoning nature. One thing is certain. By withdrawing his commission because of the controversy this sign provoked, the French government again advertised it as the exclusive property of a vicious 20th century sect. Whoever wants to feel excitingly wicked without taking a risk can scribble two zigzags on a wall and believe they are threatening the jews, the gypsies, the homosexuals and the elected government of France.

But there is more to Mr Finlay than his art and its symbols. Like many in the public eye he is sometimes invited, sometimes goaded into public utterance. On the radio last week he said he had no faith in democratic government. Leftwingers like me will hate this lack of faith, for we believe the world's worst woes come from democracy not being practised. But Mr Finlay admires Robespierre and wants a revolutionary government of the rational French 18th century sort, with vigorous, high-principled statesmen cutting each other's heads off in the cause of freedom. No Tory can like him for that. He increasingly resembles Hugh MacDiarmid, who was expelled by the communists for his Scottish nationalism and by the nationalists for his communism, and lived so determinedly where extremes meet that the majority of easy-going middling people found him a mockery or embarrassment. Mr Finlay, like Mr MacDiarmid, lives like a hermit in an old farm building near Biggar, and has been brought to his country's attention by foreigners who think his art important and a press which cares nothing for it, but loves his fights with authority.

I believe nobody can share or greatly understand Mr Finlay's political stance. Why care for him? Because he is our finest landscape poet, and since David Harding left Glenrothes New Town, Scotland's only practising one. He knows how to make any piece of ground, whether large or small, a beautiful thought-provoking place to linger or wander in. I wish the Strathclyde Region was not trying to tax his garden as if it was a shop, office or factory, just because occasional visitors see it, admire it, and give him work.

# A Radio
# Talk on Allegory*

THERE IS NO SUCH TRAIN as that one in my play as I am sure you know. British railway carriages still have switches passengers can use to stop the train, the drivers stay in their cabins and are not equipped with guns. So why should a writer imagine such a carriage, fill it with imaginary people and contrive an ending which kills them? Many real people go on journeys by rail, ship or plane which end in unexpected and undeserved death. Why add an impossible imaginary accident to all these real ones?

The simple answer is, for fun. Most of us are pleasantly excited by disasters which don't hurt us and the people we know. We are shocked, feel sympathy, are a bit worried to find such things can happen in this world, but a nasty wee selfish bit feels, for a while, a bit more safe and superior because it has not happened to us. That is why most of the world's stories, films and plays deal with warfare, crime and the breaking up of homes and families. Those of you who read Judge Dredd comics are accustomed to tales of crime and disaster in an imaginary future twenty years from now, in a world which is a bit like ours but much, much worse. You may have heard my play as a thriller, perhaps a rather dull one because people kept talking about clocks and money and cups of coffee. If it bored you, I apologize. If you enjoyed it as a thriller, I'm glad.

∗A talk on Scottish BBC Schools Radio, following my half-hour play, **Near the Driver**.

If some of you start remembering it because you feel it is worth thinking about, then you are the listeners I most want. And I would also like you to discuss it with each other, and disagree about it, because a good play or story always means different things to different people, and the better it is the more they sometimes disagree. The best and strangest story in the world is the story of Jesus which is told in four short books in the Bible. Wars have been fought between nations who found different meanings in that story.

However, my short radio play is a lot shallower than that. I am not going to tell you what it means to me, but I'll tell you two stories which may be a clue. One is fact, the other fiction. I'll start with the factual.

Fifteen years ago a serious accident happened in the United States of America, an accident which that government – like all governments of countries with nuclear power stations – had said could never happen. A nuclear power station was found to be in a dangerous condition. A nearby town was quickly evacuated, and for two days an explosion was feared which might have destroyed the life of a whole state. The experts, however, got the thing under control. While this was happening, of course, government spokesmen throughout the world appeared on television to explain why this could never happen in their countries. The British cabinet minister responsible for atomic energy explained that the American power station was using a gas-cooled system which was far less safe than the water-cooled system we British used, so we had nothing to fear. I will not tell you this cabinet minister's name, or whether he belonged to the Labour Party or the Conservative Party because it does not matter – none of our large political parties is against nuclear energy as a source of power. So no matter who was in power, the person holding that job would have said the same, because at that moment his job was to stop people like you and me from feeling worried. A few months later the same minister announced that the British nuclear power stations were changing to a new gas-cooling system to be bought from an American corporation, because the American system was safer and cheaper.

And now I'll tell you a fantastic story which nobody will believe. It is from a book called *Gulliver's Travels*, and was printed in London two hundred and fifty years ago. Gulliver is an English seaman who is wrecked on the shore of an island peopled by men and women who are six inches high, but have a very complicated civilization. Politicians rise to power in Lilliput (as this kingdom of wee folk is called) by walking a tight-rope. If they fall off, they get the sack, because they're usually too damaged to climb on again, but the more tricks a politician can do on the tight-rope, the more powerful he gets. The prime minister, who has been in power for a very long time, can not only stand, walk and run on the tight-rope but turn complete somersaults. In 1730 readers of *Gulliver's Travels* were quite sure Lilliput was a funny but convincing picture of the Britain they lived in – that balancing on a high wire, then jumping round to face the opposite way, was very like what the politicians then ruling Britain did. Think about that. Could it still be true?

# ADDENDUM

This talk followed my last radio play broadcast by the BBC, though three earlier BBC producers had turned it down. I wrote it in 1975 and sent it to Stewart Conn, who had hitherto produced five of my plays on Scottish BBC radio. He returned it saying London would not let him produce it. Some years later, learning that Shaun McLaughlin now worked for Bristol BBC I sent it to him. He wrote back saying he would gladly broadcast it, but must first do some "wheeling and dealing" with chiefs in London. Then he wrote to say London had refused permission, and I had no chance of that play ever being broadcast. So I stopped writing radio plays. More years passed, then a new director of Scottish BBC radio plays wrote to say he greatly liked my novel *Lanark*, so wanted to commission a new radio play from me. He was English, a son of Canterbury's Archbishop, so I sent him *Near the Driver*. He heartily thanked me for it in a second letter, then sent a third saying that "the self-elected cognoscenti" of BBC London still banned it. In 1983 West Deutsches Rundfunk broadcast a German translation, *Beim Zugfiihrer*, then it was printed in the Scots literary magazine, *Chapman*. Another Scottish BBC radio producer read it there and told me she wished to broadcast it for schools. I told her, "London won't let you." She said, "But London doesn't monitor Scottish school radio broadcasts." So the play was broadcast to Scottish schools, along with my little talk in 1989, fifteen years after it was first rejected by the BBC's special branch censor in London, who thought it unfit for adult listeners.

# A Friend
# Unfairly Treated[*]

PEOPLE TRYING TO WRITE TRUE accounts (instead of entertaining stories) should first say who they are and what led them to write. I am a 55-year-old Glaswegian who trained at Glasgow Art School and afterwards worked at illustrations, mural decorations, portraits and landscapes. I liked representing familiar folk and surroundings, and my work became known to people in my native city who visited galleries, though not much known elsewhere. I subsidized my art work with part-time writing. In the spring of 1977 I was phoned by Elspeth King of Glasgow's local history museum, in the People's Palace, Glasgow Green. She asked if I would like a steady job as Glasgow's first artist-recorder. Indeed I would.

The job of artist-recorder had been invented by Elspeth, and is an example of how she solved problems thought insoluble by the People's Palace's former curators. Since the First World War our local history museum had received no funds to buy new artifacts or paintings. It was funded through Kelvingrove Gallery and Museum, which had to pay the huge price of holding and preserving the Burrell Collection, so most of Glasgow's 20th century and much of its late 19th century life was not represented. But the Government had now started a Job Creation scheme to reduce unemployment, a scheme which would pay the first three months' wages of any worthy new job an employer proposed. On a 9 o'clock to 5 basis I made portraits of modern Glaswegians (some typical, some famous) in surroundings of their own choice, and painted cityscapes of buildings and streets soon to be destroyed or transformed. In return, I had a steady income, a studio in a well-lit part of the People's Palace store, and a future for my work in a public collection.

The job also brought me companionship. The store was where Mike Donnelly, Elspeth's helper, assembled and cleaned stained-glass windows, ceramic panels, posters and documents he had salvaged from buildings scheduled for demolition. At that time a lot of Glasgow was being demolished. Elspeth sometimes gave Michael manual help with his salvage work, as none of their staff was paid to retrieve things from dirty, unsafe buildings. Neither, of course, were Mike and Elspeth, but being the only keepers of Glasgow's local culture they felt bound to do it. The things they salvaged were the core of important exhibitions, exhibitions they set up at astonishingly low cost to the rate payer, as they had done nearly all the basic handwork and headwork themselves.

The store was where some of the staff had their coffee breaks, so of course I heard about the Palace and its problems: dry rot in the main structure, and leaky panes in the winter garden conservatory. The first part was administered by Kelvingrove Museum, the second by Glasgow Parks department. These made decisions without consulting Elspeth King who did not officially exist for them. She had come to the Palace in 1974 to assist the former curator, Robert Wilkie. When he retired she had inherited his job, not his title, so was never asked to official meetings discussing the Palace's condition or future. Newspaper reports indicated that the District Council were discussing a motorway through Glasgow Green which might leave the Palace awkwardly isolated. They discussed knocking it down and putting its contents in store until a modern museum was built. One councillor suggested the Palace was in bad hands because a display of Glasgow stage comedy material showed Billy Connolly's comic welly boots. Perhaps the councillor thought Harry Lauder's comic walking-sticks were devalued by the proximity. News of these talks disturbed Elspeth King, who was told nothing directly. She felt the Palace was in danger. She and Mike Donnelly identified with it and worked to save it by increasing the value of the exhibitions and making the place popular. They succeeded. Though a small local history museum it is now the fifth best attended in Scotland after Edinburgh Castle, The Burrell, the Scottish National Museum and Kelvingrove.

In September 1977 I stopped being artist-recorder, became resident writer in Glasgow University and my regular connection with the Palace ended as suddenly as it started. I no longer worried how Elspeth and Michael were managing, as occasional visits to their museum showed they were doing well. To briefly summarize their achievements:–

In 12 years she and her small staff put on forty-one special exhibitions, mostly done through work with local communities, sports and photographic clubs.

The People's Palace won the European Museum of the Year Award in 1981, the British Museum of the Year Award in 1983, and was a main feature in seven networked television films. When Ken Currie had become one of a well publicized group of new Glasgow artists; in 1987 she commissioned from him a painted history of Scottish working life on eight panels round the inside of the People's Palace dome. This was the biggest mural commission for a Glasgow public building since the decoration of the City Chambers banqueting hall almost a century earlier. Elspeth helped make other local museums in Rutherglen Park and Provand's Lordship, but the establishment of Springburn local history museum was perhaps her biggest outside effort. The curator, Mark O'Neill, was chosen on her advice.

Her main achievement was in re-organizing the Palace's permanent exhibition. When she took over it had all the interest of a big lumber-room full of things too fascinating to throw away but which no other public places wanted: the domestic organ James Watt built, Lister's carbolic spray, a regimental snuff-box made from a ram's head. They had not been presented in a way which gave a continuous idea of Glasgow's history. By 1990 Elspeth had displays about its religious foundation, the Reformation, trading and industrial growth until recent times. She was still not an official curator, but assistant to one who had retired years before.

In the year when Glasgow became the (official) European Capital of Culture its council advertised a new job: Keeper of Glasgow's Social History, to control all Glasgow's local history museums, but especially "the very popular People's Palace." Responsible for the appointment was Mr Spalding, the new head of Glasgow's museum service. When asked if Ms King would not get the job automatically he said, "No jobs for the girls. We must be democrats and make jobs open to all." He promoted the keeper of the Springburn museum to the job. This shocked those who knew his decision was not democratic. If democracy means a popular choice, Mr Spalding and the keeper of the Burrell Collection were less well known than Elspeth. If a St. Andrews university degree and achievements are a qualification, none are better qualified.

So her supporters thought:– local writers, Socialists (real ones), Tories (Scotland still has Tories), and twenty-one Labour councillors who have been threatened with dismissal from the party if they speak to the press on the matter. Her supporters achieved nothing. After fourteen years as a curator she is now made deputy of a man she once promoted. This is because that, though a member of no party she is keen on the independent traditions of Scottish working-class life, so suspected of wanting Scottish home rule, which the Labour party leaders fear. She dislikes sale of public properties, and the Labour council leaders want to sell much of Glasgow Green near the Palace to a group*that will turn it into a commercial amusement park. Elspeth has no sense of how to promote herself. Hooray for public servants who give the public a superior class of service, and are not political careerists. Scotland is rotten with the other sort.

*This was prevented because that part of the Green was found to have been polluted by industrial waste. Elspeth's work for the Palace became impossible. She resigned, and has now served the public equally well in Dunfermline and Stirling.

# McGrotty and Ludmilla*

ONCE UPON A TIME a producer of television plays planned a series of them based upon the popular nursery tales, but in modern settings. Goldilocks and the Three Bears, for instance, became the story of an innocent young social worker who, on visiting an unemployed family of social security scroungers, hardly escapes with her life. Told of this project by my London literary agent, Francis Head, I imagined the Aladdin story with the hero a junior civil servant, wicked uncle Abanazir a senior one, and the magic lamp a secret government paper which gave whoever held it unlimited powers of blackmail. The television producer rejected the idea so I made of it a radio play which Francis sold to London BBC. Directed by Shaun McLaughlin, *McGrotty and Ludmilla, or The Harbinger Report* was broadcast on the 18th of July, 1975. I give the date to show that, though a blatant plagiarist, I did not plagiarise *Yes Minister*, the later TV comedy series with a Westminster setting.

The plot of my romance is from the Arabian Nights but I first discovered the world it shows in *But Soft – We Are Observed*, a satire on the British state written by Hilaire Belloc, illustrated by G.K. Chesterton, and first published in 1928. Like most political satire, from

* *Epilogue to a novella published in 1990, Glasgow by Dog and Bone, a small publishing house started by my friend Angel Mullane and her friends, which lasted for over 2 years, and published with this 2 books of poems, 2 crime thrillers, a recipe book, a spiritual treatise all of which I designed, and 2 joke books which I did not.*

Aristophanes' *Wasps* to Pohl and Kornbluth's *The Space Merchants*, it is set ahead of the author's time. Belloc describes Britain under the premiership of Mary Bull, leader of the Anarchist party. The Anarchists speak out for the freedom of the individual, and are the successors of the Unionists who were previously Conservatives and originally Tories. The official opposition (which speaks for social justice and equality) are the Communists, formerly the Labour party, who succeeded the Liberals who began as Whigs. The leaders of both parties unite to maintain the unearned incomes of the British investing classes, for they belong to them. The government and opposition connive to get profitable contracts for wealthy corporations while pretending in parliament to protect equal freedom and justice for everyone under the rule of law. This means big government transactions are made under a cloak of secrecy, a cloak held in place by magistrates, the police, and various spy networks. These networks, like all unions of cheats and liars, are incompetent and treacherous, but hurt their victims more than their employers.

The hero of the book is a guileless young man and new to London. The secret intelligence agencies (one of them American) mistake him for the emissary of an eastern oil-bearing country, a place whose bandit chiefs will be recognised as a government by other governments as soon as they sell their mineral rights to western corporations. The perplexed hero is swiftly brought to palatial offices and homes where he meets the chief manipulators of British finance, news and politics. Unlike Mungo McGrotty he never understands his false position well enough to exploit it. His ignorance is mistaken for cunning. To stop him dealing with other people he is sent to jail for resisting police harassment, and only released when the real emissary arrives in Britain: a devious Asiatic broker who talks in terms the British chiefs understand perfectly.

When I read this novel in the fifties I thought it a funny but out-of-date caricature of an obsolete system. In the late forties the British Labour party, without violent revolution or dictatorship, had established (I believed) a working alternative to monopoly capitalism. Most education and health care, all broadcasting, most transport, fuel, power and a lot of housing were funded and owned by our local and national governments, who were supposed to prefer the good of all to the profits of some. The British Commonwealth (wealth held in common) was larger, than it had been since the privatisation of the common lands in the eighteenth and early nineteenth century. The nineteen fifties was a time of full employment, when many of the rich whined publicly about how poor they were. Evelyn Waugh, comparing life in those days with his golden memories or pre-war Britain, said he felt he was living "in an occupied country" – a catch phrase which then meant a country conquered by outsiders. I thought great riches and poverty abolished in Britain: that no important politicians had secrets worth hiding: that most secret agents were inventions of fiction writers. I thought Britain an unusually decent country. I did not know that Britain was in a temporary state of reaction to the huge indecency of the Second World War and that of the Depression which led to it.

National and local British governments have since connived to sell our Commonwealth to private speculators for the profits they will make from them. Our national health and education services have become shabby beggars pleading for alms. Our district councils are no longer funded by a Victorian rates system which taxed richer properties more highly: we have a Hanoverian poll tax to which rich and poor pay the same. At each phase of the Commonwealth sell-off Labour leaders have silenced, or rejected as extremist, those supporters who want public reacquisition put on the party's programme in terms which would discourage shareholders. These leaders explain that it can only come to power with the help of people the Tory policies have made richer, so the more right-wing the Tory party has become, the more right-wing the Labour party has become. On every major issue which divided the two main British parties (nuclear disarmament, entry into Europe, self-rule for Scotland) the Labour and Tory leaders have been on the same side. The only political fun has been public scandals over our Ministry of Spies. Since the Burgess and Maclean scandal subsequent revelations show that British espionage is larger, richer, more active and incompetent, and in our government's opinion, more essential to it – not because the government has important secrets to hide from foreign enemies, but because they prevent most British people learning and discussing decisions made, things done for (we are told) our own defence and security.

Orwell's *1984* made horrid fun of life under any modern dictatorship by caricaturing Britain during the

wartime coalition. In *But Soft – We Are Observed*
Belloc caricatured Britain as it usually is: a plutocracy pretending to be a democracy by manipulating a two party parliament which offers voters little to choose between but styles of rhetoric. Indeed, it now looks more like a sober portrait than a caricature. My novella is certainly a caricature, though it caricatures nothing but the ability of the British rich to enlist in their ranks awkward, useful or threatening outsiders.

In February 1987, the stage version of McGrotty and Ludmilla was produced by Michael Boyd at the Tron Theatre, Glasgow, with this cast:

Mungo McGrotty .... ................. Kevin McMonigle
Arthur Shots ................................. Russell Hunter
Ludmilla ....................................... Julia St. John
Miss Panther, Miss Bee, Mary Fox .. Vivienne Dixon
The Minister ................................. Sandy Neilson
Aubrey Rose, American artist ........ Bill Murdoch
Charlie Gold, Harbinger ............... Sean Scanlon

Peter Ling designed the set and the production suggested details for this book. Arthur Shots' global cocktail cabinet, McGrotty's bottle of booze brought to the wrong kind of party, Ludmilla's riding habit and sexual employment of drugs were devised by one of those named above, or by some in conjunction. And McGrotty's face on the front jacket is copied from Kevin McMonigle in the part.

In Chapter 32 the distortion of Lord Acton's axiom on power is taken from Pohl and Kornbluth's fine novel *The Space Merchants*.

To furnish Chapter 33 I stole a Dutch landscape with cows from *Little Dorrit*. My heavy villain's lapse into blank verse when deeply excited is from Thackeray's *The Rose and The Ring*. So (I suspect) is my assumption that most very powerful people, like all the rest of us, are moved by the appetites of greedy adolescents, but do more damage with them.

I will look kindly upon the advances of producers who think McGrotty and Ludmilla would make a good television film, but the advances should be made through my present London agent, Xandra Hardie.*Francis Head died of lung cancer in 1978. She smoked a lot. I wish she had not died, but cannot wish she had smoked less. I found her helpful, tolerant, and enjoyable company. Self imposed abstinence might have soured some of that. Goodbye.

* Xandra Hardie stopped being a literary agent for me or anyone else in 2004, in order to write **Bertie, May & Mrs Fish**, which she published using the name Alexandra Bingley. It is a fine book about her parents which gives private insights into the English officer class, a powerful clan almost invisible to most in Britain of my class.. My literary agents in 2014 (and possibly the rest of my life) are Jenny Brown in Edinburgh, who mainly deals with my non-fiction, and Zoe Waldie of the Rogers, Coleridge and White agency in London, who mainly deals with my fiction.

# Jack Withers'
# Culture City 1990<sup>*</sup>

THESE VERSES BY JACK WITHERS crackle and spit
with anger at the present state of Glasgow, and at
the local governors who helped make it and who give
frequent signs of being pleased with themselves. I am
acting as a doorman to the book because I think he
does well to be angry. Older Glaswegians with some
knowledge of their past need no introductions, but
Glasgow is less than a fifth of the Scottish people, less
than a fiftieth of the English and Welsh. It may help *A
Real Glasgow Archipelago* to travel further east than
Baillieston, farther south than Castlemilk if I give
context to names like The Bridge to Nowhere, Lally,
McFadden, King, Donnelly; and some events during
our city's year as Culture Capital of Europe.

All life depends on cultivation so there is no such
thing as a cultureless land, but we only think a place
highly cultured when it exports things and ideas to
people outside. The high Midwest Scottish culture
began in the second half of the eighteenth century
when the Glasgow councillors paid to have their river
straightened and deepened, because the city could not
export before it became a port. Coal and iron were
mined under the fields of nearby Lanarkshire, and
James Watt conceived the separate steam condensing
chamber when working for Glasgow University. For

* *Introduction to* **A Real Glasgow Archipelago**, *poems by Jack Withers published
1993 by* **Argyll Publishing**, *Glendaruel, with woodcuts by Ian McCulloch*

nearly two hundred years Strathclyde exported ships, machines and household goods along with the scientific discoveries and examples of public enterprise which made the material exports possible. By 1859 Glasgow Council had abolished private water companies and turned Loch Katrine into a reservoir supplying water to every class of citizen – thus escaping cholera epidemics which struck other British cities. Our public transport, street-lighting, parks and libraries were emulated by cities in America.

All this had mainly been the work of Liberal businessmen, but by the early twentieth century Clydeside had the best educated skilled workforce of its size in Britain and power passed to the Independent Labour Party who sent into parliament a majority of radical socialist MPs. Their main achievement, the Wheatley Acts, is named after one of them. It allowed local authorities throughout Britain to build good-quality low-rent housing which private landlords could not provide at a profitable rate. The Labour Party has managed Glasgow from that time to this.

But it is important to remember that the Scottish founders of this party were men of truly independent mind who believed in land nationalization, Scottish Home Rule, and opposed the First World War – some had gone to jail rather than fight in it. Some had even helped organise the Clydeside rent strike which made Lloyd George introduce rent control over the whole of Britain. Of course Glasgow was not the only city where folk believed that a people's government should manage industry and finance to stop the irresponsible wealth and damaging poverty which sprouted in the

1920s and 30s. Between 1939 and 1945 Britain would have collapsed had the government not controlled rents, wages, prices and industry. Boyd Orr was made Minister of Health. When studying medicine in Glasgow University he had seen malnutrition in the slums, and had later jolted the government into giving free school milk and dinners to the children of the poor. Under his guidance the generation who grew up between 1940 and 1945 was the healthiest on record – one reason why the British had very little faith in Tory competition when the War ended, and voted in the Labour Party to maintain the full employment and health care they had enjoyed when at war.

And now I will bring us back to Glasgow here and now by getting personal. Like most middle-class offspring of working-class parents I am a creature of the Welfare State. My birth place was in Riddrie, a Glasgow housing scheme built under the Wheatley Acts, and so posh that I had a feeling of superiority to people who lived elsewhere. A postman, a nurse, printer and tobacconist lived up our close. My father worked a machine which cut the cardboard boxes in Lairds, at Bridgeton. He did unpaid work for the Scottish Youth Hostel Association and the Camping Club of Great Britain. He knew Glasgow's Deputy Town Clerk, who lived in a semi-detached nearby on the Cumbernauld Road. My mother had been a shop girl who sang in the Glasgow Orpheus Choir. Besides going to the local cinema we went to the Citizens Theatre, the D'oyly Carte Opera Company and any visiting theatre showing the plays of Bernard Shaw.

I therefore knew that Glasgow culture, industry

and art were maintained by folk like us in Riddrie. When the National Health Service gave me a course of anti-asthma injections my mother could hardly have afforded; when I discovered that through Glasgow Public Libraries I could order and read any great books I had heard of without paying a penny; when the taxpayers (of whom my father was one) paid my Art School fees and an allowance which he could not, singly, have paid – I did not take this exactly for granted. I knew these good things had been won by hard social struggle and was proud that Glasgow folk had been part of this struggle. But by 1960 the independent radicals who were part of that struggle had died out. They have not been replaced.

Since the Second World War Glasgow councillors have taken no social initiative that was not decided in London, and decided by governments they were elected to oppose. At first their job was to maintain what the liberals had achieved while enlarging the city's housing stock, and extending motorways according to government policy. Yes, Glasgow urgently needed good new housing, but private firms profited by building them and to keep profits high living space was narrowed and Glasgow put up multi-storey flats when American cities had begun knocking theirs down. To let through the new motorway several local communities and good buildings were destroyed – though Glasgow has fewer car owners per head than any city of equal size in Europe. The original plan was continually changed in ways that left many odd cul-de-sacs. The most obvious was a huge platform of concrete stilts which for twenty

years spanned the motorway south of Charing Cross –
part of a shopping mall which perhaps materialized in
a different form somewhere else.

These mistakes were natural. Glasgow Council was
so used to being goverened from London and
subsidised through Whitehall that the opinions of their
electorate (who did not want to live in tower blocks)
seemed unimportant. Especially since the same
electorate would never vote Tory. So they employed
who they thought were the best people, English
architects, planners and associates of international
corporations putting up tower blocks from Morocco to
Brazil. By the 70s the old Strathclyde industries were
subsidiaries of companies who were stripping their
assets before shifting them south. Our material exports
had shrunk to a trickle, our public welfare was dictated
from London.

Yet before the Thatcher era most Glasgow Labour
councillors probably thought themselves Socialists. No
longer. They too now believe in a world fit for financial
houses to prosper in. Shareholders can only keep up
profits by claiming new territories. Since Britain,
despite its huge armament, has now no territories it
can safely conquer outside its borders, the government
is helping the profiteers take over the public territories
within. The Glasgow Labour government has done its
best to help, and was rewarded by being declared
Culture Capital of Europe.

The best short account of how this happened is
in a novel by a friend of mine who has allowed me to
quote it with some very slight changes. It is a dialogue
between a London art dealer and Linda, an English art

administrator employed by Glasgow District Council.

"Tell me about the European Culture Capital thing," says the dealer. "Why Glasgow? How has a notoriously filthy hole become a shining light? Is it an advertising stunt?"

"Certainly, but we have something to advertise!" says Linda. "It all began when John Betjeman discovered Glasgow in the sixties and found what nobody had ever suspected. The city centre is a masterpiece of Victorian and Edwardian architecture. But in those days it was under such a thick coating of soot and grime that only the eye of a master could penetrate it. Even more off-putting were the people. In those days most Scottish imports and exports passed through Glasgow, and the good middle bit was squashed up tight against docks and warehouses and the tenements of those who worked in them. What would visitors think of London if Trafalgar Square were on the Isle of Dogs? If every day hordes of horny-handed men in filthy overalls percolated up and down Regent Street and half filled the Fleet Street pubs? But London is vast, so the classes segregate themselves easily and naturally. They couldn't do that in Glasgow so respectable Londoners passed through it in fear of their lives. It is perhaps not logical for well dressed British people to dread the working classes, but when they flagrantly outnumber us the recoil is instinctive.

"Anyway, nothing could improve Glasgow before all its old industries got taken out, but they have been. And before that happened all the people who worked in them got decanted into big housing schemes on the verge of things. So the middle of

*Glasgow is clean now and will never be filthy again! The old warehouse and markets and tenements and churches are being turned into luxury flats and shopping malls and a surprising variety of very decent foreign restaurants. Which is where we come in – I mean the English.*

*"You see Glasgow is in Scotland and from our point of view Scotland is slightly like Rhodesia in the early years of the century. Most British industry and money is in the south of England now, so it's crowded! But we English detest crowds. At heart each of us wants to be a country squire, with wide-open spaces near our house and grounds, and if possible a village atmosphere where we can relax with a few like-minded friends. But a place like that costs a fortune in England and the nearer London you go the more astronomical the fortune gets. All the nice English villages have been bought. But by selling quite a small property in London you can get enough to buy..."*

*"Yes yes yes!" says the dealer impatiently, "I know about property development in the north. I own a small tax-avoidance forest near Inverness, but where does the culture come from?"*

*"From the Thatcher government," says Linda promptly, "and from Glasgow District Council. Glasgow once had the strongest local government there was, outside London. It owned a huge public transport system, housing schemes, docklands and lots of other things Thatcher is allowing it to sell. Like local governments everywhere it is being steadily abolished, but since the people's elected representatives usually draw salaries until they die and get all sorts of perks*

they don't complain. Maybe they don't notice! However, they want to show they can do more than just sell public property to private speculators, so they have gone in for culture with a capital C – and tourism. Commercially speaking culture and tourism are the same.

"The European Culture Capital notion was started by Melian Mercouri, the Greek minister for arts. Athens had been stone-cleaned, she wanted the tourists to know it, she suggested to Brussels that Athens be the first culture capital, then other countries could have a shot. Nobody objected. Italy chose Florence; the Netherlands, Amsterdam; Germany, Berlin; France predictably chose Paris. But being culture capital is expensive. You must first advertise yourself. Put on extra shows and concerts. Invite foreign guests. Stage boring receptions. Margaret Thatcher isn't keen on all that crap; anyway London has enough of it. Like a sensible monetarist she put the job up for grabs and offered it to the lowest bidder. Bath and Edinburgh put in for it, Cardiff, Birmingham and Glasgow. But only Glasgow gave a quiet little promise that if it got the job it would not ask the central government for cash. So Glasgow, which the Labour Party had ruled over for half a century, was given the job by the Tory arts minister who announced that Glasgow had set an example of independent action which should be followed by every local authority in the United Kingdom. We're funding the enterprise out of the rates and public property sales and sponsorship from banks, oil companies, building societies and whatever we can screw out of Europe.

"And Glasgow deserves the job! It's the

*headquarters of Scottish Opera, Scottish Ballet, Scottish National Orchestra, the Burrell Collection, the Citizens Theatre, the Third Eye Centre, and an international drama festival – all of them directed and mostly administered by the English, of course. Sometimes the natives get a bit bolshie about that but I'm very firm with them. I say quietly 'Listen! You Scots have been exporting your own people to England and everywhere else for centuries, and nobody has complained much about you! Why start howling just because we're giving you a taste of your own medicine?' They can't think of an answer to that one."*

*"But surely the natives have some local culture of their own?"*

Glasgow indeed had a culture of its own and a local history museum, the People's Palace on Glasgow Green, which was devoted to it. In charge were two very knowledgeable people, Elspeth King and her assistant Michael Donnelly.✶✶✶✶✶✶✶✶✶✶✶✶✶✶✶ ✶✶✶✶✶✶✶✶✶✶✶✶✶✶✶✶✶✶✶✶✶✶✶✶✶✶✶✶✶✶ ✶✶     *Information deleted here is in*     ✶✶ ✶✶ **A Friend Unfairly Treated** *starting page 236* ✶✶ ✶✶✶✶✶✶✶✶✶✶✶✶✶✶✶✶✶✶✶✶✶✶✶✶✶✶✶✶✶✶ ✶✶✶✶✶✶✶✶ And now I will talk personally again.

In 1988 I, Tom Leonard and Philip Hobsbaum were invited to meet the organiser of an exhibition planned for the Glasgow Culture Capital year. Alison Miyauchi was a friendly, intelligent Japanese Canadian who told us that Glasgow, despite the splendid renovations, still had the remains of a bad reputation, and the exhibition was intended to counteract this. It would be financed by Glasgow District Council and be called The Words and the Stones because Glasgow contained so many beautiful buildings and fine writers. Being a stranger to the city she would value our advice. Alas, we had none to give her. I said that Glasgow's best civic architecture this century had been good pre-war housing schemes built as a result of the Wheatley Acts. How could the District Council celebrate its achievement as a public landlord while selling its best housing stock to private buyers? Tom Leonard said that what outsiders thought of Glasgow was their problem not his. So we had nothing to do with the schedule for the exhibition which appeared some months later. It announced that Glasgow culture would be shown in five historical phases: 1) the Romans to the Norman Conquest 2) the Middle Ages – the Cathedral City 3) the 18th century enlightenment 4) Victorian enterprise 5) the future.

Since the Normans got no foothold in Scotland by conquest the schedule was obviously the work of foreigners, and they clearly wished to celebrate a history quite free of nasty strife. Archbishop Turnbull, who founded the University, might be celebrated, but not Archbishop Wishart, who was William Wallace's chancellor in the Scottish War of Independence. The Reformation (when Catholics killed Protestants, Episcopalians killed Presbyterians and Catholics, Presbyterians killed Catholics and Episcopalians) would be omitted, with the fact that all three sects had at different times defied the London government. The mercantile Glasgow of Adam Smith and the tobacco lords would be shown, but nothing of Glasgow's gains from the slave trade. Glasgow shipbuilding would be lauded, but not the great municipal achievements which had been or were about to be privatised, and certainly not the struggles of the political radicals who had put the Glasgow Labour Party in power – the party using the Glasgow people's money to fund this show.

In 1980 the show opened in the vaults under Glasgow Central Station. To stop *The Words and the Stones* being shortened to the acronym TWATS the show was renamed *Glasgow's Glasgow*. Though intended to pay for itself by the sale of entrance tickets, the District Council have since admitted that it lost £6,000,000. Nor is it strange that a transatlantic lady with an English assistant had been put in charge. The show, like the Culture Capital year itself, was not meant to send Glasgow goods and examples outward, but designed to pull foreigners and their money in. And surely foreigners must know what they want in Scotland better than the natives! During the Year of Culture three other public scandals showed the local government's contempt for local achievement. The leader of the Glasgow Labour Party and head of the District Council, Mr Patrick Lally, was involved in every one. The deputy leader, Jean McFadden, supported him.

Scandal One. The Elspeth King Affair. The District Council advertised for a new head for the Glasgow People's Palace. Elspeth King, who had done the job splendidly for twelve years, was told she might apply for it. But it went to a young Irishman she had herself employed two years earlier. She was now his assistant, and to give him a larger office in the same building (for the People's Palace is not a huge museum) the Glasgow eighteenth century gallery was dismantled. Some Glasgow Labour councillors thought this a scandal, opposed it in the City Chambers, and informed the press. Mr Lally announced that Labour councillors would be dismissed if they talked about such things in public – only the official party spokesman could do that. Michael Donnelly denounced the administration's action in a *Glasgow Herald* article and was sacked for it. Elspeth King resigned soon after. (The attendance at the People's Palace has since shrunk to nearly half its former size).

Scandal Two. The Glasgow Green Affair. While the newspapers were still intensely debating Scandal One, Mr Lally announced plans to sell off a great part of Glasgow Green near the People's Palace to a set of financiers who would cover it with expensive hotels, restaurants and a commercial pleasure park. (Plans to sell off Glasgow's oldest, biggest and most central park go back to the nineteenth century when a seam of coal was discovered underneath. Public opposition prevented it. In the 1970s and 80s a ring road extension was planned which would have isolated the park and the People's Palace. Public protest has again halted the Glasgow Green sell-off, but not parts of Bellahouston and Kelvingrove Park.)

Scandal Three. The International Concert Hall Affair. Mr Lally was chairman of the board which gave Glasgow a grand new concert hall. Strathclyde Regional Council offered to pay for its furnishings and a mural decoration for the foyer. Artists were invited to submit designs and a jury of architects, painters and academics from Edinburgh, besides Glasgow, chose

Ian McCulloch, who painted it. At a public banquet
celebrating the completion of the hall in the final month of the Culture Capital Year, Mr Lally announced that the mural would be taken down twelve months later. Members of the Strathclyde Regional Council, the jury and Ian McCulloch were all present – only McCulloch walked out in disgust. Later some of the rest made complaining sounds. (Lally got his way. The mural is now crowded into a small vestibule of the Tramway Theatre where it cannot be seen from a distance and where the damp air of a building about to be renovated endangers it.)

Such insults to local artists and historians are worth mentioning as part of much greater insults to the unemployed, poorly paid and badly housed – folk who, if they vote for anyone, vote Labour, but who the Labour party merely pretends to serve. Mr Lally denied that the millions spent or lost on the Culture Year could have been used to make damp proof the public housing in the schemes whose owners will never be able to buy it. The reasons for this are too complicated to give in detail and may be summarized thus. Governments, local and national, must first help the prosperous before they know what is left for the poor, which is why the Labour Council after deploring the Poll Tax worked so hard to collect it.

Yet 1990 and 91 showed that the Labour Party was not quite a sodden firework. In defiance of their councillors and MPs, the branch meetings of Scotland and England set up a resistance which stopped the Poll Tax working; forced a change of law which will make big property owners pay higher taxes than the small.

Tommy Sheridan, one of the leaders of this resistance, got jailed for it and has since been elected to the District Council.\* He is currently addressing meetings to oppose the sale of Glasgow's greatest municipal achievement – the waterworks and Loch Katrine which supplies them – to private profiteers. Glasgow District Council has forbidden him the use of schools as meeting places as he may again persuade people to break what is not yet, but may become, a law. This is why Jack Withers does well to be angry.

✳ *Tommy Sheridan's career as a politician ended in 2006 after he unwisely hob-knobbed with a friendly* **News of the World** *journalist, leading to stories about his private life which, however true, are thought irrelevant to the politcs of statesmen in nearly every other nation than the United Kingdom, where broadcasters publicize all unfaithfulness to a puritan code of honour if it is sexual, not financial.*

# Something Leather[*]

A FEW YEARS AGO I NOTICED MY stories described men who found life a task they never doubted until an unexpected collision opened their eyes and changed their habits. The collision was usually with a woman, involved swallowing alcohol or worse, and happened in the valley of the shadow of death. I had made novels and stories believing each an adventurous new world. I now saw the same pattern in them all — the longest novel used it thrice. Having discovered how my talent worked it was almost certainly defunct. Imagination will not employ whom it cannot surprise.

I told folk I had no more ideas for stories and did not expect them. I said it to Kathy Acker. Kathy, pointing out a new way, asked if I had thought of writing a story about a woman. I said no, that was impossible because I could not imagine how a woman felt when she was alone. Such announcements were truthful but not honest. I hoped my talent was only as dead as Finnegan, and would leap from the coffin and dance a new jig if the wake got loud enough. Meanwhile I arranged a show of paintings, began a collection of English vernacular prologues, turned old work into film scripts and came to owe the Clydesdale Bank a sum oscillating between a few

---

**\*** *Headed* **Critic-Fuel – An Epilogue** *ended the novel, issued by Jonathan Cape, London 1990. This epilogue uniquely gives a new fictional conclusion.*

hundred and a few thousand pounds. This was not poverty. Most professional folk live in debt nowadays. Banks and building societies encourage it because debts make them richer. My state only depressed me because my parents had been working class folk who, though not religious, avoided debt like the devil. I too could have avoided it by renting a smaller flat, using public transport instead of taxis, eating at home instead of restaurants, drinking alcohol four or five times a year instead of nearly every day. Alas, I felt nostalgia but no desire for the decent carefulness which had bred and educated me. I wanted to be a middle-class waster, but a solvent one.

In Queen Street station one morning I glimpsed a girl stepping jauntily through the crowd in high heels and a leather suit which fitted her so snugly in some places, left her so naked in others that it seemed a preliminary to lovemaking. Soon after or soon before I began imagining how a woman might feel when alone. This came from accompanying a friend on a shopping expedition. Some women – even women who know what looks best on them – enjoy a man's company when buying clothes, though the man stops being a distinct character to them. He becomes an audience, or rather, a small part of a vaster, more satisfying audience in their heads. I penetrated What Every Woman Wants, The House of Fraser, and Chelsea Girl with the guilty reverence I would feel in a mosque, catholic chapel or synagogue, yet the odour was familiar and friendly. I had sniffed it as a small boy in my mother's wardrobe. I was fascinated by women pondering sombre or vivid or subtly pale colours,

fingering husky or frail or soft or sleek fabrics, holding
loosely or crisply or tightly tailored second skins to
their bodies. I felt a long slow sexual ache in these
shops, a sad ache because no earthly coitus could
satisfy all the desires and possibilities suggested by the
many garments. The ache, of course, was mine, but I
was sure many women felt it too and perhaps felt it
stronger. Most women have fewer devices than men to
divert them from affection. I imagined a woman whose
world was full of that ache, whose life was years of
ordinary frustrations patiently endured before a chance
suggestion led her further and further away from the
familiar things she normally clung to. The woman need
not have been beautiful or her adventure perverse, but
these notions brought my imagination to life again.
While writing the first chapter of this book I enjoyed a
prolonged, cold-blooded sexual thrill of a sort
common among some writers and all lizards.

At that time I thought *One for the Album* (then
called *Something Leather*) a short story. On completing
it I imagined more adventures for June, but the first
episode had internal order and was a thriller of *The Pit
and the Pendulum* sort, ending when the reader was
likely to be most intrigued. Believing it could be
popular I sent it to a famous London literary agency,
suggesting they try selling it to an expensive glossy
magazine with a transatlantic circulation: *Vogue* or
*Esquire* or better still the *New Yorker*. After a few weeks
I learned it had been sent to a couple of British literary
magazines whose editors, though friendly
acquaintances of mine, had not embraced it with cries
of "yes please".

In 1987 Tom Maschler, the Chairman of Jonathan Cape Ltd, asked if I had started writing fiction again, a question he had asked annually since 1985. I sent him the new story. He liked it, thought it could be the first chapter of a novel, offered money in advance. We haggled. I obtained enough to live without debt for a couple of years while still eating and drinking too much. Only the need to write an unforeseen novel now depressed me. The further adventures I had imagined for June were too few to be a novel. I will describe these adventures, then how the novel I got written in a way which cut most of them out.

First came the orgy with Senga and Donalda (I had not yet thought of Harry) which changed June's looks and left her nothing to wear but dark glasses, high-heeled shoes and the suit I had glimpsed on the girl in Queen Street station. The wicked thrill of imagining a modest, conventional woman forced to dress like that was followed by speculations on how it might change her behaviour. For the better, I thought, if she had health and vitality. Self-conscious conventionality is bred from vanity and cowardice. It assumes everyone may be watching us closely and must be given no strong reason for finding us attractive or repulsive. I thought of June as very lonely because she has cultivated reticence to compensate for her beauty. She evades or retreats from nearly everything she dislikes, never opposing or changing it. Conventional cowardice has imprisoned her intelligence, so the discovery that her mere appearance disturbs conventional, timid and stupid people feels like release. Stepping jauntily through the streets in her defiantly sexual suit she enjoys a freedom which is far more than sexual. Next day, instead of brooding over Senga and what will happen when they meet at the end of the week, June returns to work as if nothing had happened. Her office job prevents loneliness and earns money, but today she approaches it with a mischievous interest in how her work-mates will cope with her.

She is legal adviser in a government office created to help poorly paid folk who have been badly treated by other government offices. Efficiently run it would trouble several high-ranking public servants. If run by a clever ambitious Senior Executive Officer it would trouble them often. They have given the post to Mr Geikie who never expected to rise so high. Toward colleagues and superiors he feels sensations of inferiority mingled with adoration. If they smile and call him by his first name he feels perfectly safe. He is sure he can best serve the public by giving such people no trouble at all. When June joined his office he told her in a worried, preoccupied voice, "Our main job is to defuse potentially painful confrontations by arranging alternative procedures. This is not easy. It cannot always be done quickly."

She discovers he deals with troublesome cases by post-poning decisions until the applicant's legal aid fees expire, after which most of them have lost hope and accept a very small sum in compensation. If applicants have a generous lawyer who sticks by them and complains more vigorously Mr Geikie frankly admits that the fault is his, says the delay has been intolerable but cannot be helped: his office is understaffed. When June started there she worked with Mr Geikie and three clerical assistants. The clerical staff are now twice as many, their typewriters have been replaced by word processors and their title changed to Administrative Assistants. The office has also been joined by two Higher Executive Officers who have nearly learned Mr Geikie's methods, but if one looks like bringing a troublesome case to a conclusion it is given to the other with instructions to tackle it differently. The office hums with activity and Mr Geikie can still complain he is understaffed. His superiors have now such confidence in him that his office will soon become a Department with himself the Principal of it. He will also have a greatly enlarged staff and one of his underlings promoted to Senior Officer and Deputy Assistant. He will obviously promote the most anxious and servile of his underlings, the one most like himself. June has never seemed servile, never said what she does not believe. She has avoided giving offence by being silent. Before returning to the office this morning she is trusted but not much liked by her workmates. She deliberately arrives ten minutes late, takes off coat and hat in the lift going up, carries them across the large room where the Administrative Assistants are working. She conveys who she is by saying "Good morning!" in the bright curt voice she always uses. They usually reply, but not today. She enters her room and shuts the silent starers out.

This room feels as good and friendly as a workplace ought to feel after a strenuous holiday. Here are things she can tackle, routines to help her do it efficiently. She settles at the desk to which Mr Geikie sends all cases too small to worry him, cases of official tyranny she can correct or compensate for. Through the intercom she first tells the other Executive Officers that she has returned and is now perfectly well, then she studies her desk diary and the contents of the in-tray, then dictates letters into her recorder. An hour later she calls in her Personal Administrative Assistant (or secretary) and explains how she wants the letters handled. She ignores the girl's fascinated stare by sitting sideways to it, until Jack Bleloch bursts in and says, "Excuse me for bursting in June but could you tell me if – "

He then gapes, mouths silently for four seconds, mutters an apology and leaves without closing the door. As the secretary shuts it June asks in a thoughtful voice, "Do you think he prefers me in the charcoal grey skirt and sweater?"

The secretary sits down, giggling heartily. June joins her in this. The secretary, who is last to stop, says, "Did you meet someone?"

This is a daring question. June has never spoken about her private life before, though all the office know she is divorced. After a thoughtful silence June says slowly, "I did, yes. But it may not be important."

"Not important?" whispers the secretary, staring.

"Don't judge by appearances," says June, then they both laugh loud and long, the secretary so uncontrollably that June eventually gestures her to leave. Shortly after this Tannahill jauntily enters, stares hard at her and at last says slowly, "My god! No wonder Bleloch is shitting himself. I really like this new style of yours – I've got a hard-on just looking at you. When are you and me going to have our weekend together?"

June gets up, opens the door and says in a voice almost loud enough to be heard by the clerical staff outside, "Jim Tannahill, you must feel very witty and manly and daring when you say things like that or you wouldn't keep calling in and saying them so often, but I find them boring and disgusting. I should have told you that years ago. I know you haven't enough work to fill your day but I'm luckier in that respect. Clear out of here and come back when you've something useful to say, but not before next week, or the week after."

He goes out past her like a sleep-walker. For the rest of the morning the Administrative Assistants (all women) seem larger and noisier than usual, often erupting in untypical laughter. The other Executive Officers (all men) seem rodent-like and furtive.

Ten minutes before lunchtime the Senior Executive Officer says over the intercom, "May I see you for a moment em June please?"
She goes to his room.

He sits staring hard at a sheaf of typed pages on the desk before him. June sits opposite, takes a cigarette packet from her breast pocket, asks, "May I smoke?" "Oh yes oh yes," he murmurs, pushes an ashtray toward her, stares out of the window for a while and then stares back at the sheaf. These shifts let him see June briefly from left to right and later from right to left. He blushes at the first glance, starts sweating at the second, eventually says to the sheaf of papers, "I'm em very glad you've recovered from your trouble Miss em June I mean."
"Thank you Mr Geikie."

"Are you sure you have recovered? I overwork you shamefully and em you are perhaps too em em con con conscientious."

"Quite sure Mr Geikie."

"But! – " he looks up for a second " – There is a change in your appearance Miss em em June I mean."

"I have been shaved bald for medical reasons but that will not affect my work," says June briskly and without forethought. This is the first lie she has deliberately told. She is surprised how easily it comes.

"Alopecia?" murmurs Mr Geikie, taking another peep.

"I refuse to discuss it," says June serenely.

"But there are other changes in your appearance Miss em June I mean."

She realizes he keeps calling her Miss because she is giving him the sensations of a very small boy with a mature schoolmistress. She draws thoughtfully on her cigarette, tips ash into the tray and says, "If I dressed as usual with a head like this Mr Geikie I would look pathetic – pitiable. This way every bit of me looks deliberate. You don't think I look pitiable, do you Mr Geikie?"

"No but surely a wig, perhaps?"

"I hate wigs. I hate all kinds of falsehood," declares June, so amused by how easily she lies that to prevent a wide grin she compresses the corners of her mouth, producing a smile which probably seems scornful. He cringes before it. Then rallies, straightens his back, places clasped hands on sheaf of paper, clears throat, gazes half an inch to the right of June's head and says, "However! The image our office (which will soon be a Department), the image our office presents to the general public is not consistent with your em new and em disturbing aspect."

"Our office presents no image to the general public, Mr Geikie," says June firmly, "Our clothes and hairstyles are as unknown to the people we deal with as our faces and personal characters. The public contacts us through lawyers who contact us by letter and occasional phone calls. And since we work in a commercial office block forty-five miles from Saint Andrew's House not even our civil service colleagues know or give a damn for my appearance."

"True Miss em June I mean but! Suppose!" says Geikie so eagerly that he now looks straight at her face, "Just suppose! As might one day happen! I fall ill and you have to represent our office before an arbitration tribunal! Or at an interdepartmental function! It might even be a Royal Function! Holyrood Palace!"

"I never knew you were considering me for promotion Mr Geikie!" says June, opening her eyes wide.

The idea is new to him also. He gets up, walks to the window, looks out, turns and says mildly, "Nothing definite has been decided, M ... June. Many things are still possible, I trust?"

His face shows unusual vitality – his imagination has started working. June feels inclined to pat him on the head but shakes her own head, smiles and says, "You're a wicked man Mr Geikie. You're toying with me. How can you think of promoting me when you have Bleloch and Tannahill to depend on?"

"I am not toying with you! I never toy. Surely you've noticed, June, that you do all the work which justifies the existence of this place? I and Bleloch and Tannahill do nothing but defuse potentially explosive confrontations. The fact is that Her Majesty's Government is cutting back the social services so vigorously that it is detaching itself from a big class of people it is supposed to govern. All I and Bleloch and Tannahill do is erect facades to the fact. I'm not proud of myself."

June stares at him in wonder. She knows the truth of what he says but did not know he knew it.

He sits down behind his desk again looking as ordinary and dejected as he usually does but watching her wistfully sideways. She knows he has always thought her dazzling. He sometimes starts conversations aimed at asking her out for a meal, managing them so circumspectly that she easily changes the subject before he reaches it. He is the kind of married man who jokes about how much his wife dominates him. June decides she can do him good without granting sexual favours. She says carefully, "You are a stronger man in a stronger position than you've noticed, Mr Geikie. May I call you David?"
"You know that option has always been open to you em June."
"An office is not the best place to discuss office politics. Can we meet for a meal tomorrow night in the Grosvenor Steakhouse? Nobody we know will see us there. I'll wear a turban, David, and dress so conventionally nobody will notice me at all."

He pays her a predictable compliment.

So when June returns home from work she has more to think about than Senga. (Remember there is no Harry in this development of the story.) On the following night she starts persuading Mr Geikie that he will be in no social or financial danger if he prefers the public good to the comfort of his colleagues and superiors. When they bid each other goodbye with a handshake she knows the post of Deputy Principal will be hers.

On Friday Senga phones June and asks, "Do you still hate me?"

"No."

"And you'll meet me? Not just to get your things back?"

"Oh yes."

Senga tells June to go that evening to a street where a car will collect her. June says firmly, "No, I want to meet you without your little friend."

She tells Senga to meet her instead in the lounge of a hotel, then goes to the hotel with a suitcase and books a room. She spends an hour or two in it making herself as beautiful as possible. She puts on a little black dress she perhaps bought that afternoon. It distresses Senga, who comes to her in the lounge saying sadly, "Why aren't you wearing it?" "Do you mean the suit? My work suit? I felt like wearing something romantic tonight."

"Work suit?"

"Yes. I wear it to the office to frighten the men."

"You've changed!"

"Yes, you changed me and I'm glad – I'm grateful. Why are you looking so worried?"

"Mibby I've changed you too much. I was always scared of you, June, you were so lovely. And now I'm terrified."

Senga is trembling. June says kindly, "I've booked a room upstairs – let's go there."

They go to the room, kiss, undress and make
love nervously at first, then relax into gently exploring caresses which they prolong with variations for three or four hours.

"We don't need to be cruel to each other, do we?" asks June at one point and Senga says, "Not when it's just you and me now, like this. We're just starting together so we're fresh and equal. But sooner or later one of us will be up and the other down because nobody in love ever stays equal, and I'm the one who will be down this time because all my days I've managed to keep up and I'm so tired. I'll be forty next week. Oh I love you."

She weeps and June, who has never been happier, cuddles and comforts her, says they will love each other always and equally no matter what happens, and while she says so truly believes it.

And that was all I could imagine happening between June and Senga, but I easily imagined June and Mr Geikie three months later.

They are in Edinburgh, attending sessions of a tribunal arbitrating on the first case brought before it by Mr Geikie's new department. It concerns an honest, hard-working woman who loses her ability to earn money. Her hands get scalded in a restaurant whose owner has not provided the protective gloves required by health regulations. Her schooling has told her nothing about health regulations or employers' responsibilities so years pass before she is told she should have claimed compensation; meanwhile she loses her home, her four young children and most of her sanity with the assistance of officials paid to help her keep them. June has drawn up a detailed history of the case, given a précis of it to the judges and would gladly give further details if asked, but the tribunal finds her Principal's statement of the case satisfactory. "Cutbacks in social welfare funding are no excuse for incompetence!" he concludes, "The main cause of this tragedy is a sinister absence of contact between the five offices dealing with the case, contact which could have been made at any time by the simple expedient of lifting a telephone. These offices – and the officials staffing them – work hard and long at the grass roots level of their departmental em em em remit. It would be invidious to single out for blame the names of particular individuals. But my esteemed colleagues the departmental chiefs – and some of our more highly esteemed superiors – cannot hold themselves aloof from some measure of responsibility. My department can only work by drawing such facts to their attention. May they attend to them!"

"Well done," says June as they leave the building, though she wishes he had mentioned some individuals by name.

"Yes!" says Geikie. "I was astonished to hear myself lashing out so vigorously in every direction. Yet in the men's washroom only five minutes later Macgregor of Industrial Injuries smiled and nodded to me as if I had left him quite unscathed! What a remarkable man he is. I say June, can I buy you a meal tonight to celebrate? I'll take you to my club. I'm a member of a very posh Edinburgh club. I was astonished that they let me join."

They are staying at the Sheraton Hotel and arrange to meet beforehand in the foyer. Since June's

promotion she has not worn the leather suit but keeps
it near her as a talisman. Feeling mischievous tonight she puts it on, and as her hair is again a conventional length has it shaved off by the hotel barber. On meeting her in the foyer Geikie says, "Oh dear I doubt if they'll let us into my club with you looking like that." She takes his arm saying, "Nonsense Dave. Women can look how they like and you're respectable enough for both of us."

The club is five minutes walk away on Princes Street. Fewer passers-by stare and pass comments than would happen in Glasgow, but enough of them to stimulate Geikie's adrenal glands. His spine straightens. His face takes on a look of stoical endurance. His noble bearing and her careless one carry them past the doorman, the cloakroom attendants and up a stair to the dining room. Through large windows they see the lit mansions and battlements of the castle standing high in the air between black sky and black rock. At a corner table sit two businessmen with a lawyer who attended the tribunal that day and a Scottish politician who was once a cabinet minister and famous for interesting but unwise press announcements. The first three exchange nods with Geikie. The fourth turns completely round and gazes at June who deliberately sits with her back to him. She and Geikie consult menus.

Then Geikie murmurs, "Oh here comes Lucy."
"Lucy?"
"Short for Lucifer – that's what he likes to be called."
"Excuse me for butting in unasked and unannounced," says the politician pulling a chair to their table, aiming

to sit on it and almost missing.

"Oopsadaisy David! David you MUST introduce me to your charming companion, even though she is staring at me as if I'm a kind of insect. And she should, because I AM a kind of insect. Looper T. Firefly, exiled President of Freedonia at your service Ma'am."

He blows her a kiss.

"June Tain my Deputy Principal," says Geikie coldly.

"God's boots Geikie! You are kicking out in EVERY direction these days. I hear you've actually brought a case to arbitration! Remarkable. BUT! The name of Geikie will enter the history of our race through your courage in promoting to senior rank a lady who has destroyed the STUPID old fuddy-duddy notion that our civil service is staffed by desiccated spinsters of BOTH sexes who dress to show they are dedicated, desiccated spinsters. Too few people have realized that a dozen years ago a new age dawned for Britain, HEIL MARGARET! She has given Britain back its testicles by turning government offices and free enterprises into businesses run by the same people. Highly profitable. And now every man with money and initiative can enjoy his woman and his bottle and his woman and his tax-avoidance scam and his woman and his special boyfriend (AIDS permitting) without having his fun spoiled by hypocritical spoil-sport neighbours and a ghastly spook called PUBLIC OPINION. Because at last at last at last Public Opinion recognizes what poor Fred Sneeze told us a century ago, God is dead. So now we can all do what we like. By the way, when I say God is dead I don't mean every God is dead – that would be Blasphemy and I am a Believer. I refer only to Mister Nice-Guy in the sky, the wet-eyed, bleeding-heart bastard who told us to love our neighbours and enemies because the scum of the earth are going to inherit it. That God, thank God, is AS DEAD AS SOCIALISM and even the Labour Party is delighted, though it can't openly admit it yet. You are still looking at me as though I am an insect, my dear. Quite right, quite right. A glow-worm. My little tail is indeed aglow. Your fault, my dear."

"Lucy," says Geikie, "we want to eat."

"Not yet, Geikie!" says Lucy firmly, "Because I have something important to say. Fin de siecle! End of age, start of other and what rough beast, June Tain, is shambling toward Bethlehem to be born? I'll tell you at the end of my next paragraph. I talk in paragraphs. Please remember all I say because tomorrow I won't recall a word.

"Now a lot of idiots think the British spy system sorry BRITISH INTELLIGENCE system is full of Russian double-agents. Nonsense. We 've had a lot of these but our relationship with the Yanks ensures that it's the CIA who know most of our secrets and we have learned quite a few of theirs. Do you remember Scottish Referendum, June Tain? When it looked like London might let us off the hook, haha? Well, a friend of mine – a fine fellow and a brave soldier – showed me the CIA plans for Scotland if it won some independence for itself, and the astonishing thing was – "

Mr Geikie, who has become restless, mutters, "Better not tell us these things Lucy."

"Pipe down Geikie you are not in the same

LEAGUE as your charming assistant and me, she is a Hell's Angel and I am a DRAGON-FLY, a bright spark spawned by the burning breath of the Beast of the Bottomless Pit. A fine statesman, Pitt. Do you know, June Tain, that the Yanks were going to be quite kind to independent Scotland? A lot kinder than to Guatemala, Nicaragua etcetera. They were NOT afraid of us becoming a socialist republic because they felt we'd be even easier to manipulate than England – fewer chiefs to bribe was how my friend put it – and no trouble at all compared with Ireland, especially the north bit. And what I want to tell you is this."

Lucy leans across the table and tells June in a hissing whisper, "The CIA scenario for an independent Scotland has not been scrapped and you are filling me with mysterious insights."

He stands and speaks in a solemn and quiet voice which grows steadily louder.

"I am a Douglas on my mother's side, a descendant of that Black Douglas who was Stabbed to The Death by The Hand of A King. And if you tell me it was some other Douglas who was stabbed to death by Jamie the First or Second or Third or Fourth or Fifth I DON'T CARE! I STILL FEEL PROPHETIC! I PROPHESY THAT JUNE TAIN – "

He points a finger at June and says more intimately, "I prophesy that you, June Tain," then notices his friends are beckoning him and more people are entering the restaurant. He murmurs, "Forgive me – I'm boring you," and returns to his friends.

That was all I could imagine of June's story. I thought of extending it by having her use Senga and

Donalda to entangle and corrupt important legislators, thus provoking a feminist socialist revolution. I could not believe in it. Yet from June visiting the leatherwear shop to Lucifer's speech was less than a quarter of what I had been paid to write. If I could not expand that by imaginative growth I must expand it by mere additions. June's story had a pornographic content. Such fancies come easily to me. Could I add more of them? I wrote the dialogue between the white American women which I later used in "Culture Capitalism", but tired of it. Such fancies are repetitive, and I had already written a novel using them. I decided to enlarge the book with anything interesting I could put on paper, however irrelevant: - essays, bits of autobiography, perhaps a play or two. More than a decade ago most of what I earned had been payment for television and radio plays. I had long wanted to give them new life in a book. In the early seventies a one act play called *Dialogue* had been broadcast by Scottish BBC radio, networked by Granada television, taken on tour by the short-lived Scottish Stage Company. I prosed it into the present tense, called it *A Free Man with a Pipe*, found it easy to think the Man is June's unsatisfactory ex-husband, that he is trying to forget her by half-heartedly seducing someone else. But her voice on the telephone finally demolishes him.

This suggested a form of book I had not written before. After the chapter showing Senga and Donalda seducing June in the late 1980s (the fashions in the streets give the date) the book would flash back to them in earlier years, each chapter showing one of my three women involved with men who failed them in very different but commonplace ways. As I dug for more material among past dramas I began hoping to show a greater than usual variety of those who make our Britain. I had tried that in my first and longest book, but had lacked the knowledge to build (as Dickens built in *Little Dorrit*) leaders of finance, government, law, and fashion into a continuous plot involving the factories, slums and slum landlords, the jailors and the jailed. I had patched over my ignorance with abbreviations and metaphors. But a book of episodes showing the lives of three women converging over twenty-five years might describe, without fantasy, shifts and dependencies between many believable people. Once again my book would contain no real leaders of government, finance, law, fashion etcetera, but my setting was Scotland, so how could it? Like most Scots and many English I assumed most such leaders work in London and are no use to us. I should have remembered that much of Scotland is useful to them.

The chapters called *The Proposal*, *The Man Who Knew About Electricity*, *In the Boiler Room* and *A Free Man With a Pipe* stick so close to original plays that they contain nearly every word of the original dialogue. *Mr Lang and Ms Tain* uses half a play, *Quiet People* the start of one. If any readers of *Quiet People* feel worried for the Liddels I can show them typed proof that the Liddels and their lodgers were good for each other, separating with friendship on both sides, though suddenly.

But Harry was a new, unexpected idea. In the earliest version of the first chapter she did not even appear in a photograph. She was invented for *Class Party* because a quartette allowed more permutations

than a trio, but she said little because I had no idea
where she came from or what job she did when not playing perverse games with Senga. I knew she was a rarer social type than the other women, it helped the plot for her to be rich, i84t was a useful economy to think a horrid upbringing had made it hard for her to talk. For a while I never bothered imagining a past for her, but had a rough idea she might be the administrator of a large hospital. One day I was talking to a friend about what makes rich people different from you and me, especially the rich whose wealth is a habit of mind because it is a settled inheritance. My friend had met some of them in a boarding school she had attended, also in an art gallery where she occasionally worked. I too had met some and been fascinated by the occasional remark which showed they were foreign to me. I had walked in a big private garden with an owner who had devoted it wholly to trees and shrubs because plots of flowers gave his gardener too much work. I asked if he grew vegetables. He said, "I did once. It was too much trouble. You can get them in a shop for a few shillings."

I had known a young woman who disliked all the people her parents liked, saying she preferred the company of "ordinary people". She sulked when expected to make a cup of Nescafé for herself, said she could not possibly do that, proved it by floating a spoonful of the powder in a mug of lukewarm water. These people were individuals, not types, but Scott Fitzgerald started his story *The Rich Boy* with, "Describe an individual and you may end with a type; describe a type and you are likely to end with –

nothing." I remarked to my friend that perhaps the very rich, after leaving school, found it hard to take others seriously after boarding school, because at last they could easily replace or escape from whoever did not perfectly fit them. This might explain the astonishingly unaffectionate treatment some of them gave their young. As I brooded on this I suddenly imagined Harry's mother saying at her birth, "Oh God a fucking little gel," and began conceiving my distant cousin of a queen. My direct experience of her class was slight, though its speech rhythms had resounded through all the homes where I lived from babyhood. Lord Reith was a Glasgow minister's son but the BBC system he created was for decades dominated by the dialect of English private boarding schools. I had also met the English rich in the pages of Wilde, Firbank, Hemingway's *Fiesta*, and Evelyn Waugh.

I did not expect to write much about Harry at first. I planned to shift her in one chapter from her nasty Scottish nanny and chilling mother to a boarding school, thence to the Warburg or Courtauld Institute, thence to being an arts administrator in Scotland. But the boarding school acquired a distinct geography where I invented active bodies to support interesting details. "Amanda's kid" and "new money" had been phrases I invented or borrowed to show what a snob Harry's mother was. In the shrubbery the two phrases became Hjordis with The Fortress, Linda with the speech and character she is evicted from. I grew so attached to Harry that I made her an artist and took three chapters to move her north. The chronology of the book (shown below) turns out neatly, even so, apart from *Quiet People*. The age of Donalda's child and some other details required the date to be 1971, so it was placed out of sequence to avoid putting two Donalda stories together.

| CHAPTERS | YEARS | HEROINES |
|---|---|---|
| *One For The Album* | 1989 | June, Senga, Donalda |
| *A Distant Cousin of a Queen* | 1963 | Harry |
| *The Proposal* | 1965 | Senga |
| *The Man Who Knew About Electricity* | 1967 | Donalda |
| *Mr Lang and Ms Tain* | 1973 | June |
| *In the Boiler Room* | 1977 | Senga |
| *Quiet People* | 1971 | Donalda |
| *The Bum Garden* | 1963–1989 | Harry |
| *A Free Man With a Pipe* | 1989 | June (off stage) |
| *Culture Capitalism* | 1989 | Harry, Senga |
| *Dad's Story* | 1989 | Donalda, Harry |
| *Class Party* | 1989 | June, Donalda, Senga, Harry |
| *New June* | 1989 | June, Donalda, Senga, Harry |

The last chapter ended sooner than I planned. When June returned to the shop where the novel began I saw Mr Geikie and Lucifer were irrelevant. June was now a new woman, and to describe how she used her newness would limit it. There was a hint that after Senga and Donalda had worked to liberate her, June (the professional person) and Harry (the inherited wealth person) would cut themselves off from the poorer folk and have fun together. It is an unfair end
to this tale but it is how, in Great Britain,
things are normally
arranged.

# Of Pierre Lavalle*

ARTHUR NOEL LAVALLE, painter and art publicist, was born in Sunbury-on-Thames in 1918. His father was a Belgian mechanic, a refugee from that German invasion which began the First World War. His mother was district nurse from the Scottish part of Berwick-on-Tweed. As a child he stayed there with his granny and says he remembers the rigours of the Presbyterian Sabbaths.

In 1929 industrial depression put Arthur Lavalle's father, and many other mechanics, out of work. The family moved to Valenciennes, an industrial district of France, where the father's accent did not hinder him in finding employment. Between his 11th and 21st year young Lavalle had French schooling and began to paint landscapes in the English style – 'rotten paintings' he says of them now. He joined a political group which thought all organizations which control by force (governments, armies, police etc.) should be replaced by many small, locally elected communes. The Valenciennes anarchists thought art was anything people did or made: that if a modern teaspoon was dug up 500 years later, archaeologists and art critics would, quite rightly, admire its form, symmetry and the cunning that had made it. An acquaintance who thought French bicycle races a great art form collected

---

* An introduction to a catalogue of paintings shown in The Pearce Institute, Govan, South Glasgow, 1990.

tyres from machines of well-known racers and hung them on his walls. Such ideas did not help an artist who wanted to make a flat surface beautiful by stroking it with paint, but they stimulated thought. A Jewish friend, after looking at a young Lavalle's early landscapes, asked him why he never used his imagination? The question astonished him, but he found it helpful.

In 1938, a British anarchist who saw the likelihood of a Nazified Europe, he shifted to London, joining the British army in 1939. It may have been inconsistent for an anarchist to join an army but many Christians who thought it wrong to kill did so too. His knowledge of French got him work with the Defence Ministry. After the war he continued as a civil servant with the Ministry of Information, then the Charities Commission. His life now easily divided into three periods: 11 years of English childhood, 9 of French education, 8 of British military and civil service. The third period would have been bleak without friends and associates. He married a professional violinist. He knew Lucian Freud, Dylan Thomas, Tambimuttu (the editor of *Poetry London*), and the BBC intellectuals who met in the Wheatsheaf Pub. These had strong Glasgow connections, for a lot of British broadcasting was done from Glasgow in the war years. He knew Guy Aldred, editor of *The Word*. He was friendly with an anarchist group containing Emma Goldman, Herbert Read (with whom he quarrelled), Ethel Mannin, novelist who nicknamed him Pierre. He adopted it. In France his baptismal name of Arthur had asserted his foreignness. In Britain he, the son of exiles,

made his foreignness a garment, accepted the nick-
name Pierre and wore a beret.

In 1947 he was nearing 30 and had begun to
find London oppressive. His marriage had ended. He
was tired of pen-pushing and wanted to make a fresh
start as a full-time painter, breaking completely with
his past. He came to Glasgow. I quote him: "Glasgow
at that time was the 2nd city of Britain. I had heard so
much about it, the Gorbals, the Red Clydeside, Louis
MacNeice. It was, and still is, a very interesting city. I
wasn't going to bury myself. Things that used to
happen in Glasgow were important." Once again
Clydeside was building most of the Empire's warships,
so there was a revival of the industrial power, political
confidence, and artistic vigour which the end of the
1914-18 war had depressed. With the bombing of
London, Glasgow no longer seemed a grubby place.
The painter J D Fergusson and his wife Margaret Morris
returned here from France: the painters Josef Herman
and Jankel Adler from occupied Europe. They
stimulated discussion groups, art shows and
performances in studios and meeting places near
Sauchiehall Street. Colquhon, McBride and Joan
Eardley were students at the Art School. A new theatre
was begun called the Unity because the government
was trying to create national unity with socialist
legislation, some of which encouraged fine arts in
some places they had never reached before. The
Glasgow Unity gave a professional start to the careers
of Duncan Macrae, Roddy Mcmillan and other fine
actors, the director Joan Littlewood, the painters Tom
MacDonald and Bet Low. Its biggest success, *The*

*Gorbals Story*, was taken to London, filmed, and inspired a Sadlers Wells Ballet. Pierre's view of Glasgow as a culture capital where art and socialism were uniting to abolish the slums was not eccentric in 1947. He was then renting a studio at the top of a Sauchiehall Street tenement facing the Art School.

After that something happened which can be illustrated by an anecdote. When the Scottish Arts Council was formed after the war it had no permanent office and was composed about six people, James Bridie and Naomi Richardson among them. It met alternately in a room in Glasgow and a room in Edinburgh. Ten years later it had a snug Edinburgh office with permanent receptionist, secretaries, departments chiefs, and Mrs Kemp, the director. An artist I knew (Alan Fletcher) met her at the opening of an exhibition. In a charmingly friendly way, "From Glasgow are you?" she asked. "How do you manage there? Whenever I visit Glasgow I feel in Omsk or Tomsk or some such place."

London domination of and indifference to the rest of Britain had returned. What most Londoners now knew of Glasgow culture was a half-forgotten play set in the Gorbals. That an Edinburgh official took the same ignorant view was natural, but many Glaswegians also adopted it – even artists. At Glasgow Art School between 1952 and 57, I and other students wanted Glasgow to produce original Scottish work, but no teacher told us, nothing we read indicated, that Glasgow had done that many times, even in the dismal 30s. I saw retrospective shows of work by Cowie, Fergusson and Pringle in Kelvingrove Museum, was excited by such good painting, yet felt they could not be truly great because the retrospective was not in the Tate Gallery. Too many Glasgow intellectuals disparaged each other and despised themselves. How could we who did not oppose the widespread opinion of how unimportant we were? Some solved that problem by going to London or America. Pierre Lavalle was the only one I met who understood that for all but a lucky few it is as hard to be a good artist anywhere else as it is in Glasgow, and that fine art was worth making, whoever ignored it.

But Pierre refused to be ignored. Small, urgent, full of learning and ideas about the painting he did, very keen to see other people's work and discuss their own ideas. Pierre attended the few cafes, pubs and studios near Sauchiehall Street where some hopeful art students and striving artists still sometimes met. We found him likeable, stimulating and annoying. In weak moments, feeling exiled from our community by our talents, yet each hugging a talent protectively like a secret vice, we wanted only to moan to a fellow sufferer. Pierre thought exile too commonplace to mention. He wanted to discuss OUR WORK.

He had as much to moan about as anyone else. After some satisfying sales in the 40s and early 50s, he was gripped by the new cultural ice age. Glasgow's commercial art galleries had dwindled from three to one, and the municipal galleries had a policy of showing no local contemporary work. He still sold some paintings through group exhibitions in Edinburgh, London, France and Canada, but this provided no livelihood. He had met Marguerite his second wife, who bore him a daughter, Cherie, in 1955. His only dependable income was from part-time art lecturing for Glasgow University extra-mural department: work for which he travelled from Dumfries to Oban. He was one of the artists who in 1959 hung an exhibition from the railings of the Botanic Gardens. He was in the group which conceived the new Charing Cross Gallery, established with Arts Council aid. This became The Compass Gallery under Cyril Gerber's management. In 1963 and 64 Pierre became the only critic to steadily publicise Scottish painting.

The last sentence needs explaining. At that time Cordelia Oliver and Martin Baillie reviewed art for *The Glasgow Herald*, and Robert Gage for *The Scotsman*. They often had too little space to give more than a quick opinion, they were commissioned too irregularly to offer a steady survey, and (worst of all) had no colour reproductions, seldom even a monochrome, to show the reader what they were talking about. The *Scottish Field* gave Pierre a monthly page to deal with an artist's work while developing an argument or giving an illustrative parable. It had colour reproductions of paintings, and a photo of the artist. If a history of Glasgow art is ever written, the author will find Pierre's *Field* articles the best single guide to the 60s. He wrote of Scottish painters from elsewhere, but the *Field* was based in Glasgow, so he surveyed it more completely.

He wrote about the recently dead, such as J. D. Fergusson, the established such as Davie Donaldson, talented survivors such as Tom MacDonald and Bet Low, talents about to be recognised – Pat Douthwait was one – also others with a long, tough trail ahead of them: Bill Crozier, Douglas Abercrombie, Alasdair Taylor and Carol Gibbons. In 1963 he wished good-bye and good luck to Fred Pollock, a young painter leaving for London. After a quarter of a century when Pollock's expressionism was unfashionable, it is at last being esteemed and bought in England.

I first saw Pierre's paintings in a Glasgow gallery in 1953. I remember low, bare hills painted in thin oils on the smooth side of hardboard panels. Each with an almost monochrome colouring, and haunted by surprising creatures, of an old Flemish demon sort. I did not like these but cannot forget them. I next saw his paintings 10 years later and liked them greatly. He had discovered a technique which suited his vision, a strong colourful one, and he had discovered it through his daughter. She was attending Peel Street Nursery School, in Partick, and her teacher had accepted Pierre's offer to help with Christmas decorations. He decided to paint the nativity story in the style of the Bayeux Tapestry, on a long strip of paper to be fixed along the wall like a frieze. As this was for children it was easy for him to paint playfully, with the brightness and clarity he had always enjoyed in Matisse, Kadinsky and Paul Klee, but had never before thought to use for himself. 'Magic Realist' is a literary school, but is apt for the paintings of Pierre. They have the brightness and clarity of fairy tale illustration yet the subject matter is seldom fantastic and usually landscape. Working chiefly with enamels, he builds zones of sea or sky, field or city, using small triangles or lozenges of colour divided from each other by a vividness without optical confusion. But there is no point in describing what those who like painting should see for themselves. The best are subtle, beautiful harmonies. All are a pleasure to the eye.

This exhibition in the Pearce Institute in Govan, is of work completed up to the middle 70s when Pierre stopped painting. He was suddenly exhausted and depressed by continual exile, by his artistic and spiritual generosity which too many people ignored or thought merely comic. His wife Marguerite never ignored it and is still his closest friend and helper, though their marriage ended while he was still painting.* It was Marguerite and Brian Petherbridge who arranged this exhibition.

*Pierre Lavalle died on Tuesday 26th March 2002.

# Of Andrew Sykes*

IN 1960 I WENT ON HOLIDAY TO Ireland with Andrew Sykes, a tough small stocky man with a thick thatch of white hair and a face like a boxer's. Like myself he dressed comfortably rather than smartly. We had met when he was a mature student at Glasgow University and I a very callow one just out of Glasgow Art School. We were from a working class who benefited when two post-war governments (Labour and Tory) agreed that all who qualified for professional education might have them whether or not they or their parents could pay. Andrew, who had been a sergeant with the British army in India, eventually won a doctorate through a paper on trade unions in the building industry, getting his knowledge by the unacademic ploy of working as a navvy. His army experience and a course in economics had also given him insights into the workings of our officer and financial class. He took malicious glee in gossiping to me about the insider trading by which this minority manipulate the rest. My notion of Britain had been formed at the end of the Second World War when our government announced the coming of a fairer society and the creation of social welfare for all. I had thought Britain was now mainly managed by folk who had mastered difficult processes through training and

* This is a long episode to a very short story, **Edison's Tractatus**, in **Mavis Belfrage, A Romantic Novel With Five Shorter Tales**, Bloomsbury, 1996.

experience. Andrew explained that, as often today as in the past, most British civil service and business chiefs had stepped into senior positions because they had been to three or four expensive schools and a couple of universities in the east midlands: institutions where exams mattered less than their parent's wealth and friends they made. He persuaded me that Britain was not (as most of our politicians and publicity networks say) a democracy, but an electoral aristocracy.

I thought Andrew disliked this unfair system since he was entering a profession through a socialist act of parliament. On our Irish holiday (we were guests of friends Greta and David Hodgins at Nenagh in Tipperary) I was surprised to find he hated any group who wanted to change the dominant system. He even hated the Campaign for Nuclear Disarmament. He forgave me for being a member but we could not discuss it. The only political hope we shared was a wish for Scottish self-government. I enjoyed what I saw of Ireland but enjoyed his company less than expected. His hobbies were wrestling and judo. He told me that bodybuilders convert steak into muscle by a lifting weights immediately after a meal. I will say more about him because he gave me more than the first sentence of *Edison's Tractatus*.

He became Strathclyde University's first Professor of Sociology in 1967, retired in 1989, died in 1991. His closest relatives were aunts with whom he lodged in a Glasgow tenement until they died long before he did. His job gave him prestige and colleagues. His holidays with the Hodgins in Tipperary gave him a family whose children regarded him as an uncle, a community which treated him as an equal. From a Labour Party member he became a xenophobic Tory. In the university staff club he once aimed a judo kick at a black visitor who was quietly minding his own business. His special study was trade unions, so in the 1980s he became a consultant of the U.K. government, telling Margaret Thatcher how to weaken them. He took self-conscious glee in the bowler hat, striped trousers, black jacket and waistcoat he wore on visits to Downing Street. I fear he harmed our democracy, but not me. Until 1974 he was my only steady patron, buying paintings and lending money when I was in need, usually taking a drawing as repayment. He lent money as if it was an ordinary, unimportant action, leaving my self-respect undamaged. I can't type so he got his secretaries to type my poems, plays and the early chapters of *Lanark*, my first novel. They were typed onto stencils from which, when photocopying was expensive, they printed all the copies I needed without charge. In 1974 he arranged for the Collins Gallery of Strathclyde University to give the largest retrospective show my pictures have ever had, getting a Glasgow Lord Provost to open it.

Yet in his last fifteen years I hardly saw him, maybe because I no longer had a family to support so had less need to push my work onto him. He retired as professor, became a recluse and solitary drinker, his human contacts being a cleaning lady and weekly phonecall from Greta Hodgins in Ireland. I felt sad and guilty when he died. He had given me much more than he ever received from me.

Here are items which went into *Edison's Tractatus*.

**1** In the 1960s I heard that *Wittgenstein's Tractatus* was a very brainy book. I thought it might not be too brainy for me but never got hold of a copy.

**2** I am too shy and pessimistic to start conversations with strangers but when public transport or an eating house places me beside an attractive one I sometimes fantasize about talking to them. This habit led to my first television play and a novel which is still in print. In 1982 I worked with Liz Lochhead, Jim Kelman and Tom Leonard on a revue called *The Pie of Damocles*. I scribbled a sketch in which a young woman at a café table asks a depressed young man to pass her the sugar bowl and he insists on discussing what this might lead to before refusing. My friends did not think it funny. I discarded it.

**3** I started hearing the word interface in the 1970s. It seemed to be used by people erecting a barrier round their work practice while talking across it. The barrier made the job they had mastered feel safer but conversation across it sometimes made new work, as forensic medicine had been developed from the interface between policing and doctoring. My facetious attitude to new words led me to link activities between which no interface was possible – the gap between Aztec pottery and Chinese obstetrics, for instance, seemed unbridgeable. Around the same time I heard a lecturer amuse a university student by referring to something as "an example of interdisciplinary cross-sterilization".

**4** For several years I have been perplexed by the adjective post-modern, especially when applied to my own writing, but have now decided it is an academic substitute for contemporary or fashionable. Its prefix honestly announces it as a specimen of intellectual afterbirth, a fact I only noticed when I reread my brainy character saying so.

**5** A few years ago I heard that a scientist had shown how a butterfly stamping on a leaf in a tropical rain forest might precipitate a hurricane in North America. This may or may not be true.

**6** In the first months of 1994 I conducted a creative writing class at St Andrews University. Going home by train to Glasgow one day I sat opposite a young woman who was writing in red ink on a block of graph paper. I could not read her words but they were shaped with unusual clearness and regularity. She was slightly bigger than average, neatly dressed and with no apparent make-up or anything to catch the eye. I felt a strong prejudice in her favour, believing, perhaps wrongly, that she was unusually intelligent. I suddenly wanted to put her in a story exactly as she had appeared. She exchanged words with a young man beside her. Their conversation did not interest me.

I broke my journey home at Markinch to visit Malcolm Hood in Glenrothes Hospital. Two years earlier he had been paralysed by a cerebral stroke: his brain was in full working order but his body could give no sign of it. He was now able to speak and move a little. On this visit I read him a story from Somerville and Ross's Experiences of an Irish R.M. and occasional comments and snorts of laughter showed his enjoyment. When students at Glasgow Art School forty years before we had often read aloud to each other from amusing authors. My favourites were Max

Beerbohm and Rabelais. Malcolm's were Dickens and Patrick Campbell. Campbell – an Anglo-Irish humourist not much read now – probably gave us our first taste of Blarney, which I define as the employment of an Irish idiom to make an unlikely story more convincing. The Somerville and Ross Tale was full of it.

When I boarded a homeward-bound train at Markinch *Edison's Tractatus* was germinating. I scribbled most of it in a notebook before reaching Glasgow, and as I did so imagined an Irish voice saying it, an Irish voice deliberately constructing an improbable tale. That is why I gave it an improbable title. Were I to read it aloud I would do so in my Scottish accent voice, but when writing *Edison's Tractatus* the sentences moved to a second-hand Irish lilt.

7 This lilt must come from more than a fortnight in Tipperary thirty-five years ago and from renewed pleasure in the Blarney of Somerville and Ross. Flann O'Brien's writings are an ingredient because, though Joyce, Synge and O'Casey use Blarney on occasions, O'Brien is the only Irish genius whose work is Blarney throughout. In the previous six months I had also read with pleasure *This Fella I Knew*, a short story by my friend Bernard MacLaverty who never talks Blarney and hardly ever writes it. This story is an exception. It appears in *Walking the Dog*, published in 1994.

8 A week after scribbling the first version of *Edison's Tractatus* a student in my St Andrews class asked how I got ideas for stories. I gave a long confused answer because each novel, short story or play seemed to form differently. What set it going might be a story I had read which I wanted to tell differently, or a day-dream, or

dream remembered on waking, or a fantasy I had evolved during conversation, or an incident which had befallen someone else but was unforgettable because of its oddity, humour or injustice. Ideas have sometimes come from commissions to write on a particular subject. Thereafter the idea grew through an alternation of writing and deliberate day-dreaming. If a narrative drew in many memories, ideas and phrases which had lain unused in my brain it sometimes expanded to a novella, novel or play. All but my first novel came that way. The first came from childhood faith in a long printed story as my surest way of getting attention. I day-dreamed and scribbled it for years before accumulating enough ideas and experiences to finish it. I have also developed stories by telling or reading parts to friends before completion. Most authors I know avoid this because displaying unfinished work reduces their enthusiasm for it, but some listeners' suggestions have expanded my tales in ways I might not have discovered myself.

The student's question produced this account of what went into *Edison's Tractatus*. There is probably more than I am conscious of, but I believe the brainy hero is merely a caricature of traits which Andrew Sykes and I had in common. We were both inclined to turn sexual urges into clever, sometimes boring monologues. The urge to deliver an uninterrupted monologue is the energy driving most teachers, story-tellers and politicians. *Edison's Tractatus* is obviously a portrait of someone too wordy for his own good, which also explains the addition of this bit of intellectual afterbirth.

# The Fall
# of Kelvin Walker*

FOR ALMOST SEVENTY YEARS before Margaret Thatcher's government changed the licensing laws most Scottish pubs shut at 9.30pm. At that hour in the Hogmanay of 1954, outside The State Bar off Sauchiehall Street, I was being very drunk when I first met Robert Kitts. He and companions I knew took me to several parties in the homes of strangers, and as I sobered up we formed the kind of friendship only possible between a couple of imaginative young men who recognise each other's genius. We were both students of painting (he in the London Slade), were both writing novels based on our childhoods, were both enthusiasts for Kafka, Herman Melville and Scott Fitzgerald whose *Tender is the Night* had been recently reprinted and recognised as a classic. The conversations started that night only ended when he returned to London, but on that night or the next we agreed that the natural outcome of our shared interest in visual and literary art was film making. Which Robert Kitts went on to do.

In 1963, I was a social security scrounger, recently sacked from my job as scene painter and supporting my wife and newborn son by drawing National Assistance benefit from my Sauchiehall Street labour exchange. One morning I got a telegram from Bob Kitts asking me to phone him at the London BBC,

---

* *A 1991 prologue to an edition of the novel, first published 1985 by Canongate.*

reversing charges. I did so from a street call box. He said his boss, Huw Wheldon, might let him make a documentary film about my work, but wished to see me first. Could I come to the London TV Centre at noon, the day after tomorrow, a Thursday? I told him I could not: at 9.30am then I must collect my National Assistance grant from the labour exchange. (In those days unemployed labourers, tradesmen and professional folk all got their weekly state assistance in notes handed over the counter of a labour exchange.) Bob told me to phone him back in an hour. I did. He then said that on leaving the labour exchange I should take a taxi to Glasgow Airport, where a seat would be booked for me on a 10.30 flight. If I kept the taxi fare's receipt I would be reimbursed. At London's Heathrow I would be met by a Hertz Car chauffeur who would drive me to the TV centre where Bob would introduce me to Huw Wheldon.

These were the great days of BBC Television. It had only two channels, colour was still to come, but none of its producers thought commercial television worth competing for so the quality of its productions were best in the world. Huw Wheldon, head of documentary and music programmes, was partly responsible for this. Like the BBC's founding governor, Lord Reith, he thought broadcasting should provide more than popular entertainment. Wheldon catered for what he called "the small majority" of folk who not only enjoyed the best art of the past, but innovative art now. His liking for new ideas started the careers of Ken Russell, David Jones, Melvyn Bragg and also Bob Kitts, who would have become as famous as the rest had he not worked to promote an obscure actress (his first wife) and obscure artists, one of them me. For a while I enjoyed the luxury of air flights, taxis, meals in posh restaurants and talking as an equal to Huw Wheldon. The heady experience of starting a new career in the London of 1960's television (which then seemed to welcome outsiders) was a delusion, but useful.

Before going to London I amused my wife by saying that on meeting Wheldon I would speak before he had time to open his mouth, saying, "Before we proceed to the process of question and answer which is the purpose of this meeting Mr Wheldon, I must refer you to this stain on my jersey caused by *mince* which fell off a neighbour's fork as I was dining earlier today. I had no time to change, so it is not my fault. But explanations like this must seem like swatting midgies to a man of your experience. I notice a small but perceptible stain on your neck tie. Might that be a bond between us?" This fantasy gave me the idea of a naive, brazen, pushy young Scot, with limitless self confidence because London was liberating him from a restrictive home life in Scotland. The thought of this character persisted with me. A year or two after Bob's film was broadcast, memory began giving me details for more adventures. Twice a total stranger has introduced himself by saying, "Excuse me, but do you mind if I engage you in conversation?" Both times I had been in a café with friends who were also artists, as in those days our beards proclaimed. A man of about forty, a married coal miner, needed to tell someone about his helpless love for a hospital nurse, could tell nobody he knew, but thought strange artists might sympathise. A young man told us he had come to Glasgow from Greenock, because he wanted to meet artistic people. That, I saw, was how Kelvin would introduce himself to an attractive girl in a Soho café. She – Jill – was based on Jane Mulcahy, a real English friend and for a while the partner of Alan Fletcher, a great artist I knew who had died young. I had once made notes for a play about someone like me attracting someone like her away from someone like him, but gave it up as a bad job. I now saw it was just the job for my Kelvin Walker.

I wrote the play quickly for television (no Scottish theatre existed to stage it) and posted it to the BBC drama department. Not having a television set I did not know my play was half an hour too long to be broadcast but James Brabazon, a BBC producer wrote to say he thought it could be cut down to fifty minutes, and could he come to Glasgow and discuss this with me? Of course! Once again I enjoyed the delusion of starting a splendid new career. When Mr Brabazon asked what actors I would like in my play I said I knew none, but would like Scottish actors in the Scottish parts.

*The Fall of Kelvin Walker* was networked in 1968 with Judy Cornwall as Jill, Harry Corbett as Jake Whittington the painter, Corin Redgrave as my hero. The other 2 Scottish parts were played by an Englisman (well) and an Ulsterman (badly) because London BBC could find no Scottish actors available. But for 12 years this play led to Stewart Conn commissing me to write half-hour plays for Scottish BBC, and a good London literary agent, Francis Head, who got me commissions to write plays for the BBC and Granada in England.

# Poor Things: Acknowledgements

THE AUTHOR THANKS BERNARD MacLaverty for hearing the book as it was written and giving ideas that helped it grow; and Scott Pearson for typing and research into period detail; and Dr. Bruce Charlton for correcting the medical parts; and Angela Mullane for correcting the legal parts; and Archie Hind for insights (mainly got from his play *The Sugarolly Story*) into the corrupted high noon of Glasgow's industrial period; and Michael Roschlau for the gift of Lessing's *Nathan the Wise* (published in 1894 by MacLehose & Son, Glasgow, for the translator William Jacks, illustrated with etchings by William Strang, which suggested the form (not content) of the McCandless volume; and Elspeth King and Michael Donnelly, now of the Abbot House local history museum in Dunfermline, for permission to use some of their earlier circumstances to reinforce a fiction. The shocking incident described by Bella in Chapter 17 was suggested by the Epilogue of *In a Free State* by V. S. Naipaul. Other ideas were got from *Ariel Like a Harpy*, Christopher Small's study of Mary Shelley's *Frankenstein*, and from Liz

*Placed before the introduction to the novel issued by Bloomsbury in 1992, this truly acknowledges friends and books from whom I got ideas or words. It is my happiest novel, the three main characters all being good people yet not boring, though the narrator is – compared with the other two – unintelligent. It is my only attempt at a historical tale. These 2 prelims start putting the book into the retrieved manuscript school of fiction. When* **The Herald** *printed the first chapter Elspeth King, Mike Donnelly, Archie Hind promoted the veracity of the novels most fantastic parts by denouncing me for being wrong in some ordinary details. A few readers thought these friends had turned against me. The* **Introduction** *follwing starts as fact. I omit its fantastic ending.*

Lochhead's *Blood and Ice*, a play on the same subject. Three sentences from a letter to Sartre by Simone de Beauvoir, embedded in the third and fourth paragraphs of Chapter 18, are taken from Quentin Hoare's translation of her letters published by Hutchinson in 1991. A historical note on Chapter 2 is extracted from Johanna Geyer-Kordesch's entry "Women and Medicine", in the *Encyclopaedia of Medical History* edited by W. F. Bynum. The epigraph on the covers is from a poem by Denis Leigh. The author thanks a close friend who wants not to be named for a money loan which allowed him to finish the book without interruption.

# Introduction

THE DOCTOR WHO WROTE THIS ACCOUNT of his early experiences died in 1911, and readers who know nothing about the daringly experimental history of Scottish medecine will perhaps mistake it for a grotesque fiction. Those who examine the proofs given at the end of this introduction will not doubt that in the final week of February 1881, at 18 Park Circus, Glasgow, a surgical genius used human remains to create a twenty-five-year-old woman. The historian Michael Donnelly disagrees with me. It was he who salvaged the text which is the biggest part of the book, so I must say how he found it.

Life in Glasgow was very exciting during the nineteen seventies. The old industries which had made the place were being closed and moved south, while the elected governors (for reasons any political economist can explain) were building multistorey housing blocks and a continually expanding motorway

system. In the local history museum on Glasgow
Green the curator Elspeth King, her helper Michael Donnelly, worked overtime to acquire and preserve evidence of local culture that was being hustled into the past. Since the First World War the City Council had given the local history museum (called the People's Palace) no funds to buy anything new, so Elspeth and Michael's acquisitions were almost all salvaged from buildings scheduled for demolition. A store was rented in Templeton's carpet factory (which was soon closing down) and to this place Michael Donnelly brought troves of stained-glass windows, ceramic tiles, theatre posters, banners of disbanded trade unions and all sorts of historical documents. Elspeth King sometimes gave Michael help with this work, as the rest of her staff were attendants sent by the head of the art gallery in Kelvingrove and not paid to retrieve objects from unsafe buildings. Neither, of course, were Elspeth and Michael, so the very successful exhibitions they put on cost the City Council little.

While passing through the city centre one morning Michael Donnelly saw a heap of old-fashioned box files on the edge of a pavement, obviously placed there for the Cleansing Department to collect and destroy. Looking into them he found letters and documents dating from the early years of the century, the refuse of a defunct law office. A modern firm had inherited what remained of the old business, and thrown out what it did not need. The papers mainly concerned property dealings between people and families who had helped to shape the city in its earlier days, and Michael saw the name of the first woman doctor to graduate from Glasgow University, a name only known to historians of the suffragette movement nowadays, though she had once written a Fabian pamphlet on public health. Michael decided to take the files away by taxi and sift through them at leisure; but first he called the firm which had put the boxes out and asked permission. It was denied. A senior partner (a well-known lawyer and local politician who will not be named here) told Michael that his look through the files had been a criminal act since they were not his property and intended for the municipal incinerator. He said every lawyer was sworn to keep a client's business private, whether the lawyer inherited the business or not and whether the client lived or died. He said that the only sure way to keep old business private was to destroy proof that it had happened and if Michael Donnelly saved any part of it from destruction he would be charged with robbery.

\*\*\*\*\*\*\*\*\*\*\*\*\*\*\*\*\*\*\*\*\*\*\*\*\*\*\*\*\*\*\*\*
\*\*\*\*\*\*\*\*\*\*\*\*\*\*\*\*\*\*\*\*\*\*\*\*\*\*\*\*\*\*\*\*
\*\*                 *Truthful so far, the rest of this*                 \*\*
\*\*                 *introduction becomes fiction*                 \*\*
\*\*\*\*\*\*\*\*\*\*\*\*\*\*\*\*\*\*\*\*\*\*\*\*\*\*\*\*\*\*\*\*
\*\*\*\*\*\*\*\*\*\*\*\*\*\*\*\*\*\*\*\*\*\*\*\*\*\*\*\*\*\*\*\*

# Of
# Anthony Burgess*

B ORN IN MANCHESTER, 1917, son of a shop-
keeper (newsagent-tobacconist) who was also a
pub pianist, Burgess was educated as a Catholic, got a
Second-Class Degree in English Language and
Literature at a Manchester University. He spent several
complicated years of service in the British Army
starting as a nursing orderly in World War 2 and
ending as a teacher with rank of sergeant-major in
Malaya. After that he became a teacher of English in
what we British called The Middle East – Brunei, then
Malaya. He learned the languages of these countries –
became an expert linguist. In Shaw's *Pygmalion* (the
film adaptation) the great linguist says of a more
internationally employed linguist, "He can learn any
language at all in a fortnight – the sure sign of an idiot".
I disagree. I think one of his most interesting books is
*A Mouthful of Air*, in which he briefly but respectfully
surveys many Eastern and European languages
including Scots Lallans, in an argument that schools
should teach the phonetic way of writing words, to
hear how people in other countries pronounced them.

In the late 1950s he collapsed while teaching in
Brunei and was invalided back to Britain with what
was diagnosed as an inoperable brain tumour. In
roughly twelve months he wrote to support his widow

*This is an obituary for a journal I have forgotten, so this text has been reconstructed
from memory.

three novels, the first of 32, contemporary and realistic, historical but convincing, also satirical futuristic, because he lived for another thirty years though his first wife died. He published many kinds of books, two of them autobiographies. He reviewed books and broadcasts for *The Observer*, *The Guardian* and *The Listener*.

The last was a weekly magazine published by the BBC to review its broadcasts and to print the texts of interesting talks, latterly most of which were on the *Third Programme*. In 1964 Burgess reviewed *Under the Helmet* a TV documentary about my poetry and painting directed by my friend Robert Kitts. I remember the article was illustrated with a reproduction of my Cowcaddens Streetscape, which most excited me. Burgess responded to the programme by suggesting my poetry deserved closer attention, while doubting if the device of suggesting I was dead was a good idea. When I met him in 1981 neither of us remembered that indirect encounter.

He had been invited to Glasgow by the Scottish Publishers Association to give a talk at the McLellan Galleries, and I was introduced to him at a small meal beforehand because my first novel *Lanark* had just been published, and Burgess had reviewed it, saying I was the first major Scottish novelist since Walter Scott. In the restaurant where we were introduced his first words were, "Congratulations! You don't have an agent, I hope?" He seemed to me big, full of power yet harmless because ramshackle – not well organised. I liked that as it is how many people see me. He was thoroughly English but not posh, lacked the Oxbridge smooth manner that many folk acquire without having

been to English private schools of the kind advertised
as public, because only rich families can pay to get their children into them. Anthony Burgess was what was once called A Man of Letters. Sam Johnson, Goldsmith, Orwell were such. They lived by their writing in a hand-to-mouth way that made writers with secure incomes (mostly academics) think, "These people are not in our class." But on that occasion Burgess and I exchanged no memorable ideas.

Several years later Theatre About Glasgow, a subsidiary of the Glasgow Citizens Theatre, decided to take on tour a stage version Burgess had made of his novel *A Clockwork Orange*, and commissioned me to paint the scenery. The director told me of a phone conversation with Burgess who (I think) then lived in Malta, in which he told Burgess I was busy on the scenery. According to him this information was followed by some seconds of silence before Burgess roared, "Why isn't he writing?" My writing has never had a greater compliment.

# Of Jack Vettriano*

WE DO NOT WORRY about death and earning our living before walking and speaking. Our parents do these things for us, allowing us to feel the universe holds everything we need. For a year or two, sometimes longer, we are allowed to enjoy life played as a game played for the fun of it, for as soon as they learn to walk healthy children prefer to hop, run and skip. I once saw someone skipping alone under a lamppost at night and singing, "I've a laddie in America, I've a laddie o'er the sea, I've a laddie in America, and he's goantae marry me." She was obviously lonely so needed to sing of hope for the future and America was part of this.

For her "shades of the prison house," as Wordsworth put it, were closing round the growing child. Soon authority would tell her, "We sentence you to hard labour for life in field, factory, office or home. This will get you the money to enjoy some freedom in your *spare* time." Most of us remember at least one horrid shock by which someone with authority over us demonstrated how unfree we were. Those who don't have freedom must dream of it, for freedom is the human essence. Freedom for many people used to mean America. The USA was invented by people hoping for a better life, even though they bought slaves to

∗ *From* **Fallen Angels**, *1994, a book of paintings by Jack Vettriano, edited by W. Gordon Smith in which several writers chose one as the subject of a short essay.*

make lives better still. From Scotland, Italy, every part of Europe, the poor and dispossessed poured into America until the gates were suddenly closed to them in the 30s. But the land of freedom and opportunity for all lived on in the Hollywood movies.

At the height of the world's worst economic depression before ours in 2013, Hollywood spun out Westerns, domestic comedies and crime thrillers showing the U.S.A. as a land of only two classes, the good and the bad, who all spoke the same language. A cowboy, sheriff, gangster, lawyer, office clerk or company boss, citizen or Senator might be good or bad, but if good they were buddies at heart, and spoke the same language. They married beautiful good women and lived happily ever after without working too hard. The bad guys also spoke the same language, unless they were English villains or more foreign still.

Most British adults and their children found that good or bad American fantasies were more convincing than fantasies about life in Britain. They knew too much about Britain where freedom, beauty and happiness seemed the property of a class which speaks a language taught in universities and private schools.

We know that the people Jack Vettriano paints are American because their clothes and the style of the women recall Hollywood films of the 1930s to 1960s era, a time when worldwide images of sexual excitement, adventure, fast cars, free and lavish lives were exported from the U.S.A. through posters, cartoon books, magazines, adverts, but films especially.

The good-time girls, lonely women in dance halls, bars and hotel bedrooms could easily be Scottish.

So could his men. The interiors and exteriors where we see them could easily be found in places we could all have visited in childhood or find in Britain today. The bright warm steady sunlight of his outdoor scenes strikes us as American because we don't expect it in Britain, but when we were children on holiday we expected it and got it.

There is nothing special about two young men playing cards on a bench by the seaside. Many young men play cards while on holiday. It's a cheap and comradely pastime if you don't stake big sums. Waistcoat and tie was the uniform of the respectable working man on holiday before the 1960s; only posh or bohemian types went in for open-necked shirts, even on very sunny days, but would a couple of Scottish or English friends have played a card game on a public bench in Portobello?

No, only in America could a couple of pals expose themselves so shamelessly. Apart from some sadistic rituals in private rooms Vettriano shows scenes of very possible and commonplace freedom and glamour. If he didn't translate them into American we wouldn't believe him. And now, thank goodness, this former mining engineer with a talent for colour can sell his American scenes to people who talk the language of the British universities and expensive private schools. They, too, must have had fantasies of a classless free society. I wish we would all get together and make one.

# Lean Tales: Postscript

IN 1971 DOCTOR PHILIP HOBSBAUM, who had recently started teaching English at Glasgow University, invited once a fortnight to his home a group of writers, mostly young and unpublished, to read and discuss each other's work. Scotland was the third British kingdom, or province, where he had conducted writing groups after leaving the Cambridge of Doctor Leavis. In London his circle included Peter Redgrove, Peter Porter, George MacBeth and Edward Lucie-Smith. In Belfast there were Seamus Heaney, Stewart Parker, Michael Longley and Bernard MacLaverty. In Glasgow he brought together a number who lodged in the same square mile of tenements and terraces but, before entering his high corner flat on Wilton Street, had in many cases not seen or heard of each other. There was the American poet Anne Stevenson, the Skye poets Catriona Montgomery and Aonghas MacNeacail, with Liz Lochhead, Tom Leonard, Donald Saunders, Marcella Evaristi, Chris Boyce, Alasdair Gray and Jim Kelman. Kelman was in his twenties, had been born in Glasgow and usually lived there though he had detailed knowledge of part of the USA, Wales, the English Channel Islands and London. He had recently become a family man, a position he still holds. Gray was an older Glaswegian who lived by painting and by selling infrequent plays to broadcasting companies. These two at first were indifferent to each others work.

Gray was writing a novel which used the devices of fantasy to overlook facts which were essential to Kelman's prose.

An author who liked Kelman's work was Mary Gray Hughes, one of North America's best short story writers. She visited the Glasgow group as a guest of Philip Hobsbaum and Anne Stevenson, and through her representations Puckerbrush Press of Maine published in 1973 Jim Kelman's first collection of stories, *An Old Pub near the Angel*. This book is now sought by libraries with an interest in Scottish fiction, but on first appearing it brought the author little money or fame. A first book by an original writer, issued by a small foreign publishing house which cannot afford expensive advertising and distribution, will not be reviewed by many big newspapers and magazines, and will be lucky to pay for its printing costs. Even so, *An Old Pub near the Angel* did good. It proved to those who cared for such things that Jim Kelman was a professional writer. Ten years passed before his next book of tales found a publisher, but single pieces appeared regularly in the annual Collins Scottish Short Story Anthology and such publications as *Words* magazine and *Firebird*.

In the middle seventies three former members of Philip Hobsbaum's group, Lochhead, Gray and Kelman, were tutoring part-time for Glasgow University adult education department. It was Liz Lochhead who first read and showed her colleagues the story "Arabella" which starts on page 113 of the book you now hold. She had been given it when visiting a class of writers in the Vale of Leven, a shallow valley of small factory towns along the river flowing from Loch Lomond into the Clyde at Dumbarton Rock. If you enjoyed that story you will know why Lochhead, Gray and Kelman were greatly excited. Most writing classes produce at least one entertaining story which might have been published in days when fiction magazines half filled the station bookstalls. "Arabella" was better than those. We learned that the author had come recently to story-writing, and worked as a clerk and shop-steward in a local electric clock factory. She was twice married, once widowed, with two self-supporting children and three still at school. Our first reaction was to call her a natural writer, which on second thoughts was silly. Nobody writes naturally. It is an art which is learned. Those who do it best have continued teaching themselves after leaving school, and the main teaching method is enthusiastic reading.

Agnes Owens had obviously read enough, and read intelligently enough, to clear her language of the secondhand phrases used by ordinary writers to disguise their lack of ideas. When Gray and Kelman read more of her work (for eventually they also visited the small class in the Vale) they felt she sometimes used too many adverbs, and Jim Kelman has been unremitting in his efforts to make her like Chekhov more and Graham Greene less; but tutoring, where Agnes was concerned, had little to do with the quality of her writing. Being new to writing, in a district where nearly every sort of industry was closing down, her response to those who liked her stories was, "So who will print it? And how much will they pay?" They had to teach her that if she steadily posted her work to a certain number of small magazines, always with a stamped addressed envelope for return, she might get two or three stories published in four or five years and be paid thirty or forty pounds. They had to teach her that the magazines most interested in new talent were liable to cease publication before printing her. They explained that Scotland's really famous writers – those whose stories and poems were referred to by critics and lecturers – had either some sort of unearned income or did hackwork for education and publicity establishments. They told her that in Britain those who feed and house themselves solely by writing have to turn out two or three paperback novels a year, novels which critics and lecturers ignore. They said they knew she was a writer like themselves, but they could not welcome her aboard a sturdy ship called HMS Literature. Such a ship exists, but is a work of communal imagination, and those who talk like captains of it are misleading or misled.

Agnes Owens's talent was too tough to be killed by learning that writing was not a full free life but just another sort of that daily life she knew like the back of her hand. In the next ten years she was paid thirty or forty pounds for a couple of magazine stories, and had a story accepted by an editor who vanished before printing it. She wrote radio plays which were returned by producers with letters expressing great interest – in the next play she sent them. Her first novel, *Gentlemen of the West*, was returned by a publisher who said he might consider printing it if a famous Scottish comedian said something about it which could be used as advertisement. She posted the typescript to the comedian who put it on that pile of unsolicited correspondence which no famous person has time to answer. Industry in the Vale of Leven started closing even faster than in the rest of Britain. Westclox Limited went into liquidation and Agnes did what our dynamic prime minister would do if the Thatcher family had to go on the dole: she hunted for part-time cleaning jobs. She worked for a while in the house of the comedian who had received her typescript a few years before, and got it back.

Meanwhile Jim Kelman and Alasdair Gray, who had started writing ten and twenty years earlier than Agnes Owens, became luckier sooner. In 1983 Polygon Books, the Edinburgh University Press, published Kelman's second collection of stories, *Not Not While The Giro*, and signed a contract for his second novel, *The Busconductor Hines*. Polygon is the only university press in Europe owned and run by the students. Perhaps because it does not need to make a profit it has recently become the most adventurous of small Scottish publishing houses, producing editions of native authors who are well known, but (from the viewpoint of publishers who will collapse if they make no profit) not well known enough. Kelman showed *Gentlemen of the West* to a Polygon editor who loved it, and Agnes's first novel was published in the spring of 1984. By this time a collection of Gray's stories had been issued in hardback by Canongate of Edinburgh and bought for paperback by King Penguin. A director of a London publishing house asked him if he had enough stories to make another collection. Gray said no. There was a handful of stories he had intended to build into another collection, but found he could not, as he had no more ideas for prose fictions. From now on he would write only frivolous things like plays or poems, and ponderous things like *A History Of The Preface*, or a treatise on *The Provision Merchant As Agent Of Evil In Scottish Literature From Galt To Gunn*. Even if his few unpublished stories were stretched by the addition of some prose portraits and poems they would still not amount to a book. The director asked Gray if he could suggest two other writers who would join him in a collection. And now you know how *Lean Tales* was made.

# Of Bill MacLellan*

BILL MACLELLAN, PUBLISHER; born March 20, 1919, died October 16, 1996 the publisher, Bill MacLellan, aged 81, has died of a cerebral haemorrhage at Kello Hospital, Biggar, Lanarkshire. He leaves behind a widow, the concert pianist Agnes Walker, and two daughters. Between the start of his firm in 1941 and its bankruptcy in 1969 he had published original poetry by Hugh MacDiarmid, Sorley MacLean, W S Graham, George Campbell Hay, George Bruce, Sydney Goodsir Smith and Maurice Lindsay: also fiction by J F Hendrie, Edward Gaitens and Fionn MacColla: also plays by Ewan MacColl and Robert McLellan (no relative): also books of Scottish history, art and folklore, the most notable being the Dewar Manuscripts. This would give Bill MacLellan a place in any thorough history of Scottish letters, but no such history exists. Though he is mentioned in biographies and bibliographies of MacDiarmid, hardly anyone under the age of 35 remembers him and he has no entry in *Chambers Scottish Biographical Dictionary* or *Who's Who in Scotland*.

There are two reasons for this neglect. No prominent people in Scottish public life noticed him, apart from Hugh MacDiarmid who, despite being recognised in the early 1920s as Scotland's greatest poet since Burns, was regarded by most people in public life as a troublemaker who they wanted to ignore.

\* *This was an obituary in the 1996* **Glasgow Herald***, here slightly enlarged.*

Only after the 1960s did a Scottish university get a department devoted to Scottish literature and which therefore needed MacDiarmid, but the academics who published critical editions of his works ignored the fact that MacLellan had published earlier anthologies of MacDiarmid's poems, his long *In Memoriam James Joyce*, and the magazine *Scottish Arts and Letters*, three editions of which MacDiarmid edited in the late 1960s. When there appeared hardly any Scots publishers or journals cared for modern Scots arts and letters.

The other reason was his absence of a business mind. His father was a Glasgow city councillor who ran a printing firm at 240 Hope Street, in the same block as the Theatre Royal. He died when Bill was 14. His mother continued the family business until he took it over at the age of 20, by which time he had attended Glasgow High School and the London School of Printing. Throughout the thirties his firm specialised in shade cards for J & P Coats and Paton & Baldwins, the thread and yarn manufacturers. His pacifism made him a conscientious objector in 1939, but after a spell in prison the authorities let him return to his useful and harmless profession in a city which was quite unlike the industrially depressed Glasgow of the inter-war years, and even less like the post-industrial Glasgow of today. The government was responsible for this. It had united the country behind its war effort by taking control of all productive industry and land. It had abolished private competition by deliberately paralysing the money market, restricting wages and rents and prices, and by controlling manufacture through agreement with the trade unions. It was also promising a new era of social equality and full employment. This Tory initiative was the foundation of the post-war welfare state, which led to the swinging sixties, which in the Thatcher era was widely advertised as the cause of everything wrong with Britain. But while fighting a Fascist dominated European empire it seemed a good idea: especially in Glasgow which was again at the centre of vigorous mining, steel-producing and shipbuilding communities. It was also Britain's main transit port. English, Americans and Poles were billeted there.

This was how Bill met Jadwiga Harasowski. All I know of her is her name and that she got Bill to print Polish classics and newspapers for the Polish troops. It was through her that a commercial printer discovered he had resources to publish books – and in those days he was surrounded by people who wanted them. Without official backing, many arts centres had sprung up in private houses and forces' service clubs near Sauchiehall Street, and Bill's office was one of them.

The best account of it can be found in Joan Littlewood's autobiography, *Little Me*. Wishing to start a people's political theatre in 1945, Joan despaired of London and sent scouts around Britain to find somewhere better. I will quote her.

**Jimmie and Bill Douglas skipped to Glasgow one weekend and came back born-again Scots. They'd undergone conversion in a river of whisky at 240 Hope Street.**
**"What goes on there?"**
**"It's William MacLellan's place."**
**"A pub?"**

**"A publishing house. Not only is there a poet on every street corner," said Bill, "but they're all sleeping at MacLellan's, among the presses, wrapped in their own galley proofs."**

About the same time The Unity Theatre started the professional careers of Duncan Macrae, Roddy McMillan and other fine actors. Its *The Gorbals Story* was taken to London, filmed and inspired a Sadler's Wells ballet, with decor by Colquhoun and MacBride who had recently graduated (with Joan Eardley) from Glasgow Art School. The Unity production of *Uranium 235* anticipated *Oh What A Lovely War* and McGrath's *The Cheviot, the Stag and the Black Black Oil*. The text was published by MacLellan. The painter J. D. Fergusson and his wife had returned to Glasgow. MacLellan published Fergusson's study of modern Scottish painting: Fergusson designed some covers of MacLellan's magazine *Scottish Arts and Letters*. His publishing successes were never commercial successes and I suspect the thread manufacturers' shade cards let the firm last as long as it did.

But the advertising and distribution of the books was often left to the authors, who resented getting little or no money for them. Ian Hamilton Finlay's first book contains a story about a hungry young writer failing to get paid by a kilted publisher with clear blue eyes and an absent-minded manner. Bill would describe this story in detail to acquaintances who pretended not to have read it, ending with the remark "... and then I realised this publisher was meant to be me!" The similarity inspired him with a slightly bewildered amazement which was, I think, his main attitude to

life. Working in a confused and turbulent period, when
hardly any other publishers outside or inside Scotland
cared that Scottish arts and letters existed, Bill
MacLellan did the best he could for them and lost his
family's profitable little business in the process. We
must wait for a thorough history of our
native culture before his part in it
is properly recognised.

# Working Legs*

BIRDS OF PARADISE is a professional theatre company providing professional drama training for people with physical disabilities. It also tours with professional productions. Formed in 1989, in 1993 it became a limited company and a registered charity, taking a new name from Ronald Laing's book *Sweet Bird of Paradise* which it had partly dramatized. When I was asked to write a play for it in 1996 the Council of Management was as follows:

Forrest Alexander, *wheelchairbound by multiple sclerosis.*

Iain Carmichael, *chairman, car salesman with some experience of theatre company management.*

Andrew Dawson, *art director and fully qualified drama therapist.*

David Maclean, *director at the Alpha Project resource centre for people with disabilities.*

Patsy Morrison, *administrator.*

Sylvia Sandeman, *paraplegic, disability consultant with Spinal Injuries Scotland.*

Only Mr Dawson and Ms Morrison were salaried.

The suggestion that I write a play for the company came from Forrest Alexander. He knew me as a novelist and thought that, since novels and plays

---

*Epilogue to a 1997 book of the play printed by Dog and Bone, Glasgow, which was then subsidised by the Glasgow City and Scottish Arts Councils. This ends by predicting a play for the company by Archie Hind, never made as he and a new director could not agree.*

equally depend on characters, dialogue and settings, any saleable novelist could write a successful play. This is not always true, as Henry James discovered on the first night of his play *Guy Domville*. Had I only written prose fiction I would have rejected Forrest's suggestion. However, in the days of a long-forgotten Labour administration I had seven radio, eleven television, four stage plays networked or performed, and was a highly inefficient minutes secretary of The Scottish Society of Playwrights, a small trade union started by CP Taylor and Tom Gallagher. My career as professional dramatist ended in 1978 with the death of Francis Head, my London agent, but I still felt able to write plays so Forrest introduced me to the company.

From the 6th of June to the 22nd of August I had nine meetings with actors and friends of the company, always at 5pm on Thursdays, always with Andrew Dawson or Patsy Morrison present, and all but once at the company office near Glasgow Cross, in a large room where we sat round a table among the vivid creations of a disabled folks' art class.

To the first meeting I brought only one idea. The play must have strong parts for as many disabled actors as possible, so should be set in a world where the able-bodied were a pitiable minority. The company thought this amusing. Forrest Alexander suggested a wheelchair benefit tribunal to which the able-bodied would (unsuccessfully) appeal. Mrs Anne Marie Robertson suggested that the tribunal might be a dumb one which spoke to the appellants through an artificial voice box. This grotesque notion was along lines I wanted, but I needed to know the everyday embarrassments of being disabled so that my able-bodied hero could suffer these also. I was told how hard it is for people in wheelchairs to get service in pubs if not accompanied by an able-bodied friend. Mrs Robertson, who has been wheelchair-bound for many years, spoke of some normal people's inability to accept that she was married with three children. When asked, "How did you manage that?" she had to smile and shrug her shoulders. She once had to refuse a good job because acceptance meant flitting to a house where light-switches, taps, cooker and other essential things were out of her reach and there was no money to re-equip it.

At this first meeting I also heard that my idea was not original. Vic Finkelstein, senior lecturer in disability studies at the Open University, had set a story in a village designed for the badly disabled. The able-bodied who cared for them were endangered by low doors, ceilings and wheeltracks linking the buildings. Central Television had issued a video cartoon of this story. It makes the same social point as *Working Legs* while being more informative about needs of disabled folk, but differs in plot and characters. I have consciously stolen from Mr Finkelstein the low door in scene 2 and Able's offer to wear a safety helmet.

A week later I met Alistair Fleming, a student of architecture before being hit by a car. It had left him partly paralysed and had damaged his short-term memory. He knew my novel *Lanark* because he had read it before the accident and he told me his own story in a jocular way, saying he had been very lucky – in his parents. When hospital treatment stopped doing him good his mother gave up her job to nurse him at home, and both parents had used their savings to fight a long legal battle with the car's insurance company. They won. Alistair now lives in a house adapted to his needs and employs a truly Christian minder. At a third meeting I met Mrs Alice Thompson who suggested her own medical experience could give my play a happy ending. A married woman and working nurse, she had undergone an operation for a heart condition and suffered a stroke during it. She recovered consciousness seven months later without the use of her legs.

This gallant willingness to make fun of terrible experience made my job easy. I wrote the first two scenes in time for the fourth meeting. From then on we sat round the table reading scenes aloud as they were added and discussing how the play should go. Ernest Kyle, who suffers from emphysema and is also a writer, suggested that Able's legginess should have led to the breakdown of an earlier marriage. Ernest invented the concept of wheel-training, wrote the tender dialogue which ends scene 4 and gave detailed information upon how our government is deliberately breaking down the social welfare services. As we read on it grew easy to see readers in particular parts. John Campbell seemed right for Able McMann because prosthetic surgery in both legs lets him walk with a completely natural appearance, yet his thoughtful, anxious face indicates life is not easy. Anne Marie seemed suited to the manager or Meg. It was she who suggested Able's ankles be handcuffed.

The *Birds of Paradise* Company has received generous grants from Glasgow City and Scottish Arts

Councils. This has helped the company to enlarge its staff and engage with forty-five drama workshops throughout Scotland. The number is growing. These cater for a wide range of disabilities while containing many people without them. At present most of them are rehearsing *Working Legs*; but the parent company has commissioned a new play from the author Archie Hind which will go into rehearsal when *Working Legs* goes on tour in 1998.

The grants have also helped us publish this book in time for Christmas 1997. Plays are usually published after the first stage production, but the condition of Scottish theatre makes the reverse order just as sensible. It remains for me to thank Christopher Boyce for advice on how to make scene 10 more convincing, and for suggesting the reappearance of Miss Shy at the end; also Angela Mullane for help with legal details; also Doctors Bruce Charleton and Gillian Rye for dialogue in the surgical operation scene; also Scott Pearson and Joe Murray who between them typed and typeset this book under the author's hideously exacting regime.

# Jonah, Micah and Nahum

THE THIRTY NINE BOOKS THAT King James' bible calls The Old Testament show the state of the Jews between 900 and 100 BC and preserve legends from more ancient times. They were edited into their present form by scholars defending their culture from an empire ruling land once theirs; an empire of people equally clever and literate; Greeks whose books were as various as their Gods. Jews were then unique in worshipping a single God: their folklore, laws, politics and poetry kept mentioning him. The editors arranged these books in the chronological order of the subject matter, producing a story of their people from prehistoric times and making their God the strongest character in world fiction. It began with a second century BC poem telling how he made the universe and people like a poet, out of words, followed by a fifth century BC tale of how he made man like a potter, out of clay. It then showed God adapting to his worshipers from the stone age to their own.

Adam, Cain and Noah find God punitive but soothed by the smell of burnt flesh, mostly animal. He connives with the

*Published 1999 by Canongate, this was part of a small paperback set, each a book of the Bible (in the 1611 version, authorized by King James) each introduced by a modern author. I chose* **Jonah**, *my favourite part of the Bible. To this I was asked to add two shorter adjacent books. My introduction provoked some adverse publicity. An Orthodox Jewish spokesman and fundamental Muslim one said that by saying Abraham tricked wealth out of a king by prostituting his wife, I was insulting a great prophet. I do not see how anyone can read* **Genesis** *Chapter 20 and disagree, but I was glad my introduction had made priests agree who were of faiths that sometimes did not. I found it strange that no Christian fundamentalist spoke out agreeing with them.*

tricks of Abraham and Isaac, polygamous nomads who get cattle or revenge by prostituting a wife or mistreating foreigners or relatives. When Moses leads Jewish tribes out of Egypt God commands them like a pharaoh, promising unlimited protection for unlimited obedience. He is a war God when they invade Palestine, smiting them with plague when they do not kill every man, woman, child and animal in a captured city. Their leaders (called Prophets because God tells them the future) are patriarchs and commanders until they get land and cities of their own where (as in other lands) wealth is managed by official landlords and priests who exploit the poor. New kinds of prophet then arise: poets inspired by moral rage who speak for the exploited. They say that if Jewish rulers don't obey God by being just and merciful he will use the might of foreigners to smash their new-made kingdoms. That happens. From 680 BC to 1958 Jews are ruled by foreign empires, first Assyrians and at last British. They outlive so many empires that Norwegian Ibsen calls them the aristocrats of world history for they can survive without land or government.

That was not wholly true. They were governed by the words of their prophets, especially those in the last Old Testament books who said the Jewish God is also God of all people, even people who oppress them; that God has created Jews to keep his words alive until the whole world learns justice and mercy by obeying him; that before then Jews should welcome suffering as punishment for sin or tests of faith. This must have sounded a strange new policy to those who wanted back nations founded (as all nations have been

founded) by killing folk. No wonder many Jews
assimilated with foreigners, and that the faithful sometimes sang psalms begging God to leave them alone.

The Book of Jonah is a prose comedy about a Jew who wants God to leave him alone and cannot grasp the scope of God's new policy.

Jonah is an unwilling prophet. His Jewish conscience orders him to denounce the wicked Assyrian empire in its capital city so he at once sails towards a different city where he hopes foreign gods will prevail over his own. This breaks the first of the ten commandments: You shall have no other God than me: hence the tempest. The international crew see it is aimed at someone aboard. Many verses describe their reluctance to fling Jonah out, even when he tells them it is the one way to save themselves. The book is insisting that mercy is not just a Jewish virtue; but out Jonah goes and God saves him in the belly of a fish. Here the prophet chants a psalm saying God can save those who cry on him from the belly of hell. This hell is not the eternal torture chamber later adopted by official Christianity. For Jews hell is the worst that living people can suffer. Jonah IS suffering it, unless the fish intestines are a cosy place. But now he knows that God is always with him, so he need not fear death.

Then comes a parody of Exodus. The God of Moses sent Pharaoh a message then hardened Pharaoh's heart to reject it, giving Moses an excuse to show God's power by inflicting plagues until all Egyptian first-born children and cattle are dead. God uses Jonah to send the Assyrians a message that softens their king's heart. The king leads his people into abandoning their evil ways, so God repented of the evil he said he would do unto them, and he did not. This contradicts the Mosaic code which says evil MUST be rewarded with evil.

So Jonah learns he is not a scourge in the hand of God like Moses, Joshua and Samson but a reformer, and like many reformers he looks a bit stupid. It is now obvious that the enemy king who thought his people might be persuaded to deserve mercy knew more about God than God's Hebrew prophet. Jonah's short but influential career ends not with a bang but with his dismal whimper: "I know thou art a gracious God, merciful (et cetera.) Therefore now, O Lord, take, I beseech thee, my life from me, for it is better for me to die than to live." God cuts this self-pitying cackle with a short question: "Doest thou well to be angry?" Jonah is too cowardly or childish to admit anger and squats outside the city determined to die by sunstroke if the promise of destruction is not fulfilled. Not even the mercy of miraculous shade cast over him softens this determination. The shade is withdrawn. In a fever Jonah hears God repeat something like his last question. He now answers truthfully and is favoured by words framed like another question. They suggest reasons for both God's action and inaction; most evil is caused by folly; widespread slaughter is not the best cure if a prophecy of disaster can prevent it. We are not told if Jonah learns these lessons because they are meant for us.

Believers and unbelievers have argued pointlessly about the truth of Jonah's book because they did not know great truths can be told in fantasies.

It was known by editors who put Jonah before two
realistic books about Assyria and the destruction of cities.

Micah starts a prophetic sermon in verse by denouncing the Jews who live in Samaria; God has let Assyria enslave them for disobeying him; soon the princes and priests of Jerusalem will be conquered, for they seek wealth and luxury instead of justice and mercy and think God's forgiveness can be bought by animal sacrifices. Micah foretells a disastrous but not hopeless future. After much warfare the whole world will find peace by accepting the one true God, for a Jewish ruler from the little town of Bethlehem will become lord of every nation. This prophecy must have inspired hope and dread in every imaginative child born afterward in Bethlehem.

Nahum came eighty years later. He was probably an Assyrian slave when all Jewish territory had been conquered, just as Micah foretold. Nahum saw the destruction of Nineveh by the combined armies of Babylon and Persia. These killed the people and washed the city away by channeling the River Tigris into it. The only grand truth in Nahum's triumphant song is that nations who keep living by armaments will perish by them. Most governments think this only true of foreigners. I quote from Tom Leonard's *On the Mass Bombing of Iraq and Kuwait, Commonly Known As "The Gulf War" with Leonard's Shorter Catechism*. AK Press published it in 1991.

**Q.** What did Britain take part in on Tuesday, February 19, 1991?

**A.** It took part in what was at that point "one of the most ferocious attacks on the centre of Baghdad", using bombers and Cruise missiles fired from ships.

**Q.** What did John Major say about the bombing the next day?

**A.** He said: "One is bound to ask about attacks such as these: What sort of people is it that can carry them out? They certainly are consumed with hate. They are certainly sick of mind, and they can be certain of one thing – they will be found."

(He was talking about 5lb of explosives left in a litter basket at Victoria Station in London. This killed one person and critically injured three.)

Major lead a government containing people privately enriched by weapon-sales to both Britain's army and the army of the dictator we fought. We fought him again before Christmas 1998 when our most highly respected newspapers said that, though wicked and undemocratic, this dictator had better stay in power to stop Iraq falling apart and increasing the cost of our petrol. Meanwhile, since our troops in 1991 fired bullets tipped with uranium, more babies are being born in Iraq with distorted bodies and heads, others without heads.

When a child Ernest Levy lost faith in a purely national god by living through Auschwitz and Belsen. He became a cantor in a Glasgow synagogue and now believes God is the innocent, creative, spiritual part of everyone. This sounds like the merciful God of Jonah but can any God be merciful to a nation that does not repent of the evil it does? That makes, sells and uses what kills, cripples and warps even the unborn? From Jonah, Micah and Nahum Jesus learned what governments of Britain and the USA refuse to learn from Jesus. They act like Moses and Elijah, deliberately killing and diseasing thousands of civilians who cannot harm them. They do it without the old Hebrew excuse of being slaves wanting freedom or wanderers needing a homeland, without the Crusaders' excuse of defending True Faith, without the Liberal excuse of spreading democracy. The one idea behind this is that any number of foreigners can be killed to keep up global company profits, though politicians give nicer-sounding reasons. The inevitable victory of big arms-selling nations over small arms-buying ones has provoked counter-attacks. Just now these have killed very few, but enough to prove that this world ruled by greed is hatching one ruled by revenge. Old and New Testaments should teach us to reform our ways for our children's sake.

I belong to a small nation that for centuries has exported more soldiers and weapons than the defence of it ever needed, and now contains more destructive nuclear missiles and launching machines than any nation outside the USA. England has the good sense to contain hardly any. I hope the reform of Britain starts in Scotland.

# The Book
# of Prefaces*

BOTTOM *There are things in this comedy which will never please. First, Pyramus must draw a sword to kill himself which the ladies cannot abide. How answer you that?*
STARVELING *I believe we must leave the killing out, when all is done.*
BOTTOM *Not a whit: I have a device to make all well. Write me a prologue, and let the prologue say, we will do no harm with our swords, and that Pyramus is not killed. That will make all well.*
A MIDSUMMER NIGHT'S DREAM by SHAKESPEARE

IT IS DONE. ENDED. FINISHED. COMPLETE. Thank goodness, for I think goodness is god's kindest name. He, She or It (choose your favourite pronoun: just now I feel inclined to worship god the tree) has sterner names, like Reality, Nature, and Eternal Truth, compared with which each of us is a poor wee frail body – even such mighty truth-tellers as Moses, Jesus, Mohammed, Shakespeare, Jefferson, Robert Burns and Jane Austen. I apologise to any Christian I offend by naming Jesus as a human being, but his last words upon the cross persuade me that, whatever he did later, he too is one of us. So I thank GOODNESS for letting me live to the end of this book, for though stern Reality, Nature, Truth & Co generate and allow goodness they do not let us depend upon it, as a multitude of hungry, homeless, voteless people know in every nation except, maybe, some Scandinavian ones.

I need do nothing now but give, as I promised

*Epilogue to my longest work of non-fiction (640 pages) published 2000AD by Bloomsbury. It had taken only a few years less to finish than my first novel.

in my opening advert, the motives and circumstances that led to this book, then apologise for the result.

In the early 80s I borrowed from Campbell Semple *The Philosophy of Natural History* by his remote ancestor, William Smellie, whose preface suggested the plan of this book. I saw at once it was a book I would want if someone else made it, but nobody had. Desire for a non-existent thing is the best motive for making it, even if a wish for fame and cash drives the maker too. When relaxing from other work I began to take note of good prefaces from Chaucer's *Canterbury Tales* to Vonnegut's *Breakfast of Champions*, which was how I first imagined this book starting and ending. I soon saw that most readers would, like myself, enjoy it more if they were given more information than Smellie's plan suggested. The ancient device of a marginal commentary or gloss seemed the best way to add this without breaking the flow of the most essential part.

So when a literary agent (Fiona Morrison) asked if I had ideas for a work of NON fiction (meaning a historical or biographical or critical work too speculative to be called factual) I suggested this one. When she asked for an introduction and specimen commentaries to show to publishers I quickly wrote the advert starting on page 7 and glosses on prefaces to *The Cloud of Unknowing*, Hobbes' *Leviathan* and *The Lyrical Ballads*. They were mainly, though not exactly, as printed here. Each gloss began with the sentence This was written in an age of great revolutions because I believed then, and believe still, that every generation sees an amazing change of social circumstances. The advert was cheekier. It wondered why university professors had not undertaken this anthology long before, and suggested they were unable to see the value of a book which could be made so easily – for I then thought it could be easily made. In the six centuries between Geoffrey Chaucer and Kurt Vonnegut literacy, I believed, had steadily grown with expanding populations, so the number of important books must also have steadily increased. I already knew many of the books and it would not be hard to find others that university professors agreed were best. I would photocopy their prefaces from reprints in public libraries, arrange these chronologically, then crib commentaries from the *Encyclopaedia Britannica* which Smellie had also pioneered. Anyone with a Scottish Higher Leaving Certificate in English and Lower Leaving Certificate in History can do that, especially if they were educated at Whitehill Senior Secondary School, east Glasgow.

From this you may deduce, dear reader, that though I was then over fifty I still believed in the progressive view of history – believed that each generation had added good new social and scientific and artistic works to those of the past, thus giving more people comfort, security and freedom for the future. Any honest news report about life in most Asian, African and South American lands proved that view was not inevitable, that it was being horribly disproved in many places, but my own family history showed such progress had occurred in Britain, and would enable me to make this book.

For my grandparents had been born in the middle of Victoria's reign. My mum's dad was a foreman shoemaker who brought his wife from Northampton to Glasgow when English employers blacklisted him for trade union activities. He also brought his daughters to tears by reading them Hardy's *Tess of the D'Urbervilles*. They did not regard Dickens and Hardy as English literary classics but as entertainingly truthful describers of the world they knew, Dickens showing the mainly comic aspects, Hardy the mainly tragic. My dad's dad was an industrial blacksmith and elder of a Congregational kirk: the kirk Cromwell worshipped in because the congregation chose its own priests. His political heroes were William Gladstone and Keir Hardie, both of whom wanted Scotland and Ireland to have independent governments, and British manual labourers to be as healthily and comfortably housed as their bosses, if not quite as spaciously.

Like most of the literate working class my grandparents thought themselves middle class, though my dad's parents lived with five children, my mother's parents with three, in small one-room-and-kitchen rented flats without inside lavatories and baths, where water and food was heated by the kitchen fire. Most of the wealthy depended on such primitive heating and cooking before 1900, though their servants saved them from the sight of it. My dad, born 1897, left school at twelve, worked a weigh bridge in a Clydeside dock, and joined the army in 1914. He survived Flanders, lost his parents' faith and became a Fabian Socialist, earning money between 1918 and 1939 by operating a machine in a cardboard box factory. In his spare time he worked without pay for co-operative out-door holiday organisations: The Camping Club of Great Britain, Scottish Youth Hostel Association and others.

That Trade Union shoemaker, Liberal blacksmith and Co-operative Fabian box-cutter were three types who created the first British Labour government: a party of MPs who preferred Ruskin to Marx and in 1924 passed parliamentary acts enabling town & rural councils to build the kind of housing scheme where I was born in 1934. Though my parents had only two children our flat had three rooms beside a lavatory – bathroom with hot tap water, a kitchen with that also and an electric cooker. Like most of the British working class we were further enriched by the second World War and its aftermath. My parents then paid for my health treatment and excellent education through their income tax, which I took for granted as the fair and democratic way of doing it. In their small book collection was Burns' Poems, Carlyle's *French Revolution*, Dickens' *Bleak House*, all Ibsen's plays in Archer's translation and the plays of Bernard Shaw.

My dad was also a member of the Readers Union Book Club which brought into our house in the late 1940s the works of James Joyce, Hemingway, Orwell and Arthur Waley's translation of the Chinese Monkey epic and poetic anthology. Meanwhile Whitehill School was trying and failing to teach me Latin and Greek, but did introduce me to English literature from Chaucer to Conrad; and in Riddrie public library I discovered exciting translations of Heine's *Reisbilder* and Sartre's *Nausea*. I would be ungrateful if I did not mention the BBC Third Programme. This broadcasting network was set up with the help of émigré intellectuals of a Socialist sort driven out of mainland Europe by Fascism, but their outlook was, in the broadest sense of the word, catholic. It only broadcast in the evening between the hours of six and eleven, and broadcast nothing but music and plays and lectures which were labelled (in the slang of the forties and fifties) highbrow, but which contained no erudite jargon, so I hugely enjoyed it.

Like many others in those days I believed Britain had attained a high new state of civilisation from which it would never descend. For over a century folk had striven against corporate greed to make this a land where everyone's health care and education would be decided by their needs and abilities, not their parents' wealth. This state lasted for nearly forty years. It helped millions of working class children join the professional classes. It let a grocer's daughter become Britain's prime minister, let me become an artist and author who would turn Smellie's idea into a book.

In 1987 Fiona Morrison got a publisher's advance to let me work steadily on the book. I began by arranging prefaces I had chosen in chronological order, which gave my progressive view of history its first hard knock. Dates of the earliest works were not exact, but exact enough to show Chaucer did not lead a procession of great writers, he walked in a crowd of them – Langland, Barbour, the Gawain poet and others. After Chaucer's death in 1400 the crowd shrank to a widely spaced line of pedestrians. Two centuries passed before such a good crowd of vernacular English authors jostled again, apart from a wee flurry of them in Lowland Scotland around James IV's time. Why?

I took so long to find out why that I used up the advance of my first publisher (Canongate of Edinburgh) though I also added the long introduction on Hebrew, Greek, Roman and Christian writing and prefaces to Anglo-Saxon works. In 1990 I tackled the effects of the Norman Conquest, and later discharged my debt to Canongate by giving it a science-fiction novel. I then raised money by writing more fiction and in 1995 resumed work on this book for Bloomsbury of London. It has now been announced so confidently for so many years that respected guides to modern first editions began saying it was published in 1989. (Joseph Connolly suggests £20 or less is a good second hand price, R.B.Russell puts it at £10.) Only now, on Tuesday 21st of December 1999, as I sit in bed recovering from flu, is the book being finally completed.

Copyright costs have forced me to abandon my plan for a section of prefaces by great 20th-century authors, including those who now write Australian, Asian, African and Caribbean kinds of English. The book is only completed for the third millennium through help from nearly every writer I know well, and four in Glasgow University English Literature Department contacted through my friend Philip Hobsbaum. I admit to having tampered a little with some of their contributions (Janice Galloway says her commentaries on Bronte and George Eliot have Gray fingermarks all over them) but have nowhere contradicted their opinions. My main sorrow is that Chris Boyce, who gave notes for the commentary on Cowley's preface to the History of the Royal Society, and Iain Crichton Smith who glossed Keats' and Conrad's prefaces, can neither receive a copy of this book, nor thanks for their help with it.

I have slighter regrets. Like most who have

worked for years on a job I see how much better it
could be made if begun over again. I would include prefaces by William Morris and Henry James, and commentaries on all the twentieth century prefaces I cannot afford to print, and sixty four pages of notes at the end to support all my glib assertions in earlier pages. I would spend weeks redrawing the illustrations on pages 175 and 267 to enhance their clarity, and would find something better than Dicky Doyle's old Punch cover to introduce the Liberal English section which should have been called Liberal English, Irish, Scots and American. But I sympathise with Bloomsbury for stopping me continuing to revise for another year or two.

These sixteen years of intermittent work have seen the dismantling of a Russian military empire established with USA and British aid in 1944. It has seen the world-wide triumph of international capitalism with United States and British armed forces as its most militant powers, so there has been no reduction of world warfare. Britain is entering a new constitutional period after a gigantic reduction of local government democracy, also the biggest sale of public property to private businesses since the dissolution of the monasteries in 1540, the abolition of common land in the 1820s. Even Britain's public water supply, the greatest achievement of Victorian socialism, has been privatised, so a French company now owns a British reservoir. Despite protests by librarians the best of branch library stock have been sold and replaced by the kind of cheap paperback most newsagents sell. Despite protests by teachers our local school buildings are sold to private property developers, and schools in poor areas cannot supply their pupils with proper books, though deals with local businesses will equip them with continually replaceable word processors at the tax-payers' expense. I consider this anthology a memorial to the education British governments now think useless for British working class children. But it has been my education, so I have to believe it was one of the best in the world.

*I started making maps when I was small*
*showing place, resources, where the enemy*
*and where love lay.*
*I did not know time adds to land.*
*Events drift continually down*
*effacing landmarks, raising the level like snow.*

*I have grown up.*
  *My maps are out of date.*
    *The land lies over me now.*
      *I cannot move. It is time to go.*

# Sixteen Occasional Verses*

POSTSCRIPT on what occasioned these foregoing verses

THE FIRST OF MARCH 1990

In 1990 the heads of print workshops in Glasgow and Berlin co-operated to make an artful book. They paid two professional writers and two professional artists from each city to live for a month in the other city and give the book (titled *Vier + Four*) writings and pictures based on their foreign experiences. That is how I came to be in the sky to Berlin on the first of March, and was later a guest of the Berlin Literarische Colloquium on the shore of the Wannsee when Berlin (her great partition wall about to be demolished and USA troops still deploying armaments in her suburbs) was the most politically complex city in Europe. I intended to write a verse diary of my Berlin experiences for *Vier + Four* but was unable to write more than this introduction to it.

WINTER HOUSEKEEPING

I used two houses in the winter of 1990-91, one rented from Glasgow District Council, one by the woman I was to marry. That made her home mine too, so I soon had as few as most people.

WAITING IN GALWAY

In April 1994 we went to Galway Literary Festival and enjoyed quiet afternoons in an uncrowded, unhurried

---

* *Published 2000 by Morag McAlpine.*

pub with many intricate little corners. Blows can never be evaded for long and one will inevitably kill us, but in the snug of that small drinking shop and bedroom of a small hotel I felt that between blows peace can exist for life to be good, if addiction to peace is avoided.

SOUTH AFRICA APRIL 1994

More people have lived during the twentieth century than in the whole half million years before it, and more have been violently killed. The largest killings were in wars started by capitalist empires and by single party dictatorships. After 1950 several states created and maintained by violence ended without violence destroying them: the British and USSR empires, the dictatorships of Greece, Spain, Portugal, South Africa. I wanted to celebrate the fact that unjust systems at last exhaust those who inherit them, that no human state is solid.

GENESIS

The start of the Jewish Genesis and the Christian Saint John's Gospel that expands on it have been used by people in authority to suggest that the order of the universe derives from dictatorial words of command: an idea loved by those who want to be obeyed and many who like obeying them. Existential philosophy opposed that by saying the universe that generates us has no order but the order our own minds decide to impose. This view, though perhaps bracing for brave souls trying to change a crushing state of mind or society, may have led to the woolliness of some Postmodern theories. My wee poem suggests order is a pattern unfolded in simultaneous material and mental events, and neither has priority. No doubt this idea too is liable to corruption.

## POSTMODERNISM

In 1995 I attended a conference about links between visual and verbal art. It was held in Elmira College, New York State, USA and ended in a debate dominated by a speaker who talked only about Postmodernism. He seemed sure that critics and lecturers were now entitled to read any idea they liked into a work, and illustrated the playful freedom this allowed by reading out twenty or thirty pithy, often humorous definitions of postmodernism, which he first said were quotations of writing by his students and finally declared were invented by himself. His energetic speech led to a discussion which said nothing about the links between vision and word and ignored descriptions of our intricate universe and how well or badly we live in it. Ideas Homer, Jesus, Shakespeare, Mark Twain etcetera thought important seemed irrelevant to the Postmodern speech game. Then chaos theory was mentioned with enthusiasm by one who seemed to think it a liberation from logical constraint instead of a logical way to solve problems.

I remembered Pope's Dunciad. This described fashionable criticism so divorced from common sense that it snuffs out the Word that Saint John said was the light of the mind, thus returning the universe to that earliest state which Jews thought a dark depth and the Greeks a mere chaos.

The first seven lines of this poem are quotations from the start of Saint John's Gospel in King James authorised version, the tenth line from Pope's Dunciad but shifted to the past tense.

DEAR COLLEAGUE

Philip Hobsbaum wrote a bitter, funny poem in the voice of someone interviewing an applicant for a teaching job. The applicant is rejected because, though an experienced teacher, he has also written books. My poem ends by paraphrasing the end of Philip's, which uses the conventional phrase ending most business letters in English.

POEMS 9-15 INCLUSIVE

These seven poems were suggested by the titles and images of prints by Ian McCulloch. They were written in August 1998 for Ian's book of prints, *The Artist in His World* published by Argyll, of Glendaruel.

TO TOM LEONARD

While excepting God as the energy, form, matter of the universe and believing all religious beliefs are partly true, I dislike the division of God into father, son and holy ghost: a division I feel too human and masculine, yet also too abstract and theoretical to imagine. In October 1999 I was delighted to read *God the Tree* in translations from the poetry of Rilke. Rilke imagined a sixteenth century Russian monk who speaks of god's Italian branch having an unusually sunny growth compared with the Russian branch, which none the less has its own unique growths. The brought to mind
Scotland and Tom Leonard and let me
end this collection hopefully.

# Fifteenth
# February 2003[*]

MY PARENTS TAUGHT ME that deliberately getting attention by unusual actions was bad manners – they called it showing off. By pleasing teachers, broadcasters, and others in authority I am now a published author and Professor of Glasgow University. Why should I walk with many others through the centre of Glasgow, complaining about a government that lets me vote to keep or change it once every five years? I am not driven by *esprit de corps*, team spirit, don't enjoy feeling part of a crowd. I think most goodness, truth and beauty has been achieved by folk like Jesus, Galileo and Van Gogh who were out of step with multitudes. Soldiers marching together appal me as much as a line of high-kicking chorus girls appal most feminists. I only take part in political demonstrations when feeling it wicked to stay away: a state first experienced in 1956.

I was then a student who, twice a week on his way to Art School, called at a clinic for asthma injections to reduce allergies causing asthma. As I bared my arm for the needle one morning a nurse treating me said,

*"'What do you think of the war?'*
*'What war?'*

∗ *Originally a* **Herald** *article published 17 February 2003, I first used it as a non-fiction tale in* **The Ends of our Tethers, 13 Sorry Stories** *published 2003 by Canongate Books, then made it a fictional episode in the life of John Tunnock in Chapter 14 of* **Old Men in Love***, published 2007 by Bloomsbury.*

*'The war with Egypt. We invaded it two days ago – we and the French and the Israelis.'*
*'But… but what's the BBC saying about it?'*
*'The BBC hasn't said anything about it yet, but it's in all the morning papers.'"*

This war is called the Suez War because Britain and France were fighting to get back control of the Suez canal which Egypt had nationalised the year before. Israel was fighting because Egypt had barred it from what had been an international waterway. Like the USA's war with Vietnam the Suez War was never openly declared. The British public and Parliament only heard of it on the third day when the government could no longer keep it an official secret. I hurried out of the clinic, excited by my certainty that public opinion would drive that government (a Tory one) from office in a week. I was naïve. Fellow students at the Art School were excited by the news, not all were horrified by what I considered a lawless action, even when the BBC broke silence and announced the RAF was bombing Alexandria, chief seaport of a nation without an air force. A friend who I thought was socialist said cheerfully, "The old lion is wagging its tail again!"

Like journalists writing for some popular newspapers he thought the war a revival of imperial health. I heard an anti-war rally was being held in Glasgow University Union, rushed there and found it a rally against the USSR invasion of Czechoslovakia, which was happening at the same time. Like everybody else there I too decided to forget the bombed Egyptians in my sympathy for the invaded Czechs. The Suez invasion killed 22 Britons, 10

French, about 200 Israelis and 921 Egyptians, yet Britain and its allies lost that war because the United Nations, the Vatican and the United States condemned it – also the British Labour Parliamentary Party. Yes, I voted Labour then because Labour (I believed) had created a welfare state and abolished government by stock exchange (unlike the USA) and was part of a nation providing a democratic alternative to single party dictatorship (unlike the Soviet Union). I was grateful to the Labour Party for my healthcare, my further education and for condemning the Suez War.

I was happier still when a large majority of local Labour parties voted for Britain to abandon nuclear weapons: another good example we were giving to the world. But the Labour Party leaders rejected the majority opinion of the ordinary members who had voted them into Westminster. On this matter Labour MPs sided steadily with the Tories. By 1965 the London parliament's ability to turn local Socialists into British Tories had moved me to vote for Scottish home rule, which we are far from having achieved in 2003.

Britain now has a government to the right of Mrs Thatcher's, for hers spent more on social welfare than Mr Blair's. So did John Major's. Blair supports President Bush who has decided to break the Geneva Conventions by not just invading a country that cannot invade ours, but also occupying it in order to change the government. Bush declares that Iraq has acquired genocidal weapons of the kind the USA, Russia, Britain, France, India, China, Israel also possess, which makes us terribly nervous. To paraphrase Miss Jean Brodie, "Do not do as I do, little nation, do as I say."

Can anyone doubt that if the USA and Britain backed a United Nations plan to inspect and catalogue the dangerous weapons of every nation it would be implemented? Of course every nation would have to include the USA and Britain and Israel. Saddam possesses evil weapons because Britain and the USA sold them to him and the means of making them. In the 1980s he was our ally and used them to exterminate many innocent Kurdish people, but now, in 2003, Kurds are fleeing into Iraq to escape from the government of our ally, Turkey. Certainly he arrests people on suspicion and imprisons them without trial or legal advice, but since 11 September 2001 George Bush's government also does that.

That Iraq contains more oil than any other single nation – that the USA would fall apart without cheap petrol – is one reason for this war. Another must be a widespread desire in the USA to see some brownish turbaned Islamic folk suffer what happened on 11 September 2001. An internationally orchestrated police investigation would not look sufficiently dramatic on television. The invasion of Afghanistan was not enough. It killed more civilians than those who died in the World Trade Centre, but bigger explosions, larger troop movements are needed by a President whose cuts in social welfare funding have damaged his popularity without curing a depressed US economy. The next election must be weighing very heavily on his mind.

A third of the British troops taking part in this war and occupation will be Scottish, though Scotland has a tenth of Britain's population. The Scots were hiring themselves out to foreign armies many centuries before our union with England. I regret that tradition so I am going to Glasgow Green, and thanks for a sunny day, God.

Arriving with the wife and lawyer friend I am amazed by the many crowds spreading from the triumphal arch before Glasgow High Court to the People's Palace in the east and Clyde on the south. All demonstrations contain weirdly dressed people who delight the hearts of antagonistic reporters, but here they are so outnumbered as to be invisible. Yet this multitude is splendidly un-uniform, though I hear the women of the Eurydice Socialist Choir singing a peace song and some vendors of the Scottish Socialist Party newspaper. There are people of every age, from toddlers in prams pushed by parents to elderly men like me. Some carry doves made of white polystyrene, there are many printed placards saying 'Make War on Want, Not Iraq', 'Not In My Name, Mr Blair' 'No Blood for Oil' and asking for Palestinian liberation. Some are less serious. A nice woman upholds 'I Trust No Bush But My Own', a stout bearded gent shows the 'Dumfries Ageing Hippies Against the War' logo. Two boys of ten or eleven walk carefully side by side wearing a single sandwich board made of card with slogans written in fibre-tip pen. They seem to have no adult presiding with them.

There seem no adults presiding over anyone, so we join the crowd at its thickest beside Greendyke Street where the procession should start, edging in as far as possible and looking around for guidance. It is provided, unexpectedly, by the police. They form a barrier between the crowd and the street and let us through in numbers that can start walking ten abreast, thus filling the width of the road without flooding pavements on each side.

We await our turn in this good-natured, very patient crowd. I can see none of the friends I had arranged to meet on the Green, see several others in my line of business: novelist Bernard MacLaverty, A. L. Kennedy, the poet Aonghas MacNeacail, several teachers and lecturers. Some senior citizens carry a banner saying THE TAYSIDE PENSIONERS' FORUM. My lawyer friend tells me Blair proposes to abolish old age pensions because workers' contributions are now too small to pay for them, I suppose because of inflation. This steadily reduces the wages of the poorest paid while used as a reason for taxing the wealthy less, thus letting them invest more in private business of global extent. So New Labour may undo the main achievement of Lloyd George's Liberal government in 1908! We talk about the arms industry: how the 1930s depression only ended when Britain and the USA prepared for war. How both nations have been preparing for wars or fighting them ever since. How making and exporting weapons is now Britain's main industry. I recalled that the Principal of Glasgow University, Professor Sir Graham Davies, chairs the Universities Superannuation Scheme, providing pensions for many British academics, and which (a handbill tells me) has £60 million invested in British Arms Enterprise. Some students a month ago were threatened with expulsion from Glasgow University for protesting against such investments. Should I not have supported them? But I have drunk and talked cheerfully with Principal Sir Graham Davies, who supported me, James Kelman and Tom Leonard when we were Creative Writing Professors. I did not want to criticise him publicly. I am an arselicker too.

I get letters nowadays from people wishing to discuss or discover views of Scottish identity, as if more than five million folk could possibly have one. But if asked what chiefly characterises my nation I will repeat what I wrote in 1982: arselicking. We disguise it with surfaces of course: surfaces of generous, open-handed manliness; surfaces of dour, practical integrity: surfaces of maudlin, drunken defiance: surfaces of quiet, respectable decency. The chorus of a Scottish national anthem proposed by a Dundonian poet comes to mind

*Hermless, hermless, naebody cares for me.*
*I gang tae the library, I tak oot a book*
*And I gang hame for ma tea*

– as I usually do. There have been eminent Scots with strong independent minds but now the most eminent are the worst arselickers. Our Labour MP's lick Tony Blair's bum. Tony Blair licks the bum of President Bush. Licking U.S. Presidents' bums is a British Prime Ministerial tradition.

At last the police are letting us through and, roughly ten abreast, we process down Greendyke Street then up the Saltmarket to Glasgow Cross. Occasionally those around us burst into wild cheering, seemingly inspired by folk waving encouragement from upper tenement windows. Our stream divides neatly to pass the gawky clock tower of the Tollbooth, all that remains of Glasgow's seventeenth-century

Town Hall, magistrates' court and city jail.

In John Prebble's book about the Glencoe massacre I read that two British officers were imprisoned there in 1692. They had opened their sealed orders before reaching Glencoe village and found themselves ordered to put men, women and children to the sword. They broke their swords and told their commander at Fort William that no decent officer should obey such an order. So they were sent south by ship and jailed for a while in this Glasgow Tollbooth. Prebble says there is no other record of them so they may have escaped further punishment. I would love to see a big plaque on that tower commemorating these two brave soldiers. Scotland's castles, cathedrals, public parks, city centres contain many war memorials, some of the most elaborate commemorating a few officers and men who died in Africa and Asia while killing hundreds fighting on their own soil without the advantage of gunpowder. Are these two officers the only British soldiers to disobey a dishonourable order? Then I remember hearing that in the Gulf War authorised by the last President Bush, four British officers resigned their commissions in protest against the dropping of cluster bombs (which "mince up everything that lives within a three-mile strip") onto Iraqi ground forces, though most UK and US airmen queued up enthusiastically to airstrike those who could not strike back. One bomber said they looked like swarms of cockroaches.

From the helicopter that sometimes passes above us we too probably resemble cockroaches as we ascend the High Street, turn left down Ingram Street, turn left then right again. Our biggest roar goes up as the Civic Chambers come in sight. Why are no Glasgow Town Councillors waving from those upper windows? My wife reminds me they are on holiday because this is a Saturday. Why are there none in our procession? (I am delighted to learn later there is one, at least.) Approaching George Square from the east we can now see a silhouette of the procession crossing the summit of Blythswood Hill a quarter mile ahead.

Coming abreast of an Irish pub we call in for a refreshment, emerging half an hour later to join the procession behind the banner of Unison, the local government employees' union. A small brass band is playing a melancholy Scots ditty and I am astonished to find myself on the brink of tears. This sentiment owes nothing to a recent sup of lager. Our huge movement is composed of Scottish workers, tradespeople, professional people who identify with them – all people I feel at home with. These folk will suffer most if our businessmen take the advice of an expert in Scottish Enterprises, formerly known as The Scottish Development Agency. He has advised Scottish businesses to have their goods made by workers in Eastern Europe or Asia.

We arrive in a desert of car parks covering the site of the former Princess Dock, a vast basin surrounded by huge cranes where giant ships unloaded cargoes and took them aboard during the Suez War when Glasgow was a great international port and centre of manufacture. The huge car parks are more crowded with multitudes than Glasgow Green. Beyond them I see some big arched metallic structures that seem to have slid out of each other, a building locally nicknamed The Armadillo. I realise for the first time that this Armadillo is the Glasgow conference centre. A line of yellow-jacketed police is looped protectively around it. From the height of an open-topped double decker bus near the river someone is making a speech, but loud speakers are banned so few phrases are audible. Some storms of applause are heard and we hope the Prime Minister hears them and sees how many we are. We later learn that –

(**A**) Tony Blair did not speak to the Scottish Trade Union conference that afternoon, as scheduled, but changed it to ten in the morning so he could leave the district, and perhaps Glasgow, before we left the Green.

(**B**) The speaker aboard the bus was Glasgow's Lord Provost, or the leader of the Scottish Socialist Party Tommy Sheridan, or a spokesman for the Church of Scotland, or for Scotland's Asiatic communities, or for CND, because all made speeches from there.

After half an hour we come away, moving against the flood of people still approaching from the City Centre, for the procession has been longer than its three mile route. The ruler of Britain will learn nothing from this peaceful rally, or those in New York, Sydney and most major European capitals. Are the commanders of armies in great and small, rich and poor nations right to think only destructive violence can defeat destructive violence? No. Tyrants ruling by force and torture in Greece, Spain, Portugal, South Africa, Russia collapsed without invasion and warfare. What that Jewish extremist, Jesus, preached from a small hill near Jerusalem, was not idiotic.

# Of Susan Boyd[*]

SUSAN BOYD, television playwright, was born in
1949 and died of a brain haemorrhage on 18 June
2004 in Glasgow's Southern General Hospital.

Her mother was actress Katy Gardiner; her father
playwright Eddie Boyd, who left his family too early to
be an influence, though she met and became friendly
with him in her mid-twenties. Susan lived at first with
her mother and grandmother in Riddrie, one of the
earliest and pleasantest of Glasgow's municipal
housing schemes, and in a Loch Lomond-side holiday
cottage near Rowardennan. Granny, a schoolteacher,
had been wife of the archaeologist Harrison Maxwell.
Susan's home was well furnished with books and
radical ideas, artistic and political. When Granny died,
mother and daughter moved to an equally well-
furnished flat in Great George Street, Hillhead, from
which Susan attended Hillhead Secondary School then
Glasgow School of Art.

She left the last after two years, having made life-
long friends there but now sure she was going to
become a writer. Like many with uncommon
ambitions she went to London, partly to show
independence from her tolerant and strong-minded
mother, and partly because London in the 1960s
seemed far more exciting than Glasgow. It dominated

*This obituary of a friend I had known since her childhood in Riddrie, my native
housing scheme, was certainly written soon after her death in 2004, but I cannot
remember where it was published, and maybe it was not.*

the British publishing and entertainment industries by which she hoped to live. Several Glasgow friends were there already for the same reason, documentary filmmaker John Samson and his wife Linda among them. But first Susan lived for ten years on low earnings from factory, warehouse and street market – in work as a postman, a supply teacher and (for several evenings) a life model at a Civil Service art class in the War Office basement. Her mother's influence once got her employed by BBC television's wardrobe department. Pay was good, hours few, bosses and colleagues pleasant, but the job involved typing long lists of properties. She soon left because that stupefied the imagination her writing needed, so until able to support herself by writing full-time, she preferred a variety of less middle-class jobs.

Thus she eventually equipped herself to write plays with London settings. Like many authors, her first effort was a semi-autobiographical novel, never finished, and short stories published in short-lived literary magazines. Her first success was *Another Day*, a BBC 2 Play of the Week, which attracted attention by showing love between a white woman and black man. It also showed the kind of modern life Susan could dramatise. In 1985 the *EastEnders* series began and she was in its writing team from then until her death. She also wrote episodes of *Casualty*, *Paradise Club* and *Crown Court*, several single television plays and eleven for sound radio.

By 1990 she was earning enough to buy a flat in Partick, Glasgow, where a computer now let her confer as closely with colleagues as she had done in London, with a few flying visits there for script conferences. Susan liked her work and brought to it (as all who work well in television must) the integrity and cynicism of a good professional journalist or policeman. In recent years she had to struggle with many new *EastEnders* producers and directors whose bright ideas (she thought) ignored common sense and continuity of character.

Susan Boyd lent money willingly, without assurance of return, and also gave it. Though shy she was kind to lonely, eccentric and desperate folks. A London neighbour specialised in finding homes for feral cats; Susan adopted three, which she brought to Partick. She was always careful to keep in touch with friends. When John Samson* died she was careful to locate and inform all his friends in Scotland of the funeral and flew down to it, despite being troubled by intermittent headaches. She died two days after returning. She is survived by a loving mother, brother, sister, daughter, two grandchildren, three very old domesticated feral cats and many, many friends.

Watchers of *EastEnders* may soon
notice a lack of continuity
with former episodes.

---

\* *John Samson, 1946 – 2004, was a Scottish filmmaker and resident in London. He deserves mention in more than a footnote for his calm, completely uncensorious documentaries about how people are mostly mocked or denounced for unusual sexual needs or preferences in which they harmlessly enjoy themselves.* **Dressing for Pleasure** *is the best known. His method was to film them and their doings with their own voices explaining and discussing these. He would be better known if Scotland, as seemed possible 12 years ago, had acquired its own film industry.*

# The Declaration
# of Calton Hill

IN OCTOBER 2004 QUEEN ELIZABETH I of Scots
and II of England opened Scotland's new parliament
building at the foot of Edinburgh High Street, while
across the valley from it the Scottish Workers Socialist
Party held a counter-demonstration on Calton Hill. The
Scots parliament was then dominated by a Labour-
Liberal coalition whose First Minister was then Jack
McConnell. The S. W. S. Party was led by Tommy
Sheridan. Members of his party at this demonstration
were a minority. Most of us belonged to no established
political group while agreeing with the aims of the
great French Revolution as is still declared on coins of
the French Republic – *LIBERTY, EQUALITY, FRATERNITY*,
which to me is the modern equivalent of St. Paul's
Faith, Hope and Charity.

I was flattered and excited when Mr. Sheridan
said his party was planning to publish a Declaration of
its Intent for Scotland, and suggested that I and James
Kelman might consider drafting it, though we must
submit it within 2 or 3 weeks. So Jim and I talked the
matter over and came up with several drafts. Here is
one of the last that passed between us. I believe it
contains most of the text which the Scottish Workers
Socialist Party received from us, though not much of
our wording was used in the neat little document the
S. W. S. P. (God rest its innocent, well-meaning soul)
finally printed and distributed.

We, the Undersigned, want
A Scottish Commonwealth where people of every
origin, trade, profession and faith work
for each other's welfare.

We believe this State needs a parliament elected by Scotland's
people, and recognising these people as
its only sovereign.

We believe this parliament's members and agencies should be the
servants, not masters, of Scotland's people, through a written
consistitution that promises everyone the right to freely vote, speak
and assemble; the right to know all the doings of its
government and its agencies, with all the sources of its
members' income, since a public servant's income is the
business of the public.

We believe that under this constitution, Scotland's parliament
should completely control Scotland's
revenues, and use them –

1 To negotiate as an equal with other governments.

2 To defend the health, property and safety of life in Scotland
by limiting or acquiring land or properties within Scottish
borders that are owned by outside corporations or government
agencies.

3 To work to make public housing, transport, education,
legal aid and healthcare as good as any
purchasable by private wealth.
None of these three requirements has priority.

We do not want an independent Scotland because we dislike the
English, but because we want separation from that Union of
financial, military
and monarchic establishments
calling itself Great Britain.

# Introduction to
# *The Knuckle End*<sup>*</sup>

IN 1988 PHILIP HOBSBAUM, poet and professor of English, gave at Glasgow University a public talk on literature and the teaching of it in Scotland. These two often came apart, he suggested, as university students were taught nothing but criticism, so their own writing was usually a paraphrase of their teacher's opinions. Intelligent writing could be better nourished by instruction that invited the composition of original prose and verse, though he acknowledged that this work would be much harder to mark through examinations.

Some of this mainly academic audience must have been annoyed at this argument for changes in established practices, for though not a new argument the speaker's experience made it hard to dismiss. Tutored at Cambridge by Dr. Leavis (whose faith in living literature was a religion) Philip had published poetry and criticism, taught literature in Ulster and Scotland, been a member and instigator of writing groups in London, Belfast and Glasgow – unofficial groups that had stimulated obscure authors now widely known. Seamus Heaney has written that in mid-sixties Ulster "one of the strongest agents of change was Philip Hobsbaum... he moved disparate elements into a single

---

✳ *Published in 2004 and subtitled* **A Meaty Collection of the Best Writing in Scotland***, my introduction explains how this thick, eccentric, unsatisfactory little volume, first intended by me and others to publish Glasgow University creative writing passed into the control of a publisher and designer who retitled it, illustrated it with colour photographs of butcher meat, and typeset it in ways the originators never anticipated.*

action. He emanated energy, belief in the community, trust in the parochial, the inept, the unprinted... I remember his hospitality and encouragement with the special gratitude we reserve for those who have led us toward confidence in ourselves." From several writers in Glasgow he earned the same respect, not least because, through his group, we became friends with each other. I was one of these, so when the English Literature department of Glasgow University started a creative writing course in 1995 I assumed Philip Hobsbaum was mainly responsible.

He denies this. The scheme for the new course was worded jointly by him and Willy Maley a comparatively new member of the English Literature department. The scheme was rejected by a curriculum committee. Maley reworded it, resubmitted it and did so three times, each time suffering rejection. For a fourth attempt he submitted the original version, which was accepted: says Philip Hobsbaum. "No good story is ever completely true," says Doctor Johnson, but this tale will surprise no one with experience of interdepartmental committees.

**Creative Writing**

Here let me answer a question that even experienced scholars sometimes ask: Can the writing of good new poems and stories be taught? Surely the creative imagination works like God – so mysteriously that all true writers, when adolescent schooling ends, must henceforth be completely self-instructed, or only instructed by earlier literature they discover by themselves. For there have been such writers.

But words are no more mysterious to a

professional writer than sounds to musicians, their bodies to footballers, living flesh to surgeons. It is usual for such professionals to train under experienced practitioners, and sometimes required by law. In the same way an older writer can speed the learning of a novice by showing a thriftier use of language and more things to do with it. True, some students cannot learn, some tutors cannot teach. Both incompetents seldom coincide in a university writing course because:-

(1) Though admission depends firstly on ability to pay fees, students are also selected from a larger number of applicants because a portfolio of work they submit shows talent that can develop.

(2) Very few of a university's staff are wholly useless. And half the learning in a course comes from the novice being, often for the first time, in a community of writers: people of different sexes, ages, social classes and even nations who, having the same aims, encourage each other by both example and shared ideas.

**Three Professors**

Creative writing courses took root in other Scottish universities. When Philip Hobsbaum retired in 1999 the Glasgow course was made a joint enterprise with Strathclyde University thus adding Zoe Wicomb and Margaret Elphinstone to the staff, lecturers who were also fiction writers. Then in 2001 Glasgow University advertised a new post of Creative Writing Professor, hoping that other well-known authors with teaching experience would apply. By that time Glasgow had many. Here are three.

Tom Leonard – poet, critic, biographer, anthologist –

was already part-time tutor in the course. James Kelman, Booker Prize novelist, had taught Creative Writing at Texas University. I, another author, had conducted a similar course at St Andrews. A professor's salary would have helped all three of us and I was attracted by the title's grandeur – I came from a class which thought the highest forms of social life were honest Socialist politicians, doctors or teachers, and that professors were the highest kind of teacher. But for all three of us the job had a major snag. A full-time professor of Creative Writing would not have time to creatively write. Then Marie, James Kelman's wife, pointed out that for thirty years we had been friends who sometimes worked together, and if we offered to share equally the professor's title, work and salary the university might employ all of us since it would get three notable writers for the price of one.

**Which Came To Pass**

I fear we entered the Creative Writing Course like bulls entering a crowded mini-market. We had agreed beforehand to wait a full academic term before trying to make changes, thus learning how the course usually ran. We broke that wise resolution almost at once. Student work was receiving a percentage valuation by awarding marks out of sixty for creative work, marks out of forty for critical essays. Since artistic work can only be evaluated in pounds, shillings and pence by salesmen, we wanted to give excellent work a distinguished pass, work that had improved through study a simple pass, and to fail those who did not improve. We wanted critical essays to be a voluntary not essential part of examinations. The fight for this system was supported by Glasgow University colleagues Willy Maley, Adam Piette, Rob Maslen and the head of English Literature, Susan Castillo. Hard work by Tom Leonard and Rob Maslen brought Glasgow University Senate to confirm the new scheme, which resembled the earlier one by Hobsbaum and Maley when they started the course.

This outcome may have led Strathclyde University to separate its writing course from Glasgow's in 2002. It also annoyed students who, halfway through a two year course, felt their efforts to master criticism were now a waste of time. We disagreed. Criticism, especially self-criticism, is essential to good writing and should be kept sharp by study. When study provoked critical essays we considered them part of a student's exam portfolio, and only made them voluntary to free those wanting to concentrate on other kinds of writing.

And we conducted classes where works by students and better known authors were discussed. James Kelman organised three weekend conferences at which Scottish, English and Irish filmmakers read or showed their works and answered questions on them. The University Principal, Graham Davies, authorised a grant that paid for these events, and for readings by the poets John Agard and Les Murray, and by the great American story writer, Grace Paley. Like our colleagues in the course we coached students one at a time, and thus read much surprisingly good new work that we thought should be published.

**Publication**

Most writing courses publish booklets of work and the

Glasgow course had already produced two. Such
publications, sold chiefly at student readings, seldom pay their costs but let novice writers see, show and keep their work in a neat professional format. We wanted the students' best work more widely distributed in a more lasting form. The Principal's grant had left some money for this. I knew from experience one businessman who occasionally gave money for artistic work without hope of return: Colin Beattie, owner of public houses. Between 2002 and 2004 he gave the project £3000. We held meetings to discuss practical details, one addressed by editors of *Confluence*, an earlier course publication. To select work for a book – decide on layout – calculate printing costs – discover a publisher or else ways to distribute and advertise the book – to raise more money if more was wanted – we needed a committee. To form one a meeting was held in the University staff club. Less than half in the course attended, nobody opposed those who were willing to serve, and all are among those who brought this book to publication, even if they have nothing published in the preceding pages. I list them alphabetically, believing some will one day be more widely known: Angela Blacklock Brown; Colin Clark; Rodge Glass; Jamie Johnston; Nick E Melville; James Porteous; Gary Steven; Richard Todd.

At a later date it was suggested that the fewness of women on the committee, especially older women, was a young men's conspiracy but it happened solely because there were no older, willing women at that crucial early meeting. Only one of the committee was proposed by a member of staff: I suggested Colin

Clark because his portfolio of work had shown he understood typography.

Colin Clark explained that he had found a publisher and distributor: Freight, a new firm of graphic designers who had recently, and successfully, entered publication with *The Hope That Kills Us*, a collection of stories about Scottish football. Freight would pay half the production cost and publish the course's anthology but wanted it to include work by former students who were now widely known. Since the book must have a limited number of pages, some work by present members of the course would have to be excluded. This caused much debate. Some thought that, having paid to be part of a writing course, students should be free of commercial pressures, and professors should not help to finance a publication that excluded anybody, even if this made professional distribution impossible. And what if the well-known former students invited to submit work submitted work of poor quality? And what qualified anyone in the editorial committee to be selectors and rejectors?

The debate, though intense, was not acrimonious. The professors did not want to force particular decisions upon the meeting, but I wanted proposals voted upon so sometimes cut short debates which, if continued, would have prevented that. Most of the course finally voted to let the Freight publication go ahead under Colin Clark's guidance, with the selection of work being made by reputable authors unconnected with the university: also to have a small student publication in which every present member of the course would be allowed the same number of well printed words.

The smaller work, typeset by James Porteous with a cover design by Richard Todd, was published in 2003 entitled *The Human Machine*. Works in the book you now read were selected by novelist and storywriter Bernard MacLaverty, by poet and journalist Aonghas MacNeacail, and by literary agent Jenny Brown.

So now you know all that lies behind this fine publication. A Scottish Arts Council grant has enhanced the production and let the editorial committee pay the contributors £50 each. Very good! Too many anthologies are produced by folk who think contributors sufficiently well-paid by a copy of it.

The title was chosen because it sounded memorable. A joint of meat's knuckle end was once the animal's knee so has the most bone, the least flesh. Sidney Smith called Scotland, "That knuckle end of England – that land of Calvin, oatcakes, and sulphur." A lot of Scottish writing does deal with hard people in hard situations, but you will find this book contains a lot of tasty mental nourishment, some of it succulent.

**An Epilogue**

At a pleasant party in 2001 the new professors were introduced to their university colleagues and each made a little speech. I said we had decided never to resign from our job but hold onto it until we were kicked out: to which Dorothy McMillan of English Literature responded, "Why do you think the rest of us are still here?" My speech was wrong. At the start of our second academic year we were happy, having changed the marking system, and got poet playwright Liz Lochhead and novelist Janice Galloway working as tutors with us. We expected now to concentrate on teaching without the worries of administration. But no. We had depended greatly on our secretary Lynda Perkins who now left to have a baby. Administration was mainly handled by Willy Maley or others in the department of English Literature. We were asked to admit more students than we felt able to teach properly unless Creative Writing had more tutors. A strong, firm Professor with staying power and a good political head was needed cope with this. Three old friends only eager to write and teach could not. In the autumn of 2003 Kelman and Gray resigned from our posts. Tom Leonard stayed on as a tutor only. The university saved money by stopping our salaries as soon as it received our letters of resignation, though we had offered to complete the academic year. The extra month would have let us assess the work of the students we had tutored. But I have no doubt that it was fairly assessed by the English Literature lecturers who were our former colleagues. In 2004 Lynda Perkins returned as secretary to the full-time professor who replaced us in the Creative Writing chair. He will therefore find the job less trouble than it became for us.

Our one and three-quarter years as titled professors introduced us to many interesting new writers. I believe those we personally tutored found us helpful. I later employed two of them (Rodger Glass, Richard Todd) as helpers with my writing and visual art work. We three professors also learned about government pressure to make all but a few old richly endowed universities self-supporting from fees the students pay. The result, of course, is a poorer quality of teaching.

# Of Philip
# Hobsbaum*

POET, CRITIC AND SERVANT OF SERVANTS OF
ART, Philip Hobsbaum died last week, a day before
his 73rd birthday. His ancestors were among those
adaptable, intelligent people driven out of Eastern
Europe by anti-Jewish laws and prejudices around
1900. His father, an electrical engineer in the East End
of London, had Philip taught boxing at an early age,
to cope with the bullies he had suffered from himself.
A GPO management job took the family to Bradford
where Philip, after doing badly in his first four years at
Belle Vue Grammar School, suddenly did so well that
a scholarship took him to Downing College,
Cambridge where he studied under the great critic and
pioneer of "close reading", Dr. Leavis, continuing his
studies at Sheffield with that other poet, fine critic and
close reader, William Empson.

While teaching in London he brought out his
first book of poems, *The Places Fault*, and was a
member of a writers group sometimes called The
Movement who wanted poetry to use simpler, more
demotic speech, and organised a regular writers study
group, thus influencing and being influenced by such
well-known writers as Peter Redgrove, Peter Porter,
Edward Lucie-Smith and George MacBeth. In 1962 he
lectured in Queen's University, Belfast. In an essay

✱ *This essay contains some of an obituary for* **The Independent** *newspaper
commissioned from me and printed 28th June 2005. The Seamus Heaney quotation
is from* **Belfast***, the essay published in* **Preoccupations, Selected Prose, 1968-78***.*

about the group of writers Philip started there, Seamus Heaney says that before then:–

*A lot of people of a generally literary bent were islanded about the place... I don't think many of us had a sense of contemporary poetry – Dylan Thomas's records were as near as we seemed to get to it... We hung or sleepwalked between notions of writing that we had gleaned from English courses and the living realitites of writers from our own place who we did not know, in person or in print.*

*Those of us who stayed around saw that state of affairs changed by the mid-sixties and one of the strongest agents of change was Philip Hobsbaum. When Hobsbaum arrived in Belfast, he moved disparate elements into a single action. He emanated energy, generosity, belief in the community, trust in the parochial, the inept, the unprinted. He was impatient, dogmatic, relentlessly literary: yet he was patient with those he trusted, unpredictably susceptible to a wide variety of poems and personalities and urging that the social and political exacerbations of our place should disrupt the decorums of literature. If he drove some people mad with his absolutes and hurt others with his over-bearing, he confirmed as many with his enthusiasms. He and his wife Hannah kept open house for poetry and I remember his hospitality and encouragement with the special gratitude we reserve for those who have led us toward confidence in ourselves.*

In 1968 Philip left Belfast to teach English in the University of Glasgow. His marriage had just broken up, which may have moved him to a new beginning.

Glasgow University has a student-run magazine founded in 1889 and called, for short, *Gum*. An edition it published in 1968 had an article with this heading:–

PHILIP HOBSBAUM
Interview - G. Hargie, A. Nicolson

**Q. Are you glad that you came to Scotland, Doctor Hobsbaum?**
**A.** No, not at all.
**Q. Why is that?**
**A.** Scotland doesn't need visitors. Nobody but Scotsmen can help Scotland.
**Q. Why do you say that?**
**A.** Scotland is a beaten country. It's been beaten ever since its people sold Mary Queen of Scots to the English and gave John Knox free rein to break down a civilization.
**Q. So you think we were civilized once?**
**A.** Undoubtedly – the literature shows it. And your greatest century was the century of Gauvaine Douglas, Henryson and Dunbar.
**Q. Do you think nothing's happened since?**
**A.** Of course – but all abroad. The great Scotsmen have been expatriate. In what sense is David Hume a Scottish Philosopher?
**Q. What about Burns?**
**A.** Sonsie, braw – I once turned down ten guineas rather than lecture on him.
**Q. Or Scott?**
**A.** Somebody ought to translate him into English. Or into Scots – *Wandering Willie's Tale* is a masterpiece, isolated in his work.

**Q. What about the modern period?**

**A.** There is no modern period – merely a senseless debate between MacDiarmid and Muir about whether to write in Scots or English. The fact that the debate was possible shows the impoverishment of your language and literature.

**Q. Do you not think MacDiarmid is a great writer?**

**A.** Certainly I do. My students don't. And he has been treated by his fellow countrymen with the discourtesy characteristically shown by Scotsmen to their great artists. No wonder Rennie Mackintosh died an alcoholic.

**Q. And yet you say Scotsmen can save Scotland?**

**A.** They might be able to. Certainly Englishmen can't. I've never been in such a philistine dump as Glasgow in all my life.

**Q. That's a bit strong?**

**A.** It should be stronger. Do you imagine that I have had so much as a conversation with any of my fellow artists in this city ? To converse sensibly I have to go to Dublin or Leeds.

**Q. What's the difficulty?**

**A.** Where do I meet them? Do you notice one extraordinary thing about Glasgow is the total absence of a social context?

**Q. Well, if you're looking for an English style pub –?**

**A.** I wouldn't find one. No, quite. But instead what have you got? Swine-troughs, swill factories. And what swill!

**Q. But surely the Close Theatre Club –?**

**A.** And who do you imagine I can meet there? There simply is no centre here where intelligent people can come across each other.

And this is like no other town I ever was in.

**Q. So you wouldn't rate the university very highly?**

**A.** Let's put it this way. I should hate to think that most of my colleagues were ignoramuses covering ignorance and idleness with a thin layer of complacent irony.

**Q. But?**

**A.** That's it. I'd hate to say it.

**Q. Why did you come?**

**A.** I didn't know it was going to be like this.

**Q. Why don't you leave?**

**A.** I shall do my best to leave, next year.

**Q. So you haven't fulfilled yourself then?**

**A.** I haven't fulfilled my expectations, no. But I'm worked like a dog and received nothing but envy and bitterness in return.

**Q. This is primarily a teaching university?**

**A.** Teaching University, what does that mean? If teaching isn't fertilized by research, research by teaching, both ossify. The University is a valley of dry bones.

**Q. What do you think of the students?**

**A.** Poor little devils, victims of the system. The grizzly bear eats them before they know they're alive.

**Q. What do you mean?**

**A.** Look – they go to their local school, get crammed for their local university, come reluctantly,
contribute nothing socially or culturally, leave with some kind of degree, and all the time live with mummy and daddy. What do they know of life? What will they ever know? Am I to teach Joyce and Lawrence to a bunch of ciphers?

**Q. What do you think they should do?**

**A.** If they must stick to Scotland, at least go to some other university. Then they'd have a chance of fending for themselves, of making new social contacts.

**Q. How if financially they have to come here?**

**A.** I don't believe it. But if they must, then let them leave the country when they've graduated. They can always come back when they've grown up.

**Q. 'Scotland needs them' ?**

**A.** Scotland does need all its young people, if only to rescue the country from the bunch of dead-heads and lame-brains who run it now.

**Q. What have you in mind?**

**A.** Let's name no names. But I notice when – by sheer chance, it must be – the Citizens Theatre employed a director with some courage and originality, the board of management fired him. Who are they, for God's sake? Have they never heard of the freedom of the artist?

**Q. The freedom of the artist to lose money?**

**A.** Their pop shows lost even more. Look at *The Knack* a couple of years ago. I don't notice that bunch of characters training an audience. They're too comfortably entrenched. Arty, maybe: but not artists.

**Q. So do you think there's no room for artists in Glasgow?**

**A.** Yes, yes, dozens of them. But we have to fight the milieu. We have to let them know that education is not separable from art. We have to shake up some of those dull thicks who pose as patrons of the arts. We have to combine posh *Scottish International* with underground *Henry's Magazine*. We have to appoint artists as permanent staff of our university. We have to appoint a good young Scottish director to our Theatre and give him his head – and let him appoint playwrights to his staff. We have to sweep away the tired old men who've represented Scottish culture for so long – you can hear them on George Bruce's *Arts Review* any given month – and replace them by young men who are still doing things. We – but I really mean you – have to do this.

**Q. You don't include yourself. So Scotland's defeated you?**

**A.** Let's not be smug about it. I was a force in London, because London is an anthology of exiles. I was able to help out in Ireland because the Irish are only too glad if anyone takes notice of them. But the mixture of insularity, philistinians and complacency here has been a bit much for me.

**Q. You find the fault in the modern Scotsman?**

**A.** The modern Scotsmen I've met don't want anything to happen. They always find good reasons for not having done anything. That crushes all creativity.

**Q. Would you vote Scottish Nationalist?**

**A.** I intend to. The Scots deserve Scotland.

**END**

The A. Nicolson in the heading is now better known as the Gaelic poet Aonghas MacNeacail, once also called Black Angus before his bushy beard and hair turned snow white. He told me he and other *Gum* editors met Philip in a pub to discuss an interview, and at the end of an interesting talk he gave them the foregoing questions and answers, telling them, "Print that!" which they did. It was obviously written at a bleak time in his life when its one bright spot was having the American poet Ann Stevenson as his companion. But it was also a bleak time for Scottish culture. The view he gives of it here was not false, indeed, is still partly true, in that hardly any Scottish artists have administrative posts in Scottish institutions.

But luckily Philip did not leave Glasgow in 1969, for by 1970 he had found a group of writers as strong as those in Belfast – Liz Lochhead, Tom Leonard, James Kelman and many others. All these (and I include myself) had gained confidence in our distinctive voices before we met him, but we only slightly recognised each other before he brought us together. Several of them who are less widely known are still among my closest friends.

I am sure Philip's vote got me the job of Glasgow University's Writer-in-Residence in 1977 when I desperately needed a steady income for work that would not stunt my writing ability. He even lived to see three published authors he respected made joint Professors of Creative Writing at Glasgow University, though he died after the three of us gave up Professoring as a bad job because new financial pressures to enlarge classes while lowering the quality of teaching was more than we could stand. I wish he had used his university post as a base from which to edit a literary magazine as he had done at Cambridge, where he published the early poems of Ted Hughes and Peter Redgrove. In 1968 the notion that he would work until retirement in Glasgow University, and die in Glasgow a few years later, would have struck him as a nightmare.

# Self Portraiture*

LONG BEFORE LEARNING TO WRITE I was given paper, pencil and crayons by parents who liked me using them, so from then until late adolescence I made pictures of imaginary worlds where my miraculous powers won battles, immense popularity and the love of gorgeous queens. These pictures showed queer people, monsters, machines, architecture and landscapes: never images of me because my appearance was childish and ordinary. Art was my escape from the ordinary, which included family and the pleasant modern Glasgow housing scheme where we lived. What was commonplace bored me. Only its cinemas and public library gave me exciting visions of exotic worlds.

But I enjoyed showing my artistic ability to folk with different ideas for pictures, and when sixteen made a self-portrait in a way suggested by Robert Stuart, head of Whitehill Secondary School art teaching. With Indian ink, pen and brush and using a small mirror, I drew my face lit strongly from one side, painting the areas of shadow on the other side a solid black. Such portraits were meant to be turned into lino-cut prints, though I did not do that. The dense

*This essay was commissioned for **DIVIDED SELVES: The Scottish Self-Portrait from the 17th Century to the Present**, published by the Talbot Rice Gallery of Edinburgh University in 2006 for the Fleming-Wyfold Art Foundation. Edited by Bill Hare and Polly Bielecka, essays by Vicky Bruce, Cairns Craig, Gavin Miller, Jonathan Murray and me. Illustrated with my self-portraits from the age of 16 to 70, my essay aimed to contradict the notion that Scotland has more split personalities than other lands.

shadows added no strength to a slightly bun-shaped face whose most distinct feature was a pair of spectacles. But less than three years later that technique suited my mood when making a self-portrait at Glasgow School of Art.

By then my mother had died. For several weeks the need to earn money had looked like stopping me becoming an artist. My face was now thinner and more angular. Having left Whitehill I had lost my companions there and not yet found others, hence this bid to interest onlookers in my stoical loneliness. The lamp-lit night scene behind was to justify the ominous facial shadow; it also shows my imagination at last using bits of Glasgow: exciting, recently discovered older bits. Most of the building behind the head was in Drygate, a small valley between Duke Street and the Necropolis. Duke Street at the top has been replaced by a section of the Monkland canal. More than Bob Stuart's teaching went into this picture. When much younger I had unconsciously learned a lot from children's book illustrations about combining areas of solid black and white with linear shading, especially Rudyard Kipling's *Just So Stories*. Later I discovered Blake's *The Gates of Paradise*, works by Aubrey Beardsley and Munch. Though more painter than graphic artist, Munch's stark contrasts of dark and light in his canvases fascinated me; so did his subject matter. If interiors, streets and landscapes in Norway circa 1900 provided a great artist with strong subjects, why should not 1950s Scotland? I had also learned the same lesson from Joyce's *Portrait of the Artist as a Young Man*. I now knew the world once dismissed as ordinary contains all the best and worst adventures that could happen to me.

So while still painting apocalyptic and fabulous events I came also to draw, as accurately as possible, people I knew and liked in their own homes. It was my way of stopping them leaving me. Four years after art school I entered a marriage that lasted nine, and made many pictures of my wife and son, a few of myself. Good white expensive cartridge paper usually intimidated me because my first efforts were torn up as mistakes. Most were drawn on blank wallpaper, on newsprint paper, or on a tough, slightly porous paper from a wad found in a derelict factory. Having made some lightly pencilled guidelines soon rubbed out, I drew the whole thing without stopping in an hour, more or less, using a black ballpoint or else a Radiograph pen. The last, a recent German invention used by architects and engineering draftsmen, resembled the ballpoint in making firm lines that did not darken or lighten with the hand's pressure like pencils, or change thickness with the angle of the nib like script pens. These drawings from life had no conscious exaggerations, and the only consciously eliminated details were very fine wrinkles my strong line would have grossly thickened. If the final drawing looked complete the portrait was finished; if not it was pasted onto a rigid panel and the figure made more distinct (more *real*, I thought) by tinting hair, clothes, adjacent furniture and background, using two or three mediums: watercolour, emulsion, acrylic, oil paint, crayon. These tones and colours were added in the sitter's absence, and darkened or brightened to add believable variety without obscuring what William Blake called 'the *bounding* lines.' He deliberately used an adjective with two meanings, because the outlines of a pictured body can both circumscribe its colours and have an urgent vitality of their own.

This third picture, though drawn on untypical white paper, shows my usual method. My reflection was copied from a mirror laid flat on a drawing board so viewers see it as I did, from beneath. The ceiling beyond was the same pale plaster as the cornice and centre moulding: I painted it yellow to make the head look much nearer, then tinted hair, face etcetera grey to indicate the shadow cast by the electric bulb overhead. Details outside the reflecting glass (the mirror's beaten copper frame, artist's left sleeve, paper on which the mirror lies) are left plain outline except for the solid black Radiograph and a grey tint on the hand holding it.

The least frequent kind of self-portrait shows an artist placed dramatically with someone he knows. At the most prosperous time of his long career Rembrandt painted himself seated at a banqueting table with his young wife on his knees, both richly dressed. One hand clasps her waist, the other holds high a glass of wine, he faces the onlooker over his shoulder, laughing heartily. Nearly two and a half centuries later Goya dedicated a double portrait to a doctor who helped him through a bad illness, and is shown supporting the suffering artist in bed and gently holding a glass of medicine to his lips. Fig.4 shows a less sympathetic double portrait: me and the standing figure of my first wife in the basement kitchen of 160 Hill Street. Our skins are the colour of the newsprint paper, the surface of the door behind most of Inge was solid grey as shown, but our chequered linoleum floor would have obscured her black-stockinged ankles, so was painted silvery blue. Door frame and skirting board were white as shown, the actual wall not much darker, but here made black to strengthen a composition nearly pulled in two by the divergent expressions of our faces. The look of angry dissatisfaction on Inge's face was often hers but other drawings showed her content or wistful or sad: seldom happy, because happiness is the most fleeting expression on any adult face.

Good portraits, unlike good caricatures, never reduce a face to one or two simple expressions of cunning, mirth, greed, kindness, brutality etcetera: feelings that change our features from moment to moment until brought to rest in sleep, or steady concentration, or in the sort of meditation that can be induced by staying still to be portrayed over a long time. This state of rest contains all a sitter's potential expressions so are not so easily read. They show unique people at a certain age with some general traits like social confidence tinged with melancholy or good humour, but seldom more and often not as much – hence arguments about whether or not Leonardo's *Mona Lisa* is smiling or Hal's *Laughing Cavalier* laughing. Social class is usually suggested by clothing. From Holbein's portrait of Henry VIII we might guess he had been a much-admired, jolly, companionable man; not that he was becoming a cruel, suspicious megalomaniac. But what of SELF-portraits?

The greatest novel of all, *War and Peace*, had a

shy, plain heroine whose face becomes lovely when she forgets herself. She never notices her attractive appearance because, when approaching mirrors (says Tolstoy) 'As with everyone, her face assumed a forced, unnatural expression as soon as she looked in a glass.' With everyone? I expect so. This would explain why, when unexpectedly confronted by our reflection in a mirror we did not know was there, it takes a moment to recognise ourselves. So how can artists deliberately confronting themselves in mirrors avoid a forced, unnatural expression? Answer: easily, because we can only depict our faces bit by bit, starting with an eye or eyebrow, the edge of a mouth or nostril, the curve of a cheek. Our eye explores our contours like an insect crawling round each, while our hand sets down what the insect discovers. Careful concentration will banish anything stiff and unnatural from the artist's face, just as it departs from the face of anyone who gets accustomed to a portrait sitting. There is one important difference.

Since a very complicated arrangement of mirrors is needed to paint oneself in profile, most self-portraits show artists looking searchingly into their own eyes, and in many of Van Gogh's the expression is gloomy and haunted. It changes after his hospitalisation. Beardless, with bandaged ear, he now has a sad look of loss and resignation, but in both sorts it would be phoney to suggest that this face is the face of a Dr Jekyll discovering Mr Hyde in himself. Both are as true to him as are all of Rembrandt's, from the time he shows himself as a rich jolly toper to the great final portraits of an old man calmly confronting himself and death and posterity. Any artist making an honest self-representation is more completely in mental harmony (I believe) than any politician making speeches, or any boss giving orders, or anyone doing repetitive labour that excludes their imagination and intelligence.

Having referred to self-portraits by many great artists I now have the conceit to speak of my own best: the only one to attempt subtle *chiaroscuro*. It was drawn at night, in bed, by the light of the small bedside lamp whose plastic shade is part of the composition. It was drawn from a mirror laid on my lap so again presents an upward view of someone who is now distinctly glum and middle-aged. This is not quite all of my character for in company I seem to talk and laugh a lot, perhaps a sign of nervousness. And like all folk truly devoted to their work – not just artists – there lies in doing it a satisfaction we prefer to other forms of happiness.

# New Kelvingrove*

IN 1946 I WAS ELEVEN, LIVING IN RIDDRIE, an eastern housing scheme whose people thought it very posh, as I hope they still do. I usually spent spare time in my bedroom, at a small version of a senior executive's desk my dad had made when his hobby was carpentry. Here I sat scribbling pictures and illustrating stories of magical worlds where I was rich and powerful. One day mum put some of my scribblings in a handbag and took me by tram to Kelvingrove. She had read in a newspaper that Miss Jean Irwin held an art class on Saturday mornings in Kelvingrove, and I believe (though she never said so) that class would get me out of the house and give me more friends. Children in it were supposed to be recommended by teachers, but my mum was an independent woman. A half hour tram ride brought us to Kelvingrove, not yet open to the general public, but she swiftly got admission from an attendant who explained where to go. We went up broad marble stairs and along to a marble-floored balcony-corridor overlooking the great central hall, and I heard exciting orchestral music. At the top of more steps we saw twenty or thirty children busy painting at little tables before very high windows, painting to music from a gramophone, as record players were then called. I

* Most of this was published as an article in **The Herald** 2006, and its material was partly used in Chapter 3 of my **Life in Pictures** published by Canongate in 2010.

drifted around looking at what these kids painted
while mum showed my scribbles to Miss Irwin, who let me join her class. For the next five years Saturday mornings were the happiest time of the week. Friday night was bath night. Next day I rose to a clean change of underwear, shirt and socks, so left the house feeling unusually fresh. If the day was warm enough to go without a jacket I felt the whole city was my home, and that in Kelvingrove I was a privileged part of it. The art class children came an hour before the public were admitted, I was always earliest and could therefore take the most roundabout way to the painting place, starting with a wide circuit through the ground floor.

I first turned right through a gallery with a large geological model of Strathclyde near the door. It had a pale blue river, firth and lochs, and layers representing rocks painted to show how the valley and hills had been laid down in prehistoric times pink sandstone predominated. Beyond were glass cases of fossils, including an ichthyosaurus, and uncased models. The tyrannosaurus was most impressive, and a great ugly fish with two goggle eyes near the front of his head instead of one each side, and big human-looking buck teeth. I left that gallery by an arch under the skull of a prehistoric elk with antlers over six feet wide.

Then came modern natural history, the shells and exoskeletons of insects and sea-beasts, a grotesque yet beautiful variety showing the unlimited creativity of the universe. Some I hardly dared look at and would have preferred them not to exist. A spider crab had legs splayed out as wide as the antlers of the elk. Then came stuffed birds and animals in cases with clues to their way of life. I seem to remember a fox bringing a pheasant's wing in its mouth to small foxes under a shelf of rock or under a tree root. Big animals were in a very high gallery behind large glazed arches. An elephant with its young one, a giraffe and gazelle had a painted background of the African veldt; an arctic scene had walrus, seal and polar bear with fake snow and ice floes. A Scottish display had stag, doe and fawn, capercaillie and grouse among heather.

I have no space to describe my delight in the sarcophagi, ornaments, carvings and models of the Egyptian gallery – the splendid model samurai seated in full armour before the ethnography gallery with its richly-carved furniture, weapons and canoe prow from Oceania and Africa – the gallery full of large perfectly detailed models of the greatest ships built on Clydeside. The ground floor displays assured me that the world had been, and still was, full of more wonderful things than I could imagine for myself.

After these wonders the long uncluttered floors of upstairs picture galleries were a satisfying change. I was too young to enjoy looking at many pictures. Realistic ones seemed a waste of time – the world is full of mothers and children, pompous adults, bowls of fruit and vases of flowers, flayed and limbless cattle hanging in butchers' shops – why stare at paintings of them? But I loved the two huge Salvator Rosa landscapes. I imagined climbing into them, paddling through the pools of what seemed shallow rivers, passing the small figures of John the Baptist, Jesus and

Disciples and making secret dens for myself in the hollow trees and cavernous rocks. I also enjoyed, as all children can and many adults do, Noel Paton's *Fairy Raid*, that moonlit wood full of amazing supernaturals. Only as I aged and matured did I come to appreciate Rembrandt's *Flayed Ox*, Turner's *Modern Italy*, Whistler's *Carlyle* and many more of Kelvingrove's great paintings.

I had become intimate with the galleries in the last days of Tom Honeyman's audacious curatorship. More important than his acquisition of Dali's Crucifixion was the other modern art he brought to Glasgow – his shows of work by Picasso, Matisse and Van Gogh raised storms of publicity. When taking my private unofficial stroll through the upper galleries one morning I found three were hung with all Edvard Munch's greatest paintings and prints. It was a maturing experience. Before then I had been mainly excited by views of the fantastic, erotic heavens and hells in books of pictures by Blake, Aubrey Beardsley and Bosch. I wanted to make my life exciting by painting catastrophic biblical events in modern Glasgow settings – the deluge, for instance, flooding Kelvingrove Park up to the level of Park Circus. Munch painted hell in the rooms and streets of Oslo, a city not unlike Glasgow, and he was a realist! His white suburban villa with scarlet Virginia creeper, shown at night by street lighting, was creepy and sinister but not fantastic. Munch, like adolescent me, was obsessed with loneliness, sex and death – his people look lonely, all his women are victims or vampires. He showed me great art can be made out of common people and things viewed through personal emotion.

Apart from temporary shows like Munch's the main Kelvingrove displays were almost unchanged for most of my life, apart from the model ships being shifted to the Transport Museum when it opened in the sixties. They were replaced by weapons, armour and military uniforms. I think the main arrangement had been achieved between the two world wars and maintained because no curator – not even audacious Honeyman – thought of a better one. In more than fifty years of visiting I always found something new and interesting among displays and paintings I had seen before. When Kelvingrove shut for renovation in 2003 I feared what change might bring, being an old-fashioned Socialist with conservative instincts who has disliked some renovations.

For over two centuries Glasgow had a culture of scientific discovery, industrial production and radical politics. Its municipal water supply, street lighting, parks and public transport made it a pioneer among modern cities. Municipal housing schemes (Riddrie was one) had replaced the terrible housing of its working classes. But by 1990 the big industries had gone, a Tory government with Labour connivance had privatised public services and property, so the town council, having power to do hardly anything else, decided to renovate Glasgow by attracting property developers and tourists. Glasgow was declared Europe's Culture Capital so the Council brought in culture managers to promote the city as just a nice place to be. This meant ignoring Glasgow's great industrial and municipal Socialist past. A new head of art galleries and museums made only one lasting change to Kelvingrove — paintings usually kept in store were hung on the walls of corridors, close together and high up, like stamps in an album. He also demoted Elspeth King, acting curator of the People's Palace on Glasgow Green. She had enriched this local history museum, at hardly any cost to the Council, with good displays of Glasgow's past that some Labour councillors wished to forget from the vandalism of the Reformation to Billy Connolly's welly boots. Elspeth has been my friend since she employed me as Glasgow's city recorder in 1977, so I was prejudiced against the 1990s renovation of Glasgow and against Julian Spalding who, by not leaving well enough alone, had harmed a museum. So I also feared for the Kelvingrove renovation.

But when shown round it last week before the official opening I was delighted at first. The basement has been splendidly renovated. Stores, workshops and offices it once contained are now in Nitshill, and the floor space given to a gallery shop, restaurant, rooms for visiting parties of schoolchildren and spaces for visiting exhibitions. There is a wall of ceramic tiles each made from pictures by children in Glasgow primary schools. The basement is at ground level on the river side of the building, allowing a new easier entrance from which public lifts now rise to the upper floors. This is all good.

I first noticed on the ground floor how the carved stone walls and gilded ceilings are now free of industrial grime I had thought their normal colour, and how displays are completely rearranged. Some paintings had been brought down from the sky-lit galleries because (I was told) it was found fewer folk went up there. If we ignore a minority who could not face stairs before public lifts were installed, this must be because many – like me as a boy – are bored by paintings. So why not surprise them by showing some with museum displays? On the ground floor are more good paintings by John Quentin Pringle than I knew the gallery owned, well displayed beside Rennie Mackintosh furniture. Pringle and Mackintosh were contemporaries, so why separate them from Glasgow artists in upstairs gallery? Many foreign tourists are interested in Mary Queen of Scots – why not group paintings of her downstairs with a doll in the kind of clothes she wore? There is still one painting of her upstairs in an exhibition about Scottish History – or was it Scottish Character? Many labels had still to be put in place, but perhaps my memory is at fault. Everything I saw was entertaining but confusing. I forget where I saw my old friends the spider crab, also the Irish elk whose skull is now mounted on a complete skeleton.

Nearly all I remember is now recombined unexpectedly with new acquisitions. A Glasgow squadron Spitfire hangs above the hall where the large animals had been. It would have been conventional to arrange the weapons, armour and uniforms under it, so elephant, bear, turtle, etcetera are now in the middle of the floor with no indication of their former habitats, though a label tells the elephant's sad story from circus days to when he went mad and was shot in a zoo. A gull also hung below the Spitfire and a low case contained many different, beautifully-coloured butterflies. Labelling was not complete when I was there so later visitors may read explanations that link Spitfire, exotic big animals, gull and butterflies.

Weapons and armour now appear among horned and tusked beasts with overhead shark in a display called CONFLICT AND CONSEQUENCES suggesting (despite what labels say) that men dress to kill as naturally as other species grow spikes and shells. Hedgehog, wasp, jellyfish, cactus could be added, tortoise, snail, oyster and much of the old natural history collections which must now be in store. Elsewhere a display named STYLE had a 1920s Anderson racing car, its bonnet surrounded by dummies wearing Victorian crinolines and 18th century panniered gowns. The granite sarcophagus could have been there to show the style of Egyptian coffins, but I am glad to say most Egyptian things have been kept together, with some overcrowding.

In the top galleries national schools of painting – Italian, Dutch, French, Scottish – have not been mixed together because someone thought traditional groupings dull. Standing display panels now break up the floors, letting more works be shown, but depriving them of spaciousness, because visitors must constantly turn corners. Most large paintings here are now not so easily seen from a distance, the Salvator Rosas had to leave their Italian chums and now hang below, each on a separate stair. Where once pictures appeared with only a tiny label giving the painter's name we now have big explanatory notices with distracting, superfluous colour photos showing parts of paintings beside them. Between other paintings are conspicuous metal brackets to hold pages of information about the painter's work. Pictures I love now seem owned by a domineering teacher who thinks nobody can enjoy pictures without being insistently lectured.

But there is now room for a display about the Holocaust, with small pictures recalling Belsen experiences by a lady artist who survived them and came to Glasgow. A Koran once looted by a Scottish soldier in the far east reminds us of Scotland's part in founding the British Empire. Another small display proves all Scottish soldiers were not nasty: it shows three Catholic devotional panels painted by Italian prisoners of war for their chapel in a British prison camp, and given in gratitude to the officer commanding the camp. All this is politically correct.

I am tempted to sum up my response to the new Kelvingrove in the words of an ancient muppet: "Very in — ter — est — ing... but stupid!". Unfair and untrue. From being a sequence of large, sensibly linked exhibitions, Kelvingrove is now a chaos of displays, mostly clever, some daft, all amusing, apart from the paintings upstairs that I think horribly displayed. The general style proclaims that the world exists for smart folk who can rearrange it as they like. In one word Kelvingrove is now post-modern, the highest and most insulting compliment I can pay. Children, tourists and even some who remember what it was will find it fun. My regrets are those of any old man who believes things were once better ordered.

# London Won't Let Us*

S COTS ARE TIRED of talk about Scots independence. Yes, Scotland's industries have declined as the Westminster government's power has increased. Some of us have grown used to it, some think it cannot be changed, some are comfortable enough to think the matter unimportant. Let me just entertain you with old stories from my days with the BBC.

When my first TV play was accepted by a London producer in 1966, he asked what actors I would like in the main parts. I knew too few to say, but the play was about three Scots in London so I suggested Scots actors should play those parts. In London for the rehearsals I learned Corin Redgrave would play Kelvin Walker (the hero), another English actor would play Sir Hector McKellor, and an Irishman would play Kelvin's father. This was because the producer knew no suitable Scots actors in London, and had decided to please me with at least one Scottish actor by choosing from an actors directory one whose second name began with Mac, on the assumption that he must be Scottish. It turned out that the English actors could play totally convincing Scottish parts, but the Mac was from Northern Ireland and could only sound like a dour Ulsterman. His small, crucial part had to be cut shorter. *The Fall of Kelvin Walker* was broadcast in

* Despite the opening disclaimer, this was written about 2007 as part of a debate on our need for a truly independent Scots Parliament. It was not published.

1968 and a letter from an English viewer asked why I had ruined a good play with an unconvincing end.

Despite the spoiled end of that play, it led to another about the love of a woman, a son and his dad.

\*\*\*\*\*\*\*\*\*\*\*\*\*\*\*\*\*\*\*\*\*\*\*\*\*\*\*\*\*\*\*\*
\*\*\*\*\*\*\*\*\*\*\*\*\*\*\*\*\*\*\*\*\*\*\*\*\*\*\*\*\*\*\*\*
\*\*         *See the second paragraph of*         \*\*
\*\*    **Instead of an Apology**, *pages 118 - 119*  \*\*
\*\*\*\*\*\*\*\*\*\*\*\*\*\*\*\*\*\*\*\*\*\*\*\*\*\*\*\*\*\*\*\*
\*\*\*\*\*\*\*\*\*\*\*\*\*\*\*\*\*\*\*\*\*\*\*\*\*\*\*\*\*\*\*\*

Early in the 1970s Cecil Taylor and Tom Gallagher founded the Scottish Society of Playwrights, a union of dramatists who found it hard to get work produced north of the Tweed. One of our members was Eddie Boyd who wrote the earliest and best episodes of *The View from Daniel Pike*, a networked crime series with a Glasgow setting. London BBC producers soon dropped Eddie, commissioned scripts from writers who mainly knew Scotland from books, after which the series was discontinued. The Society arranged a meeting of its members with Alasdair Milne, controller of BBC Scotland who would eventually become the BBC's Director-General. This honest man explained the BBC had no single national drama office to which playwrights could send work, and the best way to interest more producers in it was by hobnobbing socially with them, in London.

I was then having short radio plays with Scottish settings produced by Stewart Conn, then head of Scottish BBC radio drama. In 1975 I sent him *Near the Driver*, a conversation between folk on a future London-to-Scotland express train. Here they meet a polite official called "the driver" who explains that the train is remotely controlled by a computer in the Midlands, and his main job is to announce price increases – soon, after the train leaves Euston, inflation raises the cost of tea and coffee by 50%. Later still he announces that the train is on the same track as one coming the opposite way and will collide with it in ten minutes. He tells them that there is no cause for alarm, gets them strapped to their seats with safety belts that will not unfasten, and before steel shutters cover the windows to protect them from broken glass, retires to the guards' van to ensure that he, at least, survives to attend an official enquiry into the disaster. The play ends with a vast explosion.

\*\*\*\*\*\*\*\*\*\*\*\*\*\*\*\*\*\*\*\*\*\*\*\*\*\*\*\*\*
\*\*\*\*\*\*\*\*\*\*\*\*\*\*\*\*\*\*\*\*\*\*\*\*\*\*\*\*\*
\*\*      *See ADDENDUM on page 235 to*      \*\*
\*\*          **A Radio Talk on Allegory**          \*\*
\*\*\*\*\*\*\*\*\*\*\*\*\*\*\*\*\*\*\*\*\*\*\*\*\*\*\*\*\*
\*\*\*\*\*\*\*\*\*\*\*\*\*\*\*\*\*\*\*\*\*\*\*\*\*\*\*\*\*

In the late 1970s I was writer-in-residence at Glasgow University, an experience that suggested my story *Five Letters from an Eastern Empire*. It is told in the first person by the poet laureate of a vast nation who finds the highly cultured head masters employing him are not benign, but murderously selfish. Roger Scrutton, the Conservative critic, praised it as a satire 'on Soviet Russia or China', and I thought it had much in common with western nations. In 1983 I discussed broadcasting it with Michael Goldberg, a Scottish radio talks producer. He had been an adviser on science broadcasting in London until 1977 (he told me) when a referendum looked like giving Scotland its own parliament. This would have enlarged the scope of Scottish broadcasting so he had been sent North to manage some of it; but a last minute clause to the referendum bill resulted in the majority who voted for a Scottish parliament not getting it. Mr Goldberg had to go on working for BBC Scotland in ways he had not at first expected.✶✶✶✶✶✶✶✶✶✶✶✶✶✶✶✶✶✶✶✶ ✶✶✶✶✶✶✶✶✶✶✶✶✶✶✶✶✶✶✶✶✶✶✶✶✶✶✶✶✶✶ ✶✶        *See the last paragraph of*        ✶✶ ✶✶        **Not Another Scotland**, *page 35*        ✶✶ ✶✶✶✶✶✶✶✶✶✶✶✶✶✶✶✶✶✶✶✶✶✶✶✶✶✶✶✶✶✶ ✶✶✶✶✶✶✶✶✶✶✶✶✶✶✶✶✶✶✶✶✶✶✶✶✶✶✶✶✶✶

A year later (1985) my novel *The Fall of Kelvin Walker* was published and I met Tom Kinninmont, a BBC Scotland producer, who thought it could be turned into a great TV play with Bill Paterson in the title role. He did not know it had been broadcast by London BBC seventeen years earlier. I showed him the original script and,  suddenly glum, he said "London's done it already? Oh dear, it won't let us do it again!" I asked why? The first production had been spoiled by a producer who did not know enough Scots actors to play Scottish parts, so it could now be done again better, especially as I had improved the end when writing a theatre version taken on tour by the short-lived Scottish Stage Company. Also, hardly any viewers in Britain would remember the play now. But Tom Kinninmont told me that when he referred the matter to London, London refused him permission. He certainly told me so. The playwright Peter McDougall tells me he knew a Scottish producer who said he had referred a matter to London, but Peter found he had never done so, in case London said no. This self-censorship is common where local bosses kow-tow to bosses in a foreign government. In Britain local chiefs afraid to take local initiatives are not held back by fear of arrest, show-trials or physical punishment. They are made timid by fear of somehow damaging their careers.

I believe many people in Scottish industry, law, medicine, local government and politics find they cannot do some things because "London" really will forbid them. I believe there will be many others who avoid local initiatives because they think "London" dislikes these. The Scottish Labour Party contains many such folk who like this situation. They are able to draw bigger and bigger salaries while doing less and less local good, while implementing London policies*. No wonder they dread a degree of self-govermnent that would force them to support independent local action,

and help poorer workers the Labour party
was created to represent.

* It has long been notorious that many Scots MPs in London seldom voice an opinion while steadily voting as their party chiefs demand. In the early 1960s, when Glasgow was still a productive industrial city ruled absolutely by the Labour party, a folk-singer came up with a song whose first verse is

I am a Scottish MP
from a city grey and black
and I shut my mouth when I'm in the south
in case they send me back.

# Of Archie Hind*

IN 1928 ARCHIE HIND WAS BORN in Dalmarnock, an industrial part of east Glasgow. His father, a stoker on locomotive engines, worked for fifty-one years on the railways, with an interval as a soldier in World War One. Though liked by workmates and friends he was so bad a husband that when her son Archie was seven and older brother nine their mother left home with her two-year-old daughter. Ten years later the parents were reconciled; meanwhile the boys lived with their father and his widowed mother. The home Mrs Hind had abandoned, while decent and clean, was like most tenement homes in Glasgow between the wars, a room and kitchen with communal lavatory on an outside landing. Baths had to be taken in public bathhouses and Archie sometimes used these less than he wished, to stop people seeing bruises from his father's beatings. These stopped when he and his brother grew strong enough to hit back.

The brutal part of his upbringing was not the most formative part and has no place in his novel *The Dear Green Place*, where the hero's father is based on a more representative Glasgow dad, a tolerant, intelligent Marxist uncle. The main-stream of working-class thought and culture in Glasgow was the Socialism of the Independent Labour Party, the party George Orwell

* An introduction I wrote to the Polygon publication of Archie Hind's **The Dear Green Place** (never out of print since first published in 1966) in the same volume as his unfinished novel **Fur Sadie**.

most favoured, and which returned seven Scottish MPs to Westminster before World War Two. After 1946 the
best of these died or joined the Parliamentary Labour Party. Like most Socialists between the two great wars Archie's people had been hopeful about the Russian Revolution and would have distrusted the U.S.S.R. more if the British government had not been so friendly to Fascist Italy, Germany and Spain.

Archie had an early love of literature and music. He and his brother both loved singing, and he learned piping in the Boys' Brigade. Leaving school at fourteen he entered Beardmores, the largest engineering firm in Britain. It had built cars, planes, the first British airship, and still made great steam engines for ships and railway locomotives. By the late 1960s Scottish steam-powered industries were obsolete, but Archie joined the firm when World War Two was giving it a last lease of profitable life. For two years he was a messenger, reporting to Head Office on the progress of shafts and propellers shaped in the forges and turning sheds. He should have become an apprentice when sixteen, but his father wanted the higher wage Archie earned by shifting to a warehouse supplying local grocers. In 1945 or 6 he could have gone to university, since the last act of the government that brought Britain through the war had enabled any student to attend colleges of further education who passed the entrance exam. He could easily have done that, but it would have meant even less money for his dad than an engineering apprenticeship. He only left home when eighteen to do his National Service in the British Army medical corps for two years in Singapore and Ceylon.

Which tells nothing about the birth and growth of his wide erudition and strong imagination through reading, close attention to recorded music and broadcasts, and intense discussion with those of similar interests. British professional folk often think creative imaginations unlikely outside their own social class – on first reading *Ulysses* Virginia Woolf thought James Joyce (despite his Jesuit and Dublin University education) had all the faults of a self-taught working man. Who in Glasgow could see the growth of an unusual mind in a twenty-year-old ex-Beardmores progress clerk, warehouseman and demobbed medical corps private? Jack Rillie could, the Glasgow University English lecturer who ran an extra-mural class in literature. Archie attended it and on Rillie's recommendation went to Newbattle Abbey, the Workers' Further Education College in Midlothian. The Principal was the Orkney-born poet Edwin Muir who, with his wife Willa, were the foremost translators of German language novels by Broch, Musil and Kafka. Archie became a friend of both.

By now he had decided to write a book that he knew would never sell enough to support him – a book that would leave him a failure in the eyes of all but those who liked unusually careful writing. Soon after Newbattle Archie married Eleanor, a girl he had met through the Tollcross Park tennis club. She accepted him and his strange ambition while foreseeing the consequences, perhaps because her Jewish mother and Irish father came from people who did not identify worldly success with great achievements. Her mother had been brought from the

Crimea to Scotland by parents escaping from Czarist pogroms, and like many Jews in Glasgow she attended left-wing meetings. At one of these she had met John Slane, a coalminer who learned to make spectacles while studying at night classes. They married and he became an optician successful enough, and rich enough, to buy Eleanor a beautiful Steinway grand piano and give it house room. But he hated her marriage to a man who supported his growing family by working as a social security clerk, trolley-bus driver and labourer in the municipal slaughterhouse between writing a novel that would never earn a supportive income. Archie and Eleanor made friends with writers and artists met through a new Glasgow Arts Centre which met in premises leased by the painter J. D. Fergusson and his wife Margaret Morris, founder of the Celtic Dance Theatre.

I met them in 1958 when they had three sons (Calum, Gavin, Martin) and young daughter Nellimeg, whose mental age was arrested at less than two years by minor epilepsy. Their last child Sheila was born five years later. I had recently left Glasgow Art School and the Hinds had the only welcoming home I knew where literature, painting and music were subjects of extended, enjoyable conversations. It was a room and kitchen flat like that where Archie had been born, but in Greenfield Street, Govan. The room held the children's bunks so social life was always in the warm kitchen which, despite many evening visitors, never seemed overcrowded. These were years when London critics thought Osborne's *Look Back in Anger*, Amis's *Lucky Jim*, Braine's *Room at the Top*, were a new school of literature created through the agency of the welfare state. These three works described working-class lads acquiring middle-class women. Archie and I thought they described nothing profound when compared with the best writings of Joyce and D. H. Lawrence, Hemingway and Scott Fitzgerald. We admired *The Tin Drum*, *Catch-22*, *Slaughterhouse 5*, and found we were both working on a novel about the only struggle we could take seriously – the struggle to make a work of art. This has been an important theme in poetry and fiction since Wordsworth's *Prelude*. It inspired Archie most in the poetry of Yeats and fiction of Thomas Mann. He liked good jazz and American Blues, the songs of Edith Piaf and The Beatles, but thought most highly celebrated contemporary work – Beckett's dramas, John Cage's music, abstract expressionist painting and Warhol's Campbell's soup icons – indicated a thinning in the rich intellectual texture of Western culture. I was not so sure, but agreed that as writers we should maintain that texture. Our novels were both about low-income Glasgow artists doomed to failure, this coincidence worried us slightly, but we had chosen that theme long before meeting each other, and had to put up with it.

In the middle 1960s the Hinds moved to Dalkeith where Archie worked with Ferranti's Pegasus, an early computer filling nearly the whole floor of a building. He left that job to finally complete his novel, and having completed it, worked as copy-taker in the *Scottish Daily Mail*, Edinburgh, while awaiting publication. In Milne's Bar he sometimes conversed amicably about sport and politics with Hugh

MacDiarmid. In 1966 the novel was published in Hutchinson's New Author series. Its title, *The Dear Green Place*, was Archie's translation of glas-chu or gles-con, Gaelic words that became Glasgow. They had previously been translated green hollow, green churchyard, greyhounds ferry, dear stream, and (in imperial days when it was the second largest and smokiest city in Britain) the grey forge or smithy. Archie's translation is now generally accepted.

All good novels are historical – describe living people in a definite place and time. *The Dear Green Place* shows a city that had grown between 1800 and 1960, becoming for almost a century the second biggest in Britain. The earliest paragraphs give the layout – a city completely unlike London, for in Glasgow the homes of labourers, tradesmen and professional folk were intermingled with parks, shops, thriving factories with smoking chimneys and districts of old industrial wasteland. The time is about the 1950s when unemployment hardly existed and most of the labour force, though poorly housed by later standards, had the better wages and working conditions promised to the trade unions by the wartime coalition government. This Scottish region of the newly established British Welfare State gives Mat Craig the chance to occasionally dodge the commercial forces that, before 1939, would have made him an industrial serf, or political activist, or even destitute. He has enough room to exercise, however painfully, what was once a bourgeois or aristocratic privilege – the free will needed to attempt a work of art. The only other twentieth-century novel I know that places a writer's struggle in an equally well imagined city is Nabokov's novel *The Gift*.

Published in 1966, *The Dear Green Place* won four prizes: The Guardian Fiction of the Year, The Yorkshire Post's Best First Work, the Frederick Niven and Scottish Arts Council Awards. The Hinds returned to Glasgow when, as foreseen, *The Dear Green Place* had not earned enough to support them. Archie wrote revues performed in the Close Theatre and a witty, precise political column for the *Scottish International* magazine. He worked for the Easterhouse Project, a privately funded meeting place started to reduce violent crime among the young when the Easterhouse housing scheme still had few shops, no cafés, playing-fields or provision for games and entertainment. Soon after, he was appointed to the position of Aberdeen City's first Writer-in-Residence, later becoming copy-taker for the Aberdeen Press and Journal.

By this time he was working on his second novel, *Fur Sadie*. Fur is how many Glaswegians pronounce for, and the title associates it with Beethoven's piano piece, *Für Elise*, in a way that will make perfect sense when you read it. In 1973 the magazine *Scottish International* published a small part, but all that Archie wrote of it is published here for the first time, for I believe it an astonishing achievement, although unfinished.

It is sometimes said that Scottish fiction has a more masculine bias than that of other lands, and though generally untrue it is true of much writing by authors like Alexander Trocchi, William MacIlvanney, Alan Sharp, Alasdair Gray and Irvine Welsh. But *The*

*Dear Green Place* makes it hard to include Archie Hind among these and *Fur Sadie* makes it impossible. Here he transposes (as musicians say) the theme of artistic struggle into the person of a small, ordinary-seeming, middle-aged yet very attractive working-class housewife and mother. In a few episodes her life between infancy and menopause is presented as richly detailed, generally admirable, stunted by too little money and leisure, yet capable of much more. Most British descriptions of working-class people suggest how horrid, or comic, or admirable that they live that way. The narrative voice of *Fur Sadie* is free of such condescension. He knows that better lives are possible, and shows Sadie working for one.

Her portrait is deeply historical. Her childhood is in the pre-television age after World War 2 when city children still played and sang in side streets where motorcars were rarities. Many professional folk did not own one. Coal and milk were usually brought to homes in horse-drawn carts. As a housewife with working sons, Sadie need no longer heat water in a kettle because she has now an electric geyser above her kitchen sink. This innovation comes with a television set in her front room, but now she has saved enough out of her housekeeping money to buy a second-hand piano and pay for tuition to play it, knowing the expense will not worry her husband. A social revolution has happened through which we see the sexual growth of a woman and man from adolescence through early marriage to late, sad maturity. No other author I know has shown a sexual relationship over many years with such casual, unsensational delicacy and truth. That is essential to this tale of childhood friendship and a long-buried talent at last combining with a good music teacher to bring Beethoven (no less!) alive in the mind and fingers of an apparently ordinary woman.

At this point, sometime in the early 1970s, Archie Hind gradually or suddenly stopped writing *Fur Sadie* and lost interest so thoroughly that he retained no copy. The first chapters published here have been edited from a photocopy he gave in the early 1990s to John Linklater, then Literary Editor of *The Herald*, who occasionally commissioned Archie to write book reviews. Even that had pages missing from the centre, but these were found printed in a 1973 edition of the *Scottish International* magazine, so though lacking a conclusion, the start is continuous.

Shortly before Archie died in 2008, John Linklater asked him why he had not finished *Fur Sadie*. Quoting another writer he replied, 'It developed a slow puncture.' I know why this happened. Creative talent has mainly been excercised by middle class folk with some spare time and money, so in Britain there is a widespread sense that manual workers who practice it are aiming "above their station in life", as Victorian snobs would have said, or aiming to become "traitors to their class" as working-class Marxists in his family did NOT say, but often hinted. In years of full employment Archie, who could earn money in so many jobs, often became what has been called, "a Welfare State scrounger," to write a book he knew he would never earn much money. This knowledge weighed more heavily on him than on arrogant me.

I was sure my work would one day be recognised by the state whose Social Welfare offices sometimes supported me. Archie was not. It is the theme of the one novel he completed.

On reading the first chapters of *Fur Sadie* in the 1970's I fell in love with the heroine. Archie had then been definite that the novel was going to end (unlike *The Dear Green Place*) on a triumphant note. How this would be achieved he never indicated, which forces interested readers to speculate. The book breaks off when Sadie's piano playing has brought her domestic life to a crisis. She can no longer keep it out of her family's earshot and even a neighbour has started complaining. How can her talent – her life – develop without splitting up what, by any decent standards, is a good marriage? For it is obvious that the important men in her life, husband, sons, and that great teacher McKay, cannot be reconciled.

Yes, the theme of this book is that of Dickens' *Great Expectations*, Hardy's *Jude the Obscure* and most novels by D. H. Lawrence – the conflict between warm but constrictive working communities and a grasp for freedom outside it that operates like a curse, for how can a daily worker achieve emancipation without joining the damned upper classes? Sadie, however hard working and talented, is too old to become a concert pianist. It seems unlikely that she would join a band of popular musicians. Could she become a singer's accompanist? Might she find support in her sympathetic older sister Mary? Her friend Anna vanished completely when Sadie's schooldays ended – might she reappear, and to what effect? None of these questions can be answered. To present a problem our society has still not solved, and present it believably and sympathetically in mid-twentieth century Glasgow, is as much as could be expected of a writer having to earn a living in many other ways.

This book ends with an example of Archie's journalism, an article from the *Scottish International* of August 1973. The owners of the Upper Clyde Shipyards had announced the end of Glasgow shipbuilding, as they were preparing to invest in yards outside Scotland. The Glasgow shop stewards led their workers to occupy the yards in a well-organised work-in. This was the first and biggest attempt to save a major Scottish heavy industry, and for several weeks that event brought Glasgow and its working-class spokesmen into the centre of British political news. The eventual failure of the effort heralded the steady asset-stripping and closure of every other major Scottish industry (coal mining, car manufacture, steel production, fabric weaving) through the rest of the century. This article shows Archie giving historic perspective to his eye-witness contemporary report.

I wish the book also contained some of his early short stories (all lost) and playscripts from the ten commissioned and performed between 1973 and 1990. I especially remember *The Sugarolly Story*, a satirical view of Glasgow's social history from the start of World War One to the creation of Easterhouse housing scheme. This was performed by the Easterhouse Players in the Easterhouse Social Centre after Glasgow City Council at last built one. There was also *Shoulder to Shoulder*, a dramatised documentary of John MacLean's life. *The Ragged-Trousered Philanthropist*, a Scottish dramatisation of Doonan's building-trade novel, was biggest and most successful: the only one acted by a professional company (7:84) in a well known theatre (The Citizens). Scripts of these have all been lost, so this book holds all Archie's available work. Lovers of literature will value it.

*The Dear Green Place*, the start of *Fur Sadie* and Archie Hind survived into a century where his forebodings about the thinning of our cultural tradition (now called dumbing-down), has come true. Intellectuals calling themselves Postmodern claim objective truths do not exist, but are opinions in disguise. They now lecture in universities upon anything they like, because they think all artifacts equally valuable, and declare many once valued negligible. In a recent history of 20th century art  an international dealer and critic celebrated the triumph of Installation and Performance Art while announcing that oil painting since Picasso is patriarchal and obsolete. Shortly before the 21st century ended a head of visual arts in Glasgow's Art School said no artist need now learn to draw. Glasgow University has a department of Creative Writing where the kind of novel Dickens, Herman Melville, D. H. Lawrence and Archie wrote is labelled literary fiction, and taught as a genre no more worthwhile than crime, horror, science fiction and love stories publishers call chicklit. When future catastrophes have moved survivors back to serious agreement about important work in life and in art, *The Dear Green Place* and *Fur Sadie* will also survive.

# Postscript to *Fleck**

A S A CHILD I WAS a glutton for stories of magic and miracles so came to know all the fairytales pantomimes are based on, besides the talking animals and animated toys of Kenneth Graham and A.A. Milne. The Bible was not among the books in our home – faith in education was my parents' only religion – but at school my religious instruction was mostly Bible readings, so I came to know many tales about fiction's oldest, most famous and most influential character, God the Dad.

He fascinated me because (unlike his son Jesus Chirist who was probably real) God's dealings with people were horribly unfair. He makes the first man and woman ignorant of right and wrong, but gives them easy access to knowledge of right and wrong in a fruit they are commanded not to taste. He has also given the garden a clever serpent (why?) who prompts them to eat it, which they do, for they can only know it is wrong to disobey God after doing so. For this crime they and their children are punished by lives of hard labour ever after. This single-parent God is obviously a twister, but a convincing twister, who contrives for his children what Ronald Laing calls a

---

✱ *This play and postscript was printed as a book by Two Ravens Press in 2008. Every theatre in Scotland rejected it and the best efforts of an important London theatre agency could not get it accepted in England, so for three years I promoted it by reading parts at Scottish literary festivals. At Edinburgh's International Book Festival in 2012 I at last produced a reading of the whole thing, and had my readers paid at the Equity rate, by getting nearly every part read by published and well-known authors.*

double bind: the situation of being wrong because they exist. Like other early gods the Ancient of Genesis liked the smell of burnt food. Adam and Eve's son Cain tilled the soil so could only offer vegetables, so God preferred his brother Abel, a shepherd who roasted mutton for him. We are not told how God showed his preference, but it made Cain so jealous that he murdered Abel. It is good that God did not retaliate by killing Cain, but marked him so that others would know he was a public danger. Much later God tells the children of Israel "Thou shalt not kill" then tells them to invade Palestine and massacre the natives.

I now know my teachers steered clear of several Biblical stories showing God at his worst, but am still surprised by how his believers justify these. In an 1879 introduction to *Deuteronomy* the Reverend C. H. Mackintosh wrote, "some persons, allowing themselves to be influenced by morbid feeling and false sentimentality… find difficulty in the directions given to Israel in reference to the Canaanites. It seems to them inconsistent with a Benevolent Being to command His people to smite their fellow creatures and show them no mercy. They cannot understand how a merciful God could command His people to slay women and children with the edge of the sword." Mackintosh then explains that folk who cannot understand this are presuming to judge God, when they should have the faith to know that everything He commanded in the Bible was right. In 1941 *The Bible Today*, published by Oxford University Press, had a commentary excusing the massacre of Ammonites, Midianites, Canaanites and Philistines because the

Israelite invasion was a "life-and-death struggle between truth and falsehood for the cultural development of God's people." Years earlier the Nazis had started promoting German cultural development by killing the Jews. The one excuse for that old God is that he caused everything, so is everyone's dad but the dad especially of Jesus, whose Sermon on the Mount should replace the punishment clauses for the Ten Commandments. But Christian, Muslim and Zionist governments have preferred the Old Testament Dad when His words can be used when invading, killing, robbing those of another faith, or of a very similar but slightly different faith.

But I could not dismiss Nobodaddy (Blake called Him that) as a fantasy like the Wizard of Oz. If God was the soul of the universe like I was the soul of my body, then newspapers and history books showed that innocent, helpless people were still being hurt and killed on a universal scale, so the soul of the universe often IS horribly unjust. This sensible assumption would not let me rest and gave me an appetite for stories about how evil happens.

Six centuries before Christ was born, Lao Tze wrote that the cause of all things is not nameable, but those who need a name should call it Mother. Alas, my education made it impossible for me to think the soul of all things was female. I also wanted to name the not-nameable in a way that made me think it essentially good. My earthly dad, Alex Gray, did not need to do that — he thought God a name for something he did not know, so need neither accept nor reject. Like many others he had lost the Christian faith of his parents when fighting in France, so had directly experienced more evil between 1914 and 18 than I have met in a life of 73 years. He seldom spoke of his war experiences, thought evil sprang from human greed and ignorance, and that wars and exploitation would end in the victory of co-operative Socialism, though the struggle for this might last centuries. He was enviably content with this faith. The struggle he believed in had achieved many good things I enjoyed – our council house, my schooling, the public libraries, the National Health Service – but the victory over Fascism that founded the British Welfare State in 1945 was soured by the needless testing of the first atomic bombs, after which the biggest nations invested huge wealth in a nuclear weapons race that was supposed to save the world from Communism, and is now supposed to save it from terrorism but is really maintained because the arms industry is Britain and the USA's most profitable source of investment, and gives them means of bullying poorer nations. Needing to believe in a creative goodness more lasting than people I searched for it through literature and art, and found much in the works of Bernard Shaw and William Blake who, surprisingly, sent me back to the Bible.

Both of them pointed out that, even before Jesus arrived, it contained more than a blood-thirsty battle god hell-bent on destruction. He is found speaking like the demon of Socrates, not in thunder but in a still, small voice. He threatens to punish an evil empire with worse evil, but spares the wrongdoers when they repent and beg for mercy. Prophets arise who, speaking for God, denounce sacrifices – say the smell of burnt offerings stink in His nostrils, because the rich Jews are using these to win His favour while exploiting their poorer brethren. He promises that if they obey Him and love their neighbours as themselves, everyone will adopt their faith and wars will cease because (as Burns puts it) "Man to man the wide world o'er / Shall brothers be for all that". Blake especially pointed me to Job, the Bible's eighteenth and most humane book.

It is a unique poem which does not ascribe evil to human disobedience and folly, but to The Lord (as God is named here) who starts by calling a conference of his heavenly sons. One of them, Satan, has been patrolling the earth and reports on it, like a secret service chief to a prime minister. The Lord (rather smugly) says Satan can have found nothing wrong with Job, a perfectly just man who not only obeys God's commandments, but sacrifices burnt offerings on behalf of his seven sons, in case one of them has secretly sinned by cursing God in his heart. Satan replies with a question, – "Is Job not highly paid for trusting you? He is spectacularly rich. Remove his possessions and see what he thinks of you then." God refuses to do that but lets Satan do it. Job's seven sons and three daughters are killed by lightning and a storm knocking their house down, while invading foreigners kill all his servants and steal his thousands of camels, oxen, asses and other worldly goods. Job, now a pauper, says, "I was born naked and will die naked. The Lord gave and the Lord takes away. Bless Him!"

So at the next heavenly conference the Lord can still boast of Job's faith. Satan points out that, despite Job's losses, he still has his health. So Satan is allowed to make Job's skin erupt in such dreadful boils from the soles of his feet to the top of his head that soft ashes are the only seat he can bear. He squats in them, scraping his scabs with a piece of broken pot. When his horrified wife tells him to curse God and die he answers, "Shall we receive good from God and not receive evil?" Worse evil comes to him in the form of three old friends who try to persuade him the evils he suffers are God's punishments for sins he must have committed – by claiming he has never sinned he casts doubt on God's justice, so deserves to suffer. At this restatement of the bad old parental double-bind The Lord intervenes on His own and Job's behalf, telling the friends they don't know what they are talking about. In a great hymn to the glory of the universe He declares that it is too vast for human minds to completely understand, so people must accept the universe and the Lord who made it. What else can they do? Beyond this point *The Book of Job* ends unconvincingly with Job being finally given more wealth and children than he originally lost. Job is the only Old Testament book where Satan appears. He appears just once again in the Bible when tempting Christ in the Wilderness. These are the Devil's only Biblical appearances. *Genesis* does not suggest that Satan was the snake who tempted Eve and Adam.

After the crucifixion Satan's power was hugely magnified by a revolutionary Christian doctrine claiming that God gave a new immortal soul to every body at birth. Greek Pythagoras, Indian Buddha also thought souls were immortal, but had been created with the universe, after which everyone who died was reborn in a different body. Most religions, including the Jewish, thought death ended the soul, though one or two great folk might be carried up bodily into heaven and live there eternally. Most funeral rites were to ensure the dead stayed dead, and did not trouble the living as miserable ghosts. Egyptians assumed the soul disintegrated with the body, so those who could afford it tried keeping bodies and souls together by having their corpses mummified and securely entombed. An early pharaoh sought immortality by having his mummy stored with many of his riches in the world's heaviest tomb. Raiders were too smart for him. A few centuries later an Egyptian scribe lamented that even the builder of the Great Pyramid was now, like the poorest slave, dust blown around the desert sands. So when Christianity declared everyone was equally immortal, whether slave or emperor, it spread fast through the Roman Empire whose basic activity was slave-making.

But immortality was a threat as well as a glad promise, since only good Christians would enter heaven after death. Fathers of the Christian church decided that, since Adam and Eve's disobedience, Satan was the God of this world because all natural forces and nearly all people were ruled by Satan, who was no longer a son of heaven allowed by God to walk the earth as His secret policeman, but a fiery rebel whose main kingdom was Hell – the lowest part of the universe in the world's centre – with the surface being Hell's suburb where new-born souls graduated to heaven or hell after death. Nearly every earthly pleasure, especially sexual pleasure, was denounced by the church as a Satanic snare. Christians still exist who think that way. When that assumption was more widespread it is not surprising that the Devil became popular, especially after Roman Emperors made Christianity official. For about sixteen centuries after that there were tug-of-wars for supremacy between Christian churches and Christian governments, but usually they got on well together, so critics of either were condemned as Devilish. The clergy found Satan indispensable. Description of Hell's tortures were the strongest part of many sermons. Thomas Aquinas, theologian and Saint, declared that viewing the agonies of the damned were half the delight of Heaven. The logic of Aquinas became the limit of Roman Catholic philosophy for centuries. Those who tried to know more were often condemned as heretics.

The story of *Faust* became widely known shortly after the invention of printing. The name of an early German printer was attached to the wicked hero of a puppet play as famous as the story of Punch, and very similar. Faust pawns his soul to enjoy twenty years of unlimited knowledge, wealth and mischief before the Devil collects it. Kit Marlowe, Shakespeare's great forerunner, was a homosexual atheist and a member of the Elizabethan secret service which finally murdered him because he knew too many state secrets. His play *Doctor Faustus* is about the price of knowledge giving his hero invisibility, air-flight and time travel. But Marlowe's Devil, Mephistopheles, after one or two fine speeches, becomes a mere prankster – not an interesting character. Apart from his two Old and New Testament appearances the Prince of

Darkness made no great appearance in world literature before Protestant Milton took him up. In Dante's *Inferno* he cannot even move, being a three-headed giant frozen upside down in the world's dead centre.

Milton's *Paradise Lost* is still England's national epic and Satan is certainly its greatest and most sympathetic character. Being enthusiasts for the French Revolution, William Blake and Robert Burns greatly admired this archetypal rebel. Blake pointed out that after creating the universe Milton's God does nothing but forbid and punish, so all creative energy is left to God's enemy. In the 20th century it was disparaged by Ezra Pound and T.S. Eliot, who thought it made better sound than sense. The critic Leavis found Milton's supernatural universe full of contradictions, also pantomime slapstick in the Heavenly war between angels and devils who try hard but cannot seriously injure each other. But the contradictions in *Paradise Lost* are all in the Bible and what Christians have since made of it, and Milton has deliberately compounded them by adding every other convincing vision of the universe offered by Greek legend, New World geography and Renaissance science. Milton probably believed what God told Job's false comforters – that understanding Him is too big a job for the human brain, but he felt it right to try, and would probably have defended the contradictions in *Paradise Lost* as Walt Whitman defended those in *Leaves of Grass*: "Do I contradict myself? Very well, I contradict myself. I am vast. I contain multitudes." Before the 20th century most Believers accepted the contradictions. Voltaire mocked them because he was a sceptic for whom God and the nature of the universe were identical. Then at the height of European Enlightenment in the late 18th century, Goethe arrived and gave the Devil a new lease of post-Christian life.

A 20th century German author (perhaps Spengler?) wrote that modern man lived in a Faustian age where human powers had been hugely increased by Devilish bargains. It is a fact that literary masterpieces after Goethe's *Faust* are about wealth and power gained or sought by wrong-doing: Stendhal's *Red and Black*, *Crime and Punishment*, *Great Expectations*, Wagner's *Ring*, all Ibsen's plays. Strangest of all, bestsellers about supernatural evil were written by folk without faith in the supernatural – *Frankenstein, Dr Jekyll and Mr Hyde, Trilby, Dracula, A Picture of Dorian Gray, The Wild Ass's Skin*. The last is Balzac's only supernatural tale. His realistic ones show that criminal bargains are worth striking if you are smart enough to keep the gains. Thomas Mann's novel *Dr Faustus* describes a great German composer born soon after Bismark unifies his nation, who deals with the Devil shortly before World War One, writes masterpieces, but finally goes insane when Hitler comes to power.

I was fourteen in 1949 when the BBC Third Programme celebrated the bicentenary of Goethe's birth in a fortnight of broadcasts about the man and his work. For several nights it broadcast the five acts of *Faust*, and its vast scope so excited me that I bought a Penguin translation of Parts 7 and 2 by Philip Wayne, and acquired Victorian translations of the whole by Bayard Taylor and John Anster. I easily enjoyed inconsistencies as bad as any in *Paradise Lost*. Like *The*

*Book of Job*, this play starts with God allowing the Devil to test the faith of a good old professor whose knowledge of life is theoretical. Mephistopheles restores Faust's youth, helps him to seduce a young and loving girl, kill her brother in a duel, then abandon her when pregnant. Maddened by shame and loneliness she kills her baby and dies in jail, refusing Faust's last-minute efforts to free her because she fears his devilish friend. It is a richer play than that bare outline, mixing supernatural events with the social variety and humour of a Dickens novel, but written in poetry only those who know German appreciate. Yet the inferior English verse translations excited and delighted me.

Goethe was a young man when he wrote this first part and a famous middle-aged German writer when it was published, staged, acclaimed. Coleridge considered translating it, Delacroix illustrated it, Berlioz and Gounod set it to music. Goethe's admirers thought that if he completed *Faust* it would be to Germany what the *Iliad* had been to Greece, the *Aeneid* to Rome, the *Divine Comedy* to Italy – a display of Germany's cultural greatness through the power of her language. In 1832 at the age of eighty-three Goethe published the end of the play, dying soon after.

With the Devil's support Faust is now shown creating modern commerce by inventing paper money, saves Europe from civil warfare by hiring a mercenary army, time-travels to Ancient Greece, learns much ancient wisdom and returns with Helen of Troy. Their son has some of Lord Byron's traits, but Faust does not need family life. He acquires land by forcibly evicting peasants, imagines he is building a great new home for mankind by reclaiming desolate seashores, and becomes too old and blind to know or care that Mephisto has financed all his grand schemes by theft and piracy. After death he is conducted upward through angelic circles dimly recalling Dante's *Paradiso*, and left reunited with the pure spirit of the first woman he betrayed. What more could any man get? We all have fantasies of absolute power and absolute approval. No wonder the slightly miserable youth I was in 1949 liked that play.

Nietzsche thought the play's weakness was a German professor needing Satan's help to seduce a woman of the servant class. I disagree. The weakness is its unstinting sympathy for a billionaire businessman always enriching and aggrandising himself without a sign of remorse and dying happy, being fooled by Satan into thinking himself a public benefactor. The first part ended with Faust regretting he harmed Gretchen, but neither before or after does he regret using Satan to get all he wants. Since Goethe gives him an immortal soul, he might at least have put him through a purgatory that taught him to repent. No. Satan tries to seize the soul he has earned by so much hard work, and the angels cheat him out of it because (they say), "He who unweariedly kept trying, we have the power to free" – an excuse for Julius Caesar, Ghengis Khan, William the Conqueror, Napoleon, Mussolini, Hitler, Stalin and all such tyrants who could honestly say, "To the end of my days I never had a moment's rest." God in Heaven starts Faust's adventure, but even Goethe flinched from showing Him at the end, telling His angels to cheat the Devil.

What finally makes Goethe's *Faust* structurally inferior to the epics of Dante and Milton is its almost total indifference to Christianity. In the first scene Faust is restrained from committing suicide by a cathedral choir celebrating Easter morning, which reminds him of his innocent youth. Thereafter Jesus has no place in his world-view, because the mature Goethe was as much a pagan as any ancient Greek or Roman.

So Goethe's *Faust* joined God the Dad as my most haunting fictions. Both had authority I recognized but could not be at peace with. Over the years God excited my imagination (which Blake said was the Holy Ghost in people) to write verses about Him with more and more sympathy. Nobody imagining God can help making Him in their own image, so of course for me He is an artist struggling with difficult materials, some of them in his own personality. I have never been able to take Satan seriously – he is all too human – but in 1999 I saw Glasgow Citizens Theatre perform Marlowe's *Doctor Faustus* in a version by Edwin Morgan. This kept all the great poetry, replacing the slapstick clowning with modern devices – the infernal contract signed in blood became a drug injection into a vein, the three books of infernal knowledge were compressed into a laptop computer. This so impressed me that I suggested to Eddie that he should now write a more satisfactory version of Goethe's *Faust*. He rejected the idea. Maybe like MacDiarmid he disliked Olympian Goethe for turning Faust into a successful businessman who goes to heaven.

In 2006 I wrote *Goodbye Jimmy* for the Glasgow Oran Mor lunch hour theatre, a play whose main character is an absentee God who is finally shown subordinate to the Great Mother of All Things. Perhaps that prompted my own attempt to translate Goethe's *Faust*. *The Prologue* and *First Act* were completed by Hogmanay 2007 and those who know Goethe will see it only contains what he invented, though I have compressed much and omitted more. Not knowing how to continue I sent it to a Director of the Scottish National Theatre, hoping for a commission to research it further. The script was returned because the Edinburgh Lyceum had recently performed another modern version by John Clifford, so I decided to change Faust's name to Fleck and make him a Scot. At the time I was working hard on a book I had been busy with for years and had promised to give the publisher at the end of April 2008. Halfway through April I faced the fact that my *Life in Pictures* book could not be finished so soon, told my publisher I would finish it in a year or two, and enjoyed a wonderful freedom that suddenly let me finish *Fleck* in four or five weeks, with secretarial help from Helen Lloyd and Roger Glass.

I am happy to have completed this play with a hero who, though not Christian, has a Christ-like moment so beats the Devil, helped by God who starts and ends the play, while saying a few lines in the last act. My Nick is identical with the Mephistopheles of Goethe. No other characters are, except perhaps God. Goethe called his national epic a tragedy, though his ending stops it being one. I call *Fleck* a comedy because
dying well is the happiest thing anyone
can do if they don't believe
in personal immortality.

# Old Men In Love –

## Sidney Workman's Epilogue*

IN HIS INTRODUCTION TO THE 2007 reprint by
Canongate of Gray's first book, *Lanark*, William Boyd
says that years before the publication in 1981 it had a
Scottish reputation as "a vast novel, decades in the
writing, still to see the light of day... an impossibly
gargantuan, time-consuming labour of love, a
thousand pages long, Glasgow's *Ulysses* – such were
the myths swirling about the book at the time, as far as
I can recall." Boyd is referring to the early seventies
when he was a student at Glasgow University.

I was then a young lecturer in English at the
Adam Smith Teachers' Training Institute, Kirkcaldy, and
knew of *Lanark* through the publication of two early
chapters in *Scottish International*, a short-lived but
influential quarterly. Finding some of my students
impressed by what they thought "the novelty" of that
sample I wrote to the editor, Robert Tait, pointing out
how much it owed to Marquez's *One Hundred Years
of Solitude* published three years before, and the first
magic realist novel to be noticed internationally.
*Scottish International* did not print my letter but Gray
certainly read it. Shortly before *Lanark* was published
in 1981 he sent me a proof copy and letter begging me
to return it with any critical remarks I wished to make.
"The severer the better!" he wrote. "I promise to take

✻ *Workman explains here how he came to supply critical footnotes for my* **Lanark:
A Life in Four Books***, published in 1981 by Canongate. It seemed right that he supply
a critical epilogue to what is surely my last novel, published by Bloomsbury in 2010.*

account of them, and acknowledge your contribution."

This request seemed honest so I honestly replied, saying (among other things) that the only apparent reason for combining two very different narratives in Lanark was the author's assumption that a heavier book would make a bigger splash. I also noted several misleading and unjustified ploys in a so-called "epilogue" between chapters 40 and 41. On receiving a final copy of the book I found my criticisms had moved Gray to change his book in one way only: he had separated my strictures and added them as footnotes to his "epilogue". But he certainly acknowledged me as their author! The novel's success in Scotland led to smiling colleagues congratulating me on my part in it. Lecturers from other colleges began greeting me with surprise because they had thought me a figment of Gray's imagination – thought the footnotes a device to deflect criticism, not voice it. Gray had lured me into a trap. That I really exist has led those who know this to see me as Gray's dupe or stooge, thus irrevocably damaging my career. Since the mid 1980s it has been obvious that my Cambridge First will never lead to a more important teaching post, and that only retirement will let me escape from Fife. This has left me with a strong but unenchanted interest in Gray's work.

In February 2007 I received a parcel through the post and, opening it, had a déja vu experience that almost set my hair on end. It was a proof copy of *Old Men in Love* and letter from Gray profusely apologising for the bad effect of *Lanark* upon my career, which had been the opposite of his intention. *Old Men in Love* (he wrote) was a chance for us both "to set the record straight". He invited me to review it, at any length I liked, with any other of his books. He promised to publish this review as an epilogue to *Old Men in Love* without comment or alteration, and since this novel would be his last (for he is seventy-two and in poor health) I could be sure of having the last word. This smooth invitation was obviously Gray's way of obtaining another critic-deflecting device. I have accepted it with open eyes, believing that a cool statement of facts will let me at last indeed "set the record straight".

The attention that Gray's first novel *Lanark* received in Scotland is not surprising. A small country of about five million souls will make the most of what literature it has, and *Lanark* appeared in 1981 when northern universities urgently needed such a book. For nearly two centuries Scots literature had been taught as a branch of English. The post-war increase in Scottish national feeling finally made it a separate university course with only some twentieth-century poetry worth lecturing upon, and hardly any fiction. England had H.G. Wells, D.H. Lawrence, Virginia Woolf, Forster, Greene and Orwell, but the only well-known Scottish author was a thriller writer, John Buchan. From Chaucer's *Canterbury Tales* to D.H. Lawrence's *The Rainbow* England has had a great tradition of great literature showing its social breadth. The nearest Scots equivalent since Burns, Hogg and Sir Walter has been a line of dour working-class novels set in depressed local communities. Brown's *House with the Green Shutters* (1901), Grassic Gibbon's *Scots*

*Quair* (1934) were the best and William McIlvanney's *Docherty* (1975) the most recent. When *Docherty* received the Whitbread award Scots critics hoped McIlvanney would go on to produce something new and surprising, but McIlvanney, tired of high critical attention and low royalty cheques, turned to crime thrillers and left a gap in modern Scots literary courses that *Lanark* filled perfectly.

In the first place it was very big, combining several genres with a short linking story. One half was in the Scottish depressed working-class tradition, enlivened by elements from Joyce's *Portrait of the Artist as a Young Man*. The other half was a Kafka-esque pilgrimage mingled with science fiction. They were linked by a Borges type of story, a fantasia on memory, and the whole was welded together by devices that began to be labelled Postmodern in the 1980s, most of these being in the so-called "epilogue". Here, like Fowles in *The French Lieutenant's Woman*, Gray described himself inside his book, writing it. He put in a large index of authors he had plagiarised, except for Fowles, and named many friends and acquaintances in a west of Scotland literary clique that east coast critics had begun to call "the Glasgow literary mafia". He disarmed criticism yet further by enlisting me, as I have described.

In 1981 senior academics had just started lecturing on popular culture, so by ostentatiously blending fairy tale, science fiction and horror film elements with liftings from twentieth century authors most fashionable with academics, Gray boiled them into that 560 page postmodern stew, *Lanark*. The epilogue with my edited footnotes persuaded critics that the author was as smart as themselves. Favourably reviewed by the London press, *Lanark* was short-listed for the Booker prize, and two years after publication was on the curriculum of Scottish literature courses. Since then most studies of contemporary Scots literature suggest *Lanark* began a new Scottish Renaissance, without exactly dating the old one.

Between *Lanark* and *Old Men in Love* Gray has published eighteen books, none more than normal length. They consist of:

Two realistic novels involving sadomasochistic fantasies,

Four books of short stories (one shared with his friends Agnes Owens, James Kelman),

Two satirical novellas about young Scotsmen in the London media world,

Two science-fiction fantasies, one set in nineteenth-century Glasgow, one in a war-games future,

Three pamphlets urging Scots home rule, the last written with Professor Adam Tomkins,

Two histories of literature,

Two collections of verse,

One autobiographical pamphlet published by the Saltire Society,

One play script.

The novels and stories above are mostly prose versions of forgotten plays written between 1967 and 1977 for early television, radio and small stage companies. He admits this in epilogues usually headed *Critic Fuel* which, like the one in *Lanark*, defuse criticism by anticipating it. Since *Lanark* he has frequently given interviews suggesting his latest work of fiction will be the last since he has "no ideas for more". These efforts to hold public attention have succeeded in Scotland, though most critics at home and abroad agree that his most pornographic novel, *Something Leather*, should be forgotten. Even so he has received a more than fair share of critical attention in two Festschrifts:

*The Arts of Alasdair Gray* (Edinburgh University Press, 1992), and *Alasdair Gray: Critical Appreciations* (British Library, 2002). The second is not a Scottish production, but like the first nearly every critic in it is Scottish and about half are friends of Gray, some of them close friends. Both books have a multitude of Gray's illustrations, which proves Gray had access to the proofs, so must have overseen the texts. A cool, serious appraisal of Gray's work cannot be found in them or, I believe, anywhere in Scotland, but they show why he has a following among bibliophiles – those who enjoy books for visual and typographical reasons quite separate from their literary value. Before appearing as a novelist at the age of forty-five Gray had not only failed as a dramatist, but as a commercial artist, portrait painter and mural painter. By bringing visual showmanship to book production he has contrived, with illustrations and jingling rhymes, to make the jackets, blurbs, boards, typography, layouts and even errata slips in his publications more entertaining than the main texts. Not since William Morris's *News from Nowhere* and Rudyard Kipling's *Just So Stories* has an author so controlled the appearance of his books, often varying them from one edition to the next, allowing collectors to always find something new. The two festschrifts are no doubt useful guides to these parasites on the tree of literature.

But outside academia and bibliomania Gray's reputation is fading. Younger folk find more up-to-date working-class realism in Irvine Welsh, better science-fiction fantasy in Iain Banks. The minority interested in brazen Postmodern obscurantism find Gray's *Lanark* far surpassed by James Kelman's *Translated Accounts* (published 2001). Of all his works only *Lanark* has never been out of print, but here – and finally, claims Gray – we have over a hundred thousand words of his very last novel.

Henry James said H.G. Wells made novels by tipping his mind up like a cart and pouring out the contents. At first *Old Men in Love* seems to have been made in the same haphazard way, but some research in the National Library of Scotland shows it is stuffed with extracts from Gray's earlier writings. The two big historical narratives are from television plays commissioned by Granada in the 1970s. The Greek one was broadcast in a series called *For Conscience's Sake*, with Christopher Logue in the part of Socrates. It extensively plagiarised Plato's *Symposium* and passages in Plutarch. For a *Queen Victoria's Scandals* series Gray then plagiarised Henry James Prince's published diaries and Hepworth Dixon's *Spiritual Wives*. He refused to let his name be attached to the broadcast because a producer or director had changed the script in ways he disliked, after which British television had no use for Alasdair Gray. The archive has three typed dialogues for a TV play about Filippo Lippi

that was never commissioned, so *Old Men in Love* has
only three Florentine chapters. These rags of forgotten
historical plays fill nineteen chapters.

The rest are stuffed with a great deal of half-baked popular science tipped in from Gray's 2000 anthology *The Book of Prefaces*, also political diatribes from pamphlets published before three general elections that were victories for New Labour. These diatribes were and are protests against the dismantling of peaceful British industries and the welfare state, a process that has made Gray and many other professional people richer. The description of an anti-war march was written for *The Herald* in February 2003, then added inappropriately to *The Ends of Our Tethers*, a collection of tales printed in 2004. (It may be no coincidence that Will Self describes a similar protest march in *The Book of Dave*, published 2006.) Like most Scotsmen, Gray thinks himself an authority on Burns, so we find an essay about Burns mostly published in volume 30 of the 1998 Studies in Scottish Literature, edited by Professor Ross Roy. The most shameless padding is in chapter 17 which reprints verbatim a section from chapter 8. The marginal note signposting this invites readers to think it a charmingly eccentric Shandyan device, but Laurence Sterne's typographical stunts in *Tristam Shandy* are never more than a page long. This repetition is beyond a joke.

Three literary ploys try to unify the whole rag-bag. The Introduction uses the text-as-found-manuscript invented by Scott for his *Tales of My Landlord* novels and afterwards plagiarised by Hogg, Pushkin, Kierkegaard, Dostoyevsky and Gray in two earlier novels. From Scott also comes the printing of portentous quotations as epigraphs, some genuine and some pseudonymous, a device done to death by Pushkin, Poe, George Eliot and Rudyard Kipling. All but the introduction are cynically sandwiched between references to the 2001 Trade Center atrocity and May 2007 Scottish election in order to give the whole thing spurious contemporary relevance. When all the above is discounted we are left with the dreary tale of a failed writer and dirty old man, who comes to a well-deserved end through an affair with a drug-dealing procuress. This story is neither tragic nor funny.

The best criticism of Gray is to quote his own and believe it. In an 1990s epilogue to *Something Leather* he says all his stories were about men who found life a task they never doubted until an unexpected collision opened their eyes and changed their habits. The collision was usually with a woman, and the transformation often ended in death. He adds that knowing how his talent works shows it is defunct because imagination will not employ whom it cannot surprise. After that Gray published nine more fictions with this hackneyed plot, *Old Men in Love* being the last. The four old men are all versions of Gray in fancy dress, with the Socratic collision homosexual, and though this novel may indeed be his last I cannot simply dismiss it (as Allan Massie dismissed Gray's 2004 *The Ends of Our Tethers*) by calling it a collection of scraps from a tired writer's bottom drawer. Neither the blurb which Gray lured Will Self into writing nor the egoism of the text will repel empty-headed fans of these egregious authors. Many may fall under the influence of its sinister propaganda for Scottish Nationalism and Socialism.

Far too many have forgotten or never known that the German acronym for National Socialism is Nazi. Yeats' *The Countess Kathleen*, first performed in Dublin 1902, was a bad poetic play that annoyed orthodox Catholics but scandalously excited Irish Nationalists. After the 1916 Easter Rising Yeats wondered if his play had stimulated rebellion among "certain men the English shot". From their comfortable studies plausible authors often give murderous lunatics high-minded excuses for atrocities. *Old Men in Love* cunningly avoids Hugh MacDiarmid's rabid Anglophobia; but as Billy Connolly, the New Labour Party and all respectable defenders of the 1707 Union point out, racist hatred of the English is what the Scottish lust for an impossible independence feeds upon. This book should therefore not be read, or if read, swiftly forgotten. Goodbye, Mr Gray.

*Sidney Workman June 2007*

*17 Linoleum Terrace, Kirkcaldy*

# An Upper
# Clyde Falls Mural

IN 1969 THIS DECORATION was made part of an old pub, *The Tavern*, Kirkfield Bank, which is one of the long narrow villages on the banks of the upper Clyde between Hamilton and Lanark. James Campbell, a local builder, now owned it and was turning the rooms upstairs into a flat for his parents, while making an old store behind the public bar into a lounge bar. He wanted a wall painting in that lounge, and the architect planning the renovation suggested he commissioned that from me – the architect had been my fellow pupil at Glasgow's Whitehill Secondary School. When a student of mural painting I had painted a *Horrors of War* room for the Scottish-USSR Friendship Society, and after winning my diploma had painted a cloudy firmament on the ceiling of Belleisle Street Synagogue, south Glasgow, and in 1963 had completed the first week of *Genesis* in the chancel of Greenhead Church of Scotland, Bridgeton. The last, so far my biggest and best job had been demolished as part of a road-widening scheme that was later abandoned, but still suggested I was qualified for a mural

*Most of this was written in 2008 to publicise the renovation of the work. Each day I was driven to the site by my neighbour and assistant, Robert Salmon. On the way home one day we heard on his car radio a BBC announcer say Alasdair Gray was renovating a recently found mural painted 40 years before. I was astonished, could not think why me and my work were now thought news-worthy by any broadcasting company. This was a novelty. Then I recalled that every news item before that had been about the onset of the financial crisis we still undergo. News presenters had needed ANY cheery story to end on. Me and my restoration job was all, in their hurry, they could find, in the abscence of a Scots celebrity giving birth.*

painting job. The area offered was 4 feet high by 25 feet long, being the space above the back of a wall-length sofa. This shape suggested to me a landscape of the Upper Clyde Falls less than a mile away, which I had first visited a few months earlier. Like many painters and writers before me I had thought these wonderful, both as natural features and parts of Scotland's national, social and industrial history. William Wallace started his guerrilla war for Scottish Independence in Lanark and used a cave in the gorge between Cora and Bonnington Linn as a hiding place. Throughout the 19th Century these were tourist attractions. After Wordsworth saw them he considered writing an epic poem about how wild natural scenery and political freedom were akin. Turner was only one of the professional landscape artists who painted the Linns – Gaelic for waterfalls. David Dale the humane factory owner, Robert Owen the founder of co-operative socialism, built their model industrial village of New Lanark in the narrow valley below Cora Linn, for they used the force of the falls to drive their factory's spinning machines. In the 1920s Scottish Electricity built a weir above Bonnington Linn which diverted the same force to a power station above New Lanark, and twice a year the station is switched off to let folk see how grand these falls once were. That is how I had seen them shortly before the commission.

I told James Campbell that any preliminary sketch I did of the mural would mislead him, because my first design would undergo many changes during the painting. I suggested he pay me a small sum in advance for my materials and food while I did the job, on the understanding that if he disliked the final result he could paint it out and pay no more. He shook my hand on that. I travelled by train to Lanark, which is a 15 minute walk from Kirkfield Bank, and in the 3 or 4 weeks of work on the painting slept on a platform above the bar of the lounge that was being constructed. The mural was completed to Mr. Campbell's satisfaction.

This is my largest painting of a landscape mainly natural, as buildings and fields are not the main features. It shows the Clyde coming from behind Tinto, the highest hill in southwest Lanarkshire, and departing to the northwest down the valley past New Lanark, behind the high ground where the old town of Lanark stands. To distort all this as little as possible I manipulated the perspective to show both the two greatest falls and the nearly two miles of gorge between them.

In 2008 The Tavern was bought by Andy Boyle, pub owner in Hamilton, who set out to give it a new look while making it a pub that would serve first-class meals. He discovered my mural by stripping off layers of paper and paint put over it by several previous owners, and liked it – even though the colours were much faded and the surface had been pierced by fixings for wall lights. At one end water penetration had ruined an area 2 1/2 feet by 4 which had been replastered. A picture restorer called in to advise recognised the work as mine and suggested I restore it, which I did with the help of two assitants: Richard Todd and Robert Salmon. No photograph of the whole original existed and too few early sketches for it, so I chiefly relied on memory and new photographs of the landscape when restoring obliterated parts. Perhaps forty years of subsequent painting let me improve on what I first did. If not, I believe it is no worse. Andy Boyle opened the former Tavern as The Riverside Restaurant in 2008. It closed in 2009 because each of three excellent young chefs he successively employed went to better paid jobs in posh hotels. In 2013 the building is still for sale.

It is not just vanity that makes me wish it were opened again as an inn at the very least. Kirkfield Bank still has a primary school where children meet, and a small general store where housewives and husbands encounter each other. There may even still be a Kirk in Kirkfield Bank. But a village lacking a pub where adults can casually meet to enjoy the company of others singly or in groups is a community losing its soul and on the way to become a commuters housing estate. The old Tavern was a lively social centre, whether my mural was a visible part of the interior or not. I hope, for Kirkfield Bank's sake, it becomes one again.

# Hillhead Subway Station Mural[*]

THIS WALL DECORATION IS THE result of many people working together, but the main artists are Nichol Wheatley and me. So first a few words about us both, starting with the oldest.

I graduated in mural painting from Glasgow School of Art in 1957 and have since painted twelve big interior walls or ceilings, two in a Church of Scotland and Synagogue that were later demolished. Three were papered over by new owners of the buildings, but in two cases newer owners still took the paper off and I restored them. Between these jobs I often worked as a writer. It is hard in Scotland to earn a living by picture making, so many such artists work as teachers.

Nichol Wheatley is thirty-five years younger than me. He too attended Glasgow School of Art and, unwilling to teach, became a bouncer in a pub, an organizer of pub bouncers, then a blacksmith. He took to mural painting in 1999. His first commission was decorating the Grosvenor Café, Ashton Lane, when I worked on the other side, in the Ubiquitous Chip restaurant, restoring and enlarging my mural on the stairs to the lavatories. On one cafe wall Nichol painted a panoramic view of Hillhead showing both sides of Byres Road between Kelvingrove Park and the

* Written when the publicity officer of Strathclyde Partnership for Transport asked for "A rationale for the Hillhead Mural", meaning, why had I decorated a main subway station with these pictures. The decorated wall was uncovered for the public in 2012.

Botanic Gardens. This disappeared when the Grosvenor café became the Vodka Wodka bar two years later, but Nichol's talent and practical skill soon won him other, larger mural commissions. He restored the decorations and paintwork of St Aloysius Church, made wall paintings for hotels in Glasgow, England and abroad, and made the mosaic floor of the Ingram Street Corinthian restaurant.

We became colleagues in 2005 when, having painted the ceiling and gallery of the Òran Mór auditorium, I needed help to put a decorative dado, mirrors and frieze on lower walls. Nichol's firm now had employees he had trained to do all kinds of mural work, and together he and they supplied exactly what I wanted. I have a plan to decorate other, higher auditorium walls which Colin Beattie, the Òran Mór's creator and owner, approved of. He and I thought completing it would take years. Nichol has suggested how to tackle it in ways that will reduce the time to one or two years only. That is still in the future.

The general public has so far not noticed the incompleteness of the Òran Mór decorations, which are the most popular I have painted, and perhaps why in 2010 Strathclyde Partnership for Transport suggested I decorate the long wall in the Hillhead station vestibule, the first of the Subway stations they are modernizing. SPT approached me through Nichol because he had worked with me, and perhaps to ensure I would complete the job by a fixed date. Artists like me find it hard to do this with large works of art, as we cannot foresee new ideas for improvements that will extend the work, breaking deadlines some employers take seriously. If SPT thought Nichol's practical help would speed things they were right. Without him it might have been finished in 2014.

The wall size is 2.105 by 12.610 metres – nearly seven feet high and nearly six times as wide. Folk going through the turnstiles faced the left side, those coming up the stair and escalator the right. Opposite the escalator the wall bends slightly outward in an area exactly filled (allowing for the grouting) by the same size of porcelain tiles that now line other walls of the renovated station – seven rows of three, 60 by 30 centimetres. By balancing this with an equal tile area at the turnstile end I shortened the centre of the mural to about twenty-nine feet by seven, and decided to fill it with a view of Hillhead, for three reasons:

**1**. The station is in the centre of Hillhead, which I know well. Kelvingrove Art Gallery and Museum, the old BBC building with Botanic Gardens had been among my favourite places since the age of eleven. I had lived and worked in the district since 1968, would enjoy depicting it, so others might enjoy the sight of it.

**2**. It would be in a tradition of civic art that once flourished in several Italian city states, especially Sienna between the 14th and 16th Century, where public buildings are still decorated with views of how the city looked in its centuries of independent municipal government.

**3**. In 2007 I had illustrated a novel, *Old Men In Love*, with a view of Hillhead, mainly copied from a photograph of Nichol Wheatley's mural in the former Grosvenor Café.

Enlarging the illustration to make my own mural

seemed so easy that I thought that with the help of one assistant, six weeks work would produce for SPT a large scale cartoon of the final mural. In his Maryhill workshop Nichol gave me ample studio space, and with the help of three assistants I produced a convincing sketch in three months. But no good big painting is just a smaller one enlarged – mere enlargement destroys its vitality. Nichol built a table whose top was the area of the cityscape, and here were joined together detailed drawings of all the buildings. They were drawn from sketches and close-up photographs, integrated with help of aerial surveys and maps. Traditional perspective would make this impossible. Four facades of the multi-storey Boyd Orr building appear together, though nobody at one time could see more than two. Also its roofline is seen from far below while behind it Glasgow University library (a higher multi-storey being on top of a hill) is seen from above. In the language of art this is a Cubist view, like Picasso portraits where one eye is shown full-face beside a nose in profile, and other features shown as the artist thought most typical. He was certainly influenced by Egyptian figure painting in which the head and legs are shown in profile, the eye and torso full-face. That is why exciseman Rousseau said, "You and I are the greatest painters in France, Monsieur Picasso, you in the Egyptian style, I in the Modern." – which proves the exciseman was not a naïve intellectual. Picasso's Cubism shocked many before adopted by cartoonists. Mickey Mouse's two circular ears were always seen from in front however he turned his head. The artist who drew Dennis the Menace and his dog Gnasher (unlike Dudley Watkins who drew Oor Wullie) also showed features with Cubist twists. My several viewpoints are not combined in faces, only in buildings, so will not appear so surprising.

The architectural drawing was in place before the end of 2011. Leaving them to be coloured digitally at a later stage I painted the sky, streets, trees and parks, and then left the job to Nichol. Painted surfaces in an entrance hall will be damaged by change of temperature and deliberate or accidental vandalism, so he had to turn my design into something more durable. Romans and Byzantines made mural pictures with mosaic tiles a quarter inch square. Arabian murals were of larger tiles – square, triangular and other straight-sided shapes arranged in brilliantly coloured patterns. My design was mostly blocks of buildings. I asked if each main block could be cut from a single tile, as large as possible, so that the different shapes of each would fit together like a giant jigsaw puzzle. I did not know I was asking for something that had never been made before. Nichol knew that, and believed he could find a way to do it. European laws required the ceramic work to be advertised for tender. Two major firms applied, said they could only work in tiles of one size, so SPT gave Nichol the job.

He first cut the paper design into sections scanned onto a computer where they were digitally joined again on screen. A helper examined each detail and erased all accidental marks. On Nichol's laptop he and I put colours into the black and white architecture, and he ordered specimen tiles from three firms, one of them Spanish. The colours they printed on these specimens were not clear enough and proved he should fire the design onto tiles from transfers. FotoCeramic from Stoke-on-Trent made the individual transfers. Cosmo Ceramics south of the Clyde are providing all other tiles for the SPT station walls. From their biggest sheets of porcelain Nichol jet-cut each jigsaw section, found the right chemistry for applying the colour transfers, and oversaw the colours fired onto each tile with Susan O'Byrne and Emilka Radlinska of Glasgow's Ceramic Studios. Every stage needed trials, errors and losses that could not be foreseen. One in ten tiles were damaged in the firing and done again. Some were done again because what I asked for did not please me. Working overnight from 10pm to 5am, Nichol and his helpers installed these tiles, with the rainbow and glimpses of the Kelvin done in traditional mosaic. The work was finished on Monday morning, 25th of June 2012, six weeks before the station renovation was complete.

The panels at each end of the mural wall – seven rows, three tiles wide – contain symbols of people and some creatures found in most cities, with the words ALL KINDS OF FOLK and FOLK OF ALL KINDS, and on the left side, the names of all the artists who made the job possible. The symbols are mostly adapted from my book illustrations with a few invented for the mural. There is a sunny sky on the left with white clouds darkening to stormy ones in the centre and ending in a night sky above Kelvingrove, where a tablet floats with the inscription HILLHEAD 2011 when the architecture was mainly drawn. Already this view is slightly out-of-date – trees shown in the grounds of the

Òran Mór were destroyed in a recent storm. Sky apart, this Hillhead has empty streets because filling them with the usual flow of people and cars would have made them disturbingly busy and needed months of extra work. To show realistically (not symbolically) some people nowadays there are portraits of five people, too few to suggest a cross-section of our society but enough to indicate different ends of it. At the left are three still often seen at this end of Byres Road – Allan Richardson, painter, etcher and street cleaner; Maria, Big Issue seller; and Muslim (seated) a flower seller shown without his flowers. At the Kelvingrove end are two elected politicians with Hillhead connections, and I avoid party propaganda by not giving their names. One is a member of the SPT committee which commissioned the mural.

A few small parts of it could be improved if Nichol and I remade them together, but I am as happy with the whole thing now as I have been with most of my big jobs.

# Of John Connolly*

JOHN CONNOLLY HAD AN unusually tough life. At the age of eleven his working-class parents were killed in the bombing of Clydebank. After five years in an orphanage boarding school he was apprenticed as an electrician, did two years of national service and in 1952 had his first piece of good luck when he met and married Janice, a cheerful and supportive wife. From 1953-59 he underwent prolonged treatment of tuberculosis which required the removal of a lung. In convalescent periods he discovered himself as an artist, practicing embroidery and painting.

From the late 1950s onward he and Janice lived in Maryhill, northwest Glasgow, where she bore him 4 children, their second son Dennis died when a baby of meningitis. John worked as an engineer with Duncan Low ltd. who made electrical heaters. This gave him access to a welding shop and much scrap metal, letting him make metal sculptures in his free time. He made more than there was space to store in the family's three room council flat. Luckily it was on the tenement's ground floor. Being a skilled handyman in any material, John cut a trapdoor in the floor of the lobby cupboard, thus gaining access to the building's damp course, a large 4 foot high cellar. By this time he

* John Connolly was one of several Scottish workers in the visual arts who became close friends of mine in the 1960s, gained a number of showings in small west Scottish galleries, sometimes with Scottish Arts Council support, but never earned enough by their art to support their families by it.

had artist friends who appreciated his work. Into that cellar they escorted others to view his larger and heavier works on their knees and by the light of an electric torch. One of them was a Scottish Arts Council official who obtained for John his first major commission, the welded sculpture Embracing Couple for Strathclyde University.

Nowadays a few painters and sculptors in Scotland make a living solely by their art. In the 20th century that was almost impossible if the artist did not go to London. Artists without inherited money almost always subsidised their art by other work, usually teaching. John took seasoned part-time employment as a lecturer in art appreciation for Glasgow University Extra Mural department, became a training officer with the Scottish Epileptic Association, but worsening health made it essential for him to get paying work he could do at home in his own time. He retrained as a watch and clock mender, left Glasgow for Arran in 1972, and from then onward lived and worked as one in his McKelvie Road bungalow in Lamlash. Many in Arran will also remember his wife Janice, who worked as an assistant in the pharmacy. She died in 2008, her funeral service being held in Lamlash Church of Scotland. John's funeral was held on 23 April 2012.

John's first one-man exhibition of work was in 1962 at the Glasgow University Chaplaincy Centre. In 1986 he took a studio in Brodick to make portrait heads exhibited in the Royal Scottish Academy. In the period between he exhibited in Hopetoun House, the Carnegie Trust Dunfermline, the Demarco Gallery Edinburgh, the North Britain Gallery Gartocharn, also with the Regent Gallery and the Glasgow Group in the McLellan Gallery. Along with the welded sculpture his portrait heads were in ciment fondu though a late Scottish Arts Council grant enabled him to work in bronze. His last exhibition was held by his friend Vicki Hudson in her Lochranza gallery, where at present some of his work is still on show, including the bronze portrait head of Ricki Demarco he also exhibited in the Main Gallery, Brodick. Most of his works are in storage.

It is common for Scottish artists to be mainly unknown on their homeland, if they have no talent for self-publicity. John was a quiet man, mainly brought to public attention by painters and sculptors of his own age who had met him in Glasgow and loved his work. Most of these, like George Wylie and me, became widely noticed as artists quite recently. The work of some fine artists is only widely noticed after their death. John Connolly's work deserves to be. He is survived by his son Ian, his daughters Annette and Elizabeth.

# Of Will Self[*]

I LIKE WILL SELF BECAUSE he has publicly praised my work and because our political views are almost the same, though not exactly. I told him that the world's overpopulation, increasing both malnutrition and warfare, should be cured by all loving couples giving birth to only one child who they could support for a generation or two. He pointed out that I thought so because I had only fathered one child, and he had fathered several he was able to support.

That disagreement apart, we are both democratic Socialists of the Anarchist sort Orwell joined in 1938 – fighters against the troops of Franco, Hitler and Mussolini who were not given weapons by the USSR because they rejected Stalin's dictatorship. I do not suggest that either of us are capable of firing a gun, but Will's public speaking and journalism shows he too sees the British electoral system now resembles that of the USA, giving voters in most of Britain the choice of only 2 major political parties, both led by millionaires who ensure government of the people by the rich, for the rich.

But while liking him, and having a friend who found his fiction shockingly amusing, I used to dislike it. Near the start of this century he told me and a large audience in a Southbank auditorium why I disliked it, saying he could only write about people he hated and

[*] *This is a hitherto unpublished review of Self's 9th novel* **Umbrella**.

despised. Of course no good author creates perfectly loveable characters because readers cannot believe in them, human perfection being impossible. For the same reason I could not believe in Will's perfectly despicable characters. I wished he showed some great author's sympathy for the folk he invented. King Lear is a horribly selfish old man at the start of his play and has probably been a horribly selfish king, absolute power corrupting absolutely. No wonder his older daughters are equally selfish, and he rejects the one too honest to fawn upon him. He only becomes tragic and pitiable when, a homeless outcast in a tempest, he realises that when a king he should have done something for outcasts, unlike Margaret Thatcher who said she wished to make life difficult for such people. Good old Shakespeare. Even his arch-villain, a bastard who blinded his father, decides before dying to be inconsistent and try to save Cordelia.

*The Book of Dave* was the first I read in which Will had mercy on his main characters. An indirect, highly inventive criticism of Old and New Testaments, it has a large cast, the most sympathetic being a small boy with a pet creature genetically programmed to like dying and becoming food for others. Then came *Walking to Hollywood* with its satire on installation art and a Jewish narrator I could identify with, in spite of or because of his occasional lunacy. But *Umbrella* is certainly his best book yet. I cannot decide whether to call it damnably, uncomfortably fascinating or damnably fascinating and uncomfortable. I damn it with exorbitant praise because I agree with the blurb in my review copy which says *Umbrella* "takes up the challenge of Modernism and demonstrates how it – and it alone – can unravel new and unsettling truths about our world." It is a relief to read a critic who does not use the senseless Postmodern label, invented by critics who could not see that the multiple viewpoints and time-shifts in *Catch 22*, *Slaughterhouse Five* and *The Tin Drum* made them just as modern as Joyce's *Ulysses* and Sterne's *Tristram Shandy*.

*Umbrella* is three hundred and ninety-seven pages not divided into chapters, with few indentations indicating paragraphs. Nearly every sentence is very long, with many insistent phrases in italics *like this*, punctuated by many dots like... that. Since deciding 25 years ago to persist with *Ulysses*, I have not read a book that needed such *close* reading before I saw the good of it. It is a story of sanity and madness and how, from the nineteenth century onward, doctors have been driven to mistaking one for the other. One of its great insights is put into the mouth of an old psychiatrist who discovers that in battle nine out of ten conscripted soldiers never fire a gun with lethal intent, so the biggest wars between the most civilized nations are, as he puts it, "perpetrated by a mere handful of psychopathic personalities, the rest being there to... make up the numbers."

*Umbrella* not only uses the modern narrative shifts of *Catch 22*, *Slaughterhouse Five* and *The Tin Drum*, it makes new for today's Britain their humane and undeclared morality, which is the only one possible.

# Of Bill Hamilton

WILLIAM HAMILTON'S NAME became known to the general public in 1976 through Richard Dawkins' *The Selfish Gene*. Written to popularize recent discoveries in Darwinian evolution, this book claimed these were mainly due to Hamilton. Some biologists questioned these discoveries in the following years, but when Bill's funeral service was held in July 2000 at the Chapel of New College, Oxford, nobody contradicted Dawkins when he said biologists and geneticists mostly agreed that Bill was the world's greatest evolutionary biologist since Darwin. Of course total agreement in any region of thought is impossible. Students of science in parts of Ireland, the USA and some Muslim states are taught that new kinds of plant and animal did not evolve from earlier ones, because God separately invented each. Otherwise, folk interested in biology will recognise the importance of Bill Hamilton and this biography.

This is the fourth Oxford University Press publication about Bill's life and work. The first three were the trilogy of his collected papers titled, *Narrow Roads of*

Bob Kitts, the subject of essays starting on pages 112 and 229, was generous to both think highly of his friends and introduce them to each other. In 1955 perhaps, I met through him a daughter and son of a remarkable family, the Hamiltons: Mary, medical student, Bill, the student biologist. Both liked literature & art. Bob showed them my early poems. I am now ashamed of these, but Mary and Bill liked them, and we became friends. Mary, became a doctor, Bill a geneticist. In 1976 **The Selfish Gene** by Dawkins told me Bill was now both famous and controversial. His article on natural history in the **T.L.S.** proved him a good writer. This review of his official biography was rejected by **London Review of Books**, printed in **The Scottish Review of Books.**

*Geneland*. Bill edited the first two, *Evolution of Social Behaviour* and *The Evolution of Sex*, in which his scientific papers were printed in the order they were written, each with his preface explaining the circumstances, with teachers who doubted the value of his research and colleagues who valued it. Not all good scientists believe that the personal struggles producing their best ideas may cast light on them. Kepler did, thinking the mental process by which he found planetary orbits were not circular but elliptical as interesting as the discovery.

*Last Words*, the trilogy's third volume, was edited by Mark Ridley with each paper introduced by a co-author or colleague because Bill had died of a disease contracted in Africa. Even without his introductions to *Last Words* these collected papers are a scientific record and self-portrait – a scientist's *Pilgrim's Progress*. Like all autobiographies it omits much that the author took for granted or thought unimportant, hence our need of Ullica Segerstrale's biography.

It is an excellent account of a character 19th century writers called an original, meaning not easily classified. As a lecturer Bill had some traits attributed to absent-minded-professors – no respect for merely conventional manners and appearances, with carelessness over a pay cheque. This combined with practical though unconventional efficiency on expeditions in equatorial rainforests, and with unusual physical strength few noticed because he never flaunted it. Once, perhaps, he quietly enjoyed disturbing an audience by explaining how he had plugged a leak in a boat while swimming under it in

Brazil, ending with the casual remark, "The danger of piranhas is greatly exaggerated." (When I mentioned this to his wife Christine last year she said impatiently, "There is no danger from piranhas if you aren't bleeding.")

Ms Segerstrale shows that Bill's originality as a thinker derived (as often happens) from highly original parents. Both were New Zealanders who, from the mid 1930s onward, brought up six children in Oaklea, five acres of Kentish woodland surrounding an ordinary two-storey house with useful outbuildings. Here their offspring found space to develop their own interests and hobbies, with parents who gladly helped when they wanted help. This gave the children freedoms their parents had enjoyed as youngsters in New Zealand, and perhaps colonial prejudices against what they called posh. They used thriftily mended broken china, dined without tablecloths when guests were not present, avoided hotels and restaurants by travelling in a car with tents and camping equipment. This came easy to a family whose engineer dad had supervised building a road for the British Empire through the mountains of Kurdistan and used prefabricated bridges of his own invention. Life at Oaklea was both tougher and more varied than that of most middle-class British children. Bill's love of natural history began in the woods of Oaklea.

More about his parents. His mother Bettina, had qualified as a general medical doctor who meant to work as a missionary, but after marriage abandoned that, becoming a full-time housekeeping mother. She loved art and literature, read poems and stories to her children, also the Bible which she thought should be part of everyone's education. Her husband's influence may have made her more of an agnostic than a Church Christian. A sentence on page 10 of *Nature's Oracle* may be misleading: "Archie and Bettina often attended a church on Sunday, sometimes taking the children." Their eldest child, Mary Bliss, tells me her father was an outspoken Atheist who never went to church. From Archie, Bill picked up engineering skills which, like natural history, stimulated an intelligent imagination also fed by paintings, poetry, the novels of Dostoyevsky and Kafka. Two of his closest friends and scientific colleagues, Hugh Ingram and Colin Hudson were practicing Christians, and in later life George Price. Bill greatly sympathised with Price, helped publicised his discoveries, could not save him from suicide when Price found living as Jesus commanded and giving all he had to the poor was too difficult.

Bill's lack of snobbery and remarkable absence of prejudices came from his family being a small republic which quietly supported its members while expecting each to earn their independence, so at the start of her book Ms Segerstrale concentrates on family matters. After Bill's professional studies get underway she gives them priority, mentioning lecturers who thought his ideas unimportant or suspect, others who valued them and all his helpful colleagues. Bill had no small talk of the kind most young people use in mating games, so was surprised to learn later that he could be 'a ladies man', after meeting women with educations more like his own. Apart from his wife Christine, Ms Segerstrale says nothing about other women in his life.

She mentions an early proposal of marriage being turned down – the woman refused to accept his condition that of the two children she would bear, the second must have a different father. Bill was not proposing a ménage a trois, but his faith in altruistic kinship made him sure different fathers would give both children a broader range of support in life. He forgot that most women willing to wed one man are instinctively monogamous. He may have abandoned that idea when Christine accepted him. Ms Segestrale leaves later biographers to scavenge for names and details which she rightly thinks gossip irrelevant to Bill's main story. Here comes some gossip of my own.

I met Bill through friendship with his sister Mary when I was a studying mural design at Glasgow School of Art and he studying genetics at Cambridge University. We were both keen on the work of William Blake and Samuel Palmer. (Palmer's best paintings were made near Oaklea, at Shoreham where Blake had visited him.) We also discussed behavior uniquely human – our capacity to eat when not hungry, drink when not thirsty, fuck in almost any season of the year and, alas, hurt or kill other people after making them helpless. It is also obvious that some of us enjoy doing so. Theists blame these traits upon the fall of man and original sin and Atheists upon the nature of things, often called Nature for short. Bill and I were Darwinian enough to think these capacities were inherited from a time when they helped people survive, but we now worried about human survival in a world where belligerent nations threatened each other with nuclear weapons. As a Socialist I thought this belligerence mainly due to needless competition causing poverty and overcrowding. Bill also thought overpopulation dangerous, but believed belligerence had a profounder genetic source.

Our talks in the 1950s have no place in Bill's biography because they did not influence his work, which explained selfish belligerence and xenophobia indirectly. He saw there was more to be learned about the nature of human and other animals by investigating capacities for self-sacrifice. Most birds live upon insects and seeds, only a minority of bigger ones are predators, yet many smaller birds give a special cry if they see a hawk circling overhead, a cry warning others in earshot of the predator, though the cry will first attract the hawk's attention to itself. Most people incline to call individuals who risk or lose their lives helping others heroes or idiots, but a species without these self-sacrificers is in danger of extinction. Every healthy meerkat community has a member who stands on its hind legs with raised head like a human sentry, looking out for predators while the rest seek nourishment with four feet on the ground. A meerkat community too small to support a sentinel is soon killed off.

While studying altruism genetically at Cambridge Bill wished to attend anthropology lectures as a second subject but the anthropology department rejected him because he was a scientist. Anthropologists saw themselves as an arts faculty working at an interface between history and philosophy. So did most biologists who believed human societies could never undergo experimental proofs required by exact sciences. This disgruntled Bill with Cambridge. He decided that evidence for genetic altruism could be best investigated in places where animal life was thickest, among the social insects of South America. *Nature's Oracle* tells how Bill's investigations were first dismissed as "politically incorrect", though that phrase was not yet in general use. A historical excursion is needed to explain why.

Malthus' *Essay on the Principal of Population* was published in 1798 when the French Revolution was underway, and still welcomed by many critics of the British government. Among these was Tom Paine who had strongly supported the war for American independence. His book *The Rights of Man* said hereditary monarchs and aristocracies used taxation to promote warfare while supporting a hoard of unproductive parasites. He said a democratic government could use taxation to abolish hereditary bosses and poverty by setting up what was called a Welfare State over a century later. Malthus argued against this that in every land more people were born than there was food enough to feed, so death from warfare and poverty were needed to keep efficient societies working. He said that if a widespread sharing of social wealth ever produced a wholly well-fed generation, their numbers would increase so much that the next would be decimated by famine.

This argument seemed conclusive to land owners, employers and politicians who had no wish to pay better wages or improve working-class conditions. It was attacked by those who saw it used to justify widespread corruption and selfishness in what Harold Wilson once called "the commanding heights of the economy." Malthus' justification of warfare was ancient – in Chaucer's *The Knight's Tale* Mars the war-god is praised for cutting down Nature's excess – but his essay was probably first to suggest that deaths from poverty were good for a nation.

The link between population and food supply in Malthus' essay gave Charles Darwin a clue to *The Origin of Species*. This book persuaded Herbert Spencer to invent the phrase survival of the fittest, which became popular with thinkers called Social Darwinists. These tended to talk as if much money, inherited or earned, was an obvious sign of people fittest to survive. This contradicted Dean Swift's remark, that if you want to know what God thinks about money, look at those who have most. Only the sycophants of multi-millionaires can believe they show human nature at its best. By the 1890s it was also proved that working-class families with good wages tended to have less, not more children than their poorer neighbours.

Darwin never wrote or said a word that would identify him with those called Social Darwinists, but his distant cousin Francis Galton was a good scientist, meteorologist and investigator of hereditary traits who added the word eugenics to the English language. Galton worried about the general health of the British people. He saw the aristocracy threatened by the dangers of inbreeding, which the European royal families had made notorious. He saw workers in the cities plagued by tuberculosis and a host of other diseases which he thought might become hereditary.

Since the 14th century Black Death London's population had grown steadily bigger, though parish registers showed that the death rate there always exceeded the birth rate. This proved that the expansion had been caused by people constantly arriving from healthier places outside. Stockbreeders knew how to strengthen traits they approved of in horses, cattle and fowls. Galton thought public health should be improved by breeding people in the same way, and endowed a Eugenic Society to foster a healthier, more intelligent race of Britons.

Galton was no more a Fascist than other prosperous Victorians blind to the fact that people of any intelligence will always chose mates for reasons that have nothing to do with public health, so eugenics never became a science. But its arguments were welcomed by people who liked dividing humanity into their own race, class or religion and those outside it, usually folk they wanted to exploit. That is how all imperial governments divide the human race. Four enforced eugenic laws. Nazi Germany set out to kill all Jews, gypsies and (before the Catholic Church protested) the incurably sick. For some decades before the 20th century ended the USA, Norway and Sweden forcibly, legally sterilised those judged mentally subnormal for reasons later found inadequate.

Fascism was defeated after World War Two and Social Darwinism rejected, but a scientist studying genetic traits common to mankind and other animals was suspected of Nazi tendencies, especially when he related these to birth, death rates and food supplies. On leaving Cambridge Bill decided his best chance of a regular income was in secondary school education, and applied to train as a teacher of science at Moray House in Edinburgh University. He was told his degree in genetics only qualified him for training to teach in primary schools. Bill appealed against this decision because his degree had depended on passes in three other sciences, but the appeal was dismissed.

*Nature's Oracle* tells how Bill gradually overcame that prejudice, though some papers now widely accepted were first denounced as Fascist. He went on researching and publishing because he thought scientifically proved facts politically neutral, no matter what moral codes people choose to base upon them. Many left-wing people like myself were probably repelled by the title of Dawkins' book which first popularised Bill's ideas, just as it may have attracted right-wing thinkers of the anti-Christian Ayn Rand kind. *The Selfish Gene* could have been more accurately named *The Altruistic Gene Functioning Between Near And Distant Relatives Of The Same Species*, a more difficult name to remember, so less likely to help a book survive.

My incapacity for mathematics unfits me to understand the whole range of the achievements that made Bill first president of the Human Behaviour and Evolution Society, but when I translate them into human terms they seem sensible. The heroism of sentry meerkats, the warning cries of small birds are like the willingness of thinkers to tell unwelcome truths, and why greedy dictatorships censor free speech. Bill thought the effects of genetic inclinations to xenophobia in social circumstances could be predicted, and did not doubt that extra-genetic altruism between those who shared unselfish ideas could act against it. He called behaviour which benefits our self and harms others selfish, which benefits our self and others, co-operation, which benefits others at our own expense, altruism. Behaviour damaging both our self and others he first called stupid then re-defined as spite. The purest example of spite is Hitler's attitude before his suicide in the bunker – he hoped every German would be exterminated because it had let him down by failing to conquer Britain, Russia and the USA. The importance of spite is known to psychologists, but mainly ignored by historians.

*Nature's Oracle* is a success story because Bill did not fade out like most of us but died still masterfully investigating the nature of things, still open to new ideas and helping to generate them. Unlike many scientists he never rejected a suggestion by someone younger because it was unfamiliar or unproved, but reacted by first examining the evidence. He gave the Gaia hypothesis some support by recognising the part played by clouds in seed-distribution. He realised the fact that the brilliant variety of autumn leaf colours is not a just a sign of decay, but a pre-winter signal to attract or repel helpful or damaging insects.

His death was partly the result of willingness to investigate an unpopular idea. He had written an introduction in 1999 to Edward Hooper's *The River: A Journey to the Source of HIV and Aids*. This book argued that the Aids epidemic had an African origin in the experiments there of pharmaceutical companies. Bill's introduction said there might be truth in the argument. His mother Bettina, still alive and a qualified GP, told him he would make many enemies by doing so. He believed the argument could be settled by onsite analysis of the dung of anthropoid apes. He was flown back from Africa with what proved a fatal haemorrhage before finding any. His line of investigation may never be reopened.

Since his death in 2000, some biologists who find his theory of altruism distasteful have been casting doubt on his kin-selection formulas in order to suggest he has undervalued co-operative traits. These include Nowack, Harvard professor of biology and mathematics, Wilson, an emeritus professor there and former colleague of Bill, and the mathematician Tomita. Their revision has been repudiated by the majority of biologists who find Bill's concepts a useful source of new thinking and experiment. The value of scientific ideas can only be tested scientifically, so those who highly value Bill's achievements need not be disturbed by attacks which will test them further.

More than scientists will find *Nature's Oracle* interesting. Bill's sister Mary calls it a tour de force, while listing some factual errors easy to correct in a future edition. Ms Segestrale should be proud of this book.

# HELL: Dante's Trilogy Part 1, Foreword

There are more than a hundred English versions of Dante's epic and every two years another appears. Readers want them because, like the Bible, they answer important questions with fascinating stories. But unlike the Bible no governments have promoted one excellent translation. None exist. To compress dramatic action, thought and dialogue into a huge urgent poem Dante invented a poetic form of three-line verses so cleverly unified by end-rhymes that most translators try to reproduce it. End-rhymes are easy in Italian because most of the words end in one of five vowels. They are harder to rhyme in English, so most translators get them with phrases seldom used in daily speech. My version mainly keeps the Dantean form colloquial by using end-rhymes where they came easily, internal rhymes where they did not. My abrupt north British dialect has cut Dante's epic down from 14,233 lines to 8,912. This shows how far the range of my intelligence is less than Dante's. Critics who cannot read the original should compare it with more accurate English translations.

Here are examples of my abruptness. In Italy the heroine's name is pronounced with four syllables: *Be-a-trich-ay* is a poor phonetic approximation to that beautiful sound. In English the name is usually spoken with two syllables, almost rhyming with *mattress*. My rhyme scheme needs three syllables: *Be-a-tris*. Other Italian names should be pronounced with as many syllables as Italians use.

Dante mentions two political parties, Ghibelline and Guelph. The main difference (as in Britain's eighteenth and nineteenth centuries) was between old and new money, the older class being landowners, the new one merchants. Like all two-party systems the difference was constantly blurred by changing local alliances or inter-marriage. I have translated these as Tory and Whig.

Other excuses for mishandling Dante's text will be in an epilogue to my *Paradise* translation.

# Postscript

MY TITLE WAS ORIGINALLY SUGGESTED by Rudyard Kipling's autobiography, *Something of Myself*, which said all he wished to make public. He may have agreed with Edgar Allan Poe on the impossibility of a truthful autobiography. Poe said: *If any ambitious man have a fancy to revolutionize the world of human thought, opinion and sentiment, let him write and publish a very little book. Its title should be simple – a few plain words – My Heart Laid Bare. But – this little book must be true to its title. Now, is it not very singular that, with the rabid thirst for no-toriety which distinguishes so many of mankind – so many, too, who care not a fig what is thought of them after death – there should not be found one man with sufficient hardihood to write this little book? To write, I say. If the book were written there are ten thousand who would laugh at being disturbed by its publication during their life or even after their death. But to write it – there is the rub. No man ever will dare write it. No man could write it, even if he dared. The paper would shrivel and blaze at every touch of the fiery pen.*

Poe's language is melodramatic, but he had analysed his own emotions as thoroughly as Sigmund Freud and come to the same conclusion – that self-conscious feelings and behaviour – our characters – are largely shaped by desires we hide because we fear that only successful criminals, politicians and people in times of social breakdown enact them.

The 20th-century acceptance of Freud's ideas has abolished some polite inhibitions, at least verbally. Many writers now tip onto their pages matters that most authors used to carefully hide, but can now be openly sold. I am such a writer, as some of my fictions show, but though the foregoing essays were written with (I hope) disarming frankness, they do not tell how often I have been silly, petty and mean.

And a full autobiography would have chapters about people I have not sufficiently mentioned, especially my mum, Amy Fleming. Writers say little about their mothers if they are not cruel because we take them for granted. They were the world and climate in which we lived, so became what we assumed about life – assumptions Sigmund Freud called subconscious. Like most men I was so aware of my great rival in her affections (my dad) that I have said much more about him. The brightly begun, obscurely ended career of Bob Kitts is one I should have said more about. There is Brian Smith, that agitating agitator and manic innovator of many things, such as *Festival Late* in 1961, where I met Inge Sorenson, my first wife. There is Winnie Wilson (who I met through Joan Clarke) and Emmie Sachs, who I met through Winnie Wilson. In 1914 Emma had shaken hands with Franz Joseph, Emperor of Austria, when she was a young voluntary nurse at the start of that war which changed everything. Her father had been a surgeon with the rank of general in the Austrio-Hungarian army. She told me about her love of Goethe's poetry, and how she had never thought she was a Jew until Fascism after World War One made escaping to Glasgow a wise thing to do. Yet she loved the Vienna of her childhood so much that in the 1980s she returned to die in a nursing home.

From my birth in the East Glasgow housing estate, I too have seen political changes almost as fantastic, and like all elderly folk I think most have been for the worse. But I knew many of those George Eliot mentions at the end of Middlemarch:– *"The growing good of the world is greatly dependent on unhistoric acts; and that things are not so ill with you and me as they might have been, is half owing to the number who have lived faithfully a hidden life, and rest in unvisited tombs"*. Democracy would let that good number rule us, but nations are ruled now by millionaires and oligarchs whose unearned incomes depend on increasing poverty. As Marx foresaw, this too will pass, perhaps before Capitalism destroys our supportive earth.

I do not know if I will live long enough to write a wholly honest autobiography. I hope not, for it could only be done after those I love most are dead.

And now some last lines of verse.

# last epigraph

Some moments stay as fresh and clear
as this morning or five minutes ago,
though crowds of later, mostly forgotten events
have killed or changed people I used to know.

In nineteen sixty-one and the month we wed
I pleased a whole roomful of folk so much that
"I'm proud of you," my young wife said.
Our son liked to walk holding my hand
for years before he was ten.
If another boy came in sight we parted,
walked like strangers until, round a corner,
he thought it alright for us to join hands again.
My marriage ended soon after.
For a year my son disliked me once – not now.
Queer how, near my own end, such old moments
stay so uselessly fresh and clear.

Sunk ships do not dream of wreck,
storms or torpedoes that sank them.
Their hulls recall wakening to the din
of rivets finally hammered in,
the glide down a slipway and how
their bow first bit into brine
that buoyed them up and out to sea –
brine dissolving them now.

Goodbye